# WEAKLEY COUNTY, TENNESSEE

# WILL AND RECORD BOOK

# 1828-1842

---

Originally Prepared By:

The Historical Records Project
Transcription Unit
Division of Women's and Professional Projects
Works Progress Administration (WPA)

**With New Index Added**

Nashville, Tennessee
1938

> *Notice*
>
> This book has been reproduced from carbon-copies of the original transcriptions of court records by the Works Progress Administration (WPA) in 1930s. In many instances, the resulting text is light, the documents are physically flawed, and foxing (or discoloration) occurs. The pages of this reprint have been digitally enhanced and, where possible, the flaws eliminated in order to provide clarity of content and a pleasant reading experience.

*Weakley County, Tennessee, Will and Record Book, 1828-1842*

Originally transcribed by:

The Works Progress Administration (WPA)
1938

Reprinted by:

Janaway Publishing, Inc.
732 Kelsey Ct.
Santa Maria, CA 93454
(805) 925-1038
www.JanawayGenealogy.com

2006, 2014

ISBN: 978-1-59641-027-5

*Made in the United States of America*

# PREFACE

Throughout tax records in this book, names were sometimes followed with the abbreviation "H's", "Hs." or "Hrs." The most likely explanation for this denotes heirs of the mentioned person. We only used the word "heirs" when it was actually spelled out.

We would like to thank the Tennessee State Library and Archives for their kind loan of the original text.

Samuel Sistler, September 2005

TENNESSEE

WEAKLEY COUNTY

WEAKLEY COUNTY WILL & RECORD BOOK

1828 - 1842

HISTORICAL RECORDS PROJECT
Official Project No. 465-44-3-115

COPIED UNDER WORKS PROJECT ADMINISTRATION

MRS. JOHN TROTWOOD MOORE
STATE LIBRARIAN & ARCHIVIST SPONSOR

MRS. ELIZABETH D. COPPEDGE
DIRECTOR OF WOMEN'S & PROFFESSIONAL PROJECTS

MRS. PENELOPE JOHNSON ALLEN
STATE SUPERVISOR

MRS. KATHLEEN W. CARADINE
DISTRICT SUPERVISOR

COPIED BY
MRS. IRENE BALDRIDGE

TYPED BY
MISS ULALUME ZUBER

November 25, 1938.

ORIGINAL INDEX

Bradshaw, Charles - Will, 1
Buckley, Jas. 154
Bayless, Willie, 164
Brasfield & others, 186
Bondurant, H. H., 189

Cartewright, Robert, 44
Delaney, Daniel, 101

Gardner, A. Bonds, 47,48, 104,
    134,136,141
Grooms, Stephen H., 135

Hendricks, Henry, 49

Jones, Thomas, 132
Johnson, W. H., 156
Johnson, J. P., 160
Jeter, Robert, 174
Johnson, Willis, 193

Killebrew, Elias, 149

Merrell, Berry, 148
Mosely, William, 200

Parrish, John, 148

Smith, Palmer, 195

Roberts, William, 150
Russell, Baker, 153
Rogers, Job, 179

Shrum, Nicholas W., 138
Stroud, Jessie R., 139
Stunston, John, 155
Scott, W. S., 158, 161, 168,
    190, 199
Sedwicks, Solomon, 192, 194

Terrell, Peleg, 146

Williams, K., 163,170
Williams, Sarah, 172
Webb, John, Will of, 77

Charles Bradshaw's ) Recorded April the 18th, 1828
Last Will & Testament) In the name of God - Amen.

I Charles Bradshaw being of sound mind and memory, but in feable health doth hereby make this my last will and testament. Revoking at the same time all others previously made. In the first place, I give and bequeath to my son John a negro woman named Easter and a negro boy named Wonder -

I give to my son Gideon T Bradshaw a negro woman named Hannah and a negro girl named Maria -

I give to my daughter Polly two negro Girls, Jinny & Caty or Catharine-

To my daughter Susanna I give one sorrel mare and one feather bed & furniture - To my daughter Rebecca I give one bay horse & one bed and furniture -

My old negro woman Frances I wish to be set free -

To my Beloved wife Lucretia I give and bequeath during her natural life three negroes (vizt) Cynta, Fanny, and James at her death I wish them set free their offspring if any in the meantime I wish divided among my five last children by my wife Lucredtia --

My stock of cattle Hogs household & kitchen furniture, I give and bequeath to my wife Lucretia, and at her death to be sold and Equally divided among all my children -

All moneys due me I wish collected as speedily as possible and after paying my Just debts, the balance I wish divided Equally among all my children -

I hereby constitute and appoint my son John Bradshaw and my friend William Baldridge senr. Executors to this my last will and testament --

In testamony whereof I have hereunto set my hand and affixed my seal the 16th day of March in the year of our Lord one thousand Eight hundred and twenty eight -

                                                            his
                                                  Charles  X  Bradshaw (Seal)

Signed sealed &c in the presence)      mark
of Wm. L. McNeill                )
Benjamin Malin                 )

---

STATE OF TENNESSEE )
GIBSON COUNTY      ) Court of pleas & quarter sessions April term
                                               1828 -

Then was the within will of Charles Bradshaw produced in open court and the due execution thereof proven by the oaths of William L. McNeill and Benjamin Malin the subscribing witness thereto and ordered to be recorded.
                                        Test Wm H. Johnson, Clk.

Page 2

1828

| Persons Name | Acres Lnd | Dec. Titl | REMARKS | No. of Ent. | Reg. | Sec. | Dist. | Town Lots | No. Lot | Free Poll | Slav. | Stor. | Stud or Jack | $ cts m |
|---|---|---|---|---|---|---|---|---|---|---|---|---|---|---|
| Anderson Bailey, | 640, | Enty, | " | 603, | 1 | 9 | 13 | " | " | " | " | " | " | 6.40 " |
| Andrews, Cullin, | 480, | " | Part of 640 Acr. | 1327, | 2, | 9 | 12 | " | " | " | " | " | " | 4.80 " |
| Asher, Samuel, | " | " | " | " | " | " | " | " | " | 1 | " | " | " | " 50 " |
| Adams, Thomas, | " | " | " | " | " | " | " | " | " | 1 | " | " | " | " 50 " |
| Acre, Jessee, | " | " | " | " | " | " | " | " | " | 1 | " | " | " | " 50 " |
| Abernathy, Littleton F. | 81½ | " | " | 1254, | 2, | 9 | 12 | " | " | 1 | " | " | " | 1 31.5 5 |
| Austin, Samuel F. | " | " | " | " | " | " | " | " | " | 1 | " | " | " | " 50.5 " |
| Austin, Vincent, | " | " | " | " | " | " | " | " | " | 1 | " | " | " | " 50 " |
| Austin, Moses Sr. | 256, | deed, | Part of Peter) Williams 640) | 327, | 2, | 9 | " | " | " | " | " | " | " | 2.56 " |
| Austin, Moses,Jr. | " | " | " | " | " | " | " | " | " | 1 | " | " | " | " 50 " |
| Adkins, Joseph R. | 30 | " | in name of Moses Ward | 1851 | 2 | 7 | 12 | " | " | 1 | " | " | " | " 80 " |
| Atchison Willis | " | " | " | " | " | " | " | " | " | 1 | 1 | " | " | 4.50 " |
| Armstrong, Thomas | " | " | " | " | " | " | " | " | " | 1 | " | " | " | " 50 " |
| Abott, Spencer, | " | " | " | " | " | " | " | " | " | 1 | " | " | # | " 50 " |
| Anderson Burrell, | " | " | " | " | " | " | " | " | " | 1 | " | " | " | " 50 " |

(Page 2) Cont.

| Persons Name— | Acres | Lnd.-Titl. | REMARKS | #of Ent. | Rge.-Sec. | Town Dist.Lots, | #of Lots, | Free Lot, | Poll, | Slav. | Stor. | Stud or Jack. | Stud 3 $,cts. |
|---|---|---|---|---|---|---|---|---|---|---|---|---|---|
| Adams, Abel | 30 | Deed | | 1851 | 2, 7 | 12 | | 1 | | | | | 2 50 |
| Adair, John, | | | | | | | | 1 | | | | | 50 |
| Arnold, F | | | | | | | | 1 | | | | | 50 |
| Adkinson, James, | | | | | | | | 1 | | | | | 50 |
| Adkinson, John, | | | | | | | | 1 | | | | | 50 |
| Adkinson, William, | | | | | | | | 1 | | | | | 50 |
| Betts, Geraldin, | | | | | | | | 1 | | | | | 50 |
| Bondurant, Benjamin, Deed | (146 3/4 in name (Randolph King 170 3/4 (25 name of Jas. ( Lawson | | | 1455, 932, | 1, 1 | 6, 8 | 12 13 | | | | 10 | 3 | | 16 207 27½ |
| Bondurant,Albert G.29,(Name of (John Terrell | | | | 1, | 1 | 7 | 13 | 1 | 1 | | | | 1 79 |
| Beldridge,Dan'l.640,Entry, | | | | 725, | 2, | 7 | | | | | | | 6 40 |
| Bowers & Wilson,1000 | | | | 292, | 2-3, | 7 | | | | 10 | | | |
| Bowers, John, 1000 | | | | | | | | | 1 1 | | | | 1 50 |

(Page 2) Cont.

| Persons Name | Acres Lnd.,Titl. | Desc. REMARKS | #of Ent. | Rge. | Sec. | Dist. | Town Lots,Lot | # of Lots,Poll | Free Slav. | Stor. | Jac. | Horse or $ Cts. M |
|---|---|---|---|---|---|---|---|---|---|---|---|---|
| Bowers, Wm. G. | 75 | | | | | | | 1 | 3 | | | 4 25 |
| Blakemore & Patterson | 867 | | 671, | 2, | 7 | | | | | | | 8 67 |
| Blakemore, James, | 164 | | | | | 3 | | | | | | 6.14 |
| Bondurant, Hilary H. | | | | | | | | 1 | 1 | | | 1 50 |
| Bery, Presley M., | | | | | | | | 1 | | | | 50 |
| Bowers, Young P., | | | | | | | | 1 | 2 | | | 2 50 |
| Blount, John G. & Thomas | 2300, Part of 3000 acres | | 591 | 1 | 5 | | | | | | | 23 |

(Page 3)

| | | | | | | | | | | | | |
|---|---|---|---|---|---|---|---|---|---|---|---|---|
| Same | 60 | Entry, | 860, | 1, | 6, | 13 | | 1 | | | | 10 60 |
| Beyless, Wiley | | | | | | | | 1 | 1 | | | 10 50 |
| Bell, Pulaski B., | | | | | | | 1 | 1 | | | | 2 |
| Beadles, William | | | | | | | | 1 | | | | 50 |
| Brend, James | | | | | | | | 1 | | | | 50 |
| Buckley, James | | | | | | | | 1 | 2 | | | 2 50 |
| Buckly, Walter W., | | | | | | | | 1 | | | | 50 |
| Brown, Comrad, | 50 | | 1794, | 2, | 7 | 12 | | 1 | | | | 1 |

(Page 3) Cont.

| Persons name | Acres of Desc. | Lnd. Titl. | REMARKS -Ent. Rge., | Sec. | Town Dist.Lots,Lot, | #of Free Poll, | Slav.Stor.Jac. | Horse or $ Cts M |
|---|---|---|---|---|---|---|---|---|
| Brandon, John W., | 50, | Entry, | | | | 1 | | 50 |
| Bunton, William, | | | | | | 1 | | 50 |
| Brown, Levi, | | | | | | 1 | | 50 |
| Barnard, John, | | | | | | 1 | | 50 |
| Barnard, William, | | | | | | 1 | | 50 |
| Brewner, John, | | | | | | 1 | 1 | 1.50 |
| Bookout, Bradley, | | | | | | 1 | | 50 |
| Bridges, Griffin, | | | | | | 1 | | 50 |
| Barnard, Zadock, | | | | | | 1 | | 50 |
| Busey, Edward, | 60, | Entry | | 12 | | 1 | 2 | 3.10 |
| Barnes, John, | | | | | | 1 | | 50 |
| Belote, Henry A., | 512, | Deed, | (Part of 640 in<br>(name of Henry<br>( Belote | 674, 2, | 7, 13 | | | 5.12 |
| Barnes, Samuel | | | | | | 1, | | .50 |
| Bondurant,<br>Robert M., | 166 3/4, | Deed, | ( Part of Jerome<br>( McClain 3,840, 775 | 2, | 7 | 1, 1, | | 3.16 7½ |
| Bradshaw, Thompson, | | | | | | 1 | | 50 |
| Bradshaw, Charles, | 100, | Deed | | 2, | 7 | | 3 | 4 |

(Page #3) Cont.

| Persons Names | Acres Lnd. | Desc of Titl. | REMARKS | #of Ent. | Rge. | Sec. | Dist. | Town Lots | Lots Lot | #of Free Poll | Slav. | Stor. | Stud or Jack | $ cts | M |
|---|---|---|---|---|---|---|---|---|---|---|---|---|---|---|---|
| Bradshaw, Gideon T. | 100 | Deed | Jerome McClain Part of 3,840 | 775 | 2 | 7 | " | " | " | 1 | " | " | 4.50 | " |
| Baldridge, Walker | " | " | " | " | " | " | " | " | " | " | " | " | " | 50 | " |
| Baldridge, William Sr. | 490 | " | " | " | " | " | " | " | " | 1 | " | " | " | 4.90 | " |
| Byron, Harvey, J. | " | " | " | " | 2 | 7 | " | " | " | 1 | " | " | " | 50 | " |
| Byrd, Bryan, | 130 | Entry | " | 608 | 1 | 8 | " | " | " | 1 | " | " | " | 1.80 | " |
| Bradshaw, John, | " | " | " | " | " | " | " | " | " | 1 | 1 | " | " | 1.50 | " |
| Bourland, James, | 25, | " | " | 917 | 1 | 6 | 13 | " | " | 1 | 1 | " | " | 75 | " |
| Blassingame, Jas. | " | " | " | " | " | " | " | " | " | 1 | 1 | " | " | 1 50 | " |
| Buckley, Nathaniel H. | " | " | " | " | " | " | " | 2 | 36) | 1 | 2 | " | " | 5.50 | " |
| Bledsoe, Jacob, | " | " | " | " | " | " | " | " | 78) | 1 | " | " | " | 2. " | " |
| Baker, John, | " | " | " | " | " | " | " | " | " | 1 | " | " | " | 50 | " |

(Page 4,) 1828

| Persons Names | Acres Lnd. | Desc of Titl. | REMARKS | #of Ent. | Rge. | Sec. | Dist. | Town Lots | Lots Lot | #of Free Poll | Slav. | Stor. | Stud or Jack | $ cts | M |
|---|---|---|---|---|---|---|---|---|---|---|---|---|---|---|---|
| Cotton, Charles, | 640 | Entry | " | 1366 | 1 | 5 | 12 | " | " | " | " | " | " | 6.40 | " |
| Crofford, Thomas | 2830 | Deed | " | " | " | " | 13 | 1 | 3 | 3 | 3 | " | " | 31.30 | " |
| Cochran, Dennis, | " | " | " | " | " | " | " | 2 | 2 | " | " | 1 | " | 4.50 | " |
| Cage, Wilson, | 104 | Entry | " | 796 | 1 | 7 | " | 2 | " | 1 | " | " | " | 1 4 | " |
| Cooper, Whitnell, | " | " | " | " | 2, | 9-10, | " | " | " | 1 | 2 | " | " | 2.50 | " |
| Carmichel, Micheal | 3480 | " | Part of 5000 acres | 115 | 2, | 9-10, | " | " | 10-11, | " | " | " | " | 34.80 | " |
| Charlton, John, | 134 | " | Part of 184 acres | 458 | 1 | 7 | " | 5 | " | 1 | " | " | " | 9.34 | " |
| Same | 165 | " | " | 1323 | 2 | 9 | 12 | " | " | " | " | " | " | 1.65 | " |
| Same | 190 | " | Part of Wm. Murfrees 987½, | 774 | 2 | 7 | 13 | " | " | " | " | " | " | 1.90 | " |
| Same | 370½ | Deed | Name of Ed Harris, | 768 | 1 | 7 | " | " | " | " | " | " | " | 3.70 | 8 |
| Same | 553 3-4 | " | Name of L. Carter, | 313 | 3 | 9 | " | " | " | " | " | " | " | 5 53.7½ | " |
| Same | 808 | " | Name of same Grant, | 309 | 3 | 9 | " | " | " | " | " | " | " | 8.8 | " |
| Same | 525 | Entry | Name of Wm. Hill, | 773 | 2 | 7 | " | " | " | " | " | " | " | 5.25 | " |

(Page 4) Cont.

| Persons Name | Acres | Titl. | REMARKS | #of Ent. | Age | Sec. | Dist. | Town Lots | Lot | #of Poll | Free Slave | Stor. | Stud or Jack | $ cts. M |
|---|---|---|---|---|---|---|---|---|---|---|---|---|---|---|
| Campbell, Geo.W. | 80 | Grant | Part | 337 | 2 | 7 | 13 | " | " | 1 | " | " | " | .80 |
| Calvert, Levi | " | " | " | " | " | " | " | 3 | " | 1 | " | " | " | 5 " |
| Calvert, John D. | " | " | " | " | " | " | " | 1 | " | 1 | " | " | " | 2 " |
| Calvert, Joseph W. | " | " | " | " | " | " | " | " | " | 1 | " | " | " | " 50 |
| Clark, Christopher R. | " | " | " | " | " | " | " | " | " | 1 | " | " | " | " 50 |
| Clark, James W. | 5000 | Entry | " | " | " | " | " | " | " | " | " | " | " | 50 50 |
| Chaplin, Moses | 104 | " | " | " | 3 | 8 | " | " | " | 1 | " | " | " | " 50 |
| Canada, Behethlum | " | " | " | " | " | " | " | " | " | " | 2 | " | " | 2 " |
| Clark, Levi | " | " | " | " | " | " | " | " | " | 1 | 1 | " | " | 1 50 |
| Cashem, Martin | " | " | " | " | " | " | " | " | " | 1 | " | " | " | " 50 |
| William Clark | " | " | " | " | " | " | " | " | " | 1 | " | " | " | " 50 |
| Clark, David, | " | " | " | " | " | " | " | " | " | 1 | " | " | " | " 50 |
| Covet, John F., | 180 | Enty. | " | 847 | 2 | 9 | 12 | " | " | 1 | " | 1 | " | 3 30 |
| Crum, Peter, | " | " | " | " | " | " | " | " | " | 1 | " | " | " | " 50 |
| Christman, Richard, | " | " | " | " | " | " | " | " | " | 1 | " | " | " | " 50 |
| Carter, Reubin, | " | " | " | " | " | " | " | " | " | 1 | " | " | " | " 50 |
| Clayton, John, | 270 | Deed | Part of 640 Thomas, Henderson | 1250 | 2 | 7 | " | " | " | 1 | 2 | " | " | 5 20 |
| Campbell, Daniel, | 100 | " | Dougherty & McCork- In name of 1S | " | 2 | " | " | " | " | " | 2 | " | " | 3 " |
| Craig, Hugh, | 146 | " | In name of same | 1097 | 2 | 6 | " | " | " | 1 | " | " | " | 1 46 |
| Craig, William, | " | " | " | " | " | " | " | " | " | 1 | " | " | " | 1.50 |
| Cartwright, Robt. | " | " | Name Adr. Denning | " | 2 | 5 | " | " | " | " | 2 | " | " | 3.64 |
| Cooper, Henry | " | " | Deed | " | " | " | " | " | " | 1 | " | " | " | " 50 |
| Cruice, Isaac, | 320 | | Part of 640 acres in name of Joseph Alsop | 1012 | 2 | 6 | 12 | " | " | 1 | " | " | " | 3.70 |

(Page 5)

| Persons Names | Acres of Lnd. | Dec. of Titl. | REMARKS | #of Ent. | Rge. | Sec. | Dist. | Town Lots | #of Lot | Free Poll- | Slav. | Stor. | Stud or Jack | $ cts M |
|---|---|---|---|---|---|---|---|---|---|---|---|---|---|---|
| Crow, Benjamin B. | " | " | " | " | " | " | " | " | " | 1 | " | " | " | 50 " |
| Castles, John, | " | " | " | " | " | " | " | " | " | 1 | " | " | " | 50 " |
| Cooper, John, | " | " | " | " | " | " | " | " | " | 1 | " | " | " | 50 " |
| Cragley, Loyd, | " | " | " | " | " | " | " | " | " | 1 | " | " | " | 50 " |
| Cable, Henry, | " | " | " | " | " | " | " | " | " | 1 | " | " | " | 50 " |
| Cain, James C., | " | " | " | " | " | " | " | " | " | 1 | " | " | " | 50 " |
| Cantrell, Joseph, | " | " | " | " | " | " | " | " | " | 1 | " | " | " | 50 " |
| Cantrell, Duke, | " | " | " | " | " | " | " | " | " | 1 | " | " | 1 | 1 50 " |
| Cravens, John, | " | " | " | " | " | " | " | " | " | 1 | " | " | " | 1 50 " |
| Cooley, George, | 100 | | Deed (Part of 274 acres) (in name of Jno.Charlton) | 321 | 2 | 5 | 13 | " | " | 1 | " | " | " | 1 50 " |
| Cravens, Joseph, | " | " | " | " | " | " | " | " | " | 1 | 3 | " | " | 3 50 " |
| Carsley, Seth T., | " | " | " | " | " | " | " | " | " | 1 | " | " | " | " 50 " |
| Croley, William, | " | " | " | " | " | " | " | " | " | 1 | " | " | " | " 50 ? |
| Cantrell, Abron. P. | " | " | " | " | " | " | " | " | " | 1 | " | " | " | " 50 " |
| Crider, David, | 50 | | Entry | " | 1 | 9 | 12 | " | " | 1 | " | " | " | 1 " " |
| Chambers, Green-bury | " | " | " | " | " | " | " | " | " | 1 | " | " | " | " 50 " |
| Curlin, Samuel, | " | " | " | " | " | " | " | " | " | 1 | " | " | " | " 50 " |
| Curlin, ZachariahH" | " | " | " | " | " | " | " | " | " | 1 | " | " | " | " 50 " |
| Conner, Isham, | " | " | " | " | " | " | " | " | " | 1 | " | " | " | " 50 " |
| Cherry, Lawrence, | 228 | " | " | 625 | 2 | 7 | 13 | " | " | " | " | " | " | 2 28 " |
| Same | 640 | " | " | 52 | 2 | 9 | 12 | " | " | " | " | " | " | 6 40 " |
| Same | 213 | " | " | 1457 | 1 | 6 | " | " | " | " | " | " | " | 2 13 " |
| Cherry, Daniel, | 640 | " | "Name of Isaac Bateman, | 561 | 1 | 7 | 13 | " | " | " | " | " | " | 6 40 " |
| Same | 640 | " | "Name of do | 676 | 1 | 8 | " | " | " | " | " | " | " | 640 " |
| Same | 640 | " | " | 672 | 1-2 | 7 | " | " | " | " | " | " | " | 6 40 " |
| Charry, Jesse | 640 | " | " | 391 | 1, | 9,10,12, | | " | " | " | " | " | " | 6 40 " |
| Cherry, Darling, | 640 | " | " | 769 | 1 | 7 | 13 | " | " | " | " | " | " | 6 40 " |
| Deverough, Thos.D/ | 500 | " | " | 969 | 1 | 5 | 12 | " | " | " | " | " | " | 5 " " |
| Dougherty, George, | 4500 | " | " Part of 5000 acres | 98 | 3 | 9 | 13 | " | " | " | " | " | " | 45 " " |
| Dunnes, Anthony | 640 | " | " | 1326 | 2 | 9 | 12 | " | " | " | " | " | " | 6 40 " |
| Dickins, Samuel, | 160 | " | " | 1082 | 1 | 6 | " | " | " | " | " | " | " | 1 60 " |
| Dickens, Samuel & Wm. | 675 | " | " | 82 | 1 | 1 | 5 | " | " | " | " | " | " | 6 75 " |

(Page #6)6==== Acres Desc.  
| Persons Name | Ld, | Title | REMARKS | #of Ent. | Rge. | Sec. | Town Dist.Lots,lot, | #of Poll,Slav.Stor.Jack, | Free Stud or | $ cts | M |
|---|---|---|---|---|---|---|---|---|---|---|---|
| Sam'l. & | | | 1828 | | | | | | | | |
| Dickens,D=Wms,W | 200 | Entry | REMARKS | 143, | 1, | 5,6, | 12 | 1 | " | 2 | 50 |
| Davis, David W. | " | " | " | " | " | " | " | 1 | " | " | " |
| Douglass, Emore | 320 | " | " | 1347 | 1 | 8 | " | 1 | " | 3 | 50 |
| Billon, Thomas | 213 | " | " | 771 | 2 | 5 | 13 | 1 | " | 2 | 20 |
| Dawson, Isaac | " | " | " | " | " | " | " | 1 | " | 3 | 13 |
| Dent, Joseph | " | " | " | " | " | " | 2 | 2.0 | " | " | 50 |
| Delaney, William | " | " | " | " | " | " | " | 1 | " | " | 50 |
| Dunn, John | " | " | " | " | " | " | " | 1 | " | " | 50 |
| Dunn, Mathew P. | " | " | " | " | " | " | " | 1 | " | " | 50 |
| Drew, James | " | " | " | " | " | " | " | 1 | " | " | 50 |
| Dunn, Thomas | " | " | " | " | " | " | " | 1 | " | " | 50 |
| Davis, Jesse | " | " | " | " | " | " | " | 1 | 2 | " | 50 |
| Davis, Isham L. | " | " | " | " | " | " | " | 1 | " | " | 50 |
| Dunn, John P. | " | " | " | " | " | " | " | 1 | " | 2 | 50 |
| Donelson,Humphrey Drew, | 180 | " | " | 392 | 1 | 9 | 12 | " | " | 1 | 80 |
| Dougherty, George | 500 | " | " | 21 | 2 | 8 | " | " | " | 5 | 00 |
| Davis, Jesse | " | " | " | " | " | " | " | 1 | " | " | 50 |
| Davis, Nicholas | " | " | " | " | " | " | " | 1 | " | " | 50 |
| Damron, Noble L. | 50 | Deed | " | " | 2 | 7 | 13 | 1 | " | 1 | " |
| Davis, Fenuel | " | " | " | " | " | " | " | 1 | " | " | 50 |
| Dickson, Ephriam,D640,Deed, Bethel Bells House, | | | | | | | | | | | |
| Delany, Daniel | 540 | " | " | 846 | 1 | 5 | " | 1 | 2 | 8 | 90 |
| Delaney, Nell | " | " | " | " | " | " | " | 1 | " | " | 50 |
| Damron, John | 35 | Entry | " | " | 1 | 8 | 12 | 1 | " | " | 50 |
| Damron, Moses | " | " | " | " | " | " | " | 1 | " | " | 85 |
| Damron, John T. | " | " | " | " | " | " | " | 1 | " | " | 50 |
| Delaney, Elijah | " | " | " | " | " | " | " | 1 | " | " | 50 |
| Damron, Charles | " | " | " | " | " | " | " | 1 | " | " | 50 |
| Damron, George | 50 | " | " | 949 | 2 | 8 | 13 | 1 | " | " | 1 |
| Dougherty, Dennis | " | " | " | " | " | " | " | 1 | " | " | 50 |
| Edmonston, Jesse | " | " | " | " | " | " | " | 1 | " | " | 50 |
| W Edwards, Thomas,C. | " | " | " | " | " | " | " | 1 | " | " | 50 |
| Eli, Eley, | 200 | Deed | " | 1 | 1 | 6 | 12 | 1 | " | 2 | 50 |

(Page 7)

| Name | Acres of Lnd. | Desc.-Titl. REMARKS | #of Ent. | Rge. | Sec. | Dist. | Town Lots | #of Lot | Free Poll | #of Slav. | Stor. | Stud or Jack | 1828 $ cts M |
|---|---|---|---|---|---|---|---|---|---|---|---|---|---|
| (Page 7) | | | | | | | | | | | | | |
| | | (Nash) | | | | | | | | | | | |
| Eaton, John R., | 293¼, | Deed, Granted to Abner) | 132, | " | " | " | " | " | " | " | " | " | 2 93 2¼ |
| Same | 293¼ | " Do to Same | 133 | " | " | " | " | " | " | " | " | " | 2 93 2¼ |
| Same | 293¼ | " Do to Same | 134 | " | " | " | " | " | " | " | " | " | 2 93 2¼ |
| Same | 293¼ | " Do to Same | 137 | " | " | " | " | " | " | " | " | " | 2 93 2¼ |
| Same | 293¼ | " Do to Same | 145 | " | " | " | " | " | " | " | " | " | 2 93 2¼ |
| Same | 293¼ | " Do to Same | 149 | " | " | " | " | " | " | " | " | " | 2 93 2¼ |
| Eastas, John H. | " | " | " | " | " | " | " | " | 1 | " | " | " | 1 00 " |
| Ezzell, Harison, | " | " | " | " | " | " | " | " | 1 | " | " | " | " 50 " |
| Edmonston, Reubin, | " | " | " | " | " | " | " | " | 1 | " | " | " | " 50 " |
| Edmontson, James | " | " | " | " | " | " | " | " | 1 | " | " | " | " 50 " |
| East, John, | " | " | " | " | " | " | " | " | 1 | " | " | " | " 50 " |
| Eliott, George S., | 80, | Entry | 929, 1 | 8 | 13, | 2 | " | " | 1 | 4 | " | 8 " | " |
| Freeman, James, | " | " | " | " | " | " | " | " | 1 | " | " | " | " 50 " |
| Fitzgerald, Wm. | " | " | " | " | " | " | " | " | 1 | 8 | " | " | 2 50 " |
| Flack, James | 355 | " | 470 3 | 9.10 | " | " | " | " | 1 | " | " | " | 3 65 " |
| Frankling, Barnard, | 500, | " | | | | | | | | | | | |
| Freeman, Charles A. | " | " | 775 1 | 5 | 12 | " | " | " | " | " | " | 5 " | " |
| Freeman, John, | " | " | " | " | " | " | " | " | 1 | " | " | " | " 50 " |
| Forrest, Elisha, | " | " | " | " | " | " | " | " | 1 | " | " | " | " 50 " |
| Fich, John W., | " | " | " | " | " | " | " | " | 1 | 1 | " | 1 " | 6 " " |
| Force, William, | " | " | " | " | " | " | " | " | 3 | 1 | " | " | 2.50 " |
| Freels, David, | " | " | " | " | " | " | " | " | 1 | " | " | " | " 50 " |
| Farmer, Aron, | " | " | " | " | " | " | " | " | 1 | " | " | " | " 50 " |
| Farmer, Hiram, | " | " | " | " | " | " | " | " | 1 | " | " | " | " 50 " |
| Folks, Shearward, | " | " | " | " | " | " | " | " | 1 | " | " | " | " 50 " |
| Flemming, William, | 37½ | Deed, Moses Fisk | 1014, 2, | 5 | " | " | " | " | 1 | 6 | " | " | 6 87 5 |
| Same | 157 | " John Cooks, | 1136, 2, | 5 | " | " | " | " | " | " | " | " | 1 57 " |
| Same | 160 | " Part of M.Thomas 640 | " | " | " | " | " | " | " | " | " | " | " |
| Same | 79½ | Entry " | 1362 2, | 5 | " | " | " | " | " | " | " | " | 1 60 " |
| Same, | 160 | Deed Part of Eldridge & Hills 640 | 1173 2, | 6 | " | " | " | " | " | " | " | " | " 79 5 |
| Same | 450 | " Heirs of G.Christian | 1057 1, | 6 | " | " | " | " | 1 | " | " | " | 1 60 " |
| Foster, James C., | " | " | 2151 2, | " | " | " | " | " | 1 | 1 | " | " | 4 50 " |
| | | | " | " | " | " | " | " | " | " | " | " | " 50 " |

Page (8)　　　Acres  Desc.　　　　　　　　　　　　　　　　#of　　　　　Town  #of Free　　　　　　　　　　　　　horse
Name　　　　　Lnd.- Titl.　R E M A R K S　　　　　Ent. Rge.Sec.Dist.Lots, Lot,Poll,Slav. Stor.Jack $ cts M

| Name | Acres | Titl. | Remarks | Ent. | Rge. | Sec. | Dist. | Lots | Town Lot | Poll | Slav. | Stor. | Jack | $ | cts | horse or M |
|---|---|---|---|---|---|---|---|---|---|---|---|---|---|---|---|---|
| | | | 1828 | | | | | | | | | | | | | |
| Fowler, James Jr. | " | " | " | " | " | " | " | " | " | " | " | " | " | " | 50 | " |
| Fowler, James Sr. | " | " | " | " | " | " | " | " | " | 1 | " | " | " | " | 50 | " |
| Foster, George | " | " | " | " | " | " | " | " | " | 1 | 2 | " | " | 2 | 50 | " |
| Force, Albert B. | 160 | Entry | " | 780 | 2 | 6 | 13 | " | " | 1 | 3 | " | " | 5 | 10 | " |
| Foster, Clabourn | " | " | " | " | " | " | " | " | " | 1 | " | " | " | " | 50 | " |
| Fowler, Samuel | " | " | " | " | " | " | " | " | " | 1 | 1 | " | " | 1.50 | | " |
| Furlong, Hudson | " | " | " | " | " | " | " | " | " | 1 | " | " | " | " | 50 | " |
| Freeman, Richard-son | " | " | " | " | " | " | " | " | " | | | | | | | |
| Garison, Isham | " | " | " | " | " | " | " | " | " | 1 | 2 | " | " | 2 | 50 | " |
| Gardner, Jeptha | 83 | Deed,(60 Jacob Bell,Jr. | " | " | 1 | 7 | 13 | 2 | " | 1 | " | " | " | " | 50 | " |
| | | (3 acres John Terrell, | | | | | | | | | 3 | " | 1, | 10 | 13 | " |
| Gardner, Alfred | " | " | " | " | " | " | " | " | " | 1 | " | " | " | " | 50 | " |
| Griggs, Thos. H. | " | " | " | " | " | " | " | " | " | 1 | 2 | " | " | 2 | " | " |
| Griggs, Wm. A. | " | " | " | " | " | " | " | " | " | 1 | " | " | " | " | 50 | " |
| Green, Jos. H. | 1000 | Entry | " | 850 | 2 | 7 | " | " | " | 1 | " | " | " | 10 | " | " |
| Same | 665 | " | " | 872 | 2 | 6 | " | " | " | " | " | " | " | 6 | 45 | " |
| Carter, William | 640 | " | Joseph Tracy | " | 3 | 7 | " | " | " | 1 | " | " | " | 6 | 40 | " |
| Garrett, Henry A. | " | " | " | " | " | " | " | " | " | 1 | " | " | " | " | 50 | " |
| Glasco, Isaac | " | " | " | " | " | " | " | " | " | 1 | " | " | " | " | 50 | " |
| Greer, James | 416, | " | Part of 618 Acres | 1- | 6&7,3½ | | | | " | 1 | " | " | " | 10 | 16 | " |
| Same | 274 | " | " | " | 1 | 7 | " | " | " | " | " | " | " | 2 | 74 | " |
| Same | 100 | " | " | " | 1 | 7 | " | " | " | " | " | " | " | 1 | 00 | " |
| Same | 500 | " | " | " | 1 | 7 | " | " | " | " | " | " | " | 5 | 50 | " |
| Same | 100 | " | " | " | 1 | 7 | " | " | " | " | " | " | " | 1 | " | " |
| Same | 100 | " | " | " | 1 | 6 | 13 | " | " | " | " | " | " | 1 | " | " |
| Greer, &CMcCorkle | 275 | " | " | 1 | 1 | 7 | 12 | " | " | " | " | " | " | 2 | 75 | " |
| Greer, David S. | " | " | " | " | " | " | " | 1 | " | " | " | " | " | 1 | 50 | " |
| Green S.Brackin | 223 | " | " | " | 1 | 7 | " | " | " | " | " | " | " | 2 | 23 | " |
| Garrison, Edward | " | " | " | " | " | " | " | " | " | " | " | " | " | " | 50 | " |
| Gilbert, Robert | 64,Deed,Daugherty& McCorkle | | | | 2, | 5 | 12 | " | " | 1 | 1 | " | " | 2 | 14 | " |
| Goldsby, James | /" | " | " | " | " | " | " | " | " | 1 | 4 | " | " | 4 | " | " |
| Goldsby, Stephen | " | " | " | " | " | " | " | " | " | 1 | " | " | " | " | 50 | " |
| Gilbert, Randolph | " | " | " | " | " | " | " | " | " | 1 | 1 | " | " | 1 | 50 | " |
| Gilbert, Jonathan, | 91½ | " | Joab Bells No 640, | 767 | 1 | 7 | 11½ | " | " | 1 | " | " | " | 2 | 41 | 5 |
| Groom, Bright | " | " | " | " | " | " | " | " | " | 1 | 1 | " | " | " | 50 | " |
| Glass, Elisha W. | " | " | " | " | " | " | " | " | " | 1 | " | " | " | " | 50 | M |

(Page 9) 

| NAME | Acres Lnd.Titl. | Dec. REMARKS | #of Ent,Rge,Dist.Lot Rge Sec. | Dist. | Town Lots,Poll,Slav.Stor.Jack | #of Free | Horse or | $ cts | M |
|---|---|---|---|---|---|---|---|---|---|
| Guinn, William, | 262½ | Bond, Thomas Hopkins, 1797, | 1, 6 | 12 | " " " " " | 1 | " | 3 12-5 | " |
| Gailey, James | " | " | " " | " | " " " " " | 1 | " | " 50 | " |
| Groom, Stephen H. | " | " | " " | " | " " " " " | 1 | " | " 50 | " |
| Herd, George D. | 16 | Deed, Absolom, Jim | 1500 1 | 7 | " " " " " | 1 | " | " 66 | " |
| Hasky, Archibald, | " | " | " " | " | " " " " " | 1 | " | " 50 | " |
| Harmon, Israel, | " | " | " " | " | " 1 " " " | 1 | 1 | 5 " | " |
| Hornbeak, James | " | " | " " | " | " 1 " " " | " | 3 | 3 50 | " |
| Hart, James, | 480 | Entry, Part of 640 Acres 1360 | 1 | 6 | " " " " " | 1 | " | 4 80 | " |
| Henderson, Thos. | 360 | " | " 2 | 9 | " " " " " | " | " | 3 60 | " |
| Same, | 640 | " | " 1 | 9 | " " " " " | " | " | 6 40 | " |
| Same | 1700 | ", Part of 2560 Acres, 640-2.3 | 7 | 13 | " " " " " | " | " | 17 " | " |
| Howard, M.H., | 228 | Deed, Cene Johnston | 219 2, | 9 | " " " " " | " | " | 2 28 | " |
| Hockney, Isaac S. | " | " | " " | " | " " " " " | 1 | " | " 50 | " |
| Harmon, Jesse, | " | " | " " | " | " " " " " | 1 | " | " 50 | " |
| Hill, William, | 640 | Enty, | " " | " | " " " " " | 1 | " | 6 40 | " |
| Hughes, Archelous M. | " | " | " " | " | " " " " " | 1 | " | " 50 | " |
| Henry, John H. | " | " | " " | " | " " " " " | 1 | " | " 50 | " |
| Huggins, Jeremiah | " | " | " " | " | " " " " " | 1 | " | " 50 | " |
| Huggins, Robt. | " | " | " " | " | " " " " " | 1 | " | " 50 | " |
| Huggins, William, | " | " | " " | " | " " " " " | 1 | " | " 50 | " |
| Hains, Andrew, | " | " | " " | " | " " " " " | 1 | " | " 50 | " |
| Henderson, Robert, | " | " | " " | " | " " " " " | 1 | " | " 50 | " |
| Henlebert, Wm. | " | " | " " | " | " " " " " | " | " | " 50 | " |
| Howard, Geo. W., | 60, deed, 40 acres Daugherty & McCorkle 250 20 acres Jno.Jenkins | | 1.2,7 1249 | 12 | " " " " " | " | " | " 50 | " |
| Hill, Henry M. | 93 3/4 | " | 1611,2,6,7 | " | " " " " " | 1 | " | 1 10 | " |
| Hill, Dilila | 77 | " Abram Newton, | 1842 2,7 | " | " " " " " | 1 | " | " 50 | " |
| House, John, | 100 | " Towner Werdon, | " " | " | " " " " " | " | " | 1 77 | " |
| Hatler, James | " | " | " " | " | " " " M " | " | " | " 50 | " |
| Hayse, William, | 64 | " Robert, Gilbert | " 2 | 5 | " " " " " | 1 | " | 1 14 | " |
| Hunter, William, | " | " | " " | " | " " " " " | 1 | " | " 50 | " |
| Henderson, Jno.R. | 100, | " | " 2 | 6 | " " " " " | 1 | " | 1 80 | " |

(Page 9)

| Name | Acres | Dec. Ind. | Titl. | REMARKS | #of Ent. | Rge. | Sec. | Dis.Lot | Lot | Town Pol | #of Free Slav. | Stor. | Jac. | Hors. or M | $ cts. |
|---|---|---|---|---|---|---|---|---|---|---|---|---|---|---|---|
| Henderson, Robt. | " | " | " | " | " | " | " | " | " | 1 | " | " | " | " | " 50 |
| Hoggard, Byers, | " | " | " | " | " | " | " | " | " | 1 | " | " | " | " | " 50 |
| Holly, Hazell, | " | " | " | " | " | " | " | " | " | 1 | " | " | " | " | " 50 |
| (Page 10) | | | | | | | | | | | | | | | |
| Hignight, John, | " | " | " | " | " | " | " | " | " | 1 | " | " | " | " | " 50 |
| Herrod, James, | " | " | " | " | " | " | " | " | " | 1 | " | " | " | " | " 50 |
| Henry, Moses, | " | " | " | " | " | " | " | " | " | 1 | " | " | " | " | " 50 |
| Harmon, Samuel, | " | " | " | " | " | " | " | " | " | 1 | " | " | " | " | " 50 |
| Harmon, Abram, | " | " | " | " | " | " | " | " | " | 1 | " | " | " | " | " 50 |
| Hulith, Thomas P., 60, Deed | | | " | " | 2 | 7 | 13 | " | " | 1 | " | " | " | " | 1 10 |
| Hulitt, Austin, | " | " | " | " | " | " | " | " | " | 1 | " | " | " | " | " 50 |
| Harper, Forester | " | " | " | " | " | " | " | " | " | 1 | " | " | " | " | " 50 |
| Hendrix, Alfred, 119 | " | " | " | " | " | " | " | " | " | 1 | " | " | " | " | " 50 |
| Hendrix, Henry, | " | " | " | " | 2 | 7 | " | " | " | 1 | 1 | " | " | " | 2 19 |
| Huey, John, | " | " | " | " | " | " | " | " | " | 1 | " | " | " | " | " 50 |
| Herd, Baley, E., 50 Entry | 930 | | " | " | 1 | 8 | " | " | " | 1 | " | " | " | " | 1 " |
| Herron, James | " | " | " | " | " | " | " | " | " | 1 | " | " | " | " | " 50 |
| Herron, William, | " | " | " | " | " | " | " | " | " | 1 | " | " | " | " | " 50 |
| Horton, Archibald" | " | " | " | " | " | " | " | " | " | 1 | " | " | " | " | " 50 |
| Horton, John, | " | " | " | " | " | " | " | " | " | 1 | " | " | " | " | " 50 |
| Horton, James, | " | " | " | " | " | " | " | " | " | " | " | " | " | " | " 50 |
| Horton, George, | " | " | " | " | " | " | " | " | " | 1 | " | " | " | " | " 50 |
| Horton, Robert, | " | " | " | " | " | " | " | 1 | " | 1 | " | " | " | " | " 50 |
| Johnson, Wm. H., 50 | 960 | | " | " | 1 | 5 | 13 | 1 | 12 | 1 | 1 | " | " | " | 3 50 |
| Julian, James, | " | " | " | " | " | " | " | " | " | 1 | " | " | " | " | " 50 |
| Jones, James, | " | " | " | " | " | " | " | " | " | 1 | " | " | " | " | " 50 |
| James, Grey, | " | " | " | " | " | " | " | " | " | 1 | " | " | " | " | " 50 |
| Johnson, John, | " | " | " | " | " | " | " | " | " | 1 | " | " | " | " | " 50 |
| Izzell, Uriah, | " | " | " | " | " | " | " | " | " | 1 | " | " | " | " | " 50 |
| Jones, William, | " | " | " | " | " | " | " | " | " | 1 | " | " | " | " | " 50 |
| Jones, Joshia | " | " | " | " | " | " | " | " | " | 1 | " | " | " | " | " 50 |
| Jowden, John, | " | " | " | " | " | " | " | " | " | 1 | " | " | " | " | " 50 |
| Jenkins, Mansfield," | " | " | " | " | " | " | " | " | " | 1 | " | " | " | " | " 50, |
| Jones, Drury, | " | " | " | " | " | " | " | " | " | 1 | " | " | " | " | " 50 |
| James, Hosea, 320 Deed # Jos.Alsap 640, 1012 | | | " | " | 2 | 6 | 12 | " | " | 1 | 2 | " | " | " | 5 70 |
| P John, Wm. L. | " | " | " | " | " | " | " | " | " | 1 | " | " | " | " | " 50 |
| Jenkins, Thomas | " | " | " | " | " | " | " | " | " | 1 | " | " | " | " | " 50 |
| Jenkins, Jesse, 50 | " | " | " | " | " | " | " | " | " | 1 | 1 | " | " | " | " 50 |
| Jenkins, John, 3300 | " | " | Different Tracks | " | " | " | " | " | " | 1 | 5 | " | " | " | 8 00 |
| | | | | | | | | | | | | | | | 38.50 |

(Page 11)

| Persons name | Acres | Dec. Lnd. Titl. | REMARKS | #of Ent. | Rge. | Sec. | Town Dis. | #of Lot, | Free Lot, | Pol, | Slav. | Hors. Stor. Jac | $ cts. | M |
|---|---|---|---|---|---|---|---|---|---|---|---|---|---|---|
| Jones, Israel, | 640 | Deed, | Robt. Browder, | 254, 1,2, | 6,7, | 13 | " | " | 1 | 3 | " | " | 9 90 | " |
| Jones, Wm., | 100 | Entry | " | 965 | 1 | 8 | " | " | 1 | 1 | " | " | 4 " | " |
| Jones, Willie, | 100 | 969 | " | 1 | 8 | " | " | " | 1 | " | " | " | 1 " | " |
| Jolly, Henry, | " | " | " | " | " | " | " | " | 1 | " | " | " | " 50 | " |
| Jones, Thornton, | " | " | " | " | " | " | " | " | 1 | " | " | " | " 50 | " |
| Jones, William, | " | " | " | " | " | " | " | " | 1 | " | " | " | " 50 | " |
| Kain, John, | 200, | " | " | 765 | 1 | 6 | " | " | 1 | " | " | " | 2 " | " |
| Killbrew, Elias, | " | " | " | " | " | " | " | " | 1 | 1 | " | " | 1 50 | 2 |
| Kenedy, James | 50 | " | Dougherty &McCorkle | " | 2 | 5 | 12 | " | 1 | " | " | " | 1 " | " |
| Kirk,George D., | 124, | Deed, | Martin Mayfield) 164) | " | 2 | 6 | " | " | 1 | 1 | " | " | 2 74 | " |
| Kamp, Frances, | " | " | " | " | " | " | " | " | 1 | " | " | " | " 50 | " |
| Kindred, Jos. C.," | " | " | " | " | " | " | " | " | 1 | 1 | " | " | " 50 | " |
| Landrum,Samuel, | " | " | " | " | " | " | " | " | 1 | " | " | " | 2 " | " |
| Lytle,Archibald, | 136, | Enty, | Part of 260 Acres, | 804, | 2 | 7 | " | " | 1 | 2 | " | " | 1 36 | " |
| Lee, John, | " | " | " | " | " | " | " | " | 1 | " | " | " | " 50 | " |
| Lea, Henry, | " | " | " | " | " | " | " | " | 1 | " | " | " | " 50 | " |
| Lee, Jeremiah, | " | " | " | " | " | " | " | " | 1 | " | " | " | " 50 | " |
| Lewis, Wiley, | 500 | Deed, | Part of Geo. Daugherty 5000, | 98, | 2 | 9 | 18 | " | " | " | " | " | " 50 | " |
| Lynn, Elum, | " | " | " | " | " | " | " | " | 1 | " | " | " | " 50 | " |
| Looney, Joseph | " | " | " | " | " | " | " | " | 1 | " | " | " | " 50 | * |
| Lovelady,Mars. | " | " | " | " | " | " | " | " | 1 | " | " | " | " 50 | " |
| Lovin, James, | " | " | " | " | " | " | " | " | 1 | " | " | " | " 50 | " |
| Lauler,Martin, | " | " | " | " | " | " | 3 | " | 1 | 1 | " | " | 6 " | " |
| Lewis, James, | " | " | " | " | " | " | " | " | 1 | 3 | " | " | 3 50 | " |
| Lynn,William, | " | " | " | " | " | " | " | " | 1 | " | " | " | " 50 | " |
| Lemmond,Robt. | " | " | " | " | " | " | d | " | 1 | " | " | " | 1 50 | " |
| Liddle, Francis," | " | " | " | " | " | " | " | 1 | " | " | " | " 50 | " |
| Loven, Joshua, | " | " | " | " | " | " | " | " | 1 | " | " | " | " 50 | " |
| Loyd, Thomas, | " | " | " | " | " | " | " | " | 1 | " | " | " | " 50 | " |
| Laxon, Wm.l&Jno." | " | " | " | " | " | " | " | " | 1 | " | " | " | " 50 | " |
| Ledbetter,Lewis," | " | " | " | " | " | " | " | " | 1 | " | " | " | " 50 | " |
| Lightner,David, | " | " | " | " | " | " | " | " | 1 | " | " | " | " 50 | " |
| Laswell, Joseph, | 50, | Enty | " | 958 | 2 | 9 | 13 | " | 1 | 1 | " | " | 2 " | " |
| " Peter | 50 | Enty | " | 957 | 2 | 9 | " | " | 1 | " | " | " | 1 " | " |
| " Sarah, | 50 | Enty | " | 955 | 1 | 9 | " | " | 1 | " | " | " | " 50 | " |

(Page 12)

| Persons Name | Acres | Dec. Lnd, Title. | REMARKS | #of Ent. | Rge., | Sec. | Dis. 13 | Town Lot, | #of Lot, | Free Pol, | Sla. | Stor. | Hors. Jack, | $ cts. | M |
|---|---|---|---|---|---|---|---|---|---|---|---|---|---|---|---|
| MLuster, Zadock, | 300, | Deed, | Landen Corten Grated | 324 | " | " | " | " | " | " | " | " | " | 3 " | " |
| McNeel, Wm. S., | " | " | " | " | " | " | " | " | " | 1 | " | " | " | " 50 | " |
| McLemore, Sugars, | 160, | Deed, | Part of Wm. Fowler 640 | 1036 | 1 | 9 | 12 | " | " | " | " | " | " | 1 60 | " |
| Same | 160, | " | -Part of Wm. Sharp 640 Acres, | 638, | 3 | 7, | 13 | " | " | " | " | " | " | 1.60 | " |
| Same | 640, | " | Wm.A. Tharp, | 630 | 2 | 6 | " | " | " | " | " | " | " | 6.40 | " |
| Same | 700, | " | Part of J.G. & Thos. Blount, 3000 acres | 591, | 1 | 5 | " | " | " | " | " | " | " | 7 " | " |
| McNeely, John, | 177½, | Bond, | Part of Jacob Bells Heirs 640 | 767, | 1 | 7 | " | " | " | " | " | " | " | 2 27 | 5 |
| Molin, Benjamin, McLemore) & Charlton, | 224, 794, | Deed, " | Part of Jerome McClain 3860 | 775, | 1&2, | 7 | " | " | 1 | 1 | " | " | " | 3 74 | " |
| Same | 160, | " | Prt. of Jacob Bells 640 Acres | 767, | 1 | 7 | " | " | " | " | " | " | " | 7 94 | " |
| McIver, John, | 272, | Enty. | | 473 | 3 | 7 | 13 | " | " | " | " | " | " | 1 60 | " |
| Same, | 372, | " | | 361, | 3 | 8 | " | " | " | " | " | " | " | 2 72 | " |
| Same, | 640 | " | | 131, | 2.3 | 6 | 12 | " | " | " | " | " | " | 3 72 | " |
| Same, | 4360 | " | | 325 | 1.2 | 5 | 13 | " | " | " | " | " | " | 6 40 | " |
| Same, | 280, | " | | 327 | 3 | 7 | " | " | " | " | " | " | " | 43 60 | " |
| Same, | 3252 | " | Part of 4336 Acres, | 752 | 1 | 9 | " | " | " | " | " | " | " | 2 80 | " |
| Marphay, Wm., | 797½ | " | Part of 987½ Acres, | 774 | 2 | 7 | " | " | " | " | " | " | " | 32 52 | " |
| McLemore, | | | Part of | | | | | | | | | | | 7 97½ | " |
| Jno. C., | 542, | Deed, | McIvers, 4336, | 752, | 1 | 9 | " | " | " | " | " | " | " | 5 42 | " |
| Moore, Somerset, | 3, | Enty, | | 1333, | 2 | 9 | 1 | " | " | 1 | " | " | " | " 3 | " |
| Moon, Wm.R., | " | " | | " | " | " | " | " | " | " | " | 1 | " | 3 " | " |
| McMullan, St. John, | 19½, | Deed, | David Delaney, | 1596 | 1 | 6 | " | 1 | " | " | " | " | " | 2 19 | 5 |
| Michel Standly, | " | " | " | " | " | " | " | " | " | 1 | " | " | " | " 50 | " |
| McLemore, Chas. | " | " | " | " | " | " | " | " | " | 1 | " | " | " | " 50 | " |
| Mizell, John, | " | " | " | " | " | " | " | " | " | 1 | " | " | " | " 50 | " |

(Page 12) Cont. Acres,Dec.　　　　　　　　　　　　#of　　　　　　　Town　#of Free　　　　　Hors.　　　　　　16
Persons Name, Lnd.,Titl.- R E M A R K S　Ent.-Rge.,Sec.Dis.Lots,Lot,Pol,Slav.Stor,Jac. $ cts. M

| Name | Acres | Title / Remarks | Ent. | Rge. | Sec. | Dis.Lots | Town Lot | #Free Pol | Slav. | Stor. | Hors. | Jac. | $ | cts. | M |
|---|---|---|---|---|---|---|---|---|---|---|---|---|---|---|---|
| McNeely, Michael, | 67, | Enty, T. Dalton, | 1476, | 2 | 9 | 12 | " | 1 | " | " | " | " | " | 97 | " |
| Mizelle, William, | " | " | " | " | " | " | " | 1 | " | " | " | " | " | 50 | " |
| Mayo, Frederick, | " | " | " | " | " | " | " | 1 | " | " | " | " | " | 50 | " |
| Moore, Jno. H., | 150 | | " | 2 | 7 | " | " | 1 | " | " | " | " | 2 | " | " |
| Morgan, Samuel, | 370, | Deed,(Part of Thomas ) | 1250 | 2 | 7 | " | " | 1 | 10 | " | " | " | 14 | 20 | " |
| Maynard, James | " | (Henderson 640, ) | " | " | " | " | " | 1 | " | " | " | " | " | " | " |
| Maynard, Wm. W. | " | " | " | " | " | " | " | 1 | " | " | " | " | " | 50 | " |
| Moore, James | " | " | " | " | " | " | " | 1 | " | " | " | " | " | 50 | " |
| Moore, John, | 72, | Deed,Part of James | " | " | " | " | " | 1 | " | " | " | " | " | 50 | " |
| | | Terrell s 2560 | | | | | | | | | | | | | |
| Mandy Thomas, | " | " | 1274, | 2 | 5 | 12 | " | 1 | " | " | " | " | 1 | 22 | " |
| McClesky, John, | " | " | " | " | " | " | " | 1 | " | " | " | " | " | 50 | " |
| (Page 13) | | | | | | | | | | | | | | | |
| Miller, Andrew, | " | " | " | " | " | " | " | 1 | " | " | " | " | " | 50 | " |
| McCrey, William, | " | " | " | " | " | " | " | 1 | " | " | " | " | " | 50 | " |
| Mathis, John, | " | " | " | " | " | " | " | 1 | " | " | " | " | " | 50 | " |
| Miller, George, | " | " | " | " | " | " | " | 1 | " | " | " | " | " | 50 | " |
| Miller, Isaac, | " | " | " | " | " | " | " | 1 | " | " | " | " | " | 50 | " |
| Miller, John, | " | " | " | " | " | " | " | 1 | " | " | " | " | " | 50 | " |
| Moon, William, | " | " | " | " | " | " | " | 1 | " | " | " | " | " | 50 | " |
| McElroy, Isham | | | | | | | | | | | | | | | |
| H. S., | " | " | " | " | " | " | " | 1 | " | " | " | " | " | 50 | " |
| Meadows,Spearman | " | " | " | " | " | " | " | 1 | " | " | " | " | " | 50 | " |
| McCormack, Charles, | " | " | " | " | " | " | " | 1 | " | " | " | " | " | 50 | # |
| Merideth, Moses, | " | " | " | " | " | " | " | 1 | " | " | " | " | 1 | 50 | " |
| Meredith, Daniel, | " | " | " | " | " | " | " | 1 | " | " | " | " | " | 50 | " |
| Miles, William, | 71 3/4 | | | | | | | | | | | | | | |
| | | Deed,Jas.Ward 55 | 563 | 2 | 7 | 13 | 1 | 1 | 1 | " | " | " | 3 | 71 | 7½ |
| Marshall, Joseph, | " | " | " | " | " | " | " | 1 | " | " | " | " | " | 50 | " |
| Mareus Phillips, | " | " | " | " | " | " | " | 1 | " | " | " | " | " | 50 | " |
| Mosley, Robt, | 856, | deed,Part of M.J.Hollis | | | | | | | | | | | | | |
| | | & Barnets,1907 | 528,1.2. | 5 | " | " | " | 1 | 10 | " | " | " | 19 | 6 | " |
| Mosley, Edward, | " | " | " | " | " | " | " | 1 | " | " | " | " | " | 50 | " |
| McDaniel, John, | " | " | " | " | " | " | " | 1 | " | " | " | " | " | 50 | " |
| Miles, William, | " | " | " | " | " | " | " | 1 | " | " | " | " | " | 50 | " |

17 in name of

(Page 13) Cont.

| Persons Name | Acres | Desc. Lnd.-Title, | REMARKS | #of Ent.-Rge.,Sec.Dis.Lot,Lot, | Town #of Poll,Slav. | Free Stor. | Hors. Jac. | $ | cts. |
|---|---|---|---|---|---|---|---|---|---|
| Mayo, William, | " | " | " | " " " " " | 1 | " | " | " | 50 |
| McDaniel, Moses, | " | " | " | " " " " " | 1 | " | " | " | 50 |
| McClain, Charles, | " | " | " | " " " " " | 1 | " | " | " | 50 |
| McIntosh, Solomon, | " | " | " | " " " " " | 1 | " | " | " | 50 |
| McDaniel, William, | " | " | " | " " " " " | 1 | " | " | " | 50 |
| McClain, John, | " | " | " | " " " " " | 1 | " | " | " | 50 |
| Mullion, Jackson, | " | " | " | " " " " " | 1 | " | " | " | 50 |
| Majors, Samuel, | 50 | Enty | " | 959 1 9 " " | 1 | " | " | 1 | " " |
| Morris, Thomas, | " | " | " | " " " " " | 1 | 1 | " | 1 | 50 |
| Mooney, Henry, | " | " | " | " " " " " | 1 | " | " | " | 50 |
| Nailing, Nelson, | 106, | Deed, | " | " 1 6 13,1 | 1 | 7 | " | 9 | 56 |
| Nailing, Willis, | 50, | " | J. R. Nailing, | 968, 1 7 " " | 1 | 2 | " | 3 | " " |
| Nailing, Jones, | " | " | " | " " " " " | 1 | " | " | " | 50 |
| Newton, James, | " | " | " | " " " " " | " | " | " | " | 50 |
| Newman, Wm., | " | " | " | " " " " " | " | 2 | " | 2 | 60" |
| Nettles, John A., | " | " | " | " " " " " | 1 | " | " | " | 50 |

(Page 14)

| Persons Name | Acres | Desc. Lnd.-Title, | REMARKS | #of Ent.-Rge.,Sec.Dis.Lot,Lot, | Town #of Poll,Slav. | Free Stor. | Hors. Jac. | $ | cts. |
|---|---|---|---|---|---|---|---|---|---|
| Nettles, Shedrick, | " | " | " | " " " " " | 1 | " | " | " | 50 |
| Nichols, Joseph, | " | " | " | " " " " " | 1 | " | " | " | 50 |
| Nichols, John, | " | " | " | " " " " " | 1 | " | " | " | 50 |
| Nolen, Henry, | " | " | " | " " " " " | 1 | " | " | " | 50 |
| Newton, James, | " | " | " | " " " " " | 1 | " | " | 2 | " " |
| Overton, John, | 488, | Grant, Landon Carter, | | 319 3 9 13 " | 1 | " | " | 4 | 88 |
| Same, | 232, | " | Same | 315 2.3 9 " " | 1 | " | " | 2 | 32 |
| Same, | 488 | " | Same, | 317 2.3 9 " " | 1 | " | " | 4 | 88 |
| Same, | 231 | " | Same, Part of | 322 2.3 9 " " | 1 | " | " | 2 | 31 |
| Same, | 622½ | " | Same, | 2 2.5 10 " " | 1 | " | " | 6 | 22½ |
| Same, | 89 | # | " | 2 9 " " " | " | " | " | 8 | 89 |
| Overton & Wharton, | 640 | " | " | 17437, 2 9 " " | 1 | " | " | 6 | 40 |
| Overly, Thos. | " | " | " | " " " " " | 1 | " | " | " | 50 |
| Osteen, John, | " | " | " | " " " " " | " | " | " | " | 50 |
| Ore, Wm. C., | 480, | Deed, Isaac Burgess | 640, 1284, 2 7 " " | 1 | " | " | 5 | 30 |
| Oneal, John, | 113 | " | " | " " " " " | 1 | " | " | 1 | 63 |

(Page 14) Cont. Acres Desc. #of Town #of Free Hors
Persons Name Lnd, Titl. R E M A R K S Ent. Rge.,Dist. Lots,Lot, Poll,Slav.Stor. Jack Hors $ cts M
                                           Sec.

| Persons Name | Acres/Desc/Remarks | #of Ent. | Rge. | Dist./Sec. | Town Lots,Lot | #of Poll | Free Slav. | Stor. | Hors Jack | $ cts M |
|---|---|---|---|---|---|---|---|---|---|---|
| Owen, Solomon H., | 240, ", Part of Solomon George | 300, 1156, | 2, | 5, 12, | " | " | " | " | " | 2 40 " |
| Owen, Daniel, | 94 3/4 " | " | 3, | 6,7,13 | " | 1 | " | " | # | 1 44 7½ " |
| Owen, Sarah, | 94 3/4 " | " | 3, | 7, | " | 1 | 2 " | " | " | 2 48 3/4 " |
| Owen, Charles, | 148, " | " | 3, | 7, | " | 1 | " | " | " | 1 98 " |
| Outhouse, Israel, | 28½, Entry, | " | 1, | 6, 12. | " | 1 | " | " | " | "78 5 " |
| Oneal, John, | " | " | " | " | " | 1 | " | " | " | " 50 " |
| Pharr, James, | " | " | " | " | " | 1 | " | " | " | " 50 " |
| Polk, A. Devereaux, | 500, " | 289. | 1 | 5 12 | " | " | " | " | " | "5 " " |
| Same | 500, " | 57 | 1 | 9 13 | " | " | " | " | " | 5 " " |
| Same, | 500, " | 119 | 1 | 9 | " | " | " | " | " | 5 " " |
| Same, | 305, " | 732, | 1 | 5 12 | " | " | " | " | " | 3 5 " |
| Polk, William, | 5000 " | 151 | 2 | 7 13 | " | " | " | " | " | 50 " " |
| Polk, Thos. H., | 300, " | 980 | 1, | 5,6, 12 | " | " | " | " | " | 3 " " |
| Peck, John, | 400, " | 1353, | 1, | 6, 12, | " | " | " | " | " | 4 " " |
| Powell, Robert, | " | " | " | " | " | 1 | 2 | " | " | 2 50 " |
| Phillips, Thos. H., 400, Deed, John Terrell, | " | " | " | " | " | 1 | 2 | " | " | 6 50 " |
| Parks, Fields, | " | " | " | " | " | 1 | " | " | " | " 50 " |
| Philpot, Jno. W. 1494, " Trustees, N.C. | 73, | 3 | 6 | " | " | " | " | " | 14 94 " |
| Payton, Bailey, 380, Entry, | " | 1 | 8 | 8 | " | " | " | " | " | 3 80 " |
| (Page 15) | | | | | | | | | | |
| Parham, Thomas, 200, Deed, Jas. Green, | " | 1, | 6,7, 12, | " | 1 | " | " | " | 2 50 " |
| Prater, Josiah, | " | " | " | " | " | 1 | " | " | " | " " " |
| Pound, Hiram, | " | " | " | " | " | 1 | " | " | " | " 50 " |
| Parish, Jesse, | " | " | " | " | " | 1 | " | " | " | " 50 " |
| Porter, John, | " | " | " | " | " | 1 | " | " | " | " 50 " |
| Purtle, X Jesse, | " | " | " | " | " | 1 | " | " | " | " 50 " |
| Parham, Amose, | " | " | " | " | " | 1 | " | " | " | " 50 " |
| Peoples, Samuel, 200, Deed,{Shelton & 1286 | | 2 | 7 | " | " | 1 | 1 | " | " | 5 00 " |
| Perry, John, ( Hineline 1000} | " | " | " | " | " | 1 | " | " | " | " 50 |
| Parker, Wm.F., | " | " | " | " | " | 1 | " | " | " | " 50 " |
| Pentecost, William | " | " | " | " | " | 1 | " | " | " | " 50 " |
| Patton, Thomas, | " | " | " | " | " | 1 | " | " | " | " 50 " |
| Price, James W., | " | " | " | " | " | 1 | " | " | " | " 50 " |
| Poindexter, Sam I | " | " | " | " | " | 1 | " | " | " | " 50 " |

(Page 15)Cont.

| Persons Name | Acres | Desc. Lnd.-Titl. | REMARKS | #of Ent. | Rge. | Sec. | Dis. | Town Lots | #of Lots | Free Pol | Slav. | Stor. | Horse Jac. | $ | cts. M |
|---|---|---|---|---|---|---|---|---|---|---|---|---|---|---|---|
| Pope, John W., | 160, | " | John Popes 500 | 332, | 2 | 8, | 13, | " | " | " | " | " | " | 1 | 60 |
| Pope, Samuel, | 160 | " | Part of same | " | " | " | " | " | " | " | " | " | " | 1 | 60 |
| Pope, John, | 180 | " | Part of same | " | " | " | " | " | " | " | " | " | " | 1 | 80 |
| Pannel, Wm. C., | 50 | Entry | | 958 | 1 | 5, | 1 | " | " | 1 | " | " | " | 1 | " |
| Pipkin, Wm. C., | " | " | " | " | " | " | " | " | " | 1 | " | " | " | " | 50 |
| Prean, John, | " | " | " | " | " | " | " | " | " | 1 | " | " | " | " | 50 |
| Pool, Ase, | " | " | " | " | " | " | " | " | " | 1 | " | " | " | " | 50 |
| Pippin, Joplin, | 200, | Deed, | William Somers, | " | 1 | 9 | 12 | " | " | 1 | 1 | " | " | 3 | 50 |
| Pool, Wm., | " | " | " | " | " | " | " | " | " | 1 | " | " | " | " | 50 |
| Pharley, Thos.M. | " | " | " | " | " | " | " | " | " | 1 | 1 | " | " | 1 | 50 |
| Phillips, Burrell, | " | " | " | " | " | " | " | " | " | 1 | " | 1 | " | 2 | " |
| Paschell, Alexander | " | " | " | " | " | " | " | " | " | " | 2 | " | " | 2 | " |
| Paschell, Jesse,M | | | | | | | | | | 1 | | | | | 50 |
| Rendel, William, | 300 | | Landon Carter | 314 | 5 | 7 | 13 | | | | | | | 3 | |
| Same | 200 | | Same | 311 | 3 | 7 | | | | | | | | 2 | |
| Roffe, Woodson, | 50, | Entry | | 966 | 1 | 7 | | | | 1 | | | | 1 | |
| Ragsdale, Joel, | | | | | | | | | | | 2 | | | 2 | |
| Rogers, Jubilee | | | | | | | | | 1 | 1 | 6 | | | 8 | |
| Rhodes,Jno.A.C. | | | | | | | | | | 1 | 6 | | | 6 | 50 |
| Rhodes Elisha | | | | | | | | | | 1 | | | | | 50 |
| Robertson, Edward | | | Part of Jas. | | | | | | | 1 | | | | | 58 |
| (Page 16) | | | | | | | | | | | | | | | |
| Ray, Jno. & Co. | 160, | Deed, | Harts 640 | 1360, | 1, | 6 | 12 | | | | | | | 1 | 60 |
| Same | 542 | | Prt.of Jno.McIvers 4336 | 752, | 1, | 9, | 13 | | | | | | | 5 | 42 |
| Same | 640 | | Prt.of Benjm. Cofields 2560 | | | | | | | | | | | 6 | 40 |
| Same | 131¼ | | Clenigle Cherrys 517, | 735, | 1, | 4,5 | | | | | | | | 1 | 31 2½ |
| Same | 160 | | Prt.of Culen Andrews 640 | 607, | 3 | 7 | | | | | | | | | |
| Same | 640, | | Name of David Broadwell, | 758, | 2 | 7 | | | | | | | | 1 | 60 |
| | | | | 986,2,3,6 | | | | | | | | | | 6 | 40 |
| Rhea, John, | 1250, | Enty. | Prt.of 2500 Acres, | 302,2,3, | | 6 | | | | 1 | | | | 12 | 50 |
| Revice, John, | 100, | Deed | William Qualls, | 1751, | 1, | 7, | 12 | | | 1 | | | | 1 | 50 |
| Rogers, Daniel L. | | | | | | | | | | 1 | | | | | 50 |
| Rogers, Thos. | 119 3/4, | deed, | John Rogers, | 848, | 2, | 9, | | | | | | | | 1 | 69 7-¼ |

(Page 16) Cont.

| Persons Name | Acres | Desc. Lnd. | Titl. | REMARKS | #of Ent. | Rge. | Sec. | Town Dis. Lots, | #of Lot.Pol, | Free Slav, | Hors. Stor.Jac, | $ cts M |
|---|---|---|---|---|---|---|---|---|---|---|---|---|
| Rogers, Jacob | | | | | | | | | 1 | 1 | | |
| Robertson, Jno.L. | | | | | | | | | 1 | | | 50 |
| Ridgway, John, | | | | | | | | | 1 | 1 | | 1 50 |
| Ridgway, Richard, | 121 | Deed | | | | 2 | 8 | | 1 | 1 | | 4 21 |
| Ridgway, Thomas, | | | | | | 2 | | | 1 | | | 50 |
| Rea, James, | 100, | | | | | 2 | 9 | | | | | |
| Ross, Wm. G., | | | | | | | | | 1 | | | 1 50 |
| Ridgway, James | 191 | | | | | 2 | 8 | | | 3 | | 4 91 |
| Russell Buckner, Sr. | 50, | | | William Ralls | | | | | | | | 50 |
| Russell, Buckner, Jr. | 3, | | | Jas.Willoughby | | | | | | | | 50 |
| Russell, George, | 80, | Grant, | | | | | | | | | | 1 30 |
| Ralls, Wm. | | | | | | | | | 1 | | | 50 |
| Roades, Abner, | 150, | Entry, | | | 843 | 1 | 9 | | 1 | | | 1 50 |
| Rolen, Tarlton | | | | | | | | | 1 | | | 50 |
| Reece, Yernel, | 200, | | | David Crockett, | 905, | 3 | 5 | 13 | 1 | | | 2 50 |
| Ren, John | | | | | | | | | 1 | | | 50 |
| Rogers, John W., | | | | | | | | | 1 | 4 | | 4 50 |
| Rorie, Reubin, | | | | | | | | | 1 | | | 50 |
| Ross, John, | | | | | | | | | 1 | | | 50 |
| Ross, Thomas, | | | | | | | | | 1 | | | 50 |
| Ross, Joshua, | | | | | | | | | 1 | 1 | | 1 50 |
| Ross, Lacy, | | | | | | | | | 1 | | | 50 |
| Rogers, Job, | 640, | Deed, | | John Jenkins, | 702,1, | | 8, 12, | 1 | 1 | 10 | | 17 90 |
| Balls, Wm. B., | | | | | | | | | 1 | | | 50 |
| (Page 17) | | | | | | | | | | | | |
| Roberts, Wm., | 50, | Entry | | 1828 | (954,8,9 | | | | 1 | | | 1 50 |
| Rightner, Wm. | | | | Two Tracts | (952 | 8 | 13 | | 1 | | | 50 |
| Sanders, Samuel, | | | | | | | | | 1 | | | 50 |
| Smith, Jas. W., | 879, | Deed, | | A.Nash,1/8 of 6000 Acre Tract, | | | | 13 | | | | |
| Smith, Wm. H., | 879 | | | 1/8 of Same | | | | | | | | 8 79 |
| Sweny, Jas. M., | 512 | | | Henry Pilars, | 640 | | | | | | | 8 79 |
| Sweeney, Jno.L. | 128, | | | Part of same | 1154,8.9,13 | 1 | | | | | | 5 12 |
| | | | | | | | | | | | | 1 28 |

(Page 17) Cont.

| Persons Name | Acres | Desc. Lnd. | Titl. | REMARKS | #of Ent. | Rge. | Sec. | Dis.Lots | Town Lot | #of Free Pol. | Slav. | Stor. | Hors. Jac. | $ | cts | M |
|---|---|---|---|---|---|---|---|---|---|---|---|---|---|---|---|---|
| Same | 128, | | | Henry Belotes, | 674, | 2, | 7, | 13, | | | | | | 1 | 28 | |
| Same | 265 | | | Blakemore & Ross, | 601, | 1,2 | 7, | | | | | | 1 | 2 | 65 | |
| Sample, Henry,A., | 50, | Entry, | | | 962 | 1 | 5 | | 1 | | | | | 2 | 50 | |
| Suthern,Benny | | " | | | | | | | | 1 | | | | | | |
| Simmons, Charles, | | | | | | | | | | 1 | | | | | | |
| Stunston, John, | 200, | Deed | | | | 2 | 9 | 12 | | 1 | 2 | | | 4 | 50 | |
| Stunston,Wm. | | | | | | | | | | 1 | | | | | 50 | |
| Sprout,Alexander, | | | | | | | | | | 1 | | | | | 50 | |
| Stanford,Hiram, | | | | | | | | | | 1 | | | | | 50 | |
| Steele, John, | 40, | Part of Porter & McGavock 344 3/4 | | | 1542, | 2, | 7 | | | 1 | | | | | 90 | |
| Steele, Geo. R., | 500, | Part of Same | | | | | | | | 1 | | | | 1 | 56 | |
| Standley, Elijah, | 106, | Enty, | | | 1406, | 2, | 7 | | | 1 | | | | | 50 | |
| Standfor, Jno. | | | | | | | | | | 1 | | | | | 50 | |
| Standley,Noah, | | | | | | | | | | 1 | | | | | 50 | |
| Smith, Hugh D., | 66, | Deed,Thomas Hopkins, 328½ | | | 1797, | 2, | 6, | | | 1 | | | | 1 | 16 | |
| Stark, Thos. | 25, | Enty, | | | | | | | | 1 | | | | | 75 | |
| Smith, James, | | | | | | | | | | 1 | | | | | 50 | |
| Sutton, Samuel, | | | | | | | | | | 1 | | | | | 50 | |
| Skaggs, Martin, | | | | | | | | | | 1 | | | | | 50 | |
| Skaggs, James, | | | | | | | | | | 1 | | | | | 50 | |
| Stanford,Thomas | 25, | | | | 918, | 1, | 6, | 13 | | 1 | | | | | 75 | |
| Smart, Stephen, | 70 | Part of | | | | 1, | 8, | 12, | | 1 | | | | | 70 | |
| Smart, Phillip | 230, | Deed,Jas. Somers | | | 3840,1471, | 2 | 7 | | | 1 | | | | 2 | 30 | |
| Smart, Joseph, | | | | | | | | | | 1 | | | | | 50 | |
| Smart, Wm. | | | | | | | | | | 1 | | | | | 50 | |
| Shenklin,David, | | | | | | | | | | 1 | | | | | 50 | |
| Shutley,Chas. | 100, | Deed,Thomas Sharp, | | | 250, 208, | 1, | 9 | 13 | | 1 | | | | 1 | 50 | |
| Shutley, David, | 150, | 70 part of same (1828) | | | | 1 | 9 | | | 1 | | | | 2 | | |
| (Page 18) | | Part of | | | | | | | | | | | | | | |
| Shutley, Jno.M. | 80 | Deed, Thos. Sharpe | | | 250, 208, | 1, | 9 | 13 | | 1 | 1 | | | 1 | 30 | |
| Shutley, Jacob, | | | | | | | | | | 1 | | | | | 50 | |
| Seeth, Wiley, | | | | | | | | | | 1 | | | | | 50 | |
| Scott, Vaughn, | | | | | | | | | | 1 | | | | | 50 | |
| Somers, James | | | | | | | | | 2,60) | | | | | | 50 | |
| Shutley, Jno. R. | | | | | | | | | 61) | | | | | 3 | | |

(Page 18) Cont. Acres Desc.                              #of                Town   #of Free                Hors.
Persons Name     Lnd.,Titl.,  R E M A R K S   Ent. Rge., Sec.Dist.Lots, Lot, Pol,Slav.Stor Jac $ cts  M

| Persons Name | Acres Desc. Lnd.,Titl., REMARKS | #of Ent. | Rge. | Sec. | Dist.Lots | Town Lot | #of Free Pol | Slav. | Stor | Jac | Hors. | $ | cts | M |
|---|---|---|---|---|---|---|---|---|---|---|---|---|---|---|
| Standley, Lewis, | Part of John | | | | | | 1 | | | | | | 50 | |
| Terrell, Jeptha, | 500,Deed, Terrells 640 | 1 | 7 | | 2 | | 3 | | | | 10 | | 50 | |
| Thomason, Pheneas, | | | | | 1 | | 1 | | | | 2 | | | |
| Thompson, Jacob, | | | | | | | 1 | 4 | | | 4 | | 50 | |
| Terrell, Patrick, | | | | | | | 1 | 1 | | | 1 | | 50 | |
| Terrell, Peleg, | 640  John Cessels 3840, | 1 | 6 | | 1 | | | | | | 8 | | 40 | |
| Terrell, John, | 4346,Enty,Different Entrys | | | | 5 | | | 7 | | | 57 | | 96 | |
| Thomas, Joseph, | 160,Deed,John Terrell, 1413, | 1 | 7 | 12 | | | | 3 | | | 4 | | 60 | |
| Taylor, Isaac, | | | | | | | 1 | | | | | | 50 | |
| Tucker, Daniel, | | | | | | | 1 | | | | | | 50 | |
| Todd, William, | | | | | | | 1 | | | | | | 50 | |
| Thomas, James D.,150,Deed,Part of Isaac | | | | | | | | | | | | | | |
| Burgers 640 | 1284 | 2 | 7 | | | | 1 | 3 | | | 5 | | | |
| Thomas, John, 538 Part of 4 tracts, 2 | | 2 | 7 | | 1 | | 1 | 14 | | | 21 | | 38 | |
| Thomas,Tristrum H.251, | | 2 | 7 | | | | 1 | 8 | | | 11 | | 1 | |
| Trantham, Flowel, | | | | | | | 1 | | | | | | 50 | |
| Tyler, Wm. | | | | | | | 1 | | | | | | 50 | |
| Tolbert, James | | | | | | | 1 | | 1 | | 2 | | 50 | |
| Tansil, John Sr., | | | | | | | 1 | 1 | | | 1 | | | |
| Tansil, Edward, | | | | | | | 1 | 3 | | | 3 | | | |
| Tharp & Jenkins, 640,Entry,Jno. Evans & Wm. | | | | | | | | | | | | | | |
| A. Tharp, 525,1, 1, 13, | | | | | | | | | | | 6 | | 40 | |
| Taylor, Thomas, | | | | | | | 1 | | | | | | 50 | |
| Tucker, Alexander, | | | | | | | 1 | | | | | | 50 | |
| Thompson,Benjm,G., | | | | | | | 1 | | | | | | 50 | |
| Thompson, Benjm. | | | | | | | | 1 | | | 1 | | | |
| Thompson, Robert, | | | | | | | 1 | | | | | | 50 | |
| Thompson, William, | | | | | | | 1 | | 1 | | 1 | | 50 | |
| Thornton, Lemuel, | | | | | | | 1 | | | | | | 50 | |
| Thornton, Benjm. | | | | | | | 1 | | | | | | 50 | |
| Thompson, Jesse, | | | | | | | 1 | | | | | | 50 | |
| (Page 19) 1828 | | | | | | | | | | | | | | |
| Ury, Joseph, | | | | | | | 1 | | | | | | 50 | |
| Uhls, Frederick J., | | | | | | | 1 | | | | | | 50 | |

(Page 19) Cont|Acres Desc. | #of | | | | Town | # of Free | | | | Hors. | 23

| Persons Name | Lnd., Titl. REMARKS | #of Ent. | Rge. | Sec. | Dist. | Lots, Lot, | Poll, Slav, Stor, Jac, | $ | cts M |
|---|---|---|---|---|---|---|---|---|---|
| Vincent, Perry, | 100, Deed, Peter King, | 914, 1 | 7 | 13, | 1 | 63 | 1 | 2 | 5 | |
| Vincent, Orien, | | | | | 2 | | 1 | | 3 | |
| Wilkins, Lewelen, | | | | | | | 1 | 1 | 1 | 50 |
| Wade, Kinchen, | | | | | | | 1 | | | 50 |
| White, Tyrell C. | | | | | | | 1 | | | 50 |
| Ward, Robinson, | | | | | | | 1 | | | 50 |
| Williams, Kinchen, | (Part of Joseph) | | | | | | 1 | | | 50 |
| Warner, Mears, | 100, Bond(L.D.Smiths 274) | 1496, 1 | 7 | 12 | | | 1 | | 10 50 |
| Warner, Samuel A, | | | | | 2 | | 1 | | 3 | 50 |
| Winchester, Jas. | 100, Entry, | 587, 1 | 10 | | | | | | 1 | |
| Same, | 226, | 641, 2, | 7, | 13, | | | | | 22 | 26 |
| Williams, Zachareel, | 240 | | | 12 | | | | 3 | 5 | 40 |
| Wharten, Jesse, | 200, Entry | 247, 2, | 3, | 13 | | | | | 2 | |
| Same | 559¼, Grant, L.Costen | 310, 3, | 10, | | | | | | 5589 12½ |
| Same | 730 Do | 325, 2, | 9 | | | | | | 2 30 |
| Wooten, Stephen, | | | | | | | 1 | | | 50 |
| Wiggins, Benjm. | | | | | | | 1 | | | 50 |
| White, Henry, | | | | | | | | 2 | | |
| Williams, Jos.G., | | | | | | | 1 | 1 | 1 | 50 |
| Williams, Allin, 50 | (Part of Peter ) | | | | | | | | | 50 |
| Williams, Allin,156,Deed( Williams 640 ) | | 327, 2, | 9 | 12 | | | 1 | | 2 | 66 |
| Willis, Mark | | | | | | | 1 | | | 50 |
| Workman, Pleasant G., | | | | | | | | | | 50 |
| Willingham, Isaac, | | | | | | | 1 | 4 | 4 | 50 |
| Williams, Peter, 100, Entry Part of 640, | | 327,2, | 9 | | | | 1 | | 1 | |
| Wilson, Joseph | 100,Deed,Jason Wilson, | 780,2, | 9 | | | | 1 | 3 | 4 | 50 |
| Wilson, Jason, | 250,Entry | 785,2, | 9 | | | | | | 2 | 50 |
| Webb, Amos, | | | | | | | 1 | | 1 | 50 |
| Webb, John, | 228, in name of Thomas Decoech | 806,2, | 8 | | | | 1 | 1 | | |
| Willoughby,Jas. 10,Deed,Absolom Jones | | 1500 2 | 7 | | | | | 2 | 4 | 28 |
| William S, Gibson A. | | | | | | | | 1 | | 60 |
| Ward, Messer, 10 | | 2 | 7 | | | | | 1 | | 50 |
| Woodward,Geo. 244,Deed,Porter & Mc-Gavock, 344 3/4, | | 1542 2 | 7 | | | | | 1 | | 60 |
| | | | | | | | | | 294 | |

(Page 20)  Acres Desc. 1828

| Persons Name | Lnd. Titl. REMARKS | #of Ent. | Rge. | Sec. | Dist. | Town Lots | #of Lot | Free Poll | Slav. | Stor. | Horse Jac. | $ | cts | M |
|---|---|---|---|---|---|---|---|---|---|---|---|---|---|---|
| Wells, Robert, | | | | | | | | 1 | 2 | | 1/4 | | | |
| Williamson, Jno., | | | | | | | | | | | 1 | 2 | | |
| Wells, Hayden E. | 200, Deed, (Part of Shelton 1440, | 2 | 7 | | 12 | | 1 | 3 | | 5 | 50 | | |
| Williamson, Meredith, | (& Lovelace 1000) | | | | | | | 1 | | | | 50 | | |
| White, John L., | | | | | | | | 1 | | | | 50 | | |
| Winters, Aron, | 112, Deed, Daugherty & McCorkle,) | | | | | | | | | | | | | |
| Wells, Andrew, | | | | | | | | 1 | | | 1 | 12 | | |
| Ward, Britton, | | | | | | | | 1 | | | | 50 | | |
| Ward, William, | | | | | | | | 1 | | | | 50 | | |
| Walker, Simeon, | | | | | | | | 1 | | | | 50 | | |
| Warford, Samuel G. | 40, Deed, Joel Pinson, | 842, | 5, | 7 | | 13, | | 1 | | | | 90 | | |
| Wainscott, Andrew, | | | | | | | | 1 | | | | 50 | | |
| Williams, Martin, H.S., | | | | | | | | 1 | | | | 50 | | |
| Welch, John, | 27½ | | | | | | | 1 | | | | 77 | | 5 |
| White, Archibald, | | | | | | | | 1 | | | | 50 | | |
| Williams, Bartlett, | 100, M B Travis, | 964, | 1, | 8, | | 13 | | 1 | 2, | | 3 | | | |
| Willingham, Wm., | 30, Deed, R. Porter, | | 1, | 7, | | 12,2, | 75, | 1 | 1 | | 4 | 80 | | |
| Whitley, Marcus, | | | | | | | | 1 | | | | 50 | | |
| Wester, William, | | | | | | | | 1 | | | | 50 | | |
| Yarbrough, David, | 714, Deed, Geo. Daugherty Division, | 150, | 2, | 7 | | | | | | | 7 | 14 | | |
| Young, Robt. C., | | | | | | | | 1 | | | | 50 | | |
| Young, A. B., | 60, Entry, | 7 | 1 | 7 | | | | | | | | 60 | | |
| Same, | 40 | 1 | | 7 | | | | | | | | 40 | | |

(Page 20) Cont.

```
117432½  Acres of land ......$1174.32½
    65  Town lots ............    97.50
   463  Free Polls ...........   231.50    Two polls taken off leaves    461
   271  Slaves ...............   271.00    Three Slaves released leaves  268
    11  Stud Horses                57.00
     2  Stoars                     20.00
```

State tax amounts to ........ $398.68¼
County tax is ............... 418.68¼
Jury tax is ................. 370.17½
Tax for the courthouse is ... 443.58¼
Poor tax is ................. 220.18½
                              ........... $1851.32½

Total amount is $1851.31½

(Page 21)

A suplement tax list for the year 1828

| Persons Name | Acres | Desc. Lnd., Titl. | REMARKS | #of Ent. | Rge. | Sec. | Town Dist. | #of Lots, Lot, | Free Poll, | Slav. | Horse Stor.Jac. | M | $ cts |
|---|---|---|---|---|---|---|---|---|---|---|---|---|---|
| Auld, Callin, | 3000, | Deed, | (half of 6 tracts (of 1000 acres each) | | | | 13 | | | | | | 30.00 |
| Anderson, Wm., | 640, | | | | | | | | | | | | 6.40 |
| Same | 171, | Entry, | | 829, | 1 | 10 | 12 | | | | | | 1 71 |
| Barnes, Stephen, | | | (Name of Scar- | | | | 13 | | 1 | | | | 50 |
| Bowers, Wm. G., | 213½, | Deed, | (berough & Sells) | 684 | 1 | 7 | 13 | | | | | 2 | 13½ |
| Same | 320 | | ½ half of Eldridge & Hill 640) | 1057 | 1 | 5 | 12 | | | | | | 3 20 |
| Blassingame, | | | | | | | | | 2 | | | | 2 |
| Butler, Robert, | 452, | Entry, | | 673, | 1 | 7 | 13 | | | | | | 4 52 |
| Bryant, Jno. H., | 1140½, | Grant, | (in name of J.G. & Thos.Blount) | 208 | | | | | | | | | 11 40½ |
| Same | 1000 | | Same | 169 | | | | | | | | | 10 |
| Barley, John, | 200, | Entry, | | 222, | 2 | 8 | 13 | | | | | | 2 |
| Cooke, John, | 40 | Entry | | 1747, | 2, | 10, | 12 | | | | | | 40 |
| Breken, James,G. | 1000 | | | 109 | 3 | 7 | 13 | | | | | | 10 |
| , Same | 240 | | | 601 | 1 | 9 | 12 | | | | | | 2 40 |
| Childress, Jas. | 90 | Deed, | Part of Elijah Robertson 500 | | | | | | | | | | 90 |

(Page 21) Cont.

| Persons Name | Acres Desc. Lnd.Titl. REMARKS | #of Ent. | Rge. | Sec. | Town Dist.Lots,Lot, | #of Free Poll,Slav.Stor.Jac. | Horse or $ Cts. M |
|---|---|---|---|---|---|---|---|
| | (In name of | | | | | | |
| Claybourn,Thos. | 1100,(Landon Carter, | | | | | | 11. |
| Same, | 409,Part of 640 | | | | | | 4.09 |
| Cassilman,Lazarus, | | | | | | 1, | 1.50 |
| Dotey, James, | | | | | | 1, | 2.50 |
| Freeman, Charles, | 100,Enty,James Long, | 963, | 1, | 7, | 13, | 1, | 1.00 |
| John Gester | | | | | | | .50 |
| Huntsman & Tatten,2100, | | | | | | 1, | 21. |
| Hendrix, Jeremiah, | 228,Ent. | 496, | 2, | 8.9 | 12 | | 2.28 |
| Hamilton, William, | 50, | | | | | 1, | 1. |
| Harrold, John, | | | | | | 1, | .50 |
| Hinderson,Thomas, | 2560 | 640, | 3, | 7, | 13, | | 25.60 |
| Same, | 860 | | | | | | 8.60 |
| Hughes, John, | 640,Name of Thomas Henderson, | | | | | | 6.40 |
| Jackson, Thomas, | 1036, | | | | | | 10.36 |
| Love,Robt. & Thos.,2596,Different Tracts | | | | | | | 25.36 |
| Lindsey, Isaac, | 44. | | | | | | .44 |
| McLemore &Vaulx, | 381,(Part of McIlhatton & ) | | | | | | 3.80 |
| | ( Bandy 1907 Acres ) | | | | | | |
| McLemore,John C., | 640,(in name of John Wilson,274 | | | | | | 6.40 |

(Page 22) 1828

| | (Part of | | | | | | |
|---|---|---|---|---|---|---|---|
| McLemore & Vaulse, 1250,(John Rheas 2500 | | | | | | | 12.50 |
| McClain, Charles, | 50, Enty. | | | | | | .50 |
| McClain, John, | 50 | | | | | | .50 |
| McConnels, Philip H., 515, | | | | | | | 5.15 |
| McDaniel, John, | | | | | | | .50 |
| McCullock, Benjm. | 640, | | | | | | 6.40 |
| McGavock, Frances, | 890, | | | | | | 8.90 |
| Montgomery,Daniel, | 124 | | | | 1 | 1, | 2.74 |
| Same, | 128, Part of Isaac Parks 640, | | | | | | 1.28 |
| Montgomery, John, | 500, William Montgomery | | | | | | 5.00 |
| Neil, Andrew, | 1654, | | | | | | 16.54 |
| Parker, Isaac, | 512, Part of 640 | | | | | | 5.12 |

(Page 22) Cont.

| Persons Name | Acres Desc. Lnd.Titl. REMARKS | #of Ent.Rge.Sec.Dist.Lots.Lot,Poll,Sla.Sto.Jac. | Town #of Free | | Horse or | $ Cts. M |
|---|---|---|---|---|---|---|
| Pettygrew, Ebenezer, | 1250,gr.(Part of J. G. &(Thos. Blount, | 260, | 13 | | | 12.50 |
| Same, | 1084, Same | 124, | | | | 10.84 |
| Same | 1056, Same | 193, | | | | 10.56 |
| Marr, George, W. L., | 200, | | | | | 2 |
| Rhodes, Henry H., | 640, | | | | | 6.40 |
| Paschall, Elisha, | 218 | | | 1 | | 2.68 |
| Thurston/Benj., | 590½, Enty. | 286, 1.2 | 9 | | | 5.90 7½ |
| Shepherd, Abraham, | 285 2/3 | | | | | 2.85 2/3 |
| Stallings, John, | | | | 1 | | 50 |
| Sommers, James, | 2800, Part of 3840 | | | | | 28. |
| Speight & McGavock, | 640, | | | | | 6.40 |
| Shepherd, William B., | (Blount) 1100, Grant,toJ.& G. Thomas) | 191, | 13, | | | 11. |
| Same, | 1000 Same | 257, | | | | 10. |
| Same, | 1000, Same | 238 | | | | 10.00 |
| Shepherd, Charles B., | 1250, Same, | 216, | | | | 12.50 |
| Same, | 1000, Same, | 183, | | | | 10.00 |
| Same, | 1250, Same, | 209 | | | | 12.50 |
| Shepherd, James B., | 1070, Same, | 249, | | | | 10.70 |
| Same, | 1140, Same, | 196 | | | | 11.40 |
| Same, | 1362½, Same, | 241, | | | | 13.62 ½ |
| Shepherd, Frederick B.. | 1125, Same | 223, | | | | 11.25 |
| Same, | 1000, Same, | 220. | | | | 10. |
| Same, | 1184½, Same, | 201 | | | | 11.84½ |

Page 23)

| Kirkpatrick, Joseph, | 640, Enty. | | 12, | | | 6.40 |
|---|---|---|---|---|---|---|
| Hughes, Archelous | 100, | | 13, | | | 1. |
| Shepherd, Richard M., | 1125,Gr.,(to J.G. & Thos. (Blount, Same, | 213, 230, | | | | 11.25 13.62 |
| Same, | 1362, Part of | 198, | | | | 2.67 |
| Same, | 267, Same | 187 | | | | 10.56 |
| Shepherd, Penelope S., | 1056 Same | 176 | | | | 12.50 |
| Same | 1250, Same part of | 198 | | | | 2.44 |
| Same | 244, | | | | | |

(Page 23) Cont.

| Persons Name, | Acres of Desc. Lnd.Titl. | REMARKS | #of Ent. | Rge. | Sec. | Dis. | Lots, | Lot, | Town #of Free Poll, Sla. Sto. Jac. | $ | Cts. | Horse or M |
|---|---|---|---|---|---|---|---|---|---|---|---|---|
| Shepherd, John S., | 1140, | Same | 173, | | | | | | | 11.40 | | |
| Same, | 1000, | Same | | | | | | | | 10.00 | | |
| Same, | 489, | Same part of, | | | | | | | | 4.89 | | |
| Wilson, Lewis D., | 1000,Enty, | | | | | | | | | 10.00 | | |
| Wilson, Sem'l.D., | 272 | | | | | | | | | 2.72 | | |
| Veulx, James, | 150 | | | | | | | | | 1.50 | | |
| Watson, Robert, | 140, | | | | | | | | | 1.40 | | |
| Willis, John, | 2500, | | | | | | | | | 25.00 | | |
| Williamson, Heirs, | 640 | | | | | | | | | 6.40 | | |

62,534½ acres of land at $100.00 per 100 acres amounts to ..... $625.34½
8 Free Polls at 50 Cts. ................................................. 4.00
Two town lots at $1.50 is ............................................. 3.00
Three Slaves at $1.00 is ............................................. 3.00

(Page 24) Tax List - 1829

| Persons Name, | Acres | REMARKS | #of Ent. | Rge. | Sec. | Dis. | Lots, | Lot, | Poll, Sla. Sto. Jac. | $ | Cts. | M |
|---|---|---|---|---|---|---|---|---|---|---|---|---|
| Adams, Thos., | | | | | | | | | 1 | | .25 | |
| Anderson, William,E. | 640,Enty, | | 805, | 2, | 7, | | | 12 | | | 4.80 | |
| Same (Heirs,) | 171 | | 829, | 1, | 10, | | | | | | 1.28 | 2¼ |
| Anderson,(Baillie,) | 640, | | 603, | 1, | 9, | 13, | | | | | 4.80 | |
| Adkins, Joseph B., | 30, | | | 2, | 7, | 12, | | | | | .47 | 5 |
| Armstrong, Thomas, | | 256,Deed,Peter Williams, | 640, | 327, | 2, | 9, | | | 1 | 1, 2, 25 | | |
| Austin, Moses Sr., | | | | | | | | | 1 | | 1.92 | |
| Austin, Moses, Jr., | | | | | | | | | 1, | | .25 | |
| Austin, Vincent, | | | | | | | | | 1, | | .25 | |
| Austin, Samuel,F., | | | | | | | | | 1, | | .25 | |
| Acre, Jesse, | | | | | | | | | 1, | | .25 | |
| Abernathy,Littleton F., | 81½, | Entry, | 1264, | 2, | 9, | | | | 1 | | .86 | 1¼ |
| Adkerson, James, | | | | | | | | | 1, | | .25 | |
| Adkerson, William, | | | | | | | | | 1, | | .25 | |
| Alexander, Adam R., | 640, | Deed,John Terrell, | 3840, | 1, | 7, | 13 | | | | | 4.80 | |
| Same, | 29½, | Deed, John Terrll, | 640, | 1, | 7, | | | | | | .21 | 9 |
| Abboth, Spencer, | | | | | | | | | 1, | | .25 | |
| Adams, Abel, | | | | | | | | | 1, | | .25 | |
| Browder, Robert, | 440,Enty. Part of 640 | | | 1, | 6, | | | | | | 3.30 | |

(Page 24,) Cont.

| Persons Name, | Acres Dec. Lnd.Titl. | R E M A R K S | #of Ent.Rge.Sec.Dis. | Town, Lots,Lot,Poll,Sla.Sto. | #of Free | Horse or Jac. | $ | Cts. | M |
|---|---|---|---|---|---|---|---|---|---|
| Bracking, James, | 150, | | , 1, 7, 12, | | | | 1.12 | 5 | |
| Bowers, Giles, | | | | | 1 | | .25 | | |
| Bondurant, Albert G., | 55, | Deed,(Terrell & Lawrence, ( 25,30, | | | 1 | 1 | 1.16 | 2½ | |
| Bookout, Bradley, | | | | | 1 | | .25 | | |
| Breken, James G., | 1000, | Grant, | 17340,3, 7 | | | | 7.50 | | |
| Same, | 240, | | 17321,1, 9, | | | | 1.80 | | |
| Bosly, John, | 220 3/4,E., | Part of 640, | 221, 2, 8, 13, | | | | 1.65 | 5 | |
| Baldridge, Daniel, | 640, | | 725, 2, 7 | | | | 4.80 | | |
| Boling, Baxter, | 480, | Part of 640, | 1082, 1, 6, 12, | | | | 3.60 | | |
| Berry, Preseley,M., | | | | | 1, | | .25 | | |
| Bowers, Elbert J., | | | | | 1, | | .25 | | |
| Bevard, James H., | | | | | 1, | | .25 | | |
| Bell, Pulaski B., | | | | | 1, | | .25 | | |

(Page 25) 1829

| Persons Name, | Acres Dec. Lnd.Titl. | R E M A R K S | #of Ent.Rge.Sec.Dis. | Town, Lots,Lot,Poll,Sla.Sto. | #of Free | Horse or Jac. | $ | Cts. | M |
|---|---|---|---|---|---|---|---|---|---|
| Bondurant, Benjm., | 145 3/4, | Deed, Ralph King, | 1455, 1, 6, 12, 16,17 3, & 49, | | | | 17.09 | 5 | |
| Bondurant, Hillery H., | 4, | John Terrells | 640, 1, 7, 13, | 11, 1. | 1, | | 11.25 | | |
| Blount, John G., | 2500, | Ent., Part of 3000, | 591,1, 5, | | | | 18.75 | | |
| Same, | 274, | | 692,2, 9, 12, | .4, | 1 | | 2.05 | 5 | |
| Same, | 60, | | 860,1, 6, 13, | | | | .45 | | |
| Bayless, C & W, | | | | 1, 23, 1, | | | 11.50 | | |
| Bayless, Willie, | | | | 1, 1 | | | .75 | | |
| Baldridge, Wm., | 490, | Part of 640, | | | | | 3.67 | 5 | |
| Bowers, John, | | | | 1, 1, | | | .75 | | |
| Blakemore & Patterson, | 867, | | 671,2, 7, 13, | | | | 6.50 | 2½ | |
| Blakemore, James, | 146 3/4, | Deed,TilmanDickson, | 639,1, 7, | | | | 1. 9 | 8 | 3/4 |
| Same, | 130, | Heirs Richd.Smith, | 640, | | | | .97 | 5 | |
| Bishop, Richard, | | | , 1, 88, | 1, | | | 1.75 | | |
| Brown, Coonred, | 50, | Ent., | | | 1 | | /62 | 5 | |
| Barnes, Solomon, | | | 1734,2, 7, 12, | | 1 | | | 25 | |
| Belote, Henry A., | 512, | Deed,Henry Belote | 640, 674,2, 7, 13, | | | | 3.84 | | |

(Page 25) Cont.

| Persons Name | Acres | Desc. Lnd., Titl. | REMARKS | #of Ent.Rge. | Sec. | Town, Dis.Lots, | #of Free Poll, Sla. Stor., "ot, | Horse Jac. | $ Cts.M |
|---|---|---|---|---|---|---|---|---|---|
| Belote, Henry, | 128, | Entry, | Part of 640 | 1154, 1, | 8 & 9,12, | | | | .96 |
| Same, | 128 | | Part of 640 | 674, 2, | 7, 13, | | | | .96 |
| Brown, Eli, | | | | | | 1 | | | .25 |
| Barnard, William, | | | | | | 1, | | | .25 |
| Barnard, John, | | | | | | 1, | | | .25 |
| Barnard, Zadock, | | | | | | 1, | | | .25 |
| Busey, Edward | 60, | Deed, | | | | 1, | 2, | | 1.70 |
| Billingsby, Bazil, | | | | | | 1, | 1, | | .75 |
| Bridges, Griffin, | | | | | | 1, | | | .85 |
| Brasel, Edward, | | | | | | 1, | | | .25 |
| Bren, James. | | | | | | 1, | | | .25 |
| Buckley, James, | | | | | | | 2, | | 1. |
| Beadles, Basset A., | | | | | | 1, | | | .25 |
| Beadles, William, | | | | | | 1, | | | .25 |
| Bynum, Thomas, | | | | | | 1, | | | .25 |
| Baker, John, | | | | | | 1, | | | .25 |
| Buckley, Nathaniel H., | | | | | 2, 36, | 1, | | | 3.50 |

(Page 26)

| Persons Name | Acres | Desc. Lnd., Titl. | REMARKS | #of Ent.Rge. | Sec. | Town, Dis.Lots, | #of Free Poll, Sla. Stor., "ot, | Horse Jac. | $ Cts.M |
|---|---|---|---|---|---|---|---|---|---|
| Bennet, George, | | | | | | 1, | | | .25 |
| Bowers, Young, P., | | | | | | 1, | 2, | | 1.25 |
| Bryant, John H., | 1140, | Gt., | J.G. & Thos. Blount,208, | | 13, | | | | 8.55 |
| Same, | 1000, | | Same | 169, | | | | | 7.50 |
| Byrd, Nazareth, | | | | | | | | | .25 |
| Berry, William, | | | | | | | | | 2. |
| Bradshaw, Thompson, | | | | | | | 4, | | |
| Barham, Benjamin, | | | | | | 1, | | | .25 |
| Barger, Daniel, | | | | | | 1, | | | .25 |
| Barns, John, | | | | | | 1, | | | .25 |
| Bondurant, Robert M. | 166 3/4 | Deed, | | | 13, | 1, | | | 1.99 8 |
| Bowers, Wm. G., | 50, | | Wm. Williams | 961, 1, | 7 | 2, | 3, | | 2.37 5 |
| Same, | 380, | | Eldridge & Hill,640, | 1057, 1, | 6, 12 | | | | 2.40 |
| Same, | 213 3/4, | | Scarbrough & Sells, | 684, 1, | 7, 13, | | | | 1.60 |
| Same, | 250, | | Henry White, | 919, 1, | 6, | | | | .18 7 |

(Page 26) Cont.

| Persons Name | Acres | Desc. Lnd. Titl. REMARKS | # of Ent | Rge., Sec. | Dis. | Town Lot | # of Free Poll | Sla. | Sto. | Horse or Jac. | $ Cts. | M |
|---|---|---|---|---|---|---|---|---|---|---|---|---|
| Baker, James, | 16½, | Entry | | | | | | | | | .37 | 3 3/4 |
| Brown, Levi, | | | | | | | 1, | | | | .25 | |
| Bourland, James, | 25, | | 917,1, | 6, | | | 1, | | | | 43.7½ | 7½ |
| Beauchamp, Thomas D., | | | | | | | 1, | | | | .25 | 7½ |
| Bradshaw, John, | | | | | | | 1, | 2, | | | 1.25 | |
| Byrd, Bryan, | | | | | | | 1, | | | | .25 | |
| Calvert, Joseph, W., | | | | | | 1, 67, | | | | | 1.50 | |
| Caldwell, David P., | | | | | | | 1, | | | | .25 | |
| Cotton, Charles, | 640, | | 1366,1, | 5, | 12, | | | | | | 4.80 | |
| Clark, James W., | 5000, | | 104, 3, | 8, | 13, | | | | | | 37.50 | |
| Cherry, Clemigle, | 520, | | 617, 3, | 7, | | | | | | | 3.90 | |
| Claiborn, Thomas, | 200, | Grt., Landon Carter, | 311, 3, | 9, | | | | | | | 1.50 | |
| Same, | 300, | Same, | 312, 3, | 9, | | | | | | | 2.25 | |
| Same, | 300, | Same, | 314, 3, | 9, | | | | | | | 2.25 | |
| Same, | 30, | Same, | 324, 3, | 9, | | | | | | | 2.25 | |
| Same, | 409, | Part of 640 | 322,2 &3, | 9, | | (10,11, | | | | | 3.06 7½ | |
| Charlton, John, | 134, | Enty,Part of 184, | 858, 1, | 7, | | 4,(40 & 96,1, 1, | | | | | 7.80 | |
| Same, | 165, | | 1323, 2, | 9, | 12 | | | | | | 1.23 7½ | |
| Same, | 190, | Deed(Part ofWm. (Murfrees 987½, | 774, 2, | 7, | 13 | | | | | | 1.42 | |
| Same, | 370½ | Edward Harris, | 768, 1, | 7, | | | | | | | 2.82 | 8 3/4 |

(Page 27)

| Charlton, John, | 553 3/4 | L. Carter | 313, 3, | 9, | 9 | 13 | | | | | 4.15 | 3 3/4 |
|---|---|---|---|---|---|---|---|---|---|---|---|---|
| Same, | 808 | Same, | 309, 3, | 9 | | | | | | | 6.06 | |
| Same, | 525, | Enty, | 773, 2, | 7 | | | | | | | 3.93 | 7½ |
| Same, | 213½, | Deed,Thomas Dillon, | 771, 2, | 5 | | | | | | | 1.59 | 7½ |
| Cooper, Whitnil, | | | | | | (69 | 1, | 3, | | | 1.75 | |
| Cochran, Dennis, | | | | | | 3(70,71) | 1; | 1 | | | 5.25 | |
| Clark, Levi, | | | | | | | 1, | 1, | | | .75 | |
| Cherry, Daniel, | 640, | Deed,J.Bateman, | 678, 1, | 8 | | | | | | | 4.80 | |
| Same, | 640, | Same, | 672, 1&2, | 7, | | | | | | | 4.80 | |
| Same, | 640, | E, | 561, 1, | 7, | | | | | | | 4.80 | |

(Page 27) Cont.

| Persons Name | Acres, Desc. Lnd, Titl. REMARKS | #of Ent. | Rge. | Sec. | Town Dist. | Lots, Lot, | #of Poll, | Free Sla. | Stor. | Horse Jac. | $ | Cts. | M |
|---|---|---|---|---|---|---|---|---|---|---|---|---|---|
| Cherry, Lawrence, | 228, | 625, | 2, | 7 | | | | | | | 1.71 | | |
| Same, | 640, | 52, | 2, | 9, | 12, | | | | | | 4.80 | | |
| Same, | 213, | 1457, | 1, | 6, | | | | | | | 1.59 | 7½ | |
| Cherry, Darling, | 640, | 769, | 2, | 9, | | | | | | | 4.80 | | |
| Clark, Christopher R., | | | | | | | 1, | | | | .25 | | |
| Casselman, Lazarus, | | | | | | | 1, | | | | .25 | | |
| Christman, Richard, | | | | | | | 1, | | | | .25 | | |
| Carter, Reubin, | (64 | | | | | | 1, | | | | .25 | | |
| Clayton, John, | 370, Deed,Thos.Henderson, | 1250, 2, | 7, | | | | 1, | 2, | | | 3.27 | 5 | |
| Claxton, James | 128, Enty, | | | 13, | | | | | | | .96 | | |
| Campbell, Daniel, | | | | | | | | 2, | | | 1. | | |
| Cowan, James, | 640, D, Jesse Charry, | 391, 1, | 9 &10, | 12 | | | | | | | 4.80 | | |
| Chilton, William, | 300, | | | | | | | | | | 2.25 | | |
| Cruise, Isaac, | 320, Jos.Alsop, | 640, | 1012, 2, | 6, | | | | | | | 2.65 | 6 | |
| Clifton, John M., | | | | | | | 1, | | | | .25 | | |
| Cooper, Henry, | | | | | | | 1, | | | | .25 | | |
| Cartright, Robert, | 164, A. Deming, | | 2&3, 5, | | | | 1, | 2, | | | 2.48 | 7½ | |
| Cordel, Mark, B., | | | | | | | 1, | | | | .25 | | |
| Cimbrell, Joseph, | | | | | | | 1, | | | | .25 | | |
| Clifton, Eldridge, | | | | | | | 1, | | | | .25 | | |
| Craw, Benjn. B., | | | | | | | 1, | | | | .25 | | |
| Cocks, Edward M., | | | | | | | 1, | | | | .25 | | |
| Cathey,Thos.D.&J.W. | 875,E,Part of 1000 | 680, | 2, | 8 &9, | 12, | | 1, | | | | 6.56 | 1¼ | |
| Crum, Peter, | | | | | | | 1, | | | | .25 | | |
| Coleman, John, | | | | | | | 1, | | | | .25 | | |

(Page 28) 1829

| Clark, William, | | | | | | | 1, | | | | .25 | | |
| Clark, David, | | | | | | | 1, | | | | .25 | | |
| Cavit, John F., | 180,E, | 847, | 2, | 9, | 12 | | 1, | 1, | | | 2.10 | | |
| Cook, John, | 40 | 1747, | 2, | 10, | | | | | | | .30 | | |
| Cashin, Martin, | | | | | | | 1, | | | | .25 | | |
| Carr, Thompson, | | | | | | | 1, | | | | .25 | | |
| Conner, Isham, | | | | | | | 1, | | | | .25 | | |

(Page 27) Cont.

| Persons Name | Acres,Dec. End.,Titl. R E M A R K S | #of Ent. Rge.Sec.Dis.Lots,Lot. | Town,#of Poll,Sla.Sto.Jac. | Free Horse | Horse $ Cts. | M |
|---|---|---|---|---|---|---|
| Curlin, Zacheus H., | | | | 1, | .25 | |
| Curlin, Lemuel, | | | | 1, | .25 | |
| Cuder, David, | 50, | | | 1, | .62½ | |
| Cain, James, C., | | 1, 7, | | 1, | .25 | |
| Cassels, John, | | | | 1, | .25 | |
| Cooper, John, | | | | 1, | .25 | |
| Cantrell, Duke, | | | | 1, 1, | .75 | |
| Cantrell, Joseph, | | | | 1, | .25 | |
| Cantrell, Abraham P., | | | | 1, | .25 | |
| Cravens, Joseph, | | | | 1, 3, | 3.25 | |
| Cravens, John, | | | | 1, 1, | .75 | |
| Crabtree, Anderson, | | | | 1, | .25 | |
| Cooley, George, | 100, D,John Charton,274,321, | 2, 5, 13, | | 1, | 1. | |
| Carsby, Seth T., | | | | 1, | .25 | |
| Childress, James, | 90(Elijah Robertson,Gt., ( 500 | | | 1, | .67 | 5 |
| Dunn, John, | | | | 1 | | |
| Deloach, Thomas, | 228,Ent. | 806, 2, 8, 12, | | | 1.71 | |
| Devereeux, Thos. P.500, | | 967, 1, 5, | | | 3.75 | |
| Dougherty, George, | 943, | 932, 1&2, 7, | | | 7. 7 | 2½ |
| Same | 4500,Part of 5000, | 98, 3, 9, 13, | | | 33.75 | |
| Dunner, Anthony H., | 640, | 1326, 2, 9, 12, | | | 4.80 | |
| Dickens, Samuel, | 160,D,(Barder Bolings, | 1082, 1, 6, | | | 1.20 | |
| Same, | 675,Bty(640 | 82, 1, 5, | | | 5. 6 | 2½ |
| Dunlap, John H., | 640,D, Elijah Ward, | 1032, 1, 9, | | | 4.80 | |
| David W. Davis, | | | | 1, | .25 | |
| Dunn, Thomas, | | | | 1, | .25 | |
| Davis, Terrell, | | | | 1, | .25 | |
| Dickson, Laurden, | | | | 1, | .25 | |

(Page 29)

| Persons Name | Acres,Dec. | #of Ent. | Town | Free Horse | $ Cts. |
|---|---|---|---|---|---|
| Dawson, Isaac, | | 1347, 1, 8, 12, | 1, 20, | 1 | 1.75 |
| Douglass, Elmore,320,Ent. | | | | | 2.40 |
| Dent, Joseph E., | | | 1, 1, 90, | 1, | 1.75 |
| Davis, Jesse, | | | | 1, | .25 |
| Dunham, William, | | | | 1, | .25 |
| Denning, Thomas, | | | | 1, | .25 |
| Donelson, Humphrey180, | | 392, 1, 9, | | | 1.35 |

(Page 29,) Cont.

| Persons Name | Lnd. | Acres | Dec. Titl. | REMARKS | #of Ent. | Rge | Sec | Dis.Lots | Town.Lot | #of Free Poll | Sla. | Sto. | Horse Jac. | $ Cts. | M |
|---|---|---|---|---|---|---|---|---|---|---|---|---|---|---|---|
| Davis, Isham L., | | | | | | | | | | 1, | | 2 | | 1.25 | |
| Dunn, John P., | | | | | | | | | | 1, | | | | .25 | |
| Daugherty, Geo.Divis, | 500, | | | | | 21, | 2, | 8, | | | | | | 3.75 | |
| Dunn, Mathew, | 218, | | | | | | | | | | | | | 1.88 | 5 |
| Davis, Jesse | | | | | | | | | | 1, | | | | .25 | |
| Drew, James H., | | | | | | | | | | 1, | | | | .25 | |
| Damron, John, | 35, | | | | | 1, | 7, | | | 1, | | | | .50 | 2½ |
| Damron, Moses, | | | | | | | | | | 1, | | | | .25 | |
| Damron, Charles, | | | | | | | | | | 1, | | | | .25 | |
| Damron, John T., | | | | | | | | | | 1, | | | | .25 | |
| Damron, George | 50, | | | | 949, | 2, | 9, | 13, | | | | | | .62 | |
| Doherty, Dennis, | | | | | | | | | | 1, | | | | .25 | |
| Davis, Newel, | | | | | | | | | | 1, | | | | .25 | |
| Dickson, Ephram D., | 240, | | Deed, Byhel Bells Hs, | 640, | 846, | 1, | 5, | | | 1, | 5, | | | 4.55 | |
| Doty, James | | | | | | | | | 1, | | 1 | | | 2. | |
| Delaney, Neill, | | | | | | | | | | 1, | | | | .25 | |
| Daniel, Delaney, | | | | | | | | | | 1, | | | | .25 | |
| Deck, Daniel, | | | | | | | | | | 1, | | | | .25 | |
| Edmonston,Jesse, | 9 3/4, | | Deed, John Terrell, | 640 | | 1, | 7 | | | 1, | 2, | | | 1.32 | 2½ |
| Eli, Ely, | 200, | | B, B.Coffield, | 2560, | 735, | 1, | 4 &5, | | | 1, | | | | 1.75 | |
| Edwards, Thomas C., | | | | | | | | | | 1, | | | | .25 | |
| Eliott, George S., | 50, | Ent. | | | 929, | 1, | 8,1, | 1, | 25, | 1, | 4, | | | 4.12 | 5 |
| Edmonston, Reuben, | | | | | | | | | | 1, | | | | .25 | |
| East, John, | | | | | | | | | | 1, | | | | .25 | |
| Fowler, Thomas, | | | | | | | | | | 1, | 1, | | | .75 | |
| Freeman, Charles A., | 100, | D., | James Long, | | 963 | 1, | 7,13, | | | 1, | | | | 1. | |

(Page 30)

| Persons Name | Lnd. | Acres | Dec. Titl. | REMARKS | #of Ent. | Rge | Sec | Dis.Lots | Town.Lot | #of Free Poll | Sla. | Sto. | Horse Jac. | $ Cts. | M |
|---|---|---|---|---|---|---|---|---|---|---|---|---|---|---|---|
| Freeman, Evans, | | | | | | | | | | 1, | 3, | | | 1.75 | |
| Freeman, John, | | | | | | | | | | 1, | | | | .25 | |
| Farbis, Lorenzo D., | | | | | | | | | | 1, | | | | .25 | |
| Farbis, Almarine M., | | | | | | | | | | 1, | | | | .25 | |
| Fowler, William, | 400, | Enty, | Part of 640, | | 1036, | 1, | 9, | 12, | | | | | | 3. | |
| Fowler, John, | | | | | | | | | | 1, | 1, | | | .50 | |
| Fowler, Stephen, | | | | | | | | | | 1, | | | | .25 | |
| Fitzgerald, William, | | | | | | | | | | 1, | | | | 1.75 | |
| Folks, Sheerwood, | | | | | | | | | | 1, | | | | .25 | |

(Page 30) Cont.

| Persons Name | Acres | Desc. Lnd. | Titl. | REMARKS | #of Ent. | Rge. | Sec. | Dis.Lots | Lot | Poll | Sla. | Sto. | Jac. | Town #of Free | Horse | $ Cts. | M |
|---|---|---|---|---|---|---|---|---|---|---|---|---|---|---|---|---|
| Flemming, William, | 37½, | D, | Moses Fish, | 1041, | 2, | 5, | | | | | | | 1, | 8 | 4.33 | 1¼ |
| Same, | 157, | | John Coons, | 1136, | 2, | 5, | | | | | | | | | 1.17 | 7½ |
| Same, | 160, | | (Micayah,Thomas (640 | | | | | | | | | | | | | |
| Same, | 97½ | Enty, | | 1362, | 2, | 5, | | | | | | | | | 1.20 | |
| Same, | 160, | Deed, | (Eldridge & (Hill,640, | 1173, | 2, | 6, | | | | | | | | | .73½ | |
| Same, | 450, | | Heirs ofG.Christian, | 1057, | 1, | 6, | | | | | | | | | 1.20 | |
| | | | | | 1, | 5, | | | | | | | | | 3.75 | |
| Foster, James C., | | | | | | | | | 1, | | | | | | .25 | |
| Fowler, James, | | | | | | | | | 1, | 2, | | | | | 1.25 | |
| Farmer, Hiram, | | | | | | | | | 1, | | | | | | .25 | |
| Freels, David | | | | | | | | | 1, | | | | | | .25 | |
| Farmer, Aron, | | | | | | | | | 1, | | | | | | .25 | |
| Freeman, Charles, | | | | | | | | | 1, | | | | | | .25 | |
| Freeman, Richardson, | | | | | | | | | 1, | 1, | | | | | .75 | |
| Farr, George, | | | | | | | | | 1, | | | | | | .25 | |
| Fowler, John, | | | | | | | | | 1, | | | | | | .25 | |
| Furlong, Budson, | | | | | | | | | 1, | | | | | | .25 | |
| Forle, Albert B, | 170, | Ent. | | 760, | 2, | 6, | 13, | | 1, | 3, | | | | 5 | 3. 2 | |
| Fowler, Samuel, | | | | | | | | | 1, | 1, | | | | | .75 | |
| Foley,Jesse, | | | | | | | | | 1, | | | | | | .25 | |
| Finch, John W., | | | | | | | | | 1, | | | | | | .25 | |
| Griffith, Abel, | | | | | | | | | 1, | | | | | | .25 | |
| Griffith, Owen, | | | | | | | | | 1, | | | | | | .25 | |
| Gardner, Alfred, | | | | | | | | | 1, | | | | | | .25 | |
| Garrett, Henry,A., | | | | | | | | | 1, | | | | | | .25 | |

(Page 31) 1829

| Persons Name | Acres | Desc. Lnd. | Titl. | REMARKS | #of Ent. | Rge. | Sec. | Dis.Lots | Lot | Poll | Sla. | Sto. | Jac. | Town #of Free | Horse | $ Cts. | M |
|---|---|---|---|---|---|---|---|---|---|---|---|---|---|---|---|---|
| Greer, James, | 100, | E. | | | 1, | 7, | 12, | | | | | | | | .75 | |
| Same, | 274, | | | | 1, | 7, | | | | | | | | 5 | 2. 5 | |
| Same, | 100 | | | | 1, | 7, | | | | | | | | | .75 | |
| Same, | 99 | | | | 1, | 6, | 13, | | | | | | | | .74 | 2½ |
| Same, | 100, | | | | 1, | 7, | 12, | | | | | | | | .75 | |
| Same, | 226, | | | | 1, | 7, | | (9&2 | | | | | | | 1.62 | |
| Greer & McCorkle, | 285, | | | | | | | 4,(42,91 | | | | | | | 2.13 | 7½ |
| Greer, James & David, | | | | | | | | | | | | | | | 6. | |

(Page 31) Cont. Acres Desc.                           #of           Town  #of Free                    Horse
Persons Name,       Lnd.Titl. R E M A R K S           Ent.Rge. Sec. Dis.Lots, Lot,Poll,Sla.Sto.Jac.   $ Cts  M

Gardner, John A.,                                                        1, 19,                       1.50
Gardner, Richard W.,                                                             1,                    .25
Guest, George,      150,Ent.                          1065, 2, 9                                      1.12  5
Gaston, William,    640                                301, 3, 7,  13,                                4.80
Gillespie, David,   640                                 85, 2, 8.9 12,                                4.80
Guion, Alvah,                                                            1, 26,                       1.50
Green, Joseph Heirs,1000,                              850, 2, 7,  13,                                7.50
Same,                645,                              872, 2, 6,                                     4.84  2½
Glasco, Isaac,                                                 (53,88,                  4ø/, 8ø        .25
Gardner, Jeptheh,    63,D, Bell & Terrell,     1, 7, 5,(97 98, 1,  3, 1,                             12.80
                                                              (99

Glass, Dudley,                                                           1,    9                      4.75
Glenn, Phillip B.,                                                       1,                            .25
Guin, James,                                                        1,   1,                           1.75
Gilbert, Robert,     60, R. E. C. Daugherty 112,- 2, 5,  12,             1, 1,                        1.89
Gilbert, Jonathan M.,91½,Joab Bells,640,   767, 1, 2, 7   13,            1, 2,                        1.93  6¼
Goldsby, James,                                                          1, 4,                        2.00
Goldsby, Stephen,                                                        1,                            .25
Gilbert, Randolph,                                                       1, 1,                         .75
Groom, Bright,                                                           1,                            .25
Garison, Edward,                                                         1,                            .25
Green, Caswell,                                                          1,                            .25
Glass, Elisha W.,                                                        1,                            .25
Gertner, John,                                                           1,                            .25
Galley, James,                                                           1,                            .25
Gwen, Malcolm,                                                           1,                            .25
Herd, George D., 16, D, Absolom Jones,      1500, 1, 7,  12,             1,                            .37
Horton, James,                                                      1,   1,                           1.75
(Page 32)    1829
Herd, Bailey E., 50, E.                                903, 1, 8,  13,   1,                            .62  5
Huskey, Isam,                                                            1,                            .25
Hopkins, Thomas,3750, Part of 5000,                    817, 1.2, 7/8     1,                          28.12  ½
Hart, James,     480, Part of 640,                    1360, 1, 6,  12,                                 3.60
Harmon, Israel,                                                       1                               1.75
Hughes, Archessus M.,                                                    1, 3                          .75
Horton, Archibald,                                                       1, 1,                         .25

(Page 32) Cont. Acres Desc.                          #of              Town  #of Free                      Horse
Person Name,        Lnd.Titl. R E M A R K S     Ent. Rge.,Sec. Dis.,Lots,Lot,Poll,Sla.Sto.Jac. $ Cts.  M

| Person Name | Acres/Desc. Remarks | #of Ent. | Rge. | Sec. | Dis. | Town Lots | #of Lot | Free Poll | Sla. | Sto. | Jac. | $ | Cts. | M |
|---|---|---|---|---|---|---|---|---|---|---|---|---|---|---|
| Horton, John, | | | | | | | | 1 | | | | | .25 | |
| Horton, George, | | | | | | | | 1 | | | | | .25 | |
| Henry, Hendrix, 120, D, Jerome McClain, | | 775, | 2, | 7, | 13, | | | | 1, | | | 1.30 | | |
| House, John, 100, | | | 2, | 7, | 12, | | | | | | | 1. | | |
| Hubbert, William, | | | | | | | | 1, | | | | | .25 | |
| Howard, George W. 60, | | | 2, | 6, | | | | 1, | | | | | .70 | |
| Holt, Benjamin, 252, | | | | | | | | 1, | | | | | 2.14 | |
| Hall, Wilson, | | | | | | | | 1, | | | | | .25 | |
| Howard, Littleton, | | | | | | | | 1, | | | | | .25 | |
| Hill, Henry M., | | | | | | | | 1, | | | | | .25 | 5 |
| Hamilton, William, 50, E., | | 1465, | 1.2 | 5, | | | | 1, | | | | | .62 | |
| Henderson, John K., | | | | | | | | 1, | | | | | .25 | |
| Holly, Hazel, | | | | | | | | 1, | | | | | .25 | |
| Harrod, James, | | | | | | | | 1, | | | | | .25 | |
| Hunter, William, | | | | | | | | 1, | | | | | .25 | |
| Hoggard, Byars, | | | | | | | | 1, | | | | | .25 | |
| Hurt, Samuel, | | | | | | | | 1, | | | | | .25 | |
| Hays, William, 64, Deed, | | | 2, | 5, | 12, | | | 1, | 1, | | | 1.23 | | |
| Huggins, Jeremiah, | | | | | | | | 1, | | | | | .25 | |
| Huggins, Robert, | | | | | | | | 1, | | | | | .25 | |
| Huggins, James, | | | | | | | | 1, | | | | | .25 | |
| Huggins, William, | | | | | | | | 1, | | | | | .25 | |
| Horton, Robert, | | | | | | | | 1, | | | | | .25 | |
| House, Isham, | | | | | | | | 1, | 2, | | | 1. | | |
| House, Wilbourn, | | | | | | | | 1, | | | | | .25 | |
| Hornback, James, 50, Entry, | | 970, | 1, | 6, | 13, | | | 1, | 2, | | | 1.62 | | 5 |
| Haynor, Samuel, | | | | | | | | 1, | | | | | .25 | |
| Henry, Moses, | | | | | | | | 1, | | | | | .25 | |
| (Page 33) | | | | | | | | | | | | | | |
| Huleth, Thomas P. 600, Deed, Jel Pinson, | | | | | | | | 1, | | | | | .70 | |
| Harrel, John, | | | | | | | | 1, | | | | | .25 | |
| Harmon, Jesse, | | | | | | | | 1, | | | | | .25 | |
| Hughes, John, 640, Thos. Henderson, | | 228, | 1, | 10, | 13, | | | 1 | | | | 4.80 | | |
| Joplen, John, | | | | | | | 1, | 1, | | | | | 1.75 | |
| John K. Jones, | | | | | | | | 1, | | | | | .25 | |

(Page 33) Cont.

| Persons Name | Acres | Desc. Lnd., Titl. REMARKS | #of Ent. | Rge., | Sec., | Dis.Lots, Lot, | Town, Poll, | #of Free, Sla. | Sto. | Jac. | $ | Cts. |
|---|---|---|---|---|---|---|---|---|---|---|---|---|
| Jones, Gray, | | | | | | (12,82,)1 | | | | | | .25 |
| Johnson, Wm. H., | 50, | Entry, | 960, | 1, | 5, | 4(83,84) | 1 | | | | 7.12 | 5 |
| Julian, James J., | | | | | | | 1, | | | | | .25 |
| Jones, William | | | | | | | 1, | | | | | .25 |
| Jones, Josiah, | | | | | | | 1, | | | | | .25 |
| Jones, Adonijah, | | | | | | | 1, | | | | | .25 |
| Israel, Urias, | | | | | | | 1, | | | | | .25 |
| James, Hosea, | | | | | | | 1, | | | | | .25 |
| Jennings, Andrew, | | | | | | | 1, | 1, | | | | .75 |
| Jenkins, Mansfield, | | | | | | | 1, | | | | | .25 |
| Johnson, John, | | | | | | | 1, | | | | | .25 |
| Jones, Thornton, | | | | | | | 1, | | | | | .25 |
| Jones, Williams, | 100, | | 965, | 1, | 8, | 1, | 1, | 1, | | | 3. | |
| Jones, Willie, | 100, | | 969, | 1, | 8, | | 1, | | | | .75 | |
| Jenkins, Thomas, | | | | | | | 1, | | | | | .25 |
| Jenkins, Jesse, | 50, | D, Burrel Anderson, | | 2, | 6, | | 1, | 1, | | | 1.12 | 5 |
| Jenkins, John, | 3000, | E, Different Tracts | | | | | 1, | 5, | | | 25.25 | |
| Jenkins, James, | | | | | | | 1, | 1, | | | .75 | |
| Jones, Israel, | 640, | D, Robert Browers, | 245, | 1,2, | 6,7, | | 1, | 3, | | | 6.55 | |
| Jameson, Samuel, | | | | | | | 1, | | | | | .25 |
| Kirkpatrick, Joseph (Page 34) | 640, | Ent. | 1358, | 1, | 7, | 12, | 1, | | | | 4.80 | |
| Koen, John, | 150, | | 765, | 1, | 6, | 13, | 1, | | | | 1.12 | 5 |
| Kenedy, Betholem, | | | | | | | | 2, | | | 1.00 | |
| Kirksey, John, | | | | | | 1,50, | 1, | 1, | | | 2.25 | |
| Kirk, George D., | 124, | Maxwell 164, | | 2, | 6, | | 1, | 1, | | | 1.87 | |
| Kirk, William, | 40, | Part of same, | | 2, | 6, | | 1, | | | | .55 | |
| Kele, Barney C., | | | | | | | 1, | | | | | .25 |
| Killebrew, Elias, | | | | | | | 1, | | | | | .25 |
| Kindred, Joseph G., | | | | | | | 1, | | | | | .25 |
| Kindred, Elisha H., | | | | | | | 1, | | | | | .25 |
| Kenedy, James, | | | | | | | 1, | | | | | .25 |
| Kemp, Francis, | 174, | Deed, Jno.Charlton 274,321, | 2, | 5, | 13, | | 1, | | | | 1.55 | |
| Landrum, Samuel, | | | | | | | 1, | 2 | | | 1.25 | |
| Lawler, Martin, | 98, | James Greer, | 1, | 6,7, | 12, | 2(27& (72 | 1, | 1 | | | 4.48 | 5 |

(Page 34) Cont.

| Persons Name | Acres | Desc. Ind.Titl. REMARKS | #of Ent. | Rge. | Sec. | Dis. | Town Lots | Lot | #of Free Poll | Sls. | Sto. | Horse Jac. | $ Cts. | M |
|---|---|---|---|---|---|---|---|---|---|---|---|---|---|---|
| | | 1829 | | | | | | | | | | | | |
| Landrum, James, | | | | | | | | | 1, | | | | .25 | |
| Lytle, Archibald, | 236, | Ent. | 804, | 2, | 7, | | | | | | | | 1.77 | |
| Lynn, Elam, | | | | | | | | | 1, | | | | .25 | |
| Levi, Levister, | | | | | | | | | 1, | | | | .25 | |
| Lawrence, Joseph, | 25, | | 932, | 2, | 4, | 13, | | | | | | | .18 | 7½ |
| Lynn, William, | | | | | | | | | 1, | | | | .25 | |
| Lemmond, David, | | | | | | | | | 1, | | | | .25 | |
| Lemmond, Robert, | | | | | | | | 1, 55, | | | | | 1.50 | |
| Liddle, Francis, | | | | | | | | | 1, | | | | .25 | |
| Lewis, James, | | | | | | | | | 1, | 2 | 5.82 | 3. | | |
| Lasswell, Peter, | 50, | | 957, | 2, | 9, | | | | 1, | | | | .62½ | |
| Lasswell, Robert, | | | | | | | | | 1, | | | | .25 | |
| Lasswell, Joseph, | | | 956, | 2, | 9, | | | | | | | | .62 | 5 |
| Same, | 50, | D,Wm & Mary K.Roberts, | | 2, | 8, | 9, | | | | | | | .37 | 5 |
| Lasswell,Sarah, | 50, | Ent.Donnie Lasswell, | 955, | 2, | 9, | | | | | | | | .37 | 5 |
| Loven, James, | | | | | | | | | 1, | | | | .25 | |
| Loven, Joshua, | | | | | | | | | 1, | | | | .25 | |
| Loyd, Thomas, | | | | | | | | | 1, | | | | .25 | |
| McNeeley, John, | 54,B, Joeb Bells 640, | | 767, | 1, | 7, | | | | 1, | | | | .65 | 5 |
| Moon, William, | | | | | | | | | 1, | | | | .25 | |
| McItosh, Charles, | | | | | | | | | 1, | | | | .25 | |
| Molin, Benja. | 224,D,Blakemore Sweny&Ross, | | 601, | 1,2, | 7, | | | | 1, 1, | | | | 2.43 | |
| Michel, Thomas, | | | | | | | | | 1, | | | | .25 | |
| J.C. & R & | | | | | | | | | | | | | | |
| McLemore,T.Love,555, E. | | | 300, | 3,7, | | | | | | | | | 4.16 | 2½ |
| McCulock,Janja,, | 640, | | 355, | 3,9, | | | | | | | | | 4.80 | |
| Moore,Somerset, | 3, | | 1333, | 2, | 9, | 12, | | | | | | | 2 | 2½ |
| (Page 35) 1829 | | | | | | | | | | | | | | |

| | | | | | | | | | | | | | | |
|---|---|---|---|---|---|---|---|---|---|---|---|---|---|---|
| McLemore, John C., | 3 3/4,Ent. | | 816, | 1, | 8, | 13, | | | | | | | 2 | 5¼ |
| Same, | 38, | | 823, | 2, | 7, | | | | | | | | 28 | 5 |
| Same, | 143½, | | 1071, | 2, | 9, | 12, | | | | | | | 1, 7 | 6¼ |
| Same, | 1250, McLemore & Hopkiss | | 877, | 1,2,7,8, | 13 | | | | | | | | 9.37 | 5 |
| Same, | 640,Deed, John Nelson, 274, | | | 2, | 7,8 | | | | | | | | 4.80 | |
| Same, | 2000,E., | | 322, | 2, | 5 | | | | | | | | 15.00 | |
| Same, | 160, D,James Hart,640, | | 1360, | 1, | 6, | 12, | | | | | | | 1.20 | |
| Same, | 752, John McIver,4336, | | | 1, | 9,10,13 | | | | | | | | 5.64 | |

(Page 35) Cont. Acres Desc.          #of            Town  #of Free            Horse
Persons Name        Lnd,Titl.,R E M A R K S  Ent. Rge. Sec. Dis.Lots,Lot,Poll,Sla,Sto,Jac.  $ Cts.  M

| Persons Name | Acres | Desc. Lnd,Titl.,REMARKS | #of Ent. | Rge. | Sec. | Town Dis. | Lots | Lot | #of Poll | Free Sla | Sto | Horse Jac. | $ Cts. | M |
|---|---|---|---|---|---|---|---|---|---|---|---|---|---|---|
| McLemore & Jas. | | | | | | | | | | | | | | |
| Vouk, | 100, | E, | 807, | 2, | 9, | 12, | | | | | | | .75 | |
| Same & Same, | 150, | | 627, | 2, | 8, | | | | | | | | 1.12 | 5 |
| Same & Same, | 1250, | D, John Rhea, 2500, | 302, | 2,3 | 6, | 13, | | | | | | | 9.37 | 5 |
| Same & Same, | 128, | Sion William 640, | 351, | 2, | 5,6, | 12 | | | | | | | .96 | |
| McLemore Sugars,160, | | William Fowler 640, | 1036, | 1, | 9, | | | | | | | | 1.20 | |
| Same, | 160, | Wm. Sharp, 640, | 368, | 3, | 7, | 13, | | | | | | | 1.20 | |
| Same, | 700, | J.G. & Thos.Blounts, (3000) | 591, | 1, | 5, | | | | | | | | 5.25 | |
| Same, | 1640, | Wm.A. Tharp, | 630, | 2, | 6, | | | | | | | | 4.80 | |
| McLemore & Charlton, | | | | | | | | | | | | | | |
| Same & Same, | 741, | Jerome McClain, | 775, | 1,2, | 7, | | | | | | | | 5.55 | 7½ |
| | 165, | Joab Bell, 640, | 767, | 1, | 7, | | | | | | | | 1.23 | 7½ |
| Murphy, William,797½,Ent, Part of 987½, | | | 774, | 2, | 7, | | | | | | | | 5.98 | 1¼ |
| Michel, Kisiah, | | | | | | | | | | | | | .50 | |
| Moran, James,H., | | | | | | | 2, | 1 | | | | | 10.25 | |
| McDaniel, John, | | | | | | | | | 1, | | | | .25 | |
| Morgan, Samuel; 520,Deed, | | | | 2, | 7, | 12, | | | 1, | | | | 9.65 | |
| Moore, John H., | | | | | | | | | 1, | 11, | | | .75 | |
| McGavock &Wilson,640, | Frances Lewis, | | | 1, | 8,9 | 13, | | | 1, | 1, | | | 4.80 | |
| Same, | 250, | Thomas Sharp, | | 1, | 9, | 12, | | | | | | | 1.87 | 5 |
| Moore, James, | | | | | | | | | 1, | | | | .25 | |
| Malnard, Wm.H., | | | | | | | | | 1, | | | | .25 | |
| Malnard, Jas., | | | | | | | | | 1, | | | | .25 | |
| Mandy, Thos., | | | | | | | | | 1, | | | | .25 | |
| Meadows, Spearson, | | | | | | | | | 1, | | | | .25 | |
| Moore, John, | 72,D, John Jenkins, | | | 2, | 5, | | | | 1, | | | (1, | 3.79 | |
| McClusky, John, | | | | | | | | | 1, | | | (St H,) | .25 | |
| McNeely,Michael, | 47, 2 Tracts Dalton 17 | | | 2, | 9, | | | | 1, | | | | .60 | 2½ |
| Mizelle, Williams, | | | | | | | | | 1, | | | | .25 | |

(Page 35 A)

| Persons Name | | | | | | | | | | | | | $ Cts. | M |
|---|---|---|---|---|---|---|---|---|---|---|---|---|---|---|
| McClain, George, | | | | | | | | | 1, | | | | .25 | |
| Morris, Francis, | | | | | | | | | 1, | | | | .25 | |
| Mathew,F.Michel, | | | | | | | | | 1, | 1, | | | .75 | |

(Page 35 A) Cont. Acres Desc. | #of | Town, #of Free Horse

| Persons Name | Land, Titl, REMARKS | #of Ent. | Rge. | Sec. | Dist. Lots, Lot, Poll, Sla. Sto. Jac. | $ | Cts | M |
|---|---|---|---|---|---|---|---|---|
| Majors, Samuel, | 50, E. | 959, | 2, | 9, | 13, | 1 | .62 | 5 |
| McClain, Charles, Sr. | 50, | | | | | | | |
| McClain, Chas. Jr., | | | 1, | 9, | | | .37 | 5 |
| McIntosh, Solomon, | | | | | | 1, | .25 | |
| Moss, Bennet, | | | | | | 1, | .25 | |
| Mayo, William, | 131, D, | | 2, | 9, | 12, | 1, 1, | .75 | |
| McClain, John, | 50, C, | | 1, | 9, | | 1, | 1.33 | 2⅛ |
| Miles, William, | 200¼, J.Ward & Grender | | | | 13, 1, 54, | 1, 1, | .62 | 5 |
| Miller, Andrew, | | | | | | 1, | 3.75 | 3 |
| Murrey, John, | | | | | | 1, | .25 | |
| Marshall, Joseph, | | | | | | 4, | .25 | |
| Marshall, Robert, | | | | | | 1, | .25 | |
| Mosley, Robert, | 760, D, McWharter & Barnett, (1917) | 528, 1.2 | 5 | | | 1, 9, | 10.45 | |
| Same, | 400, Byhel, Bells, | 640, 846, | 1, | 5, | | | 3. | |
| Mosley, Edward, | | | | | | 1, | .25 | |
| McMullen, John, | 19½, Daniel Delaney, | 1596, | 1, | 6, | 12, 1,29, | 1, | 1.89 | 6¼ |
| Marcus, Phillip, | | | | | | 1, | .25 | |
| Nall, Andrew, | 1654,E, | 97, | 2, | 9, | 13, | | 12.40 | 5 |
| Nelson, Nailing, | 106,(2 Tracts Cain & ( Charlton, | 765, | 1, | 6, | 2,(35 & (36 | 5, | 6.29 | 5 |
| Nalin, Willis, | 50, J. R. Nailing, | 968, | 1, | 7, | | 1, 1, | 1.12 | 5 |
| Nailing, John R., | | | | | | 1, | .25 | |
| Nailing, James, | | | | | | 1, | .25 | |
| Newman, William, | | | | | | 1, 1 | .75 | |
| Newton, James W., | | | | | | , 1 | .25 | |
| Nolen, Henry, | | | | | | 1, | .25 | |
| Nicholas, John, | | | | | | 1, | .25 | |
| Overton, John, | 488,Gt., L.Costen, | 319, | 3, | 9, | | | 3.66 | |
| Same, | 232, Same, | 315, | 2,3, | 9, | | | 1.74 | |
| Same, | 484, Same, | 317, | 2.3, | 9, | | | 3.66 | |
| Same, | 231, Same | 322, | 2.3, | 9, | | | 1.73 | 2⅛ |

(Page 36)

| Persons Name | Acres | Desc. Lnd,Titl. | REMARKS | #of Ent. | Rge, | Sec. | Dist. | Town Lots, | #of Lot, | Free Poll, | Sla. | Sto. | Horse Jac. | $ | Cts. | 42 M |
|---|---|---|---|---|---|---|---|---|---|---|---|---|---|---|---|---|
| Same, | 622½ | | Same, | 323, | 2, | 10, | 13, | | | | | | | 4.66 | 8 | 3/4 |
| Same, | 98, | Ent. | | | | 9, | 9, | | | | | | | .73 | 5 | |
| Same, | 735, | G | L. Carter, | 321, | 3, | 9, | | | | | | | | 5.56 | 2½ | |
| Overton & Wharton, | 640, | E, | | 25, | 2, | 9, | | | | | | | | 4.80 | | |
| Oan, William C., | 480, | | | 2, | 2, | 7, | 12, | | | | | | | 3.85 | | |
| Oliver, Isaac, | 77, | | | 8, | 2, | 7, | | | | 1, | | | | .82 | 7½ | |
| Oliver, Stephin, | | | | | | | | | | 1, | | | | .25 | | |
| Oneel, John, | 113, | | | 1, | 1, | 5, | | | | 1, | | | | 1. 9 | 7½ | |
| Osteen, John, | | | | | | | | | | 1, | | | | .25 | | |
| Overly, Thomas, | | | | | | | | | | 1, | | | | .25 | | |
| Owen, Charles, M., | 70, | D., | Joel Penson, | | | | 13, | | | 1, | | | | .78 | 2½ | |
| Owen, Daniel, | 47 3/4, | | Same, | | | | | | | 1, | | | | .60 | 7½ | |
| Owen, Sarah, | 47½ | | Same, | | | | | | | | 2, | | | 1.35 | 7½ | |
| Outhouse, Israel, F., | 28½ | E. | | 1, | 6, | 12, | | | | 1, | | | | .46 | 3 | 3/4 |
| Parham, Thomas, | 200, | D., | Jas. Greer | 1, | 6.7 | | | | | | 2, | | | 1.50 | | |
| Powell, Robert, | | | | | | | | | | 1, | | | | 1.25 | | |
| Parks, Fields, | | | | | | | | | | 1, | | | | .25 | | |
| Prater, Josiah, | | | | | | | | | | 1, | | | | .25 | | |
| Polk, William, | 5000, | E., | | 151, | 2, | 9, | 13, | | | | | | | 37.50 | | |
| Polk & Devereaux, | 500, | | | 289, | 1, | 5, | 12, | | | | | | | 3.75 | | |
| Same | 500, | | | 59, | 1, | 9, | 13, | | | | | | | 3.75 | | |
| Same, | 500, | | | 119, | 1, | 9, | | | | | | | | 3.75 | | |
| Same, | 305, | | | 531, | 1, | 5, | 12, | | | | | | | 2.28 | 7½ | |
| Same, | 195, | | | 732, | 1, | 5, | 13, | | | | | | | 1.46 | 2½ | |
| Polk, Thos.Heirs, | 300, | | | 980, | 1, | 5, | 12, | | | | | | | 2.25 | | |
| Peck, John, | 402, | | | 1353, | 1, | 6, | 13, | | | | | | | 3. 1 | 5 | |
| Payton, Bailey, | 380, | | | 1, | 8, | 8, | 13, | | | | | | | 2.85 | | |
| Pope, John, | 180, | | Part of 500 | 330, | 2, | 8, | | | | | | | | 1.35 | | |
| Pope, John W., | 160, | D | Part of same | 330, | 2, | 8, | | | | | | | | 1.20 | | |
| Pope, Samuel, | 160, | | Part of same, | 330, | 2, | 8, | | | | | | | | 1.20 | | |
| Parham, Amos, | | | | | | | | | | 1, | | | | .25 | | |
| Pettigrew,Ebenezer, | 1250,G., J.G. & T. Blount, | | | 194, | | | | | | | | | | 9.37 | 5 | |
| Same, | 1084, | | Same, | 193, | | | | | | | | | | 8.13 | | |
| Same, | 1250, | | Same, | 216 | | | | | | | | | | 9.37 | 5 | |

(Page 37) Acres Desc. #of Town, #of Free
Persons Name Lnd.Titl. R E M A R K S -Ent. Rge,Sec.Dis. Lots,Lot,Poll,Sla.Sto.Jac. $, Cts. M

| Persons Name | Acres Desc. Lnd.Titl. REMARKS | Ent. | Rge, | Sec, | Dis. | Lots, | Lot, | Poll, | Sla, | Sto, | Jac. | $, Cts. M |
|---|---|---|---|---|---|---|---|---|---|---|---|---|
| Parker, Isaac, | 512, E, Part of 640, | 615, | 2, | 6, | 13, | | 1, | 89, | 1, | | | 3.84 |
| Parker, Lorenzo, | | | | | | | | | | | | 1.75 |
| Parker, Gideon, | | | | | | | 1, | | | | | .25 |
| Powers, Charles, | | | | | | | 1, | | | | | .25 |
| Powers, Henry, | | | | | | | 1, | | | | | .25 |
| Peoples, Samuel, | 200, D, | | 2, | 7, | 12, | | | | | | | 1.50 |
| Perry, Solomon, | | | | | | | 1, | | | | | .25 |
| Parker, Wm. T., | | | | | | | 1, | | | | | .25 |
| Patton, Thomas, | 100, | | 2, | 6, | | | 1, | | | | | 1. |
| Price, William, | | | | | | | 1, | | | | | .25 |
| Price, James, | | | | | | | 1, | | | | | .25 |
| Patton, John M., | | | | | | | 1, | | | | | .25 |
| Pentecost, Wm., | | | | | | | 1, | | | | | .25 |
| Pate, Stephen, | 50, R. E/ Daugherty C | | 2, | 5, | | | 1, | | | | | .62½ |
| Partee, Jesse, | | | | | | | 1, | | | | | .25 |
| Parrish, Jesse, | | | | | | | 1, | | | | | .25 |
| Pursel, Auburn, | | | | | | | 1, | | | | | .25 |
| Paschall, Jesse M., | | | | | | | 1, | | | | | .25 |
| Pepipin, Loftis, | | | | | | | 1, | | | | | .25 |
| Parrish, John, | | | | | | | 1, | | | | | .25 |
| Poindexter, Samuel, | | | | | | | 1, | | 5, | | | 2.50 |
| Perry, John, | | | | | | | 1, | | | | | .25 |
| Phillips, David, | | | | | | | 1, | | | | | .25 |
| Powers, George, | | | | | | | 1, | | | | | .25 |
| Pannel, William C. | 50, E., | 958, | 1, | 5, | 13, | | 1, | | | | | .62 5 |
| Roads, Abner, | 150, | 843, | 1, | 9, | 12, | | 1, | | | | | 1.12 5 |
| Rogers, Jubilee, | 440, D, John Terrell, | | 1, | 7, | 13, | 1, | 63, | | 7, | | | 12.80 |
| Robertson, Edward, | | | | | | | 1, | | | | | .25 |
| Ragsdale, Joel, | 60, Jas. Greer, | | 1, | 7, | 12, | | 1, | | 2, | | | 1.40 |
| Roffe, Woson, | | | | | | | 1, | | | | | .25 |
| Rhea, John, | 1250, E,Part of 2500, | 302, | 2,3, | 6, | 13, | | 1, | | | | | 9.37 5 |
| Revice, John H. | 100,D, Wm. Qualls, | 1751, | 1, | 7, | 12, | 2,(86 (87 | 1, | | 6, | | | 1. |
| Rogers, John W., | | | | | | | 1, | | | | | 6.25 |

(Page 38) 1829 Acres Desc.                    #of          Town  #of Free        Horse
Persons Name  -  Lnd.,Titl. R E M A R K S  -  Ent.Rge.,Sec.Dis.Lots,Lot,Poll Sla.Sto.,Jac.$ Cts.  M

| Persons Name | Acres | Desc. Lnd.,Titl. | REMARKS | Ent. | Rge., | Sec. | Dis.Lots, | Town Lot | #of Poll | Free Sla. | Sto.,Jac. | Horse $ | Cts. | M |
|---|---|---|---|---|---|---|---|---|---|---|---|---|---|---|
| Rhoads, John A.C. | 14, | D, | John Atchison, | | 1, | 6, | 12, | | 1, | 3 | | 1.85 | 5 | |
| Russell, Buckner Sr., | 50, | | | | | | | | | | | .37 | 5 | |
| Russell, Buckner, Jr., | 3, | D, | | | | | | | | | | .27 | 2½ | |
| Ralls, William, | | | | | | | | | 1, | | | .25 | | |
| Richie, James, H., | | | | | | | | | 1, | | | .25 | | |
| Rhea, John W., | 100, | | | | 2, | 9, | | | 1, | | | .75 | | |
| Ridgway, John, | | | | | | | | | 1, | 2, | | 1.25 | | |
| Ridgway, Richard, | 121, | | | | 2, | 8, | | 1, 47, | 1, | | | 2.65 | 7½ | |
| Ross, William, | | | | | | | | | 1, | | | .25 | | |
| Ridgway, James, | 192, | | | | 2, | 8, | | | | 3, | | 2.94 | | |
| Ridgway, Thomas, | | | | | | | | | | | | .25 | | |
| Rogers, Thomas, | 119 3/4, | D, | John Rogers, | 848, | 2, | 9, | | | 1, | | | 1.14 | 7½ | |
| Rogers, Jacob, | | | | | | | | | 1, | | | .25 | | |
| Ralls, Wm. B., | | | | | | | | | 1, | | | .25 | | |
| Rogers, Job, | 640, | | John Jenkins | 702, | 1, | 8, | 13, 1, | | | 8, (1 Pleas-(ure carriage | | 12.80 | | |
| Ross, Lacie, | 40, | | | | | | | | | | | 1. | 5 | |
| Ross, Joshua, | | | | | | 1, | 9, | 12, | | 1, 1, | | | .25 | | |
| Ross, Reubin, | | | | | | | | | 1, | | | .25 | | |
| Ratten, Tatton, | | | | | | | | | | | | .25 | | |
| Ray, John, | 640, | | David Broadwell, | | 2, | 6, | 13, | | 1, | | | 4.80 | | |
| Ren, John, | | | | | | | | | 1, | | | .25 | | |
| Rachels, William, | | | | | | | | (61) | 1, | | | .25 | | |
| Shulty, John R., | | | | | | | | 2,(60) | 1, | | | 3.00 | | |
| Shulty, John M., | | | | | | | | | 1, | | | .25 | | |
| Sneed, Samuel R., | | | | | | | | | 1, | | | .25 | | |
| Stallings, John, | | | | | | | | | 1, | | | .25 | | |
| Sample, Henry A., | 50, | E., | | 962, | 1, | 5, | | | 1, | 1, | | 10.62 | 5 | |
| Speight & McGavock, | 640, | | | 828, | 1, | 10, | 12, | | | | | 4.80 | | |
| Smith, Richard, | 640, | | | 474, | 23, | 7, | 13, | | | | | 4.80 | | |
| Sanders, Saml., | | | | | | | | | 1, | | | .25 | | |
| Sanders, James, B., | | | | | | | | | 1, | | | .25 | | |
| Shepherd, Wm. B., | 1100, | Gr., | J.G. & T. Blount, | 191, | | | | | | | | 8.25 | | |
| Same, | 1000, | | Same, | 257, | | | | | | | | 7.50 | | |
| Same, | 100, | | Same, | 238, | | | | | 1, | | | 7.50 | | |
| Stuff, Henry, | | | | | | | | | 1, | | | .25 | | |

(Page 39) Acres Desc. #of Town, #of Free Horse
Persons Name Lnd.Titl R E M A R K S - Ent.,Rge.,Sec.Dis. Lots,Lot,Poll,Sla.Sto.Jac. $ Cts. M

B.

| Persons Name | Acres | Desc. Lnd.Titl | REMARKS | #of Ent. | Rge.,Sec.Dis. | Town,Lots,Lot | #of Poll | Free Sla. | Sto. | Horse Jac. | $ | Cts. | M |
|---|---|---|---|---|---|---|---|---|---|---|---|---|---|
| Shepherd, Charles, | 1250, | G, J.G. & T.Blount, | | 216, | | 1.3 | | | | | 9. | 37 | 5 |
| Same, | 1000, | Same, | | 183, | | | | | | | | 7.50 | |
| Same, | 1250, | Same, | | 209, | | | | | | | 9. | 37 | 5 |
| Shepherd, James B. | 1070, | Same, | | 249, | | | | | | | 8. | 2 | 5 |
| Same, | 1140, | Same, | | 196, | | | | | | | | 8.55 | |
| Same, | 1362, | Same, | | 241, | | | | | | | 10. | 21, | 5 |
| Shepherd, Fred'k B. | 1125, | Same, | | 223, | | | | | | | 8. | 43 | 7½ |
| Same, | 1100, | Same, | | 220, | | | | | | | | 8.25 | |
| Same, | 1184½ | Same, | | 201, | | | | | | | 8. | 88 | 2 |
| Shepherd, Penelope S. | 1056, | Same, | | 187 | | | | | | | | 7.92 | |
| Same, | 1250, | Same | | 176, | | | | | | | 9. | 37 | 5 |
| Same, | 214, | Same part of | | 198, | | | | | | | | 1.83 | |
| Shepherd, Rich'D M. | 1125 | Same | | 231 | | | | | | | 8. | 43 | 7½ |
| Same | 1362 | Same | | 230 | | | | | | | 10. | 21 | 5 |
| Same | 267 | Same part of | | 198 | | | | | | | 2.2 | 2½ | |
| Shepherd, John S. | 1140, | Same | | 173 | | | | | | | | 8.55 | |
| Same | 1000, | Same | | 213, | | | | | | | | 7.50 | |
| Same, | 489, | Same part of | | 198 | | | | | | | 3. | 66 | 7½ |
| Shaw, Daniel B. | 100 | | | | | | | | | | | .75 | |
| Standly, Elijah | 106,E, | | | 1406, | 2, 7, | 12, | 1, | | | | 1. | 4 | 5 |
| Steel, George R., | 50, | | | | 2, 6, | | 1, | 1, | | | 1. | 12 | 5 |
| Steel, John, | 40, | | | | 2, 7, | | 1, | | | | | .55 | |
| Sommers, James | 2800, | Part of 3840, | | 1497¼, | 1.2, 7, | | | | | | 21. | | |
| Swaney, James M. | 512, | D,(Henry Belote | | 1154, | 2, 8.9 | | | | | | | 3.86 | |
| Swaney, John L., | 256, | (640 | | | | 13, | | | | | | 1.92 | |
| Standley, Noah, | | | | | | | 1, | | | | | .25 | |
| Sanford, John, | | | | | | | 1, | | | | | .25 | |
| Stark, Thomas, | 258, | | | | 1, 5, | 12, | 1, | | | | | .43 | 7½ |
| Sparks, Hardy, | | | | | | | 1, | | | | | .25 | |
| Smyth, James, | | | | | | | 1, | | | | | .25 | |
| Sneed, Israel, | | | | | | | 1, | 2, | | | 1. | 25 | |
| Sprout, Elexander | | | | | | | 1, | | | | | .25 | |
| Stanford, Hiram, | | | | | | | 1, | | | | | .25 | |
| Stunson, John, | 200, | D, | | | | | 1, | 3, | | | 3. | | |
| Stunston, Henry, | | | | | | | 1, | | | | | .25 | |

(Page 40)

| Persons Name | Acres Desc. Lnd. | Titl. | REMARKS | #of Ent. | Rge. | Sec. | Dis. | Town Lots,Lot | #of Free Poll | Sla. | Horse. Sto.,Jac. | $ | Cts. | M |
|---|---|---|---|---|---|---|---|---|---|---|---|---|---|---|
| Sommers, Charles, | | | | | | | | | 1, | | | | .25 | |
| Short, Epes, | | | | | | | | | 1, | | | | .25 | |
| Self, John, | | | | | | | | | 1, | | | | .25 | |
| Smart, James H., | | | | | | | | | 1, | | | | .25 | |
| Shulty, Jacob, | | | | | | | | | 1, | | | | .25 | |
| Smart, William, S., | | | | | | | | | 1, | | | | .25 | |
| Smart, Phillip, 230, D., Jas. Sommers 3840, | | | | | 1, | 7, | 12, | | | | | 1.72 | 5 | |
| Smart, Stephen, 70, E. | | | | | 1, | 7, | 12, | | | | | .52 | 5 | |
| Segraves, Willie, | | | | | | | | | 1, | | | | .25 | |
| Shultey, Charles, | | | | | | | | | 1, | | | | .25 | |
| Sommers, James, | | | | | | | | | 1, | | | | .25 | |
| Sursey, Isaac, | | | | | | | | | 1, | | | | .25 | |
| Shultz, David, 80, | | | | | | | 13, | | 1, | | | | .85 | |
| Ship, Bennet, | | | | | | | | | 1, | | | | .25 | |
| Skaggs, James, | | | | | | | | | 1, | | | | .25 | |
| Stanford, Thos., 25, E., | | | | 918, 1, | 6, | | | | 1, | | | | .43 | 7½ |
| Stone, William, | | | | | | | | | 1, | | | | .25 | |
| Smyth, Hugh D., 66, D., Thomas Hopkins 228½, | | | | 1797, 1, | 7, | 12, | | | 1, | | | | .47 | 5 |
| Thomas, Micajah, 640, | | | | 1362, 2, | 5, | 12 | | | 1, | | | | 4.80 | |
| Taylor, Caleb Heirs, 640, | | | | 1363, 1, | 5, | | | | | | | | 4.80 | |
| Terrell, Peleg, 627½, D, J. Terrell, | | | | 1, | 6, | 13, | 1, | 74, | 1, 1, | | | | 6.95 | 6½ |
| Terrell, Jephtha, 500, Same, | | | | 1, | 7, | 1, | 93, | | 1, 2, | | | | 6.50 | |
| Thompson, Jacob, 170, Same, | | | | 1, | 6, | | | | 1, 3 | | | | 3. 2, 2½ | |
| Thomas, Mathew, | | | | | | | | | 1, | | | | .25 | |
| Terrell, John, 3802 3/4, Eight tracts | | | | | | | (15,30,) 9,(32,34 (56,57) (58,68,94,) | | 6, | | | | 45, 1 8 3/4 | |
| Terrell & Charlton, | | | | | | | 1, 95, | | 3, | | | | 1.50 | |
| Thomas, Joseph, 160, D. J. Terrell, | | | | 1413, 1, | 7, | 12, | | | | | | | 2.70 | |
| Todd, William, | | | | | | | 1, | | | | | | .25 | |
| Thomas, John, 536, | | | | 2, | 7, | 1, | 39, | | 1, 12, | | | | 10.27 | |
| Thomas, James D., | | | | | | | | | 1, 3, | | | | 1.75 | |
| Trentham, Floyd, | | | | | | | | | 1, | | | | .25 | |
| Taylor, Isaac, | | | | | | | | | 1, | | | | .25 | |

(Page 40) Cont.

| Persons Name | Acres | Dec. Lnd.Titl. REMARKS | #of Ent. | Rge. | Sec. | Town Dis. | Lots. | Lot. | #of Free Poll | Sla. | Sto. | Horse or Jac. | $ Cts. | M |
|---|---|---|---|---|---|---|---|---|---|---|---|---|---|---|
| Thompson, Jesse, | | | | | | | | | 1, | 1, | | | .75 | |
| Thompson, James, | | | | | | | | | 1, | | | | .25 | |
| Thompson, William, | | | | | | | | | 1, | | | | .25 | |
| Tucker, Daniel, | | | | | | | | | 1, | | | | .25 | |
| (Page 41) 1829 | | | | | | | | | | | | | | |
| Thompson, Robert, | | | | | | | | | 1, | | | | .25 | |
| Tausil, Edward, | | | | | | | | | | 3, | | | 1.50 | |
| Tausil, John, | | | | | | | | | | 1, | | | .50 | |
| Tharp, William A., | 480, | D. John Evans, H.S., | | | 13, | | | | | | | | 3.60 | |
| Uhs, Federick, J., | | | | | | | | | 1, | | | | .25 | |
| Vincent, Perry, | 200, | P. King & J. Terrell, | | | | 1, 31, | | | 1, | 2, | | | 4.25 | |
| Vincent, Orrin, | | | | | | | 2,(79,80) | | | 1, | | | | 3. | |
| Vincent, John M., | 100, | | | 1, | 7, | | | | 1, | 6, | | | 4. | |
| Vaughn, John, | | | | | | | | | 1, | | | | .25 | |
| Wilson, Samuel, | 272, | | | | | | | | | 2, | 4 | | | |
| Williams, Kinchen, | | | | | | | | | 1, | | | | .25 | |
| Wilkins, Lewelen, | | | | | | | | | | 1, | | | .75 | |
| Warner, Mears, | 100, | D. J.L.D.Smiths 274, | 1486, | 1, | 7, | 12,2,(37,38) | | | 1, | | | | 4. | |
| Ward, Robertson, | | | | | | | | | 1, | | | | .25 | |
| Willis, John, | 2500, | E, | 140, | 2,3, | 7,8,13, | | | | 1, | | | | 18.75 | |
| Williams, Scion, | 512, | Part of 640, | 351, | 2, | 5,6 | | | | | | | | 3.84 | |
| Watson, Robt(Heirs) | 140, | | 655, | 2, | 5, | | | | | | | | 1. 5 | |
| Wharton, Jesse, | 200, | | 274, | 3, | 9, | | | | | | | | 1. 50 | |
| Same, | 559½, | G, L. Carter, | 310, | 3, | 10, | | | | | | | | 4.19, 6¼ | 5 |
| Same, | 370, | Same, | 309, | 3, | 9, | | | | | | | | 5.47 | 5 |
| Williams, Joseph, G.,M | | | | | | | | | 1, | 1, | | | .75 | |
| Williams, Zachariah, | 240, | D, Boxter Boling | 640, | 1, | 6, | 12, | | | | 6, | | | 4.80 | |
| Wenscot, Andrew, | | | | | | | | | 1, | | | | .25 | |
| Willingham, Wm. | 30, | R. Porter, | | 1, | 7, | 12,2,(13,75) | | | 1, | 1, | | | 3.97 | 5 |
| Wilson, Lewis D., | 1000, | E, Bowers&Wilson, | | 2,3, | 7, | 13, | | | | | | | 7.50 | |
| Warner, Samuel, A., 5, D.,J. Terrell, | | | | 1, | 7, | | | | | | | | 1.78 | 5 |
| Winchester,Jas.H.S. | 296½, | E., | 641, | 2, | 7, | | | | 1, | 3, | | | 1.69 | 5 |
| Same, | 100, | | 587, | 1, | 10, | 12, | | | | | | | .75 | |
| White, Tyrel C., | | | | | | | | | 1, | | | | .25 | |
| Williamson, Meredith, | | | | | | | | | 1, | | | | .25 | |
| Woodward, George, | 144, | D.,Porter &McGavock, | | | | | | | 1, | | | | 1.33 | |
| Ward, Messrs., | 10, | | | | | | | | 1, | | | | .32 | 5 |
| Willingbly, James | 13, | | | | | | | | 1, | | | | .34 | 7½ |

(Page 41) Cont.

| Persons Name | Acres | Dec. Ind. Titl. REMARKS | #of Ent.Rge.,Sec.Dis.Lots.Lot | Town #of Free, Poll,Bla.Stos,Jac. | Horse or $ Cts. M |
|---|---|---|---|---|---|
| Wells, Hayden,E., | 200, | | | 1, 3, | 3.25 |
| White, John L., | | | | 1, | .25 |

(Page 42)

| Persons Name | Acres | Dec. Ind. Titl. REMARKS | #of Ent.Rge.,Sec.Dis.Lots.Lot | Town #of Free, Poll,Bla.Stos,Jac. | Horse or $ Cts. M |
|---|---|---|---|---|---|
| Williams, Briant, | | | | | |
| Winters, Aron, | 112, | D.,Doherty & McCorkle, | 2, 5, 12, | 1, | .25 |
| Wilson, Joseph, | 100, | D.,Jason Wilson, | 786, 2, 9, | 1, | 1.34 |
| Wilson, Jason, | 250, | E., | 785, 2, 9, | 1, 3, | 2.25 |
| Webb, Amos, | | | | | 1.87 5 |
| Webb, John, | | | | 1, 1, | .75 |
| Winsted, Johnson, | | | | 1, 2, | 1. |
| Wester, William, | 60, | | | 1, | .25 |
| Wheeler, Mark, | | | | | .70 |
| Workman, Pleasant, G., | | | | 1, | .25 |
| Williams, Mnna, | 100, | | | 1, | .25 |
| Williams, Allin, | 156, | | | | .75 |
| Whitley, Marcus, | | | | 1, | 1.42 |
| Whelly, Benjamin, | | | | 1, | .25 |
| Williams, Bartlett, | 100, | D.,Moses B. Travis, | | 1, 1, | .25 |
| Williams, Thomas, | | | | 1, 1, | 1.50 |
| Welsh, John, | 28½, | | 1, 6, 12, | 1, | .75 |
| Williams, Charles, | | | | 1, | .46 3 3/4 |
| Williams, Martin, | | | | 1, | .25 |
| Young, Abraham, B., | 40, | E. | 1, 7, | 1, | .25 |
| Same, | 60, | | 1, 7, | | .30 |
| Young, Henry J., | | | | 1, | .45 |
| Zimmerman, John, | | | | 1, | .25 |
| | | | | | .25 |

(Page 43) SUPPLEMENT LIST OF 1829

| Persons Name | Acres | Dec. Ind. Titl. REMARKS | #of Ent.Rge.,Sec.Dis.Lots.Lot | Town #of Free, Poll,Bla.Stos,Jac. | Horse or $ Cts. M |
|---|---|---|---|---|---|
| Rey, John & Co., | 2560, | Deed,Benj.Coffields | 2560,735,1, 4&5, 13, | | 17.70 |
| Same, | 542, | John McIvers, | 4336,752,1, 9&10, | | 4. 6 5 |
| Same, | 228, | Cave Johnson, | 600,1, 10, 12, | | 1.50 |
| Same, | 160, | James Harts, | 640, 1360, 1, 6, 12, | | 1.20 |
| Same, | 160, | Benjn.McCulocks, | 640, 355, 3, 9, 13, | | 1.20 |
| Same, | 131¼, | Clemigle,Cherrys, | 640, 617, 3, 7, | | .96 3 3/4 |
| Rey & Peters, | 640, | David Jeffries, | 184, 1, 9, | | 4.80 |
| Roberts,Nathaniel, | 1000, | Thomas Persons, | 240, 2, 7, | | 7.50 |
| Wilson, Samuel,D., | 272, | Ent. | | | 2. 4 |

(Page 43) Cont. Acres Desc.       #of              Town #of Free                              Horse
Persons Name    Lnd.Title, R E M A R K S  Ent. Rge.,Sec.Dis.Lots,Lot,Poll,Sla.Sto.Jac. $ Cts.   or      49
                                                                                              5.36  2½  M

Yarbrough, David, 715, D, Devis of Geo.Daugherty

434         Free Polls @ 25¢ per poll is ........................$108.50
287         Slaves @ 50¢ per poll is ...........................  143.50
74 Town lots @ $1.50 pr. lot is ................................  111.00
 4          Retail Store @ $10.00 pr Store is ..................   40.00
 6          Stud Horses @ various prices is ....................   13.00
 1          Two wheeled carriages of pleasure is ...............    2.50
 1          Tavern is ..........................................    5.00
146,955 3/4 Acres of land @ 75¢ pr hundred acres is ............ $1102.16 7½
                                                  Total amount   $1525.66 7½

State tax amounts to    $444 79  1 3/4 & a fraction
County tax amounts to    474 29  1 3/4         Do
Jury Tax amounts to      303 29  1 3/4         Do
Tax for courthouse amounts 303 29  1 3/4       Do
                        $1525 66  7 1/2

                Wm. H. Johnson Clerk

(Page 44)

Robert Cartwright's )
Last Will & Testament ) Recorded 29th of July, 1829.

In the name of God Amen - I, Robert Cartwright, of the County of Weakley and State of Tennessee being sick & calling to mind the certainty of Death do make and ordain this my last will and testament. First of all I desire my body to be buried in a decent christian burial at the discretion of my executors hereafter named. As in respects what estate it has pleased God to bless me with I give and bequeath in the following manner, towit:

First I give and bequeath to my present dearly beloved wife, Elizabeth Cartwright, during her natural life part of the tract of land whereon I now live bounded as follows: Beginning at the lower or south west corner of the peach orchard running thence east to the east boundary of my tract thence north to the corner thence with the line of my tract to the bank of a dry branch thence up the meanders of said dry branch so far that a line due north will strike the beginning containing eighty acres be the same more or less including all the buildings of every description.  Item 2nd, I do also give and bequeath unto my said wife Elizabeth two head of choice horses, two head of choice cows and calves, two choise steers and oxcart, seven head of choice hogs and three head of sheep.

Item 3rd, I do also give and bequeath unto my said wife Elizabeth two negroes, Peter and Sarah and their future increase forever.  Item 4th, I give and bequeath to my daughter Evalina Nakes all the residue of the tract of land whereon I now live, viz. Beginning at the lower or south west corner of peach orchard running east to the east boundary of my tract thence south; thence with the lines of my tract to the bank of a dry branch thence up said dry branch so far that a due north line will strike the  (Page 45) beginning containing eighty acres be the same more or less. Item 5th, I give and bequeath to my said daughterEvalina one negro boy Phillip to her and her heirs forever.

Item 6th, I give and bequeath to my daughter Penney Nettles two negro women, Sylvia and Chaney with their future increase forever. I do further give to my daughter Evalina one cow and calf.  All the balance of my stock of every description I wish divided equally between my wife and my two daughters after selling so much of it as will pay my just debts, and also I wish the present crop divided equally between my wife and two daughters aforesaid.  I do further bequeath to my wife Elizabeth all the household furniture and farming tools, everything that remains not particularly mentioned I wish sold and the proceeds equally divided.

I do hereby appoint my trusty friend William Flemming and John A Nettles my executors to this my last will and testament. In testimony whereof I have here unto set my hand and seal this 30th day of March, 1829.  Interlined before signed.

Robert Cartwright,(Seal. )

(Page 45) Cont.
William Flemming,   )
Phillip L. Turner  )
State of Tennessee )

Weakley County Court, July term, 1829. Then was execution of the foregoing will proven in open court by the oaths of William Flemming and Phillip L. Turner the subscribing witness thereto and ordered to be recorded.    William H. Johnson Clk.

(Page 46, A supplement Tax list for 1829.

| Persons Name | Lnd. | Titl. | REMARKS | Ent. | Rge. | Sec. | Dis. | Lots | Lot | Poll | Sla. | Sto. | Horse or Jac. | $ Cts. M |
|---|---|---|---|---|---|---|---|---|---|---|---|---|---|---|
| Brawner, John, | | | | | | | | | | | | | 1, | .50 |
| Cage, Wilson, | 104 | Entry | | | | | | | | | | | | .78 |
| Same, | 80 | | | | | | | | | | | | | .60 |
| Delany, Elijah, | | | | | | | | | | 1, | | | | .25 |
| Foster, George M., | | | | | | | | | | 1, | 2, | | | 1.25 |
| Huntsman &Totten, | 2100, | | | | | | | | | | | | | 15.25 |
| Haines, Samuel, | | | | | | | | | | 1, | | | | .25 |
| Mitchel, Archelous, | 240, | Deed, | Solomon George, | | | | | | | | 2, | | | 2.80 |
| Moony, Henry | | | | | | | | | | 1, | | | | .25 |
| Miller, George, | | | | | | | | | | 1, | | | | .25 |
| Mar, George W.L., | 200, | Entry, | | | | | | | | | | | | 1.50 |
| Same, | 2560, | Deed, | Thomas Henderson, | | | | | | | | | | | 19.20 |
| Same, | 640, | | Henry Rhodes Heirs, | | | | | | | | | | | 4.80 |
| Owens, Solomon, H. | 140, | | John H. Moore, | | | | | | | | | | | 1.05 |
| Willingham, William | | | | | | | | | | | | | 2 | 3.00 |
| Williams, Elisha, | 640, | Entry, | | | | | | | | | | | | 4.80 |
| Ward, Britton, | | | | | | | | | | 1, | | | | .25 |
| Total, | 6704 | | | | | | | | | 6, | 5, | 2, | | $57.78 |

(Page 47)

SHERIFFS BOND RECORDED JANUARY 29, 1830.

Know all men by these presents that we Alfred Gardner Jeptha Gardner John A Gardner John Jenkins John Terrell George G. Roulhac all of the County of Weakley and State of Tennessee are held and firmly bound unto William Carrell Esquire, Governor of the State of Tennessee and his successors in office in the penal sum of Six thousand dollars for the true and faithful payment of

(Page 47) Cont.

which we bind ourselves our heirs executors administrators jointly and severally firmly by these presents sealed with our seals and dated the 12th day of January, 1830.

The condition of the above obligation is such that whereas the above Alfred Gardner has been this day duly constituted and appointed sheriff in deed for the County of Weakley for the ensuing two years therefore should the said Alfred Gardner well and truly collect and pay over all fines & sums of money & county taxes that may become due during the time for which he the said Alfred Gardner the incumbent of said appointment then in that case the above obligation to be void otherwise to remain in full force and effect.

```
                                         A. Gardner,    Seal
Signed and acknowledged )                Jeptha Gardner, Seal
in open court           )                Jno. A. Gardner, Seal
Wm.H.Johnson,Clk.       )                John Jenkins,  Seal
                                         John Terrell,  Seal
                                         Geo. G. Roulhac, Seal
```

---

(Page 48) SHERIFFS BOND RECORDED FEBRUARY 1st, 1830.

Know all men by these presents that we Alfred Gardner, Jeptha Gardner John A. Gardner, John Jenkins John Terrel George G Roulhac and Albert G. Bondurant all of the County of Weakley and State of Tennessee are held and firmly bound unto William Carroll Esqr. Governor in & for the State of Tennessee for the time being and his successors in office in the penal sum of Ten Thousand Dollars for the payment of which well and truly to be made we bind ourselves our heirs executors and administrators jointly & severally firmly by these presents.

The condition of the above obligation is such that whereas the above bound Alfred Gardner has been this day constituted and appointed sheriff of Wealkey County by the Justices of the court of Please & quarter sessions for said county for the ensuing two years from the date hereof. If therefore the said Alfred Gardner shall well and truly execute and due return make of all process & precepts to him directed and pay and satisfy all fees and sums of money by him received or levied by virtue of any process into the proper office by which the same by the tenor thereof ought to be paid or to the person or persons to whom shall be due his her or their executors administrators attorneys or agents and in all other things well and truly and faithfully execute the said office of sheriff during his continuance therein then the above obligation to be void otherwise to remain in full force and effect.

Witness our hands and seals this 12th day of January, 1830.
```
                    A. Gardner, Seal, ; Jeptha Gardner, Seal
                    Jno. A. Gardner, Seal,; John Jenkins, Seal
                    John Terrell, Seal,:  Geo. G. Roulhac, Seal
                                          A. G. Bondurant, Seal
Signed sealed and acknowledged in)
open court                       )
 Wm. H. Johnson, Clk.            )
```

(Page 49)

## HENRY HENDRICKS LAST WILL. RECORDED MARCH THE 12th, 1830.

In the name of God Amen -

I Henry Hendricks of the State of Tennessee, Weakley County calling to mind the mortality of my body & knowing that it is appointed for all men once to die & after death the Judgment, being in good health and of sound mind & memory blest with such worldly estate as it has pleased God to bless me with, do think proper to dispose of the same in the following manner & form & do make and ordain this my last will & testament annulling all other wills heretofore by me made, and first of all I do recommend my soul into the hands of Almity God that gave it & my body to be buried in a decent christian like manner at the discretion of my executors then I will and bequeath to my beloved wife Cary Hendricks one negro girl named Silvia about seven years old also I will & Bequeath to my beloved wife Cary Hendricks one bed & all the household furniture that she possessed before we were married together with all the additional furniture that she may add to the said bed also one set of earthen plates one set of knives & forks two earthen dishes two pitchers one set of cups and saucers one cream pot one looking glass one coffee mill one three gallon pot pot hooks and pot rack one bake oven and one half dozen chairs one chest one cow & calf one spinning wheel one pair of cotton cards fifty weight of picked cotton & ten barrels of corn, washing tub one pail three hundred weight of pork one sow & pigs one piggin & one churn all of the above named property I give unto her during life & for her to dispose of as she may think proper.

I also reserve sixty rod square of land taken out of the northeast corner of the tract of land that I now live on for my wife Cary Hendricks for a home during her natural life or so long as she remain a widow & live on said land & and if she should think proper to remove off of sd land then she relinquishes all her wright to sd land into the hands of my executors

(50) for the benefit of my two sons Washing & William Hendricks and whereas my daughter Sally Cummins has received of my estate one hundred & seventy three dollars, my son Pinkney Hendricks one hundred & seventy three dollars. my daughter Elizabeth Hopper one hundred & seventy three dollars my son Alford Hendricks one hundred & seventy three dollars my son Paden Hendricks one hundred & fifty one dollars. I therefore will & bequeath to my daughter Polly Ann Hendricks one negro girl named Lilla together with her bed, bed stead & chord two counterpains & two bed quilts & one sheet at one hundred and eighty three dollars & if the said negro girl should die before my daughter Polly Ann becomes of age or marrys then one hundred & fifty dollars is to be made up to her out of the rest of my property. Also I will & bequeath to my two sons Washington & William Hendricks the tract of land whereon I now live running a line from east to west across sd land giving Washington the south end of said land & William the north end at one hundred & seventy eight dollars each/ The above named legatees Washington & William A. Hendricks not to have possession for eight years for which time Forester Hopper is to keep his part Alford Hendricks all that he clears on said tract of land & and my wife Cary to have the benefit of the field called mine till the sd Alford Hendricks clears clears as much land on his lot reserved for her as sd field & puts in good repair for tending them to exchange & said Alford to take the field the balance of the time & my son Paden Hendricks his part the term of eight years, two negroes namely Jenny & Harriett & two town lots with all the

(Page 50) Cont.
rest of my property not named to be sold and after paying all just debts & making all my ligitees up equal agreeable to the sums named here the balance if any to be divided equally among all my ligatees begotten of
(51) my body I therefore do nominate & appoint my beloved son & son in law alford Hendricks & Forester Hopper my true and lawful executors. In witness whereof I have hereunto set my hand and offered my seal this 18th day of October inthe year of our Lord, 1829.
                                                   his
                                    Henry H. Hendricks Seal
Test.          )                               Mark
Benjamin Malin )
Wm. Baldridge )

---

STATE OF TENNESSEE )
WEAKLEY COUNTY    )
                            JANUARY COURT 1830

Then was the within will proven by the oaths of Benjamin Malin & William Baldridge the subscribing witnesses thereto and ordered to be recorded.
    Wm. H. Johnson, Clk.

---

Page 52,) TAX LIST FOR 1830

| Persons Name | Acres | #of Lnd. Titl. | REMARKS | #of Ent. | Rge. | Sec. | Dis. | Lots, Lot, | Town Poll, | #of Free Slav. | Sto. | Horse Jac. | $ | Cts. | M |
|---|---|---|---|---|---|---|---|---|---|---|---|---|---|---|---|
| Adams, Thomas, | | | | | | | | | | | | | | .50 | |
| Asher, Sam'l., | | | | | | | | | 1, | | | | | .50 | |
| Alexander, Adam R., | 640, | Deed, | John Terrell, | | 1, | 7, | 13, | | 1, | | | | | 6.40 | |
| Same, | 10, | | Part of Jno. Terrell | 640,- | 1 | 7, | | | | | | | | .10 | |
| Anderson, Wm. E., | 640, | Entry, | | 828, | 2, | 7, | 12, | | | | | | | 6.40 | |
| Same, | 171, | | | 829, | 1, | 10, | | | | | | | | 1.71 | |
| Anderson Bailey Heirs, | 640, | | | 603, | 1, | 9, | 13, | | | | | | | 6.40 | |
| Abbott, Spencer, | | | | | | | | | 1, | | | | | .50 | |
| Adkison, Williford, | | | | | | | | | 1, | | | | | .50 | |
| Adkison, James, | | | | | | | | | 1, | | | | | .50 | |
| Adkison, William, | | | | | | | | | 1, | | | | | .50 | |
| Abernathy, Littleton F. | 81½, | | | 1264, | 2, | 9, | 12, | | 1, | | | | | 1.35 | 5 |
| Acre, Jesse, | | | | | | | | | 1, | | | | | .50 | |
| Austin, Samel F. | | | | | | | | | 1, | | | | | .50 | |
| Austin, Moses, Sr., | 193, | Deed, | Pet Williams 640, | 327, | 2, | 9, | | | | | | | | 1.93 | |
| Austin, Vincent, | | | | | | | | | 1, | | | | | .50 | |
| (Page 53,) 1830 | | | | | | | | | | | | | | | |
| Austin, Moses Jr., | 63, | | Part of Same, | 327, | 2, | 9, | | | 1, | | | | | 1.13 | |
| Adkins, Joseph, R., | 30, | | Messer.Ward, | | 2, | 7, | | | 1, | | | | | .80 | |
| Armstrong, Thomas, | | | | | | | | | 1, | | | | | .50 | |
| Adams, Abel, | | | | | | | | | 1, | | | | | .50 | |
| Bayliss, Cullin, | | | | | | | | | 1, | | 2, | | | 2.00 | |
| Bayliss, Willie, | | | | | | | | | 1, | | | | | .50 | |
| Bayliss, C & W., | 19½, | Deed, | Danl. Delaney, | 1596, | 1, | 6, | | | 1, | | 1, | 1, | | 11.19 | 5 |
| Bondurant, Benjn., | 371½, | Deed, | 2 Tracts Winchester, | | | | | | | | 11, | 3, | | 19.96 | 5 |
| Bell, Pulaski,B., | | | | | | | | | | | | | | .50 | |
| Bondurant, Albert, G., | 55, | Deed, | Segraves & Terrell, | | 1, | 9,12, | 13, | | 1, | | 2, | | | 2.55 | |
| Same | 640, | | Hs.Elisha Ward, | 1030, | 1, | 7, | 13, | | | | | | | 6.40 | |
| Bonderant, Hillary,H., | 4, | | Jno. Terrell, | 640, | | | | | 1, | | 2, | 2, | | 4.04 | |
| Bookout, Bradley, | | | | | | | | | 1, | | | | | .50 | |
| Breken, James G., | 1000, | Entry, | | 109, | 3, | 7, | 12, | | | | | | | 10.00 | |
| Same, | 240, | | | 601, | 1, | 9, | 13, | | | | | | | 2.40 | |
| Blount, John G., | 2500, | | Part of 3000, | 591, | 1, | 5, | 12, | | | | | | | 25.00 | |
| Same, | 274, | | | 692, | 2, | 9, | 12, | | | | | | | 2.74 | |
| Same, | 60, | | | 806, | 1, | 6, | 13, | | | | | | | .60 | |

(Page 53 A)

| Persons Name | Acres Desc. Lnd. Titl. REMARKS - | #of Ent. | Rge., | Sec., | Dis. | Town, Lots. | #of Lot, | Free, Poll, | Sla. | Horse. Sto. | Mac. | $ cts. | M |
|---|---|---|---|---|---|---|---|---|---|---|---|---|---|
| Brown, William R., | 590½, Entry, | 286, | 1&2, | 9, | 13, | | | | | | | 5.90 | 5 |
| Baldridge, Daniel, | 640, | 725, | 2, | 7, | | | | | | | | 6.40 | |
| Bowers, John, | | | | | | | | | | | | 1.75 | |
| Bradley, James, | 480, | 602, | 1, | 8, | | | | 2, | 1, | | | 4.80 | |
| Same, | 480, | 703, | 3, | 4, | | | | | | | | 4.80 | |
| Byars, William, | 100, Deed, | | | | | | | | | | | 1.00 | |
| Bowers, Young, P., | | | | | | | | 1, | 2, | | | 2.00 | |
| Brackin, James, | 150, G, | 1154, | 1, | 7, | 12, | | | | | | | 1.50 | |
| Belote, Henry, | 128, 2, Part of 640, | | 1, | 8&9, | | | | | | | | 1.28 | |
| Same, | 128, Part of 640, | 674, | 2, | 7, | 13, | | | | | | | 1.28 | |
| Baker, John, | | | | | | | | 1, | | | | .50 | |
| Bradshaw, Thompson, | 50, D. Daniel Baldridge, | 640, | 2, | 7, | | | | 1, | | | | 1.00 | |
| Burton, Charles, | | | | | | | | 1, | | | | .50 | |
| Baldridge, Andrew W.; | | | | | | | | 1, | | | | .50 | |
| Bondurant, Robert M.; | 166½, Jerome McClaines, | | 2, | 7, | 13, | | | 1, | 1, | | | 2.91 | 5 |
| Byrd, Nazareth, | | | | | | | | 1, | | | | .50 | |
| Browder, John, | 440, Enty, R. Browder | 239, | 1&2, | 6, | | | | 1, | | | | 4.40 | |
| Barley, John, | 220½, | 222, | 2, | 8, | | | | 1, | | | | 2.20 | 5 |
| Bell, John, Trustee, | 230, | | | | | | | | | | | 2.30 | |
| Same, | 100, | | | | | | | | | | | 1.00 | |
| Beadles, Williams, | | | | | | | | 1, | | | | .50 | |
| Beadles, Bassit A., | | | | | | | | 1, | | | | .50 | |
| Bynum, Thomas, | | | | | | | | 1, | | | | .50 | |
| Brand, James, | | | | | | | | 1, | | | | .50 | |
| Buckley, James, | | | | | | | | | 1, | | | .75 | |
| Bunton, William, | | | | | | | | 1, | | | | .50 | |
| Barnes, Solomon, | | | | | | | | 1, | | | | .50 | |
| Brown, Coonrad, | 50, | 1794, | 2, | 7, | 12, | | | 1, | | | | 1.00 | |
| Brawner, John, | | | | | | | | 1, | 1, | | | 1.25 | |
| Bullock, A. M., | | | | | | | | 1, | | | | .50 | |
| Barnerd, William, | | | | | | | | 1, | | | | .50 | |
| Bridges, Griffin, | | | | | | | | 1, | 1, | | | 1.25 | |
| Billingsly, Bazel, | | | | | | | | 1, | | | | .50 | |
| Barnard, John, | | | | | | | | 1, | | | | .50 | |

| (Page 54) Persons Name, | Acres Lnd, | Desc. Titl. | REMARKS | #of Ent. | Rge., | Sec., | Dis. | Town Lots, | #of Lot, | Free Poll, | Sla., | Sto. | Horse Jac. | $ Cts. M |
|---|---|---|---|---|---|---|---|---|---|---|---|---|---|---|
| Barnard, George, | | | | | | | | | | | | | | .50 |
| Blackley, James, | | | | | | | | | | | | | | .50 |
| Busey, Edward, | 60, | | | | 2, | 5, | 12, | | | 1, | | | | 2.60 |
| Brasiel, Edward M., | | | | | | | | | | 1, 2, | | | | .50 |
| Bradshaw, John, | | | | | | | | | | 1, 2, | | | | 2.00 |
| Bradshaw, Gideon, | | | | | | | | | | 1, | | | | .50 |
| Baker, James, | 16½ | | | | | | | | | 1, | | | | .66 5 |
| Baker, John, | | | | | | | | | | 1, | | | | .50 |
| Burgin, Abner, | | | | | | | | | | 1, | | | | 1.25 |
| Bourland, James, | 25, | Enty, | | 917, | 1, | 6, | 13, | | | 1, 3, | | | | 1.50 |
| Bowers, Wm. G., | 150, | | Different tracts | | | | | | | 1, 5, | | Y | | 5.00 |
| Cochren, Dennis, | | | | | | | | | | 1, 2, | | 1 | 1 | 11.00 |
| Clark, James W., | 3925, | | Part of 5000, | 104, | 3, | 8, | | Y, | | | | | | 39.25 |
| Charlton, John, | 954½, | | Different Tracts | 640,- | | | 12 | 5 | | 1 | 2 | | | 16.54 5 |
| Cotton, Charles, | 640, | | | 1366, | 1, | 5, | | | | | | | | 6.40 |
| Claibourn, Thomas, | 200, | Deed, | Landon Carter, | 311, | 3, | 9, | 13, | | | | | | | 2.00 |
| Same | 300, | | Same, | 312, | 3, | 9, | | | | | | | | 3.00 |
| Same, | 300 | | Same, | 314, | 3, | 9, | | | | | | | | 3.00 |
| Same, | 300, | | Same, | 324, | 3, | 9, | | | | | | | | 3.00 |
| Same, | 409, | | Same, | 322, | 2&3, | 9, | | | | | | | | 4.09 |
| Carmichel, Michael | 3480, | Ent. | Part of 5000 | 115, | 2, | 9 & 10 | | | | | | | | 31.80 |
| Cherry, Clermigle, | 520, | E | | 617, | 3, | 7, | | | | | | | | 5.20 |
| Carter Lendon, | Hs.559 3/4, | G. | | 313, | 3, | 9, | | | | | | | | 5.597½ |
| Same, | 808, | | | 319, | 3, | 9, | | | | | | | | 8.08 |
| Same, | 300, | | | 316, | 3, | 9, | | | | | | | | 3.00 |
| Conrad, George C., | 92¼, | Entry, | | 1912, | 1, | 7, | 12, | | | | | | | .92¼ |
| Clark, Christppher R., | | | | | | | | | | 1, | | | | .50 |
| Cooke, Willis, | | | | | | | | | | 1, 1, | | | | .50 |
| Clark, Levi | | | | | | | | | | 1, 1, | | | | 1.25 |
| Canady, Behithalum, | | | | | | | | | | 1, 2, | | | | 1.50 |
| Carr, Silas, | 50, | | | | | | | | | | | | | .50 |
| Cherry, Lawrence, | 228, | | | 625, | 2, | 7, | 13, | | | | | | | 2.28 |
| Same, | 640, | | | 52, | 2, | 9, | 12, | | | | | | | 6.40 |
| Same, | 213, | | | 1457, | 1, | 6, | | | | | | | | 2.13 |

(Page 55) 1830

| PERSONS NAME | Acres Desc. Lnd.Titl. R E M A R K S | Ent., | Rge., | Sec., | Town, Dis.Lots,Lot | #of Poll, | Free Sla, | Horse or Sto.Jac. | $ Cts. |
|---|---|---|---|---|---|---|---|---|---|
| Cherry, Daniel, | 640, Entry, | 561, | 1, | 7, | 13, | | | | 6.40 |
| Same, | 640, Deed, Isaac Bateman, | 676, | 1, | 8, | | | | | 6.40 |
| Same, | 640, Same, | 672, | 1&2, | 7, | | | | | 6.40 |
| Cherry, Darling, | 640, Entry, | 769, | 2, | 9, | 12, | | | | 6.40 |
| Conner, Isham, | | | | | | 1, | | | .50 |
| Curlin, Zacheus H. | 640, Benjn. McCullock, | 355, | 3, | 9, | | 1, | | | 6.90 |
| Craig, Ebenezer, | 13, Bond, J.Terrell 640, | | 1, | 7, | 13, | 1, | 1, | | 1.38 |
| Crider, David, | 50, | | | | 12, | 1, | | | 1. |
| Clark, David, | | | | | | 1, | | | .50 |
| Cashen, Elum M., | | | | | | 1, | | | .50 |
| Clark, William, | | | | | | 1, | | | .50 |
| Cavit, John F., | 180, Enty, | 847, | 2, | 9, | | 1, | 1, | | 3.05 |
| Cook, John, | 40, | 1747, | 2, | 10, | | 1, | | | .40 |
| Coleman, John, | | | | | | 1, | | | .50 |
| Cathey, Thomas &A.J.W., | 875, Enty, Part 1000,680, | | 2, | 8 & 9, | | 1, | | | 8.75 |
| Crum, Peter | - | | | | | | | | .50 |
| Clayton, John, | 270, Deed, Thos. Henderson, 640, | | 2, | 7 | | 1, | 3, | | 5.45 |
| Carter, Reubin, | | | | | | 1, | | | .50 |
| Christmas, Richard, | | | | | | 1, | | | .50 |
| Cruise, Isaac, | 320, Part of 640, | 1012, | | | | 1, | | | 3.70 |
| Craig, William, | | | | | | 1, | | | .50 |
| Craig, William D., | 124, Part of 320 acres | | 2, | 6, | | 1, | | | 1.74 |
| Craig, Samuel, | | | | | | 1, | | | .50 |
| Craig, Hugh, | 146, Deed, | | | | | 1, | | | 1.46 |
| Cox, Henry B., | | | | | | 1, | | | .50 |
| Cox, Edward M., | | | | | | 1, | | | .50 |
| Cox, Robert T., | | | | | | 1, | | | .50 |
| Campbell, Daniel, | | | | | | 1, | 2, | | 1.50 |
| Claxton, James, | 128, Part of 640, | | 1, | 7, | 13, | 1, | | | 1.78 |
| Cooley, George, | 170, Deed,Part of 2 tracts, | | 2, | 5, | | 1, | | | 2.20 |
| Carsley, Seth L., | | | | | | 1, | | | .50 |
| Cravens, Joseph, | | | | | | 1, | 3, | 1, | 5.75 |
| Cantrell, Duke, | | | | | | 1, | 2, | | 2.00 |
| Cravens, John, | | | | | | 1, | 1, | | 1.25 |

(Page 56) 1830

| Persons Name | Acres Desc. Lnd.Titl. | REMARKS | #of Ent.Rge., | Sec. | Town Dis. Lots, | Town Lot, | #of Free Poll, | Sla.Sto. | Horse Jac. | $ Cts. M |
|---|---|---|---|---|---|---|---|---|---|---|
| Cantrell, Joseph, | | | | | | | | | | .50 |
| Chaplin, Moses, | | | | | | | 1, | | | .50 |
| Crockett, David, 225, | | | 3, | 5, | 13, | | 1, | | | 2.75 |
| Crabtree, Anderson, | | | | | | | 1, | | | .50 |
| Cantrell, Abraham S., | | | | | | | 1, | | | .50 |
| Cooper, James, | | | | | | | 1, | | | .50 |
| Dent, Joseph E., | | | | | | 1, | 1, | | | 1.50 |
| Dunn, John, | | | | | | | 1, | | | .50 |
| Devereaux, Thos. P.500, Entry, | | | 967, 1, | 5, | 12, | | | | | 5.00 |
| Daugherty, George 943, | | | 943, 1 &2, | 7, | | | | | | 9.43 |
| Same, 4500, Part of 5000 Acres, | | | 98, 3, | 9, | 13, | | | | | .45 |
| Dunnar, Anthony Hs.640, | | | 1326, 2, | 9, | 12, | | | | | 6.40 |
| Dickens, Samuel, 160, Deed, Part of 640, | | | 1082, 1, | 6, | | | | | | 1.60 |
| Same, 675, | | | 82, 1, | 5, | 13, | | | | | 6.75 |
| Same, 200, | | | 143, | | | | | | | 2.00 |
| Damron, Isaac, | | | | | | | | 1, 1, | | 2.25 |
| Drew, James, H., | | | | | | 1 | 1, | | | .50 |
| Dell, Joseph, | | | | | | | 1, | | | .50 |
| Dell, Zebulon, | | | | | | | 1, | | | .50 |
| Dunholbarger, Daniel, | | | | | | | 1, | 1, | | 1.25 |
| Davis Fennel, | | | | | | | 1, | | | .50 |
| Damron, Moses, | | | | | | | 1, | | | .50 |
| Damron, Charles, | | | | | | | 1, | | | .50 |
| Damron, George, 50, Entry | | | | | | | 1, | | | 1.00 |
| Doherty, Dennis, | | | | | | | 1, | | | .50 |
| Damron, John T., 35, | | | 1, | 8, | 12, | | 1, | | | .85 |
| Damron, John, | | | | | | | 1, | | | .50 |
| Damron, Constantine, | | | | | | | 1, | | | .50 |
| Delaney, Elijah, | | | | | | | 1, | | | .50 |
| Davis, Jess B., | | | | | | | 1, | | | .50 |
| Dunn, Mathew, P., | | | | | | | 1, | | | .50 |
| Donelson, Humphrey, 180, | | | | | | | 1, | | | 1.80 |
| Davis, Isham, L., | | | | | | | 1, | 2, | | 2.00 |
| Davis, Jesse, | | | | | | | 1, | | | .50 |
| Delaney, Will, | | | | | | | 1, | | | .50 |

(Page 57)

| Persons Name | Acres Desc. Lnd.Titl. REMARKS | #of Ent. | Rge. | Sec. | Town,Dis. | #of Lot,Lot | Free Poll | Sla. | Sto. | Horse Jac. | $ Cts. M |
|---|---|---|---|---|---|---|---|---|---|---|---|
| Delaney, Daniel, | | | | | | | 1, | | | | .50 |
| Durham, William, | | | | | | | 1, | | | | .50 |
| Dickson, Ephriam, D., | | | | | | | | | | | |
| | 240, Deed, Byhel Bells, 640, | | 1, | 1, | 13, | 1, | 1, | 2, | | | 5.40 |
| Dunning, George, W., | | | | | | | 1, | | | | .50 |
| Deck, Daniel, | | | | | | | 1, | | | | .50 |
| Edwards, Thos. C., | | | | | | | 1, | | | | .50 |
| Eley, Eli, | 200, Bond, Benjn.Coffield, 2560, 735 | 1, | 4,5, | | | | 1, | | | | 2.50 |
| Edmonston, Jesse, 10, John Terrell 640, | | 1, | 7, | | | | 1, | | | | .10 |
| Edwards, Eli, | | | | | | | 1, | | | | .50 |
| Edwards, Eleas, | | | | | | | 1, | | | | .50 |
| Elzey, William, | | | | | | | 1, | | | | .50 |
| Edmonston, James, | | | | | | | 1, | | | | .50 |
| Edmonston, Jesse, | | | | | | | 1, | | | | .50 |
| England, David, | | | | | | | 1, | | | | .50 |
| Eliott, George S. 50, E. | | 1, | 8, | | | | 1, | 4, | | | 6. |
| English, Asa, | | | | | | | 1, | | | | .50 |
| Ezzell, Urias, | | | | | | | 1, | | | | .50 |
| Ezzell, Hanson, | | | | | | | 1, | | | | .50 |
| Edmonston, William, | | | | | | | 1, | | | | .50 |
| Ethridge, Thomas, | | | | | | | 1, | | | | .50 |
| Fitzgerald, William, 200, D.; James Greer, | | 1, | 6 & 7, 12, | | | | 1, | 3, | | | 4.75 |
| Fowler, Wm. H., | | | | | | | 1, | | | | .50 |
| Forbis, Almerick M., | | | | | | | 1, | | | | .50 |
| Forbis, Lorenzo D., | | | | | | 2, | 1, | | | | 2.50 |
| Freeman, Charles A., 100, James Long | 963, | 1, | 7, | 12, | | | 1, | | | | 1.50 |
| Freeman, John, | | | | | | | 1, | | | | .50 |
| Fowler, Thomas, | | | | | | | 1, | 2, | | | 1.50 |
| Farley, Thomas M., | | | | | | | 1, | 3, | | | 2.75 |
| Freeman, Richardson, | | | | | | | 1, | 3, | | | 2.75 |
| Force, Albert B., 160, Entry, | | 2, | 6, | 13, | | | 1, | 2, | | | 2.10 |
| Fowler, Bullard, A.; | | | | | | | 1, | 1, | | | 2. |
| Fowler, John, | | | | | | | | | | | |
| Filpot, Bennet, | | | | | | | 1, | | | | .75 |
| Freels, Garritt, | | | | | | | 1, | | | | .50 |
| Freels, David, | | | | | | | 1, | | | | .50 |

(Page 58) 1830

| Persons Name | Acres Lnd. | Desc. Titl. | REMARKS | #of Ent. | Rge. | Sec. | Dis. | Town Lotg | Lot | #of Free Poll | Sla. | Horse Sto. | Jac. | $ Cts. M. |
|---|---|---|---|---|---|---|---|---|---|---|---|---|---|---|
| Farmer, Aron, | | | | | | | | | | 1, | | | | .50. |
| Farmer, Hiram, | | | | | | | | | | 1, | | | | .50 |
| Freeman, Evans, | 100, | D, | Porter & McGavocks, | 2, | 7, | 12, | | | | 1, | 3 | | | 3.45 |
| Foster, James, | | | | | | | | | | 1, | | | | .50 |
| Force, William, | | | | | | | | | | 1, | | | | .50 |
| Finch, John, W., | 27½, | | John Rush, | 1, | 6, | | | | | 1, | 1, | | | 1.52 5 |
| Fowler, Samuel, | | | | | | | | | | 1, | 1, | | | 1.25 |
| Foley, Jesse, | | | | | | | | | | 1, | | | | .50 |
| Foley, Townsend, | | | | | | | | | | 1, | | | | .50 |
| Garrett, Henry A., | | | | | | | | 4 | | 1, | | | | .50 |
| Gardner, Alford, | | | | | | | | | | 1, | | | | 4.50 |
| Glen, Phillip B., | | | | | | | | | | 1, | | | | .50 |
| Gleeson, William H., | 500, | Enty, | Isaac Taylor, | | | | | | | 1, | 2, | | | 7.00 |
| Gerner, John, | | | | | | | | | | 1, | | | | .50 |
| Guest, George, | 150, | Entry, | | | | | 1, | | | 1, | | | | 1.50 |
| Gwlon, Avah, | | | | | | | | | | | | | | 1. |
| Glen, Robert J., | | | | | | | | | | 1, | 2, | | | 2.00 |
| Glass, Dudley Sr., | | | | | | | | | | 1, | 8, | | | 6.00 |
| Glass, Dudley Jr., | | | | | | | | | | 1, | | | | .50 |
| Gardner, Jeptha, | 63, | D, | Two Tracts | | | | | | | 1, | 2, 1, | 1, | | 8.60 |
| Greer, James, | 100, | Ent. | | | | | | | | 1, | | | | 1.00 |
| Same, | 100, | | | | | | | | | | | 3 | | 4.00 |
| Same, | 274, | | | | | | | | | | | | | 2.74 |
| Same, | 87 | | | | | | | | | | | | | .87 |
| Same, | 40 | | | | | | | | | | | | | .40 |
| Same, | 150, | | | | | | | | | | | | | 1.50 |
| Same, | 285, | | | | | | | | | | | | | 2.85 |
| Glaco, Isaac, | | | | | | | | | | 1, | | | | .50 |
| Gardner, John, | | | | | | | | 1, | | | | | | 1.00 |
| Gardner, John A., | | | | | | | | 1, | | | | | | 2.50 |
| Gardner, Richard W., 2, B. | | | J.Terrell 640, | | | | | | | 1, | | | | .52 |
| Galloway, Glidwell, 151, B, | | | D. Broadwell, | | | | | | | 1, | 2, | | | 2.00 |
| Galloway, Benjn., | 150, | | Same, | | | | | | | 1, | | | | 2.00 |
| Going, Henry J., | | | | | | | | | | 1, | | | | .50 |
| Going, Levi, | | | | | | | | | | 1, | | | | .50 |

(Page 59)

| PERSONS NAME | Acres Lnd. | Desc. Titl. | REMARKS | Ent.,Rge., | Sec. | Dist. | Town Lots, | # of Lot | Free Poll | Slaves | Sto. | Horse Jec. | $ | Cts. M. |
|---|---|---|---|---|---|---|---|---|---|---|---|---|---|---|
| Gerison, Isham, | | | | | | | | | | | | | | 50 |
| Gilliam, Grey, | 143, | | | | | | | | 1, | | | | 2293 | 7½ |
| Gilliam, Henry, | | | | | | | | | 1, | | | | | .50 |
| Goldsby, Stephen H., | | | | | | | | | 1, | | | | | .50 |
| Goldsby, James | | | | | | | | | | | | | | 3.00 |
| Gilbert, Robert R., | 64, | | | | | | | | 4, | | | | | 2.64 |
| Gilbert, Jonathan M., | 91½, | Deed, | Joab Bell, 640, | | | | | | 1, | 2, | | | | 2.91 5 |
| Gilbert, Randolph, | | | | | | | | | 1, | 1, | | | | 1.25 |
| Grooms, Bright, | | | | | | | | | 1, | | | | | .50 |
| Grooms, Stephen H., | 200, | D., | Charles Cotton, 640, | | | | | | 1, | | | | | 2.50 |
| Gailey, James, | | | | | | | | | 1, | | | | | .50 |
| Graham, Elijah, | | | | | | | | | 1, | | | | | .50 |
| Hughes, Archelous M., | | | | | | | | | 1, | 1, | | | | 1.25 |
| Hughes, Joseph B., | 100, | D., | Archelous Hughes, | 1, | 7, | 13, | 1 | | 1, | | | | | 1.00 |
| Harmon, Israel, | | | | | | | | | 1, | | | | | 1.50 |
| Hornbeak, Wm., | | | | | | | | | 1, | | | | | .50 |
| Hungerford, Cullin, | | | | | | | | | 1, | | | | | .50 |
| Huntsman & Totten, | 1700, | Ent. | Part of 2100, | | | | | | | | | | 17. | 500 |
| Harpole, Moses, | | | | | | | | | 1, | | | | | 37.50 |
| Harpins, Thomas, | 3750, | | Part of 5000, | 1&2, | 7.8, | | 1, | | 1, | | | | | 2.00 |
| Herd, Bailey E., | 50, | | | | | | | | 1, | | | | | .50 |
| Harmon, Jesse, | | | | | | | | | 1, | | | | | 2.75 |
| Higgs, Alfred, | 150, | | | 1, | 7, | | | | 1, | 1, | | 1 | | 6.30 |
| Herd, George D., | 80, | D., | J.L.D.Smith,274, | 1, | 7, | 12, | 1, | | 1, | | | | | .50 |
| Huskey, Archibald, | | | | | | | | | 1, | | | | | 3.50 |
| Hornbeak, James, | 200, | D., | 4 Entrys | | | | 1, | | 1, | 2, | | | | 1.50 |
| Horton, James, | | | | | | | | | 1, | | | | | .50 |
| Horton, Archibald, | | | | | | | | | 1, | | | | | .50 |
| Horton, John, | | | | | | | | | 1, | | | | | .50 |
| Horton, Robert, | | | | | | | | | 1, | | | | | .50 |
| Horton, George, | | | | | | | | | 1, | | | | | .50 |
| Hopper, Forister, | 119, | | | | | | | | 1, | | | | | 1.69 |
| Hendrix, Alfred, | | | | | | | | | 1, | | | | | .50 |
| Henry Moses, | | | | | | | | | 1, | | | | | .50 |
| Hamblin, Joel, | | | | | | | | | 1, | | | | | .50 |

(Page 60)

| Persons Name | Acres Desc. Lnd.,Titl., REMARKS | #of Ent. | Rge., | Sec. | Town, Dis.,Lots,Lot | #of Free Poll, | Sla., | Sto. | Horse Jec.$ | Cts. M |
|---|---|---|---|---|---|---|---|---|---|---|
| Hill &Collier,Wm.,640, | | | 2, | 9, | 12, | | | | 6.40 | |
| Howard, John, | | | | | | 1, | | | .50 | |
| Henderson,John, | | | | | | 1, | | | .50 | |
| Huggins, William, | | | | | | 1, | | | .50 | |
| Huggins, Robert, | | | | | | 1, | | | .50 | |
| Huggins, Jeremiah, | | | | | | 1, | | | .50 | |
| Huneycut, Herman, | | | | | | 1, | | | .50 | |
| Hall, Abraham P., | | | | | | 1, | 1, | | 1.25 | |
| Hall, Thomas, | | | | | | 1, | | | .50 | |
| Howard, Geo. W., 60, D. | | | | | | 1, | | | 1.10 | |
| Healt, Benjamin, 250, | | | | | | 1, | | | 3.00 | |
| Hall, Durham, | | | | | | 1, | | | .50 | |
| Hatten, James, | | | | | | 1, | | | .50 | |
| Holly, Hazell, | | | | | | 1, | | | .50 | |
| Henderson, Robert, | | | | | | 1, | | | .50 | |
| Hubbard, Williams, | | | | | | 1, | | | .50 | |
| Hamilton, William,50, Entry | | | | | | 4, | | | 1.00 | |
| Hayse, Williams, 64, | | | | | | 1, | | | 1.14 | |
| Herrod, James, | | | | | | 1, | | | .50. | |
| Hoggard, Byas, | | | | | | 1, | | | .50 | |
| Howard, Littleton, | | | | | | 1, | 1, | | 1.25 | |
| Henerson, John K.,50, | | | | | | 1, | | | 1. | |
| Harmon, William, | | | | | | 1, | | | .50 | |
| Harroll, John, | | | | | | 1, | | | .50 | |
| Johnson,William,H.70, R. Wetson, 140, | | | | | 4 | 1, | 1, | | 5.95 | |
| Jones, Calvin, 2560, | | | | | | 1, | | | 25.60 | |
| Kephin, John, | | | | | 1, | 1, | | | 1.50 | |
| Jenkins, John, 3250, | | | | | | 1, | 6, | | 37.50 | |
| Jenkins & Tharp, 480,Part of 640 J. Evans | | | | | | 1, | | | 4.80 | |
| Julian, James J., 29, J.Terrell,640, | | | | | | 1, | | | .79 | |
| Jones, Gray, | | | | | | 1, | | | .50 | |
| Jones, Thornton, | | | | | | 1, | | | .50 | |
| Jones, William, | | | | | | 1, | | | .50 | |
| Jones, Israel, 640, D. Brender, | | | | | | 1, | 3, | | 9.15 | |
| Jenkins, Jesse, 50, B. Anderson, | | | | | | 1, | 2, | | 2.50 | |

(Page 61) 1830 Acres Desc.                                        Town,          Free            Horse   64
PERSONS NAME      Lnd., Titl. R E M A R K S    Ent., Rge., Sec.Dis.,Lots, Lot, Poll,Sla.Sto.Jac.$ Cts.  M

| PERSONS NAME | Lnd. | Titl. | REMARKS | Ent. | Rge. | Sec.Dis. | Lots | Lot | Poll | Free Sla. | Sto. | Horse Jac. | $ Cts. |
|---|---|---|---|---|---|---|---|---|---|---|---|---|---|
| Jenkins, Jesse, | 320, | - | David Broadwells | 640, | | | | | | | | | 3.20 |
| Jenkins, James, | | | | | | | | | 1, | 1 | | | 1.25 |
| Jenkins, Thomas, | | | | | | | | | 1, | | | | .50 |
| Jones, Bennit, | | | | | | | | | 1, | | | | .50 |
| Jolly, Henry, | | | | | | | | | 1, | 1, | | | 1.25 |
| Jones, William, | 100, | Enty, | | | | 1, 8, 13, | 1, | | | | | | 1.00 |
| Jones, Willie, | 100, | | | | | | | | | | | | 1.00 |
| Jolly, Reuben M., | | | | | | | | | 1, | | | | .50 |
| Johnson, John, | | | | | | | | | 1, | | | | .50 |
| Jones, William, | | | | | | | | | 1, | | | | .50 |
| Jones, Joshua, | | | | | | | | | 1, | | | | .50 |
| James, Isaac, | | | | | | | | | 1, | | | | .50 |
| Jennings, Anderson, | | | | | | | | | 1, | 1, | | | .50 |
| Jordan, John, | | | | | | | | | 1, | | | | .50 |
| Jenkins, Mansfield, | | | | | | | | | 1, | | | | .50 |
| James, Hosea, | 210, | Deed, | Part of 640, | 1012, | 2, | 6, 12, | | | 1, | 1 | | | 3.35 |
| Israel Michael, | | | | | | | | | 1, | | | | .50 |
| Jemison, Samuel, | | | | | | | | | 1, | | | | .50 |
| Kain, John, | 150, | E., | | 765, | 1, | 6, 13, | | | 1, | | | | 1.50 |
| Kirksey, John C., | | | | | | | | | 1, | | | | .50 |
| Kirkpatrick, Joseph, | 640, | | | | 1, | 7, 12, | | | | | | | 6.40 |
| Kindred, Joseph C., | | | | | | | | | 1, | | | | .50 |
| Kindred, Elisha H., | | | | | | | | | 1, | | | | .50 |
| Kuykendall, Jesse | 121, | D., | in name of Snow, | | 2, | 8, | | | 1, | | | | 1.20 |
| Kirk, George D., | | | | | | | | | 1, | | | | .50 |
| Kirk, William, | 40, | | Part of 164, | | | | | | 1, | | | | .50 |
| Keath, John, | | | | | | | | | 1, | | | | .50 |
| Kimbrell, Joseph, | | | | | | | | | 1, | | | | .50 |
| Kizzee, Charles, | | | | | | | | | 1, | | | | .50 |
| Kennedy, James, | | | | | | | | | 1, | | | | .50 |
| Kemp, Frances A., | 170, | D., | A Charleston | 274, | 2, | 5, 13, | | | 1, | | | | 2.20 |
| Lynn, William, | | | | | | | | | 1, | | | | .50 |
| Landrum, Samuel, | | | | | | | | | 1, | 3, | | | 2.35 |
| Levister, Levi, | | | | | | | | | 1, | | | | .50 |
| Lyle, Archibald, | 236, | E., | | 804, | 2, | 7, 12, | | | 1, | | | | 2.36 |

(Page 62) 1830

| Persons Name | Acres, Desc. Lnd., Titl. REMARKS | #of Ent. | Rge. | Sec. | Dis. | Town, Lots | #of Lot | Free Poll | Sla. | Sto. | Horse Jac. $ | Cts. M |
|---|---|---|---|---|---|---|---|---|---|---|---|---|
| Lawler, Martin, | 98, D, James Greer, | | 1, | 6, | 12, | 2 | | 1, | 1, | | 4. | 23 |
| Landrum, Thomas, | | | | | | | | 1, | | | | .50 |
| Landrum, James, | | | | | | | | 1, | | | | .50 |
| Lasswell, Joseph, | 50, Entry, | 957, | 2, | 9, | 13, | | | 1, | | | | 1.00 |
| Lasswell, Peter, | 50, | 956, | 2, | 9, | | | | 1, | | | | 1.00 |
| Lasswell, Sarah, | 50, D. Lasswell, | 955, | 1, | 9, | | | | | | | | .50 |
| Lasswell, Gilliam, | | | | | | | | 1, | | | | .50 |
| Lasswell, Jesse, | | | | | | | | 1, | | | | .50 |
| Lasswell, William, | | | | | | | | 1, | | | | .50 |
| Lindsey, Isaac, | 44, | | | | | | | | | | | .44 |
| Lovin, Joshua, | | | | | | | | 1, | | | | .50 |
| Lovin, James, | | | | | | | | 1, | | | | .50 |
| Lawrence, Joseph, | 30, | | | | | | | | | | | .50 |
| Langley, Leonard, | 250, D., Geo. Doherty 500, | 21, | 2, | 8, | 12, | | | | 8 | | | 9.00 |
| Laemore, Charles J., | | | | | | | | 1, | | | | .50 |
| Langley, Jane J., | | | | | | | | 1, | | | 1, | 11.75 |
| Love, Robt. & Thos. | 320, E., | 169, | 1.2, 9, | 13, | | | | | 9, | | | 3.20 |
| Same, | 500, | 141, 1.2, 7.8, | | | | | | | | | | 5.00 |
| Same, | 1591, D, M.Carmichels, 5000, | 113, | 2, | 9, | 12, | | | | | | | 15.91 |
| Love, Robert, | 228, Ent. | 329, | 2, | 7, | | | | | | | | 2.28 |
| Lemond, David, | | | | | | | | | | | | .50 |
| Liddle, Frances, | | | | | | | | 1, | | | | .50 |
| Lawrence, William, | 60, Part of 640, | | | | | | | 1, | | | | 1.50 |
| McLemore & Vaulx, | 400, Deed, Huntsman &Totton, | 475, | 3, | 7.8, | 13, | | | | | | | 4.00 |
| Same & Same, | 100, Enty. | 807, | 2, | 9, | 12, | | | | | | | 1.00 |
| Same & Same, | 150, | 627, | 2, | 8, | | | | | | | | 1.51 |
| Same & Same, | 1250, D John Rhea 2500, | 302, | 2.5, 6, | 13, | | | | | | | | 12.50 |
| Same & Same, | 228, Sion Williams 640, | 351, | 2, 5.6, 12, | | | | | | | | | 2.28 |
| Same & Same, | 381, E., | 528, | 1.2, 5, | 13, | | | | | | | | 3.81 |
| Montgomery, Deniel, | 252, | | 2, | 6, | | | | | | | | 2.52 |
| Montgomery, John, | 500, D, Wm.Montgomery | 733, | 2, | 8, | | | | | | | | 5.00 |
| Moon, William, | | | | | | | | 1, | | | | .50 |
| McLemore & Cherlyon, | 744¼, Part of 3840, | 775, | 2, | 7, | | | | | | | | 7.44 2½ |
| Same & Same, | 165, 7⅞, | 767, | 1, | 7, | | | | | | | | 1.65 |
| McLemore, John C., | 3 3/4 E., | 816, | 1, | 8, | | | | | | | 3 | 7½ |

(Page 63) Acres Desc.        #of   Sec.  Town   Free            Horse
Persons Name  -  Lnd.Title. R E M A R K S - Ent.Rge./Dis. Lots, Lot, Poll,Sla.Sto. Jac. $ Cts.  M.

| Persons Name | Acres | Desc. Lnd.Title. | REMARKS | #of Ent. | Sec. Rge./Dis. | Town Lots | Free Lot | Poll | Sla. | Sto. | Horse Jac. | $ | Cts. | M. |
|---|---|---|---|---|---|---|---|---|---|---|---|---|---|---|
| McLemore, John C., | 38, | E, | | 823, | 3, 7,13, | | | | | | | | .38 | |
| Same, | 143¼, | | | 1071, | 2, 9,12, | | | | | | | | 1.43 | 2½ |
| Same, | 640, | | | 274, | 2,7.8 | | | | | | | | 6.40 | |
| Same, | 1250, | D,Thos.Hopkins,5000, | | 877,1.27.8,13 | | | | | | | | | 12.50 | |
| Same, | 2000, | E. | | 322, 2,5, | | | | | | | | | .20 | |
| Same, | 160, | D James Hart, 640, | | 1360, 1, 6, 12, | | | | | | | | | 1.60 | |
| Same, | 752, | John McIvers 4336, | | 752, 1, 9, 13, | | | | | | | | | 7.52 | |
| Same, | 100, | E, | | 2, 5, | | | | | | | | | 1.00 | |
| Same, | 80, | | | 1057, 1, 6, 12, | | | | | | | | | .80 | |
| McLemore & Love, | 555, | | | 300, 3, 7, 13, | | | | | | | | | 5.55 | |
| McLemore, Sugars | 160, | D, Part of 640, | | 1036, 1, 8, 12, | | | | | | | | | 1.60 | |
| Same, | 160, | Wm.Sharp, 640, | | 638, 3, 7, 13 | | | | | | | | | 1.60 | |
| Same, | 700, | Thomas Blount, e 3000, | | 1, 5, | | | | | | | | | 7.00 | |
| Same, | 640, | E. | | 630, 2, 6, | | | | | | | | | 6.40 | |
| Murphy, William, | 797, | | | 774, 2, 7, | | | | | | | | | 7.97 | |
| Moran, James H., | | | | | | 2 | | | | 1, | | | 12.50 | |
| McNeely, John, | | (Blakemore) | | | | | | 1, | | | | | .50 | |
| Molin, Benjamin, | 224, | D, Swaney & Ross, | | 1, 7, | | | | 1, | | | | | 2.74 | |
| Mitchell, Kissey, | | | | | | | | 1, | | | | | 3.00 | |
| Mooney, Henry, | | | | | | | 4 | | | | | | .50 | |
| Majors, Samuel, | 50, | E, | | 959, 2, 9, 13, | | | | 1, | | | | | 1.00 | |
| McCarter, Isiah, | | | | | | | | 1, | | | | | .50 | |
| Marshall, Joseph,S., | | | | | | | | 1, | | | | | .50 | |
| Marshall, Robert, | | | | | | | | 1, | | | | | .50 | |
| McCormack, Charles, | | | | | | | | 1, | | | | | .50 | |
| Miles, Wm. C., | | | | | | | | 1, | | | | | .50 | |
| McDaniel, John, | | | | | | | | 1, | | | | | .50 | |
| McClain, John, | 50, | | | | | | | 1, | | | | | 1.00 | |
| McDaniel, Cristiana, | 50 | | | | | | | | | | | | .50 | |
| Moss, Bennit, | | | | | | | | 1, 1, | | | | | 1.25 | |
| McDaniel, Hiram, | | | | | | | | 1, | | | | | .50 | |
| McDaniel, Moses, | | | | | | | | 1, | | | | | .50 | |
| McClain, Charles, | | | | | | | | 1, | | | | | .50 | |
| McClain, George, | 60, | | | 2, 9, 12, | | | | | | | | | .60 | |

(Page 64) Acres- Desc.      #of      Town,   #of Free                Horse
Persons Name    Lnd.Titl. R E M A R K S *    Ent. Rge.Sec. Dis.Lots,Lot,Poll,Sla.Sto. Jac., $ Cts. M

| Persons Name | Acres-Desc. Lnd.Titl. | REMARKS | #of Ent. | Rge. | Sec. | Town, Dis. | Lots, Lot | #of Free Poll | Sla. | Sto. | Horse Jac. | $ Cts. | M |
|---|---|---|---|---|---|---|---|---|---|---|---|---|---|
| Murrel, John S., | | | | | | | | 1, | | | | .50 | |
| McNeely, Michael, | 47, | E, T. Dalton, 10 | | 2, | 8, | 12, | | 1, | | | | .97 | |
| Mayo, William, | 130, D, | | | 2, | 9, | | | 1, | | | | 1.80 | |
| McWherter, John, | | | | | | | | 1, | | | | .50 | |
| McWherter, George, | | | | | | | | 1, | | | | .50 | |
| Mizelle, William, | | | | | | | | 1, | | | | .50 | |
| Mitchell, Standley, | | | | | | | | 1, | | | | .50 | |
| Moore, John H., | | | | | | | | 1, | 1, | | | 1.25 | |
| Morgan, Samuel, | 427, D, | | | | | | | 1, | 5, | | | 8.52 | |
| Miller, George, | | | | | | | | 1, | | | | .50 | |
| Miller, Isac, | | | | | | | | 1, | | | | .50 | |
| Miller, Andrew, | | | | | | | | 1, | | | | .50 | |
| Moore, James, | | | | | | | | 1, | | | | .50 | |
| Meadows, Spearman, | | | | | | | | 1, | | | | .50 | |
| Moore, John, | 72, | | | 2, | 9, | | | 1, | | | 1, | 7.22 | |
| McClusky, William, | | | | | | | | 1, | | | | .50 | |
| Michael, Archelous, | 240, | | | | | | | 1, | 2, | | | 3.90 | |
| McElroy, William, T | | | | | | | | 1, | | | | .50 | |
| Maynard, Wm. W., | | | | | | | | 1, | | | | .50 | |
| Mandy, Thomas, | | | | | | | | 1, | | | | .50 | |
| Montgomery, A., | | | | | | | | 1, | | | | .50 | |
| Miller, George S., | | | | | | | | 1, | | | | .50 | |
| Mathis, Daniel, | | | | | | | | 1, | | | | .50 | |
| Mosley, Robert, | 1060, D, Part of 2 tracts | | | 2, | 5, | | | 1, | 10, | | | 18.60 | |
| Marcus Phillips, | | | | | | | | 1, | | | | .50 | |
| Mosley, Edward, | | | | | | | | 1, | 3, | | | 2.75 | |
| Maxwell, Jesse, | | | | | | | | 1, | | | | .50 | |
| Marr, Peter, | | | | | | | | 1, | | | | .50 | |
| Nailing, Nelson, | 106, D, | | | | | | 2, | 2, | 5, | | 1, | 11.81 | |
| Nelling, Willis, | 50, | | | | | | | 1, | 2, | | | 2.00 | |
| Nichols, James, | | | | | | | | 1, | | | | .50 | |
| Nolin, Henry, | | | | | | | | 1, | | | | .50 | |
| Newton, James, | | | | | | | 1, | | | | | 1.00 | |
| Newton, James W., | | | | | | | | 1, | | | | .50 | |
| Overton & Whorton, | 640, E | | 25, | 2, | 9, | 13, | | | | | | 6.40 | |

(Page 65) - 1830 - Acres Desc.                    #of              Town,        #of  Free
Persons Name        Lnd.,Title, R E M A R K S  -- Ent.,Rge., Sec.,Dis.,Lots, Lot, Poll,Sla. Stor.,Jac.,$ Cts. M

| Persons Name | Acres | Desc. Lnd. | Title | REMARKS | #of Ent. | Rge. | Sec. | Dis. Lots | Town, Lot | #of Poll | Free Sla. | Stor. | Horse Jac. | $ Cts. | M |
|---|---|---|---|---|---|---|---|---|---|---|---|---|---|---|---|
| Overton, John, | 488, | G, | | L.Carter, | 391, | 3, | 9, | 13, | | | | | | 4.88 | |
| Same, | 232, | | | Same, | 315, | 2.3, | 9, | | | | | | | 2.32 | |
| Same, | 488, | | | Same, | 317, | 2.3, | 9, | | | | | | | 4.88 | |
| Same, | 231, | | | Same, | 322, | 2.3, | 9, | | | | | | | 2.31 | |
| Same, | 622½, | | | Same, | 323, | 8, | 9, | | | | | | | 6.22½ | |
| Same, | 98, | Entry, | | | | 2, | 7, | | | | | | | .98 | |
| Same, | 735, | Gt., | | L.Carter, | 321, | 3, | 9, | | | | | | | 7.35 | |
| Owens, Charles M., | 268 3/4, | D, | | three Tracts, | | | | | | 1, | 1, | | | 3.93 | 7½ |
| Osteen, John, | | | | | | | | | | 1, | | | | .50 | |
| Overby, Thos. P., | | | | | | | | | | 1, | | | | .50 | |
| Oar, Wm. C., | 480, | D, | | | 2, | 7, | 12, | | | 1, | | | | 5.30 | |
| Oliver, Isaac, 7 | 77 | | | A. Newton, | | | | | | 1, | | | | 1.27 | |
| Oliver, Alexander, | | | | | | | | | | 1, | | | | .50 | |
| Owens, Solomon H., | 149, | | | J.H. Moore, | | | | | | | | | | 1.49 | |
| Oneal, John, | 11.3, | | | | | | | | | 1, | | | | 1.63 | |
| Outhouse, Israel F., | 28½, | Ent. | | | | | | | | 1, | | | | .78 | |
| Parker, Isaac, | 512, | | | Part of 640, | 615, | 2, | 6, | 13, | | | | | | 5.12 | |
| Peck, John, | 402, | | | | 1353, | 1, | 6, | 12, | | | | | | 4.02 | |
| Payton, Bayley, | 380, | | | | | 1, | 8, | 13, | | | | | | 3.80 | |
| Polk & Devereaux, | 500, | | | | 289, | 1, | 5, | 12, | | | | | | 5.00 | |
| Same & Same, | 500, | | | | 59, | 1, | 9, | 13, | | | | | | 5.00 | |
| Same & Same, | 500, | | | | 119, | 1, | 9, | | | | | | | 5.00 | |
| Same & Same, | 305, | | | | 531, | 1, | 5, | 12, | | | | | | 3.05 | |
| Same & Same, | 195, | | | | 732, | 1, | 5, | 13, | | | | | | 1.95 | |
| Polk, William, | 5000, | | | | 198, | 1, | 9, | | | | | | | .50 | |
| Parham, Thomas, | 200, | | | James Greer, | | 1, | 6.7, | 12, | | | | | | 2.00 | |
| Parham, Amos, | 16, | D, | | A. Jones, | | 1, | 7, | | | 1, | | | | .66 | |
| Polk, Thomas H., | 300, | Entry, | | | 980, | 1, | 5, | | | | | | | 3.00 | |
| Parch, Israel, | | | | | | | | | | 1, | | | | .50 | |
| Parker, Gedeon, | | | | | | | | | | 1, | | | | .50 | |
| Parker & Bishop, | | | | | | | | | | 1, | 1, | | 1, | 2.25 | |
| Parker, Lorenzo, D., | | | | | | | | | | 1, | 1, | | 1, | 1.50 | |
| Prater, Josiah, | | | | | | | | | | 1, | | | | .50 | |
| Pursel, Abel, | | | | | | | | | | 1, | | | | .50 | |
| Paschall, Jesse M., | | | | | | | | | | 1, | | | | .50 | |

(Page 66) ACRES -Desc. -1830- # of Town, # of Free Horse

| Persons Name | ACRES-Desc. | Lnd.Title | REMARKS - Ent. | Rge. | Sec. | Dis.Lots.Lot | Town | Poll | Sla.Sto.Jac. | Horse | $.Cts. M |
|---|---|---|---|---|---|---|---|---|---|---|---|
| Price, Thomas, | | | | | | | | 1, | | | .50 |
| Phillips, Bursell, | | | | | | | | | | 1, | 4.00 |
| Perry, John, | | | | | | | | | | | .50 |
| Parrish, John, | | | | | | | | 1, | 5, | | 3.75 |
| Parrish, Henderson, | | | | | | | | 1, | | | .50 |
| Pope, John, W., | 160, | D. | J. Pope, | 500, | 2, | 8, 13, | | | | | 1.60 |
| Pope, John, | 180, | E., | Same, | | | | | | | | 1.80 |
| Pope, Lemuel, | 160, | D, | Same, | | | | | | | | 1.60 |
| Pool, Asa, | | | | | | | | 1, | | | .50 |
| Pippin, Loftis, | | | | | | | | 1, | | | .50 |
| Purtle, Jesse, | | | | | | | | 1, | | | .50 |
| Palmer, Paul, | 250, | D,21, | Geo. Daugherty, | 500,2, | 8, | 12, | | 1, | 10, | | 10.50 |
| Powers, Joseph, | | | | | | | | 1, | | | .50 |
| Peoples, Samuel, | 200, | | Shelton & Hanline, | 1000, | | | | 1, | 2, | | 4.00 |
| Powers, Charles, | | | | | | | | 1, | | | .50 |
| Powers, Henry, | | | | | | | | 1, | | | .50 |
| Palmer, Amos A., | | | | | | | | 1, | 1, | | 1.25 |
| Patton, John M., | | | | | | | | 1, | | | .50 |
| Price, William, | 40,D, | | | 1012,2, | 6, | | | 1, | | | .90 |
| Pate, Stephen S., | 50, | | | 2, | | | | 1, | 2, | | 2.50 |
| Pentecost, Searbrough, | | | | | | | | 1, | | | .50 |
| Perry, Solomon, | | | | | | | | 1, | | | .50 |
| Parker, William T., | | | | | | | | 1, | | | .50 |
| Pentecost, William, | | | | | | | | 1, | | | .50 |
| Patton, Thomas, | 50, | E. Part of 100, | | 1869, 2, | 6, | 13, | | 1, | | | 1.00 |
| Price, William, | | | | | | | | 1, | | | .50 |
| Perry, Gideon, | | | | | | | | 1, | | | .50 |
| Powers, George, | | | | | | | | 1, | | | .50 |
| Ragsdale, Joel, | 60,D, | | | 1, | 7, | | | 1, | 1, | | 1, 35 |
| Roulhac, George G., | | | | | | | | 1, | 2, | | 2. 00 |
| Rhea, John, | 1250, | E. Part of 2500, | | 1250, 2.3, | 6, | 13, | | | | 12. 50 | |
| Roffe, Woodson, | | | | | | | | 1, | | | 5.50 |
| Robertson, Edward, | | | | | | | | 1, | | | .50 |
| Rives, John H., | 100,D., | Wm. Quells, | | 1, | 7, | 12, | | 1, | | | 1.50 |
| Rogers, Isabelle, | 640, | D, | J.Terrell, | 3840, 1, | 7, | 13, 1, | | 1, | 8, 1, | | 23.40 |

[Page 67] 1830, Acres Desc.                                    Town  #of  Free
Persons Name  Lnd. Title- R E M A R K S -  Ent.,Rge.,Sec.,Dist.Lots,Lot,Poll,Sla.,Sto.Jac.$ cts. M

| Persons Name | Acres / Lnd. Title - REMARKS | Ent. | Rge. | Sec. | Dist.Lots | Town Lots | #of Lot | Poll | Free Sla. | Sto.Jac. | $ cts. M |
|---|---|---|---|---|---|---|---|---|---|---|---|
| Rogers, Jubile V.; |  |  |  |  |  |  | 7, | 1, | 1 |  | .75 |
| Ralls, William B.; |  |  |  |  |  |  |  | 1, |  |  | .50 |
| Rogers, Joel, |  |  |  |  |  |  |  | 1, |  |  | .50 |
| Roberds, William C.; |  |  |  |  |  |  |  | 1, |  |  | 2.00 |
| Rogers, John W., 52, |  | 2, | 7, | 13, | 2 |  |  | 1, | 2, |  | 6.02 |
| Ren, John, |  |  |  |  |  |  |  | 1, | 4, |  | .50 |
| Rogers, Job, 640, | D, John Jenkins, |  | 1, | 8, |  |  |  | 1, | 8, |  | 12.40 |
| Ross, Joshua, |  |  |  |  |  |  |  | 1, |  |  | .50 |
| Rogers, Thomas,119 3/4, | Jno. Rogers, | 2, | 9, | 12, |  |  |  | 1, |  |  | 1.69,7½ |
| Rogers, Jacob, C., |  |  |  |  |  |  |  | 1, |  |  | .50 |
| Ridgway, William, |  |  |  |  |  |  |  | 1, |  |  | .50 |
| Rea, James W., 100, |  |  |  |  |  |  |  | 1, |  |  | 1.00 |
| Ross, William G., |  |  |  |  |  |  |  | 1, |  |  | .50 |
| Ridgway, James, 342, | Swan, |  |  |  |  |  |  | 1, | 4, |  | 6.42 |
| Ridgway, John, |  |  |  |  |  |  |  | 1, | 1, |  | 1.25 |
| Ridgway, Thomas, |  |  |  |  |  |  |  | 1, |  |  | .50 |
| Russell, Buckner, W.,3, | Jas. Millighley, |  |  |  |  |  |  | 1, |  |  | .53 |
| Ralls, William, |  |  |  |  |  |  |  | 1, |  |  | .50 |
| Russell, George Heirs,80, | E |  |  |  |  |  |  |  |  |  | .80 |
| Roads, Abner, 150, |  |  |  |  |  |  |  |  |  |  | 1.50 |
| Ruse, Yarnel, 200, | D, D.Crockett | 3, | 5, | 13, |  |  |  | 1, |  |  | 2.50 |
| Rachels, William, |  |  |  |  |  |  |  | 1, |  |  | .50 |
| Rachels, Valentine, |  |  |  |  |  |  |  | 1, |  |  | .50 |
| Speight & McGavock,640, | E. | 828, | 1, | 10, | 12, |  |  |  |  |  | 6.40 |
| Sanders, James, |  |  |  |  |  |  |  | 1, |  |  | .50 |
| Semple, Henry A.; |  |  |  |  |  | 1, |  | 1, |  | 1, | 11.50 |
| Sneed, Samuel,R.; |  |  |  |  |  |  |  | 1, |  |  | .50 |
| Stovall, George, |  |  |  |  |  |  |  |  | 5, |  | 3.75 |
| Smith, Joseph,L. D., 20, | Part of 274, | 1, | 7, |  |  |  |  | 1, |  |  | .20 |
| Stone, Claibourn, |  |  |  |  |  |  |  |  |  |  | .50 |
| Sweney, John L., 256, |  |  |  |  |  |  |  |  |  |  | 2.56 |
| Swaney, James M., 512, |  |  |  |  |  |  |  |  |  |  | 5.12 |
| Smith, William Div. 2923, | A. Nash different tracts |  |  | 13, |  |  |  |  |  |  | 29.36 |
| Smith, James W., 2833, | Same, |  |  | 1, |  |  |  |  |  |  | 28.33 |
| Shelton, Abraham, |  |  |  |  |  |  |  |  |  |  | .50 |

(Page 68) - 1830-Acres Desc.        #of                    Town, #of Free            Horse      71
PERSONS NAME  , Lnd. Titl.,  R E M A R K S  - Ent.Rge., Sec.,Dis.Lots,Lot,Poll,Sla. Sto. Jac.$ Cts. M.

| PERSONS NAME | Acres | Desc. Lnd. Titl. | REMARKS | #of Ent.Rge., Sec.,Dis.Lots | Town, Lot | #of Poll | Free Sla. | Sto. | Horse Jac. | $ | Cts. | M. |
|---|---|---|---|---|---|---|---|---|---|---|---|---|
| Standley, Lewis, | | | | | | 1, | | | | | .50 | |
| Simmons, Thomas, | | | | | | 1, | | | | | .50 | |
| Ship, Benton, | | | | | | 1, | | | | | .50 | |
| Skaggs, James, | | | | | | 1, | | | | | .50 | |
| Skaggs, Martin, | | | | | | 1, | | | | | .50 | |
| Spete, James, | | | | | | 1, | | | | | .50 | |
| Shultey, John R., | | | | | | | 2, | | | | 2.00 | |
| Smart, James H., | | | | | | 1, | | | | | .50 | |
| Smart, William J., | | | | | | 1, | | | | | .50 | |
| Shultey, Jacob, | | | | 1, | | 1, | | | 1 | | 2.50 | |
| Searcy, Isaac, | | | | | | 1, | | | | | .50 | |
| Shulty, David, | 80 | | | | | 1, | | | | | 1.30 | |
| Segraves, Willie, | | | | | | 1, | | | | | .50 | |
| Sommers, James, | | | | | | 1, | | | | | .50 | |
| Shulty, John M., | | | | | | 1, | | | | | .50 | |
| Shultey, Charles M., | | | | | | 1, | | | | | .50 | |
| Smart, Stephens, | 70, | | | | | | | | | | .70 | |
| Smart, Phillip, | 230, | D.Jas. Sommers 3840, | 2, 7,12, | | | | | | | | 2.30 | |
| Summers, Richard, | | | | | | 1, | | | | | .50 | |
| Stunston, James, | | | | | | 1, | | | | | .50 | |
| Sunneys, John, | | | | | | 1, | | | | | .50 | |
| Stanton, Henry, | | | | | | 1, | | | | | .50 | |
| Stunston, Henry Sr., | 40, | | 2, 9, | | | | | | | | .40 | |
| Stunston, John, | 200, | | | | | | 4, | | | | 5.00 | |
| Stoker, Edmund, | | | | | | 1, | | | | | .50 | |
| Steward, Samuel, | | | | | | 1, | | | | | .50 | |
| Sprout, Alexander, | | | | | | 1, | | | | | .50 | |
| Sommers, James, | 2800, | Part of 3840 | | | | | | | | | 28.00 | |
| Stallings, John, | | | | | | 1, | | | | | .50 | |
| Standley, Elijah, | 106, | | | | | 1, | | | | | 1.56 | |
| Steele, George R., | 50,D, | Shilders 343 3/4 | | | | 1, | | | | | 1.00 | |
| Steele, John, | 40, | Part of Same, | | | | 1, | | | | | .90 | |
| Standley, Noah, | | | | | | 1, | | | | | .50 | |
| Sanford, John, | 100, | D 1985,Tavener Wisdom, | 2, 7, 12 | | | 1, | | | | | 1.50 | |
| Shaw, Archbald, | 100, | Doherty & McCorkle, | | | | 1, | 2, | | | | 2.50 | |

(Page 69) - 1830 Acres                Town   #of  Free                              Horse    72
PERSONS NAME    Lnd. Title, R E M A R K S  -  Ent., Rge, Sec., Dis.Lots, Lot, Poll, Sla. Sto. Jac. $ Cts. M

| PERSONS NAME | Lnd. | Title | REMARKS | Ent. | Rge | Sec. | Dis.Lots | Lot | Poll | Sla. | Sto. | Horse Jac. | $ Cts. M |
|---|---|---|---|---|---|---|---|---|---|---|---|---|---|
| Shaw, Daniel B., | | | | | | | | | 1, | | | | .50 |
| Smith, James, | | | | | | | | | 1, | | | | .50 |
| Starks, Thomas, | 25, | | | | | | | | 1, | | | | .75 |
| Smith, Hugh D., | 66, | D, | Part of 320, | 2, | 6, | 12, | 1, | | 1, | | | | 1.16 |
| Snell, Israel, | | | | | | | | | 1, | 2, | | | 2.00 |
| Sutton, Lemuel, | | | | | | | | | 1, | | | | .50 |
| Smith, Richey, | | | | | | | | | 1, | | | | .50 |
| Seal, James, | | | | | | | | | 1, | | | | .50 |
| Seal, William, | | | | | | | | | 1, | | | | .50 |
| Stone, William, | | | | | | | | | 1, | | | | .50 |
| Span, Moses T., | | | | | | | | | 1, | | | | .50 |
| Stanford, Thomas, | 25, | E. | | 1, | 6, | 13, | | | 1, | | | | .75 |
| Stanford, Hiram, | | | | | | | | | 1, | | | | .50 |
| Terrell, Jeptha, | 500, | D, | J. Terrell, 3840, | 1, | 7, | | 1 | | 1, | 2, | | | 8.00 |
| Turner, John, | | | | | | | | | 1, | | | | .50 |
| Taylor, Caleb Hs. | 640, | E, | | 1363, | 5, | 12, | | | | | | | 6.40 |
| Thomas, Joseph, | 160, | D, | J.Terrell, | 1, | 7 | | | | 1, | 8, | | 1 | 18.10 |
| Terrell, Patrick, | 100, | | Same, | | | | | | 1, | 1, | | | 1.75 |
| Thomas, Mathew, | | | | | | | | | 1, | | | | .50 |
| Terrell, John, | 3592, | | Different Tracts | | | | 8 | | 1, | 7, | | | 49.67 |
| Thompson, James, | | | | | | | 8 | | 1, | | | | .50 |
| Tausil, John, | 40, | | Joel Penson | | | | | | 1, | 1, | | | 1.15 |
| Thompson, Jacob, | 170, | D, | J. Terrell, | 1, | 6, | 13, | | | 1, | 4, | | | 5.20 |
| Thompson, William, | | | | | | | | | 1, | | | | .50 |
| Taylor, Isaac, | | | | | | | | | 1, | | | | .50 |
| Taylor, Chapman, | 100, | | | 1, | 9, | 12, | | | 1, | 1, | | | 1.50 |
| Taylor, Edmund, | | | | | | | | | 1, | | | | .50 |
| Taylor, Isaac, | | | | | | | | | 1, | | | | .50 |
| Tucker, Daniel, | | | | | | | | | 1, | | | | .50 |
| Thomas, John Jr., | 564, | | Different Tracts | | | | 1, | | 1, | 11, | | | 14.89 |
| Travis, Fielding | | | | | | | | | 1, | | | | .50 |
| Thomas, James D., | | | | | | | | | 1, | 3, | | | 2.75 |
| Trantham, Floyd, | | | | | | | | | 1, | | | | .50 |
| Tate, William, | | | | | | | | | 1, | | | | .50 |
| Tate, James, | | | | | | | | | 1, | | | | .50 |

Page 70) -1830-Acres Desc.   Ent#of   Town, #ofFree           Stud
PERSONS NAME   Lnd., Titl. R E M A R K S /Rng.Sec.Dis.Lots, Lot,Poll, Sla.Sto. Jac. $ Cts. M.

| PERSONS NAME | Acres | Desc./Titl. | REMARKS | Ent#of Rng.Sec.Dis.Lots | Town,Lot | #ofFree Poll | Sla. | Sto. | Stud Jac. | $ | Cts. | M. |
|---|---|---|---|---|---|---|---|---|---|---|---|---|
| Uhls, Frederick J., | | | | | | 1, | | | | | .50 | |
| Vincent, Orrin, | | | | | | | | | 2, | 2.00 | | |
| Vincent, John M., | 100, | | | 1, 7, 13, | | 2, | 6 | | | 6.50 | | |
| Vincent, Perry, | 200, | | | | | 1, | 2 | | 2, | 6.00 | | |
| Vinvent, Joseph, | | | | | | 1, | | | | .50 | | |
| Warner, Mears, | 100, | D., | J. L. D. Smith, | 274, 1, 7, 12, | | 1, | | | 2, | 3.50 | | |
| Wainscott, Andrew, | | | | | | 1, | | | | .50 | | |
| White, Tysel, C., | | | | | | 1, | | | | .50 | | |
| Wilson, Samuel D., | 272, | E., | | 2, 9, 13, | | | | | | 2.72 | | |
| Willis, John, | 2500, | | | 204, 2,3,7.8 | | | | | | 25.00 | | |
| Wharton, Jesse, | 200, | | | 274, 3, 9, | | | | | | 2.00 | | |
| Same, | 559½ | D Gt., | L.Carter, | 310, 3, 10, | | | | | | 5.59 | 5 | |
| Same, | 730, | D Gt., | Same, | 325, 3, 9, | | | | | | 7.30 | | |
| Wilson Lewis,D., | 1000, | E, | Bowers & Wilson, | 2.3, 7, | | | | | | 10.00 | | |
| Ward, Robison, | 75, | | | | | 1/, | 1 | | | 1.00 | 25 | |
| Williams, Sarah, | | | | | | | | | | .75 | | |
| Wilson, Alice, S., | 27, | D, | Joab Bells, | 640, 1, 7, 13, | | | | | | .27 | | |
| Willimgham, Wm., | 30, | | R. Porter, | 1, 7, 12, 4, | | 1, | 1, | | | 5.55 | | |
| Williams, Joseph G., | | | | | | 1, | | | | .50 | | |
| Warner, Samuel A., | 5¼, | D, | J.Terrell, | 640, 1, 7, 13, | | 1, | 2, | | | 2.05 | 2½ | |
| Wade, Kencher, | | | | | | 1, | | | | .50 | | |
| Whitley, John, | | | | | | 1, | | | | .50 | | |
| Whitley, Alphens, | | | | | | 1, | | | | .50 | | |
| Williams, Kinchen, | | | | | | 1, | | | | .50 | | |
| Webster, Richard J., | | | | | | 1, | | | | .50 | | |
| Wilkins, Bartlett, | 100, | D, | M.B.Travis, | | | 1, | 1, | | | 2.25 | | |
| Wilkins, Lewelin, | | | | | | 1, | 1, | | | 1.25 | | |
| Workman, Pleasant G., | | | | | | 1, | | | | .50 | | |
| Williams, Anne, | 100, | | Peter Williams | 640, | | | | | | 1.00 | | |
| Williams, Allin, | 228, | | Same, | | | 1, | 1, | | | 2.28 | | |
| Wheler, Mark, | | | | | | 1, | | | | .50 | | |
| Wester, William, | | | | | | 1, | | | | .50 | | |
| Winsted, Johnson, | | | | | | 1, | | | | .50 | | |
| Webb, Amosa, | | | | 12, | | 1, | 1, | | | 1.25 | | |
| Webb, John, | 288, | | Thomas Deloech, | | | | 3, | | | 3.78 | | |

(Page 71)

| PERSONS NAME | Acres Lnd. | Desc. Titl. | REMARKS - Ent.Rge. Sec.Dist. Lots, | Town, Lot,Poll, | #of Sla. | Free Sto. | Horse Jac.$ | Cts. M |
|---|---|---|---|---|---|---|---|---|
| Wilson, Joseph, | 100, | | | | | | 3, | 3.25 |
| Wilson, Jason, | 250, | | | | | | | 2.50 |
| Williams, Gibson, A., | | | | | | | | .50 |
| Wells, Hayden, E., | 200, | D, Shelton Haneline | | 1, | | 3, | | 4.75 |
| Williamson, Meridith, | | | | 1, | | 1, | | 1.25 |
| Willoughby, James, | 13, | | | 1, | | | | .63 |
| Ward, Mosser, | 10, | | | 1, | | | | .60 |
| Watts, Matvill, | | | | 1, | | | | .50 |
| Wells, Sarah, | | | | | | 2, | | 1.50 |
| Ward, William, | | | | 1, | | | | .50 |
| Ward, John, | | | | 1, | | | | .50 |
| White, John L. | 70, | | | 1, | | | | 1.20 |
| Ward, Britton, | | | | 1, | | | | .50 |
| Winters, Aaron, | 112, | | | | | 1, | | 1.87 |
| Ward, George, | | | | 1, | | | | .50 |
| Warren, Edwin, | 50, | | | 1, | | | | 1.00 |
| Williams, Martin Hs, | | | | 1, | | | | .50 |
| Welch, John, | | | | 1, | | | | .50 |
| Williams, Charles, | | | | 1, | | | | .50 |
| Warren, Benjamin, | | | | 1, | | | | .50 |
| Warren, Leroy, | | | | 1, | | | | .50 |
| Warren, William, | | | | 1, | | | | .50 |
| White, William W., | | | | 1, | | | | .50 |
| Yarbrough, Seth, | | | | 1, | | | | .50 |
| Young, Abraham B., | 100, | Two Tracts | | | | | | 1.00 |
| Zimmerman, John, | | | | 1, | | | | .50 |
| Well, William,Exctrs, | 660, | Part of Andrew Neills 1654, 2, 9, 13, | | | | | | 6.60 |
| Neill Alexander, Exctrs, | 660, | Part of Same, 1654, | | | | | | 6.60 |
| Nelson, Robert, | 500, | Enty, | 108,1&2,9, 13, | | | | | 5.00 |
| Same, | 296½ | | 255,1&2, 9, | | | | | 2.96½ |

Total amount of Acres - T. Lots Store -Free Polls ,Stud Horse State Tax,County Tax Court House Tax
120,524¼                74,            490,              8         423.18.13 , 409,14,6— 415.72,0¼ , [?]
Sl. 308, Jury Tax, 6¾¾, 395.34.4,  Poor Tax, 275.75 2 3/4

Total 1859.143¾¾

(Page 72) Suplement List of 1830

| PERSONS NAME | Lnd. Titl. | REMARKS - Ent. Rng.Sec.,Dis,Lots,Lot,Poll,Sla.Sto Jac. | Town #of Free | | | Horse $.Cts. M. |
|---|---|---|---|---|---|---|
| Arnold, Farney, | | | | 1, | | .50 |
| Blakemore & Patterson, | | | | | | |
| Clark, Wm. H., | 367, E, | 671, 2, 7.13 | | | 1 | 8.67 |
| Braim, Peter H., | | | | 1, | | 5.50 |
| Blakemore, James, 146, | 639 | 1, 7, 13, | | | | 1.46 |
| Same, 2 tracts, 260, D, Part R.Smith 2 Tracts | | 2, | | | | 4.60 |
| Brown, Nathaniel, 200, E, | 772, | 2, 6, | | | | 2.00 |
| Bondurant, Benjn. | | 3, | | | | 3.00 |
| Cook, Richard, | 161, | 777 | 2, 8, | 1, | | 1.61 |
| Conrad, George | 92¼ | 1912 N. Conrad, | 1, 7, 12, | | | .92  2½ |
| Chilton, William, | 300, | | 2, 5, | | | 3.00 |
| Douglass, Elmore,Hs.,320, | | | 1, 8, | | | 3.20 |
| Fleming, William, 1113½ | | Seven Tracts | 1, | 1, | 8 | 17.63  5 |
| Glasco, Isaac, | | | | 1, | | .50 |
| Gardner, Wm. H., | | | | 1, | | .50 |
| Killebrew, Elias, | | | | 1, | | .50 |
| Mitchell, John, | | | | 1, | | .50 |
| Owen, Daniel, | 47, D, | Joel Penson, | | 1, | | .97 |
| Ross, Lacie | 40, | | 13, | 1, | 1, | 1.65 |
| Thompson, Robert, | | | | 1, | | .50 |
| Thomas, Micajah, | 480, | | | | | 4.80 |
| Williams, Bennit, | 240, | Baxter Boling 640, | 13, | 1, | 5, | 6.65 |
| Williams, Elisha, | 640,E, | | 12, | | | 6.40 |
| Yarbrough, David, | 715, D., | Divis of Gep. Doherty,2, 7, 12, | | | | 7.15 |

Acres    Town Lots ,F.P. Sla. Sto. Studs,    Pleasure Carriage
127466,    79      501, 322, 3,   9,               1

State Taxes .............$445.44  5 3/4
County Tax, ............. 428.72.4½
Courthouse Tax, ......... 437.13.6 3/4
Jury Tax, ............... 412.10. 9½
Poor Taxes, ............. 291.14,2 3/4

Total Amount is .........$1954.56 0 3/4

(Page 73)

STATE OF TENNESSEE )
WEAKLEY COUNTY    )
                  ) RECORDED JULY 8th, 1830.

Know all men by these presents that we, Alfred Gardner, John Jenkins, John Terrell, Benjamin Bondurant and George S. Eliott all of Weakley County & state aforesaid are held and firmly bound unto John Webb Chairman of out County Court of Weakley County and his successors in sum office in the sum of five thousand dollars in the payment of which/well and truly to be made we bind ourselves, our heirs etc. jointly & severally firmly by these presents signed with our names & sealed with our seals and dated this thirteenth day of April A. D., 1830.

The condition of the above obligation is such that whereas the above bound Alfred Gardner hath been appointed sheriff & collector of taxes within said county by the Justices of the county court. Now if the said Alfred Gardner shall well & truly pay over to the Trustee of said county all moneys and taxes which by law he may be bound to collect & pay over to the said Trustee for the year 1830 within said county (To wit) the county tax, Jury tax, Poor tax, & Public building tax laid by the county court for said year within the time & according to the terms prescribed by law. Then the above obligation to be void else to remain in full force & virtue.

|                        |   |                          |
|---|---|---|
| Signed, sealed and     ) | | Alfred Gardner, Seal, |
| acknowledged in        ) | | John Jenkins, Seal, |
| open court.            ) | | Jno. Terrell, Seal |
| Test                   ) | | Benjn. Bondurant, Seal |
| Wm. H. Johnson Clk.    ) | | G. S. Eliott, Seal |

---

(Page 74)

STATE OF TENNESSEE )
WEAKLEY COUNTY    )
                  ) RECORDED JULY 8th, 1830.

Know all men by these presents that we Alfred Gardner, Benjamin Bondurant, George S. Eliott, John Jinkins and John Terrell all of Weakley County & state of Tennessee are held and firmly bound unto William Carroll, Governor of the State of Tennessee for the time being and his successors in office in the sum of one thousand five hundred dollars in which sum well & truly to be paid as aforesaid we bind ourselves, our heirs etc. jointly and severally firmly by these presents sealed with our seals and dated this thirteenth day of April A. D., 1830.

The condition of the above obligation is such that whereas the above bound Alfred Gardner hath been appointed by the Justices of the county court of Weakley County Sheriff and collector of the public taxes in said county. Now if the said Alfred Gardner shall well and faithfully pay over to the treaurer of the state of Tennessee for the Western district

(Page 74) Cont.

all taxes which he may be bound by law to collect & pay to the said Treasurer for the State of Tennessee for the year 1830 within the time prescribed by law for such payment of said state tax and according to the terms thereof then this obligation to be void else to remain in full force & virtue.

    Interlined before signed.
Signed, sealed & acknowledged in open court.

|  |  |
|---|---|
| Test. ) | Alfred Gardner, Seal |
| Wm. H. Johnson, Clk. ) | Benjn. Bondurant, Seal |
|  | G. S. Eliott, Seal |
|  | John Jenkins, Seal |
|  | Jno. Terrell, Seal |

---

(Page 75) Supplement Tax list for 1830.

| Persons Name | Land Acres | Desc. Titl. | REMARKS | # of Ent. | Rge. | Sec. | Dis. | Town Lots | # of Lots | Free Poll | Sla. | Sto. | Horse Jac. | $ | Cts. M |
|---|---|---|---|---|---|---|---|---|---|---|---|---|---|---|---|
| Berry, Martha | | | | | | | | | | | 4 | | | 3.00 | |
| Cartwright, Elizabeth | 160 | | A. Deming, | 164, | 2&3, | 5, | 12, | | | | | | | 1.60 | |
| Culer, Alonzo D. | | | | | | | | | | 1, | | | | .50 | |
| Foster, Clabourn, | | | | | | | | | | 1, | | | | .50 | |
| Hunter, William, | | | | | | | | | | 1, | | | | .50 | |
| Persons, Thomas, | 1000 | Entry, | (640) | 240, | 2, | 7, | 13, | | | | | | | 10.00 | |
| Ray, John & Co., | 160, | Deed, | Cullen Andrews, | 1327, | 2, | 9, | 12, | | | | | | | 1.60 | |
| Same | 442, | | J. McIvers 2560 Acres, | | | | | | | | | | | 4.42 | |
| Same | 640, | | Richard Smith, | 474, | 2,3,7, | 13, | | | | | | | | 6.40 | |
| Same | 640, | | David Jeffries, | 184, | 1, | 9, | | | | | | | | 6.40 | |
| Same, | 120, | | Benjn.Coffields, | 2560, | 1, | 4,5 | | | | | | | | 1.20 | |
| Same, | 228, | | Cave Johnston, | 600, | 1, | 10, | 12, | | | | | | | 2.28 | |
| Same, | 640, | | James Hart, | 1360, | 1, | 6, | | | | | | | | 6.40 | |
| Same | 160, | | Benjn.McCulloch | 640, | 3, | 9, | 13, | | | | | | | 1.60 | |
| Same, | 640 | | J. C. McLemore, | | | | | | | | | | | 6.40 | |
| Cowan James | 640 | Deed, | Jesse Cherry, | 391, | 1, | 9 &10, | 12, | | | | | | | 6.40 | |
| Haning, Samuel, | | | | | | | | | | 1, | | | | .50 | |
| Hulett, Thomas P., | 60, | | Jack Penson, | | | | 13, | | | | | | | .60 | |
| Kile, Barney,C., | | | | | | | | | | 1, | | | | .50 | |
| Miles, William, | | | | | | | | | 1, | | | | | 1.00 | |
| Pierce Abel, | | | | | | | | | | 1, | | | | .50 | |
| Pierce, John, | | | | | | | | | | 1, | | | | .50 | |
| Parks, Fields, | | | | | | | | | | 1, | | | | .50 | |
| Purcel, Abel, | 25,E | | | | | | 13, | | | | | | | .25 | |
| Stunson, Henry, | 178,D | | | | | | 12, | | | | | | | 1.78 | |
| Simmons, Charles, | | | | | | | | | 1, | | | | | .50 | |
| Tansil, Edward, | 320, | Deed, | | | | | | | | | 4, | | | 6.20 | |
| Barnett, Andrew | 864, | E, | Part of 1907, | | 2, | 5, | 13, | | 1 | | 9, 8, 1 3 | | | 8.64 78.07 | |
| Total | 6757 11 6746 | | | | | | | | | | 8 5 | | | 76.21 2.86 | |

State Taxes ............$15.27, 2½  
County Tax,............ 14.46  Jury Tax .........$14.39, 7½  
Court house tax     18.67, 7½  Poor Tax,........ 13.39, 7½ ) Total $76.21

(Page 76)

| Persons Name | Acres Desc. | Lnd.Titl. | #of R E M A R K S | Ent. Rge. Sec. Dis. | Town, Lots, | #of Free Lot, Poll, | Sla. Sto.Jac. | $ . Cts. M |

Total amount of taxes given in for 1830 up to Oct. 22nd

| | | |
|---|---|---|
| 1272270¼ acres of land @ $1.00 per 100 acres is | ............ | $1272.70 2½ |
| 80 Town lots @ $1.00 per lot is | ............ | 80.00 |
| 509 Free Polls @ .50 per Poll is | ............ | 254.50 |
| 327 Slaves @ .75 per poll is | ............ | 245.25 |
| 3 Retail stores @ 10.00 per store is | ............ | 30.00 |
| 9 Stud horses @ Jacks @ various prices | ............ | 50.00 |
| 3 Taverns @ $5.00 per tavern is | ............ | 15.00 |
| 1 Pleasure Carriage with 2 wheels @ $1.25 per wheel is | ............ | 5.00 |

| | | |
|---|---|---|
| Tax for the State is | $460.71 8½ | $462.21 6½ |
| Nelson's land added | 1.50 | |
| Tax for the county is | 443.18 4¼ | 444.68 4¼ |
| Do for the Courthouse is | 455.81 4½ | 457.77 9¼ |
| | 1.95 5 | |
| Do for the Jury is | 426.50 7 | 428.05 7 |
| | 1.50 | |
| | 1.50 | |
| Do for the poor is | 304.54 ¼ | 306.04 ¼ |
| | 1.50 | |
| | $2090.96 4¼ | $2098.77 9½ |

H. Nelson's Land is 796½ acres .... $7.96½ added all 1280.66 3/4
                                    Total on land ........... 1280.66 7½

A mistake in calculation above on William H.Johnson
Total amount of taxes for the year 1830 to-wit

| | | |
|---|---|---|
| 135008½ acres of land @ $1.00 per hundred acres is | ............ | 1350.08½ |
| 80 Town lots @ $1.00 per lot is | ............ | 80.00 |
| 509 Free polls @ 50¢ per poll is | ............ | 254.50 |
| 327 Slaves @ 75¢ per poll is | ............ | 245.25 |
| 9 Stud horses at various prices | ............ | 52.00 |
| 3 retail stores @ $1.00 $10.00 per store is | ............ | 30.00 |
| 3 Taverns @ $5.00 Each is | ............ | 15.00 |
| 1 Pleasure cariage with 4 wheels | | 4.00 Total |
| | | $2031.83 5 |

(Page 76) Cont.

| | | |
|---|---|---|
| Tax for the state is | $456.51 | 6¼ |
| Tax for the county is | 443.64 | 1¼ |
| Tax for the courthouse is | 457.02 | |
| Tax for the Jury is | 367.64 | 1¼ |
| Tax for the poor is | 304.01 | 6¼ |

Total $2031.83 5

---

(Page 77)

Recorded 14th May, 1831

## JOHN WEBB'S LAST WILL & TESTAMENT

In the name of God Amen. I, John Webb of the County of Weakley and State of Tennessee being very sick and weak in body but of sound mind and memory thanks be given to Almighty God, calling into mind the mortality of my body and knowing that it is appointed for all men once to Die - do make and ordain this my last will and testament. That is to say first and principally I recommend my soul to and into the hand of Almighty God who gave it and my body I recommend to the earth to be buried in a decent christian Burial at the discretion of my executors to be hereafter named and as touching such worldly Estate wherewith it has pleased God to bestow upon me in this world. I give devise and dispose of the same in the following manner and form:

First that all my just debts be paid together with all my funeral charges.

Item First, I give and bequeath to my son Amosa Webb, one negro boy named Aaron, one horse, one bed & furniture and one cow which he has now in possession.

Item second, I give and bequeath to my daughter Mary Davis one negro girl named Lozette and the occupant whereon they now live, one feather bed and furniture, one cow and calf which they have in possession.

Item Third, I give & Bequeath to my son John Webb my negro boy Baxter and a gray filly to be and remain his forever but Baxter being sick, should he die with the present Desease then my said son John is to have my negro girl Caroline but if said negro boy should recover, he is not to have the last mentioned negro girl Caroline.

Item fourth, I give unto my beloved wife Nancy Webb all my remaining property real & personal & perishable during her natural life or widowhood but at death then the remaining property to be equally divided amongst (Page 78) my six youngest children, towit: Jesse, Sarrah, Elizabeth, George, Holland & Bushrod Webbs.

I likewise constitute and appoint my wife Nancy Webb and my son Amosa Webb executors of this my last will and Testament hereby revoking annulling and making void all former wills Testaments or Executors heretofore made, given, granted, appointed constituted or ordained Ratefying and confirming this and this only to be my last will and Testament In witness whereof I here unto set my hand and seal this eleventh day of January in the year of our Lord, 1831.

(Page 78) Con.

Signed inthe presence of )
the subscribing witnesses )       John Webb, (Seal)
J. Wilson      )
John Ridgway  )    The word property enterlined before signed.  Test. J. Wilson.

STATE OF TENNESSEE -

Weakley County Court  April Term 1831   Then was the Execution of the foregoing will proven in open court by the oaths of John Ridgway & Joseph Wilson, the subscribing witness thereto and ordered to be recorded.   Wm. H. Johnson, Clk.
(Page 79)

|Person's name|Acres Lnd.|Desc. Titl.|REMARKS|#of Ent.|Rge.|Sec.|Dis.|Town Lots|#of Lot|Free Poll|Sla.|Sto.|Horse Jac.|$|Cts.|M|
|---|---|---|---|---|---|---|---|---|---|---|---|---|---|---|---|---|
|Ashbrooks, Moses,|||||||||||1,||||.40|5|
|Anderson, Bailey,|640,|E||603,|1,|9,|13,|||||||| 3.60 ||
|Anderson, Wm. E.,|640,|||805,|2,|7,|12,|||||||| 3.60 ||
|Same,|171,|||827,|1,|10,|12,|||||||| .86 | 1½|
|Adkison, Edward,|100,||||1,|7,|13,||||||3,|| 3.40 |5|
|Adkison, Welford,|||||||||||1,|||| .40 |5|
|Adkison, Wm. P.,|||||||||||1,|||| .40 |5|
|Adams, Harden S.|||||||||||1,|||| .40 |5|
|Austin, Vincent,|||||||||||1,|||| .40 |5|
|Austin, Moses Sr.|156,|E, Peter Williams,|640,|2,|9,|12,|||||||| .87 |7½|
|Austin, Moses, J.C.,|100,|Part of same,||2,|9,|12,|||||||| .96 |7½|
|Abernathy,Littleton,|81½,||||2,|9,|12,|||||||| .86 |3|
|Austin, Samuel,|||||||||||1,|||| .40 |5|
|Acre, Jesse,|||||||||||1,|||| .40 |5|
|Adkins, Josiah R.|30,|Messer Ward,||||||||||1,|||57|3|3/4|
|Armstrong, John,||||||||||||1,||| 1.21 |7½|
|Armstrong, Thomas,|||||||||||1,|||| .40 |5|
|Arnold, Kerney,|||||||||||1,|||| .40 |5|
|Adams, Abel,Heirs,|88,||||2,|5,|13,|||||||| .49 |5|
|Alexander, Adam R.,|650,|John Serrell,||1,|7,|13,|||||||| 3.65 ||
|Bowers, John,||||||||( 95 )||||1,||| .81 |2½|
|Bondurant, Hillery H.,|4,|E., John Terrell,|64,|1,|7,|13,|3|94,96|1,|2,||| 5.09 |2½|
|Bondurant, Benj.|501,|Different tracts||1,|6,|12,|7½,|||11,||| 19.75 |2½|
|Bondurant, Albert G.|720,|Elisha Ward Hs.,|1032,|1,|9,|12,||||1,|3,|| 6.08 ||
|Barley, John,|220,|||222,|2,|8,|13,|||||||| 1.24 |1|

(Page 79) Cont. Desc.                                           Town.  #of Free         Horse
Persons Name  Ac.Lnd. Titl. R E M A R K S       Ent.Rge. Sec. Dis.Lots,Lot.Poll,Sla.Sto. Jac. $ Cts. M.
Bell, John, Trustee,330,G, Elijah Robertson,500,  2&3,  9,  13,                              1.85  6¼
Bradbury, James, 513, E, 2 Tracts R.Smith,              13,                                  2.88  5
Butler, Wm. E., 452,       Robt. Butler,        693, 1, 7,  13,                              2.54  2½
Brown, William,K.,590½,    Benj. Herndon,       286, 1&2, 9, 13,                             3.32  1½
Brocken, James, 150,       (640)                     1,  7,  12,                              .84  3½
Brinkley, William,512,     Sion Williams,Hs),251, 2, 5&6, 12,                                2.88
Boleing, Baxter, 160,      640,                 1082,                                         .90
              6 808

(Page 80)     6808
Bowers,& Wilson, 1000, E,                        29, 2&3,  7,  13,                           5.62  5
Baldridge, Daniel,640,                          725,  2,   7,  13                            3.60
Blount, John G., 2634,     3 tracts                                     16.21                14.81 6¼
Bowers, Young P.,                                                                             2.03
Brown, Nathaniel, 200,                          772,  2,   6,  13,   (25,27)  1,       2,    1.12  5
Bayles, C & W.,                                                      4,60,61)                9.00
Bayless, Cullen, 2 3/8, John Terrell 640,        1,   7,   13,          1,    4,             3.66  7½
Bayless, Wiley,  6,     Part of same,            1,   1,   7,  13,      1,    2,             2.05  8½
Barger, Daniel D.,                                                      1,                    .40  5
Byrd, Nazareth,                                                         1,    1,             1.21  7½
Brasfield, Caleb,                                                       1,    5,             4.46  7½
Baldridge, Wm. 590, D.Baldridge, 640,                 2,   7,  13,      1,                   3.51  8 3/4
Baldridge, Andrew W.,                                                   1,                    .40  5
Bradshaw, Thompson,50, D.Baldridge, 640,              2,   7,  13,      1,                    .68  6¼
Blakemore, James, 406, 3 Tracts                                  2,                          4.28  3 3/4
Blakemore & Patterson,800,                                                                   4.50
Berry, Martha,                                                          1,                    .81 2½
Bondurant, Robert M. 1662 2/3, hs. Jerome McClain,3840, 2 7,            1,                   2.15  5
Brain, Peter H.,                                      13,  1,           1,                    .40  5
Burnit, George,                                                                             1,3.40  5
Bledsoe, Jacob,                                                                               .40  5
Byars, William, 100,       Robert Butler,452,  693, 1,7,  13,           1,                    .56  2½
Beadles, b Bassit,                                                      1,                    .40  5
Beadles, Duke,                                                          1,                    .40  5
Beadles, William,                                                       1,                    .40  5
Bynham, Thomas,                                                         1,                    .40  5

(Page 80) Cont.

| Person's Name | Ac:Lnd | Titl. REMARKS | #of Ent. | Rge. | Sec. | Dis. | Town Lots | #of Lot | Free Poll | Sla. | Sto. | Jac. | $.Cts. M |
|---|---|---|---|---|---|---|---|---|---|---|---|---|---|
| Buckley, James, | | | | | | | | | | 1, | | | .81 2½ |
| Brand, James, | | | | | | | | | 1, | | | | .40 5 |
| Brown, Coonrad, | 50, | | | 2, | 7, | 12, | | | 1, | | | | .68 6¼ |
| Brooks, William, | 222, | Pt. 510 Acres | | 2, | 7, | 12, | | | | 3, | | | 3.67 5 |
| Bryant, John H., | 2140, | G., J.G. & Thos. Blount 2tracts | | | | 13, | | | | | | | 12.03 7½ |
| Breedlove, Robert H., | | | | | | | | | 1, | | | | .40 5 |
| Betts, Samuel D., | | | | | | | | | 1, | | | | .40 5 |
| Barnard, William, | | | | | | | | | 1, | | | | .40 5 |
| Brawner, John, | 15,015 1/3 Acres . | | | | | | | | 1, | 1, | | | 1.21 7½ |

(Page 81)

| Person's Name | Ac:Lnd | Titl. REMARKS | #of Ent. | Rge. | Sec. | Dis. | Town Lots | #of Lot | Free Poll | Sla. | Sto. | Jac. | $.Cts. M |
|---|---|---|---|---|---|---|---|---|---|---|---|---|---|
| Busey, Lucy | | | | | | | | | | 3 | | | 2.43 7½ |
| Billingly, Baset, | | | | | | | | | | 1, | | | 1.21 7½ |
| Barnard, John, | | | | | | | | | 1, | | | | .40 5 |
| Bradshaw, Henry, | | | | | | | | | 1, | 1, | | | 1.21 7½ |
| Bookout, Bradley, | | | | | | | | | 1, | | | | .40 5 |
| Bridges, Griffin, | | | | | | | | | 1, | | | | .40 5 |
| Baker, John, | | | | | | | | | 1, | | | | .40 5 |
| Bourland, James, | 25, E., | | | 1, | 6, | 13, | | | 1, | | | | .40 5 |
| Bradshaw, John, | | | | | | | | | 1, | | | | .54 5½ |
| Bradshaw, Gideon T., | | | | | | | | | 1, | 2, | | | 2.03 |
| Bell, Pulaski B., | | | | | | | | | 1, | | | | .40 5 |
| Bowers, Giles, | | | | | | | | | 1, | | | | .40 5 |
| Blakemore, Willie, | | | | | | | | | 1, | | | | .40 5 |
| Blakemore, Benjn., | | | | | | | | | 1, | 1, | | | 1.21 7½ |
| Blagg, James, | | | | | | | | | 1, | | | | .40 5 |
| Barnes, Solomon, | | | | | | | | | 1, | | | | .40 5 |
| Belote, Henry, | 256, | Part of 640, | | | | | | | | | | | 1.44 |
| Catron, John, | 1000, | G, J. G. & T. Blount, | 258, | | | 13, | | | 1, | | | | 5.62 5 |
| Claxton, James, | 160, | E, Blakemore, Swaney & Ross | 601, | 132, | 7, | 13, | | | 1, | | | | 1.30 5 |
| Clark, Christopher, | | (640 Acres) | | | | | | | 1, | | | | .40 5 |
| Charlton, John, 1161 3/4 , 6 tracts | | | | | | | | 2, | 1, | 2, | | | 9.99 0¼ |
| Clabourne, Thomas, | 1009, | G, 3 Tracts , L.Carter, | | | | 13, | | | 1, | | | | 5.67 5¼ |
| Chester, Henry W. | 300, | E, John Terrell, | 3840, | 1, | 6, | 13, | | | 1, | 2, | | | 3.71 7¾ |
| Clark, Levi, | | | | 1, | 5, | 12, | | | 1, | 1, | | | 1.21 7½ |
| Cotton, Charles, | 640, | | 1366, | | | | | | | | | | 3.60 |

83

(Page 81) Cont.

| Persons Name | Acres, Desc. REMARKS | #of Ent. | Rge., | Sec., | Dis. | Town Lots, | #of Lots, | Free Poll, | Sla, | Sto, | Jac, | Horse $.Cts. | M |
|---|---|---|---|---|---|---|---|---|---|---|---|---|---|
| Cherry, Clemigle, | 520, | 617, | 3, | 7, | 13, | | | | | | | 2.92 | 5 |
| Charlton, John, | 178,Hs.Joseph Greer,1000, | 850, | 2, | 7, | 13, | | | | | | | 1.00 | 1¼ |
| Carr, Silas, | 50, | | 2, | 7, | 13 | | | | | | | .28 | 1¼ |
| Charleton & Willingham, | | | | | | 2, | | | | | | 2.00 | |
| Clark, James W., | 3925, Part of 5000 Acres | 104, | 3, | 8, | 13 | | | | | | | 22.07 | 8 |
| Childress, James, | 80, G,Elijah Patton, 500, | 337, | 2 33, | 9, | 13, | | | | | | | .45 | |
| Cherry, Laurence, | 1081, E, 3 Tracts, | | | | 13, | | | | | | | 6.08 | 0½ |
| Cherry, Daniel, | 1920, 3 Tracts, | | | | 13, | | | | | | | 10.80 | |
| Cherry, Darling, (Page 82) | 640 | 769, | 2, | 9, | 12, | | | | | | | 3.60 | |
| Cochran, Dennis, | | | | | 13, | 3 | 1, 4 | | | | | 6.65 | 5 |
| Campbell, George W., | 340, 2 Tracts | | | | | | | | | | | 1. 91 | 2½ |
| Cassel, John, | | | | | | | 1, | | | | | .40 | 5 |
| Craig, Ebenezer, | 60,E, Joel Pinson, | | | | 13, | | 1, | | | | | .74 | 2½ |
| Crider, David, | | | | | | | 1, | | | | | .40 | 5 |
| Crider, Winston B., | | | | | | | 1, | | | | | .40 | 5 |
| Curlin, Zacheus H., | 640, Benjm. McCullock, | | | | 13, | | 1, | | | | | 4.00 | 5 |
| Chambers, Greenberry, | | | | | | | 1, | | | | | .40 | 5 |
| Conner, Isham, | | | | | | | 1, 1, | | | | | 1.21 | 7⅞ |
| Cavitt, John F., | 180, | | 2, | 9, | 12, | | 1, 1, | | | | | 2.23 | |
| Cooke, Margarett, | 40, John Cooke, | | 2, | 10, | 12, | | | | | | | .22 | 5 |
| Clark, David, | | | | | | | 1, | | | 1, | | 2.90 | 5 |
| Clark, William, | | | | | | | 1, | | | | | .40 | 5 |
| Casher, Elam M., | | | | | | | 1, | | | | | .40 | 5 |
| Coleman, John, | | | | | | | 1, | | | | | .40 | 5 |
| Carsley, Seth T., | | | | | | | 1, | | | | | .40 | 5 |
| Cathey, Thomas & A.J.W., | 875, Part of 1000 | | 2, | 9, | 12, | | 1, | | | | | 4.92 | 2 |
| Cocke, Benjamin, | 112, A Winters land, | | 2, | 6, | 12, | | 1, | | | | | .63 | |
| Clayton, John, | 370, 2 Tracts | | 2, | 7, | 12, | | 1, 4, | | | | | 5.73 | 6¼ |
| Clark, William H., | | | | | | | 1, | | | | | .40 | 5 |
| Carter, Rubin, | | | | | | | 1, | | | | | .40 | 5 |
| Clayton, Martin, | | | | | | | 1, 2, | | | | | 2.03 | |
| Christman, Richard, | | | | | | | 1, | | | | | .40 | 5 |
| Casselman, Lazarus, | | | | | | | 1, | | | | | .40 | 5 |
| Campbell, Daniel, | | | | | 12, | | 1, 2, | | | 1, | | 6.62 | 5 |
| Cartwright, Thomas N/.100, | | | 2, | 5, | 12, | | 1, 2, | | | | | 2.59 | 2½ |
| Cartwright, Elizabeth, | 60, | | 2, | 5, | 12, | | | | | | | .33 | 7½ |
| Cruse, Isaac, | 320, Part of 640, | 1012, 2, | 6, | 12, | | 1 | | | | | | 2.20 | 5 |

(Page 82) Cont. Acres Desc.                         #of  Range  Town,    #of Free
Persons Name    Lnd. Titl. R E M A R K S       Ent/ Sec. Dis. Lots, Lot, Poll, Sla., Sto. Jac.  $ Cts. M.

| Persons Name | Acres/Desc. REMARKS | Ent/Sec. Dis. Lots | Poll | Sla. | Sto. Jac. | $ Cts. | M. |
|---|---|---|---|---|---|---|---|
| Cox, Edward M., | | | 1, | | | .40 | 5 |
| Cox, Robert, | | | 1, | | | .40 | 5 |
| Cooper, Henry, | | | 1, | | | .40 | 5 |
| Chilton, William, 300, | | 2, 5, 12, | | | | 1.68 | 7½ |
| Cox, Henry B., | | | 1, | | | .40 | 5 |
| Crowley, Jesse, | | | 1, | | | .40 | 5 |
| Cantrell, Abraham P., 200, | Benj. Coffield Hs., | 1, 5, 13, | 1, | | | 1.53 | |
| (Page 83) (Year 1831) | | | | | | | |
| Cooper, James, | | | 1, | | | .40 | 5 |
| Cravens, John, | | | 1, | 1, | | 1.21 | 7½ |
| Crabtree, Anderson, | | | 1, | | | .40 | 5 |
| Cantrell, Duke, | | | 1, | | | .40 | 5 |
| Cantrell, Joseph, | | | 1, | | | .40 | 5 |
| Cantrell, Richard, | | | 1, | | | .40 | 5 |
| Cravens, Joseph, | | | 1, | 3, | 1, | 3.93 | 7½ |
| Cooley, George, 170, E. 2 Tracts, | | 1, 5, 13, | 1, | | | 1.36 | 1¼ |
| Carmichael, Michael, 3400, 5000 | | 13, | | | | 19.12 | 5 |
| Dunn, John, | | | 1, | | | .40 | 5 |
| Dickins, Samuel, 875, 2 Tracts | | 1,5,6, 12, | | | | 4.91 | 1½ |
| Devereaux, Thos. R., 500, | | 967, 1,5, 12, | | | | 2.81 | 2½ |
| Doherty, George, 5562, 2 Tracts, | | 1326,2, 9, 12, | | | | 33.16 | 1¼ |
| Dunnar, Anthony Hs., 641, | | 872,2, 6, 13 | | | | 3.60 | |
| Dickson, Matton, 129, Jos. Greer Hs. (645) | | | | | | .72 | 5½ |
| Dent, Jos. E., 7 3/4, Joab Bells Hs. 640, 767, 1, 7, 13 | | | | | | .44 | 5 |
| Damron, Nobel L., | | | 1, | | | .40 | 5 |
| Darling, James S., | | | 1, | 1, | | 1.21 | 7½ |
| Davis, Fennel, | | | 1, | | | .40 | 5 |
| Douglass, Elmore, 320, | | 1, 8, 13, | | | | 1.80 | |
| Damron, John, 35, | | 1, 8, 12, | | | | .60 | 1½ |
| Damron, Moses L., | | | 1, | | | .40 | 5 |
| Damron, Constantine, | | | 1, | | | .40 | 5 |
| Damron, George, 50, | | 2, 8, 13, | 1, | | | .68 | 6¼ |
| Damron, Charles, | | | 1, | | | .40 | 5 |
| Damron, Samuel, | | | 1, | | | .40 | 5 |
| Delaney, Elijah, | | | 1, | | | .40 | 5 |
| Dougherty, Dennis, | | | 1, | | | .40 | 5 |

(Page 83) Cont. Acres Desc.                                    Town,    #of  Free
Persons Name      Lnd. Titl. R E M A R K S    Ent. Rge., Sec. Dis. Lots, Lot, Poll, Sla. Sto. Horse Jac. $ .Cts M

| Persons Name | Acres | Remarks | Ent. | Rge. | Sec. | Dis. Lots | Town, Lot | #of Poll | Free Sla. | Sto. | Horse Jac. $ | .Cts M |
|---|---|---|---|---|---|---|---|---|---|---|---|---|
| Dawson, Isaac, | | | | | | | 1, | | | | 2.21 | 7½ |
| Dill, Zebulon, | | | | | | | | 1, | 1, | | .40 | 5 |
| Dill, Joseph, | | | | | | | | 1, | | | .40 | 5 |
| Davis, George, | | | | | | | | 1, | | | .40 | 5 |
| Drew, James H., | | | | | | | | 1, | | | .40 | 5 |
| Davis, Jesse B., | | | | | | | | 1, | | | .40 | 5 |
| (Page 84) | | | | | | | | | | | | |
| Donelson, Humphrey, | 180, | E., | | 1, | 9, | 12 | | | | | 1.01 | 2½ |
| Davis, Isham L., | | | | | | | | 1, | 1, | | 1.21 | 7½ |
| Dunn, Mathew, P., | | | | | | | | 1, | | | .40 | 5 |
| Davis, Jesse | | | | | | | | 1, | | | .40 | 5 |
| Dunn, Nathaniel, | | | | | | | | 1, | | | .40 | 5 |
| Dunham, William, | | | | | | | | 1, | | | .40 | 5 |
| Delaney, Neil, | | | | | | | | 1, | | | .40 | 5 |
| Dickson, Ephriam, D., | | | | | | | 1, | 1, | | | | |
| Eley, Eli, | 200. | Benj. Coffield Hs. 2560 | 735, | 1, | 4 | 5, | 13, | 1, | 2, | | 3.03 | 5 |
| Edwards, Thos. C., | | | | | | | 1, | 1, | | | 1.53 | 5 |
| Edmonston, Jesse, | | | | | | | 1, | 1, | | | .40 | 5 |
| Edwards, Eli, | | | | | | | | 1, | | | 1.40 | 5 |
| Edmonston, Reubins, | | | | | | | | 1, | | | .40 | 5 |
| Edmonston, James, | | | | | | | | 1, | | | .40 | 5 |
| Edwards, Thomas S., | 50, | Burrel Anderson, | | 2, | 6, | 13, | | 1, | | | .68 | 6¼ |
| Edmonston, Robert, | | | | | | | | 1, | | | .40 | 5 |
| Eaves, Solomon, Jr., | | | | | | | | 1, | | | .40 | 5 |
| Easves, Thomas J., | | | | | | | | 1, | | | .40 | 5 |
| Eliott, George S., | 575, | Thos. Henderson 2560, | | 1, | 8, | 13, | 1, | 1, | 4, | | 7.88 | 9 |
| Ezzell, Harison, | | | | | | | | 1, | | | .40 | 5 |
| Eleson, Ingram, | | | | | | | | 1, | | | .40 | 5 |
| Ethridge, Thomas, | | | | | | | | 1, | | | .40 | 5 |
| Fowler, Stephen, | | | | | | | | 1, | | | .40 | 5 |
| Freeman, Charles A, | 100, | Jas. Long, | 963, | 1, | 7, | 13, | | 1, | | | .96 | 7½ |
| Freeman, John, | | | | | | | | 1, | | | .40 | 5 |
| Fowler, Wm. A., | | | | | | | | 1, | | | .40 | 5 |
| Fuller, Joseph, | | | | | | | | 1, | | | .40 | 5 |
| Fowler, Thomas, | | | | | | | | 1, | 3, | | 2.43 | 7½ |
| Fowler, Wm. H., | | | | | | | | 1, | | | .40 | 5 |
| Fonville, John B., | | | | | | 2 | | 1, | 1, | | 3.21 | 7½ |

(Page 84) Cont. Acres Desc.                                                    Town, #of Free
Persons Name  Ind. Title, R E M A R K S, Ent.Rge., Sec. Dis. Lots Lot, Poll, Sla. Sto. Jac. $. Cts. M

| Persons Name | Acres | Desc. Title | REMARKS | Ent.Rge. | Sec. | Dis. | Town/Lots | Lot | Poll | Sla. | Sto. | Jac. | $ | Cts. | M |
|---|---|---|---|---|---|---|---|---|---|---|---|---|---|---|---|
| Foster, Nathaniel H., | | | | | | | | | 1, | | | | .40 | 5 | |
| Farel, Albert B., | 160, | | | 2, | 6, | 13, | | | | | | | .90 | | |
| (Page 85) | | | | | | | | | | | | | | | |
| Farmer, Jesse, | | | | | | | | | 1, | | | | .40 | 5 | |
| Fowler, John, | | | | | | | | | 1, | 1, | | | .81 | 2½ | |
| Fowler, Bullard A. | | | | | | | | | 1, | 1, | | | 1.21 | 7½ | |
| Frizzell, Jason, | | | | | | | | | 1, | | | | .40 | 5 | |
| Freeman, Richardson, | | | | | | | | | 1, | 2, | | | 2.03 | | |
| Farmer, Hulitt, | | | | | | | | | 1, | | | | .40 | 5 | |
| Farmer, Aron, | | | | | | | | | 1, | | | | .40 | 5 | |
| Farmer, Hiram, | | | | | | | | | 1, | | | | .40 | 5 | |
| Fields, David, | | | | | | | | | 1, | | | | .40 | 5 | |
| Frizzell, Isreal, | 150, | E.½,Jno. H. Moore, 1984, | | 2, | 7, | 12, | | | 1, | 5, | | | 4.90 | 6¼ | |
| Freeman, William | | | | | | | | | 1, | 4, | | | 3.65 | 5 | |
| Freeman, Evans, | 100, | Parter & McDaniel 300, | | 2, | 7, | 12, | | | 1, | 3, | | | 3.40 | 5 | |
| Folks, Shearwood, | | | | | | | | | 1, | | | | .40 | 5 | |
| Flemming, William, | 1693½ | 7 Tracts, | | | | 12, | | | 1, | 9, | | | 16.87 | 6 | |
| Finch, John W., | 25, | John Welch, | | 1, | 6, | 12, | | | 1, | 2, | | | 2.16 | 6 | |
| Fowler, Samuel, | | | | | | | | | 1, | | | | .40 | 5 | |
| Foley, Townsend, | | | | | | | | | 1, | | | | .40 | 5 | |
| Forbis, Lorenzo D., | | | | | | | 1, | | 1, | | | | 1.40 | 5 | |
| Forbis, Amarine M., | | | | | | | | | 1, | | | | .40 | 5 | |
| Fitzgerald, William, | 2, | Jno. Terrell, 640, | | | | | | | 1, | 3, | | | 2.84,5 3/4 | | |
| Foster, Clabourn, | | | | | | | | | 1, | | | | .40 | 5 | |
| Furlong Hudson, | | | | | | | | | 1, | | | | .40 | | |
| Gardner, Alfred, | | | | | | | 3, | | 1, | | | | 3.40 | 5 | |
| Gaston, William, | 640, | Joseph Tracy, | | 301,3, | 7, | 13, | | | 1, | 3, | | | 3.60 | | |
| Gardner, John A. | 15, | 2 Tracts, | | 1, | 7, | 13, | 3, | | 1, | 3, | | | 5.92 | 6¼ | |
| Gleeson, Wm. W. | 200, | James Greer, | | 1, | 7, | 12, | | | 1, | 2, | | | 3.15 | 5 | |
| Gardner, Jiptha, | 66, | 2 Tracts, Jacob Behn, | | 767,1, | 7, | 13, | | | 1, | 2, | | | 2.40 | 1½ | |
| Gardner, Jesse, | | | | | | | | | 1, | 3, | | | 2.84 | 2½ | |
| Greer, James, | 1003, | Five Tracts, | | | | | 3, | | 1, | | | | 9.04 1 3/4 | | |
| Gellespie, Geo. T., | 830 | 3/4, G,3 tracts, | | 3, | 9, | 13, | | | | | | | 4.69 | 2½ | |
| Glasco, Isaac, | | | | | | | | | 1, | | | | .40 | 5 | |
| Glass, Dudley, Sr., | | | | | | | | | 1, | 8, | | | 6.50 | | |
| Glass, Dudley Jr., | | | | | | | | | 1, | | | | .40 | 5 | |
| Green, Alvah, | | | | | | | | | 1, | | | | 1.00 | | |

(Page 86)

| Persons Name | Acres Lnd. | Titl. REMARKS | #of Ent. | Rge., | Sec. | Dis. | Town, Lots, | #of Lot | Free Poll | Sla. | Sto. | Horse Jac. | $. | Cts. | M |
|---|---|---|---|---|---|---|---|---|---|---|---|---|---|---|---|
| Garrett, Henry A., | | | | | | | | | 1, | | | | .40 | 5 | |
| Garden, David, | 640, | E., J.C. McLemore, | | | | | | | | | | | 3.60 | | |
| Gains, James, | | | | | | | | | | | | | .40 | 5 | |
| Galoway, Glidwell | 8,150, | David Broadwell, | | 2, | 6, | 13, | | | 1, | | | | 1.24 | 8 | 3/4 |
| Galoway, Benjh., | 150, | Same, | | 2, | 6, | 13, | | | 1, | | | | 1.24 | 8 | 3/4 |
| Gardner, Richard W., | | | | | | | | | 1, | | | | .40 | 5 | |
| Gibbs, Jesse, | | | | | | | | | 1, | | | | .40 | 5 | |
| Gilliam, Gray, | 43 3/4, | Porter & McDowell, | | 2, | 7, | 12, | | | 1, | 1, | | | 1.05 | 7 | 3/4 |
| Gilliam, Henry, | | | | | | | | | 1, | | | | .40 | 5 | |
| Gunter, Frances, | | | | | | | | | 1, | | | | .40 | 5 | |
| Goodman, Samuel, | | | | | | | | | 1, | | | | .40 | 5 | |
| Grooms, Bright, | | | | | | | | | 1, | | | | .40 | 5 | |
| Gilbert, Jonathan M., | 91½, | Jacob Bell, 640, | 767, | 1, | 7, | 13, | | | 1, | 2, | | | 2.53 | 3 | |
| Goldsby, James, | | | | | | | | | | 4, | | | 3.25 | | | |
| Gilbert, Robert, | 64, | | | 2, | 5, | 12, | | | | 2, | | | 2.39 | | | |
| Goldsby, Stephen, | | | | | | | | | | | | | .40 | 5 | |
| Gilbert, Randolph, | | | | | | | | | | 1, | | | 1.21 | 7½ | |
| Garner, John, | | | | | | | | | 1, | | | | .40 | 5 | |
| Galby, James, | | | | | | | | | 1, | | | | .40 | 5 | |
| Griffith, Abel, | | | | | | | | | 1, | | | | .40 | 5 | |
| Glenn, Robert J., | | | | | | | | | 1, | | | | .40 | 5 | |
| Gardner, Jeptha, | 10 | S. McCorkle, | | 1, | 6, | 12, | | | 1, | | | | .05 | 6¼ | |
| Griffith, Owen, | | | | | | | | | 1, | | | | .40 | 5 | |
| Hendrix, Alfred, | | | | | | | | | 1, | | | | .40 | 5 | |
| Hopper, Forester, | 120, | Hs. Jerome McClain, 3840, | 182, | | 7, | 13, | | | 1, | | | | 1.08 | | |
| Harpole, Moses, | | | | | | | | | 1, | | | | .40 | 5 | |
| Hall, Britton, | 14, | John Atchison, | | 1, | 7, | 13, | | | 1, | 1, | | | 1.29 | 6¼ | |
| House, Isham, | | | | | | | | | 1, | 2, | | | 1.62 | 5 | |
| House, William, | | | | | | | | | 1, | | | | .40 | 5 | |
| Hill, James, | | | | | | | | | 1, | 1, | | | 1.21 | 7½ | |
| Harmon, Israel, | 10, | John Terrell, 640, | 930, | 1, | 7, | 13, | 2, | | 1, | | | | 2.46 | 1¼ | |
| Herd, Bailey E., | 50, | | | | 8, | 13, | 1, | | 1, | 1, | | | 2.49 | 8 | 3/4 |
| Hungerford, Cullin, | | | | | | | 1, | | | | | | .40 | 5 | |
| Hornsby, John, | | | | | | | | | 1, | | | | .81 | 2½ | |

Page 87) (1831) Acres, #of Town, Free Horse
Persons Name Lnd. Titl. R E M A R K S  Ent. Rge., Sec., Dis.Lots,Pbli,Sla. Sto. Jac. $. Cts. M
                        2100)

| Persons Name | Acres, Lnd. | Titl. REMARKS | #of Ent. | Rge., | Sec., | Dis.Lots, | Pbli, | Sla. | Sto. | Horse Jac. | $. Cts. | M |
|---|---|---|---|---|---|---|---|---|---|---|---|---|
| Huntsman, Adam, | 787½, | E. Huntsman & Totten,) | 475, | 3, | 7 &8, | 13, | | | | | 4.42 | 9 |
| Huskey, Archibald, | 67, | | | | | 13, | | | | | .77 | 7 |
| Hornbeak, William, | | | | | | | 1, | | | | .40 | 5 |
| Henry Moses, | | | | | | | 1, | | | | .40 | 5 |
| Horton, Archibald, | | | | | | | 1, | | | | .40 | 5 |
| Horton, James, | | | | | | | 1, | 1, | | | 3.40 | 5 |
| Horton, George, | | | | | | | 1, | | | | .40 | 5 |
| Horton, Robert, | | | | | | | 1, | | | | .40 | 5 |
| Horton, John, | | | | | | | 1, | | | | .40 | 5 |
| Hood, John, | | | | | | | 1, | | | | .40 | 5 |
| Hambly, Joel, | | | | | | | 1, | | | | .40 | 5 |
| Hill & Collier, | 640, | | | | | | 1, | | | | 3.60 | |
| Huggins, William, | | | | | | | 1, | | | | .40 | 5 |
| Huggins, Jeremiah, | | | | | | | 1, | | | | .40 | 5 |
| Howard, John, | | | | | | | 1, | | | | .40 | 5 |
| Huggins, Urbin L., | | | | | | | 1, | | | | .40 | 5 |
| Huggins, James, | | | | | | | 1, | | | | .40 | 5 |
| Hall, Durham, | | | | | | | 1, | | | | .40 | 5 |
| Hall, Thomas, | | | | | | | 1, | | | | .40 | 5 |
| Honeycut, Hiram, | | | | | | | 1, | | | | .40 | 5 |
| Hall, Abraham P., | 150, | Hs.Isaac Burgess 640, | | 1, | 7, | 12, | 1, | 2, | | | 2.87 | 3 3/4 |
| Hill, Henry M., | | | | | | | 1, | | | | .40 | 5 |
| Howard, George W., | 60, | | | 2, | 7, | 12, | 1, | | | | .74 | 2½ |
| Holt, Benjamin, | 252, | 2 Tracts, | | 2, | 7, | 12, | 1, | | | | 1.81 | 7½ |
| Henderson, Robert, | | 2 Tracts, | | | | | 1, | | | | .40 | 5 |
| Howard, Littleton F., | | | | | | | 1, | 1, | | | 1.21 | 7½ |
| Hubbard, William, | | | | | | | 1, | | | | .40 | 5 |
| Holley, Hazel, | | | | | | | 1, | | | | .40 | 5 |
| Henderson, John K., | 100, | | | 2, | 6, | 12, | 1, | | | | .96 | 7½ |
| Hinton, Joseph, | | | | | | | 1, | | | | .40 | 5 |
| Hays, William, | 64, | | | 2, | 5, | 12, | 1, | | | | .75 | 2½ |
| Hunter, John, | | | | | | | 1, | | | | .40 | 5 |
| Highsaw, Frederick, | | | | | | | 1, | | | | .40 | 5 |
| Hoggard, Byars, | | | | | | | 1, | | | | .40 | |
| Hamilton, William, | 50, | | | 1, | 5, | 12, | 1, | | | | .68 | 6¼ |

(Page 88) (1831)

| Persons Name | Lnd., Titl., R E M A R K S | #of Ent.Rge./Dis. | Sec. Lot, | Town lot, | #of Free Poll, | Sla. | Sto. | Horse Mac. | $.Cts. | M |
|---|---|---|---|---|---|---|---|---|---|---|
| Herrod, James, | | | | | 1, | | | | .40 | 5 |
| Harmon, Jesse, | | | | | 1, | | | | .40 | 5 |
| Harrel, John, | | | | | 1, | | | | .40 | 5 |
| Hornbeak, James, | 200, E., 4 Tracts, | | | | 1, | | | | 3.15 | 5 |
| Hughes, Samuel, | | | | | 1, | 2, | | | 1.21 | 7½ |
| Hughes, Archelous, | | | | | 1, | 1, | | | 1.21 | 7½ |
| James, Archibald, | | | | | 1, | | | | .40 | 5 |
| Julen, Richard 0, | 9 3/4, John Terrell,640, | 1, 7, 13, | | | 1, | | | | .45 | 3 3/4 |
| Johnson, William, | 76, 2 Tracts, | | 13, | 4, | 1, | | | | 4.83 | 2 ⅛ |
| Jones, James K., | | | | | 1, | | | | .40 | 5 |
| Jones, Gray, | | | | | 1, | | | | .40 | 5 |
| James, Isaac, | | | | | 1, | | | | .40 | 5 |
| Julen, James J., | 11, | | | | 1, | | | | .46 | 1¼ |
| Jenkins, Jesse, | 320, David Broadwell 640, | 2, 6, 13, | | | 1, | 2, | | | 3.83 | |
| Jenkins, James, | | | | | 1, | 1, | | | 1.21 | 7½ |
| Jenkins, Thomas, | | | | | 1, | | | | .40 | 5 |
| Jeter, Robert, | 3309½ G,3 Tracts,J.& T.Blount, | | 13, | | 1, | 4, | | | 21.86, | 2½ |
| Jenkins, John, | 3050, | | | | 1, | 8, | | | 24.06 | 1¼ |
| Jenkins & Thorp, | 526,E.,Hs. John Evans,640, | 1, 7, 13, | | | 1, | | | | 2.95 | 8 3/4 |
| Jolly, Henry, | 50, David Crider, | 1, 9, 12, | | | 1, | | | | 1.09 | 3 3/4 |
| James, William, | 100, | 1, 8, 13, | | 1, | 1, | | | | 4.40 | 5 |
| Jones, Wille, | 100, | 1, 8, 13, | | | 1, | 3 | | | .56 | 2½ |
| Jolly, Reuben, | | | | | 1, | | | | .40 | 5 |
| Jackson, Newton | | | | | 1, | | | | .40 | 5 |
| Jones, William, | | | | | 1, | | | | .40 | 5 |
| Jones, Thornton, | | | | | 1, | | | | .40 | 5 |
| Johnston, John, | | | | | 1, | | | | .40 | 5 |
| Jones, William, | | | | | 1, | | | | .40 | 5 |
| Jones, Bennet, | | | | | 1, | | | | .40 | 5 |
| Jones, Joshua, | | | | | 1, | | | | .40 | 5 |
| James, Hosea, | 52, | 1012,2, 6, 12, | | | | | | | .29 | 2½ |
| Jennings, Anderson, | | | | | 1, | 1, | | | 1.21 | 7½ |
| Jourden, John, | | | | | 1, | | | | .40 | 5 |
| Jenkins, Mansfield, | | | | | 1, | | | | .40 | 5 |
| Jameson, Samuel, | | | | | 1, | | | | .40 | 5 |

(Page 89) (1831) Desc. Town, #of Free Horse
 #of
Persons Names, Lnd. Title, R E M A R K S - Ent. Rge. Sec. Dis. Lots, Lot, Poll, Sla. Sto. Jac., $.Cts. M

| Persons Names | Lnd. | Title, REMARKS | #of Ent. | Rge. | Sec. | Dis. | Lots | Town, Lot | #of Free Poll | Sla. | Sto. | Horse Jac. | $.Cts. | M |
|---|---|---|---|---|---|---|---|---|---|---|---|---|---|---|
| Kirksey, John C. | | | | | | | | | | | | | | |
| King, Robert, | 150, | E | 765, | 1, | 6, | 13, | 1, | | 1, | | 1, | | 2.21 | 7½ |
| Kirkpatrick, Joseph, | 640, | | | 1, | 7, | 12, | | | | | | | .84 | 3 3/4 |
| Kindred, Elisha H., | | | | | | | | | | | | | 3.60 | |
| Kemp, Joseph B., | 175 | | | | | | | | 1, | | 1, | | .98 | 3 3/4 |
| Kelough, Isaac, | | | | | | | | | | | | | .40 | 5 |
| Kenedy, Sampson, | 121, | | | 2, | 8, | 12, | | | 1, | | 1, | | 1.49 | 3 3/4 |
| Kenedy, Killebrew, | | | | | | | | | 1, | | 1, | | 1.21 | 7½ |
| Killebrew, Elias, | | | | | | | | | 1, | | 1, | | .40 | 5 |
| Kingston, Simeon, | | | | | | | | | | | | | .40 | 5 |
| Kile, Barney C., | | | | | | | | | | | | | .40 | 5 |
| Kissee, Charles, | | | | | | | | | | | | | .40 | 5 |
| Kechum, Solomon, | | | | | | | | | | | | | .40 | 5 |
| Kechum, William, | 16½ | Jas. Baker, | | 1, | 5, | 12, | | | 1, | | | | .49 | 6 |
| Kemp, Francis A., | 174, | John Charlton, 274, | | 1, | 5, | 13, | | | 1, | | | | .98 | 3 3/4 |
| Lawler, Martin, | 200, | | | 1, | 6&7, | 12, | | | 1, | | 1, | | 2.34 | 2½ |
| Landrum, Samuel, | | | | | | | | | | | 2, | | 1.62 | 5 |
| Landrum, Thos. | | | | | | | | | | | | | .40 | 5 |
| Lytle, William P. | 1825, | Part of 2560 | 82, | 1, | 5, | 12, | | | 1, | | | | 10.25 | 3 |
| Love, Robert J., | 600, | 2 tracts | | | | | | | | | | | 3.37 | 3 3/4 |
| Lytle, Archibald, | 118, | Part of 236, | 804, | 2, | 7, | 12, | | | | | | | .66 | 3 3/4 |
| Lindsey, Isaac, | 44, | | 723 | 2, | 7, | 13, | | | | | | | .24 7½ | |
| Levister, Levi, | | | | | | | | | 1, | | | | .40 | 5 |
| Loyd, Thomas | | | | | | | | | 1, | | | | .40 | 5 |
| Lawrence, Joseph, | 25 | | | 1, | 8, | 13, | | | 1, | | | | .14 | 0 3/4 |
| Lasswell, Joseph, | 50 | | | 2, | 9, | 13, | | | 1, | | | | .68 | 6¼ |
| Lakey, William, | | | | | | | | | 1, | | | | .40 | 5 |
| Lasswell, Gilliam, | | | | | | | | | 1, | | | | .40 | 5 |
| Lasswell, Peter, | | | | | | | | | 1, | | | | .40 | 5 |
| Lasswell, Sarah, | 50 | Daniel Lasswell, | | 1, | 9, | 13, | | | | | | | .28 | 1¼ |
| Lews, Thomas | | | | | | | | | 1, | | | | .40 | 5 |
| Langley, Leonard, | 250, | G. Doherty, 1500, | 21, | 2, | 8, | 12, | | | 1, | | 8, | | 8.51 | 1¼ |
| Langley, James T., | | | | | | | | | 1, | | 10, | | 1,13.12 | 5 |
| Lightner, Daniel, | | | | | | | | | 1, | | | | .40 | 5 |

(Page 90)   Acres Desc.                                      #of            Town  Free                P.Carriage/Horse
Persons Name    Lnd. Titl. R E M A R K S - Ent. Rge., Sec. Dis.Lots, Poll, Sla./Sto. Jac.   $. Cts. M.

| Persons Name | Remarks | Free Poll | Sla./Sto. | P.Carriage/Horse Jac. | $ | Cts. | M. |
|---|---|---|---|---|---|---|---|
| Lawrence, Charles J., | | | | | .40 | 5 | |
| Lemmond, David, | | 1, | | | .40 | 5 | |
| Lemmond, Thomas, | | 1, | | | .40 | 5 | |
| Lawrence, William,100, E., | 2, 6, 12, | 1, | | 1, | 3.90 | 5 | |
| Liddle, Francis, | | 1, | | | .96 | 7½ | |
| Montgomery, Daniel,252, | 2, 7, 13, | 1, | | | .40 | 5 | |
| Montgomery, John, 500, Wm. Montgomery, 733, 2, 7, 13, | | | | | 1.41 | 7¼ | |
| Moran, James H., | | | | | 2. 81 | 1¼ | |
| McGavock, Francis, 890  2 Tracts | 13, 2, | | 1,1, | | 7.40 | 5 | |
| McIver, John, 9176, 6 Tracts | | 1, | | | 5.00 | 6¼ | |
| Martin, Andrew L., 320, G., Elijah Pattons 1000,28,1, 9, 13, | | | | | 51.61 | 5 | |
| McLemore & Chartton,890, E.,2 Tracts, 182, 7, 13, | | | | | 1.80 | | |
| McLemore & Greer, 50,R-Bruce Russell 200, 1669, 1, 7&8, 12, | | | | | 5.00 | 6¼ | |
| McLemore & Blackfan,160,Eldridge& Hill,640, 1075, 1, 6, 12, | | | | | .28 | 1¼ | |
| McLemore & Vaulx, 1304,  7 Tracts | | | | | .90 | | |
| McLemore, John C., 6124 3/4, 14 Tracts | | | | | 7.33½ | | |
| Molin, Benjamin, 224,Blakemore,Swaney & Ross, | | 1, | | | 34.45 | 1¼ | |
| McNeely, John, | | 1, | | | 1.66 | 5 | |
| Michael, Thomas, | | 1, | | | .40 | 5 | |
| Mitchel, John, | | 1, | | 1, | 5.21 | 7½ | |
| McClellan, Trigg, | | 1, | | | .50 | 5 | |
| Marshall, Joseph, | | 1, | | | .40 | 5 | |
| Marshall, Robert, | | 1, | | | .40 | 5 | |
| McClain, Charles, | | 1, | | | .40 | 5 | |
| McDaniel, Moses, | | 1, | | | .40 | 5 | |
| Miles, William C., | | 1, | | | .40 | 5 | |
| McIntosh, Solomon, | | 1, | | | .40 | 5 | |
| Moss, Bennit, | | 1, | | | .40 | 5 | |
| Mooney, Kenny, | | 1, | | | .40 | 5 | |
| McMillen, John, | | 1, | | | .40 | 5 | |
| Morris, Mathew J., | | 1, | | 1, | 1.21 | 7 ½ | |
| Moss, Mason, | | 1, | | | .40 | 5 | |
| Majors, Samuel, | | 1, | | | .40 | 5 | |
| Meredith, Daniel, | | 1, | | | .40 | 5 | |

(Page 91)(1831)

| Persons Name | Acres Lnd. | Desc. Titl. | REMARKS | #of Ent. | Rge. | Sec. | Dis. | Town Lot. | Free Poll. | Sla. | Sto. | Horse Jac. | $. | Cts. | M. |
|---|---|---|---|---|---|---|---|---|---|---|---|---|---|---|---|
| Moss, James, | | | | | | | | | 1, | | | | .40 | 5 | |
| McClain, George, | 60, | E., | Part of Jos. Cavitts 268, | | | | | | | | | | .33 | 3/4 | |
| Murrell, John, | | | | | | | | | 1, | | | | .40 | 5 | |
| Murrell, Benjamin, | | | | | | | | | 1, | 3, | | | 2.43 | 7½ | |
| McWhorter, Frankling, | | | | | | | | | 1, | | | | .40 | 5 | |
| McNeely, Michael, | 47, | | 2 tracts, | 2, | 8, | 12, | | | 1, | | | | .66 | 8 3/4 | |
| Mayo, William, | 130, | | Samuel McCorkle, | 2, | 8, | 12, | | | 1, | | | | 1.73 | 6¼ | |
| Mizelle, William, | | | | | | | | | 1, | | | | .40 | 5 | |
| McWhorter, John, | | | | | | | | | 1, | | | | .40 | 5 | |
| McWhorter, George, | | | | | | | | | 1, | | | | .40 | 5 | |
| More, John H., | | | | | | | | | 1, | 2, | | | 2.03 | | |
| Morgan, Samuel, | 413, | | 2 Tracts | 2, | 7, | 12, | 1, | | 1, | 5, | | | 1.79 | 1¼ | |
| McElroy, William T., | | | | | | | | | 1, | | | | .40 | 5 | |
| Miller, Isaac, | | | | | | | | | 1, | | | | .40 | 5 | |
| Miller, Andrew, | | | | | | | | | 1, | | | | .40 | 5 | |
| Mitchael, Archelous, | 240, | | | 2, | 5, | 12, | | | 1, | 2, | | | 2.97 | 5 | |
| McCluskey, John, | | | | | | | | | 1, | | | | .40 | 5 | |
| Moore, James, | | | | | | | | | 1, | | | | .40 | 5 | |
| Moore, John, | 72, | | Part of 2560 | 2, | 5, | 12, | | | 1, | | 1, | | 2.82 | 7½ | |
| Miller, George, | | | | | | | | | 1, | | | | .40 | 5 | |
| Maxwell, William, | | | | | | | | | 1, | | | | .40 | 5 | |
| McLuskey, William H., | | | | | | | | | 1, | | | | .40 | 5 | |
| Mandy, Thomas, | | | | | | | | | 1, | | | | .40 | 5 | |
| McElroy, Equilla, | | | | | | | | | 1, | | | | .40 | 5 | |
| Manard, William W., | | | | | | | | | 1, | | | | .40 | 5 | |
| Moffit, John, | | | | | | | | | 1, | | | | .40 | 5 | |
| Mainard, John, | | | | | | | | | 1, | | | | .40 | 5 | |
| Meadows, Spearman, | | | | | | | | | 1, | | | | .40 | 5 | |
| Montgomery, William, | | | | | | | | | 1, | | | | .40 | 5 | |
| Mathis, Daniel, | | | | | | | | | 1, | | | | .40 | 5 | |
| Montgomery, James, | 100, | | John Terrell, | 1, 6, | 13, | | | | 1, | | | 1 | 3.40 | 5 | |
| Mobly, Ransom, | | | | | | | | | 1, | 2, | | | 2.59 | 2½ | |
| McBride, William, | | | | | | | | | 1, | | | | .40 | 5 | |
| Mosley, Edward, | 400, | | Hs. of Byhel Bell, | 2, 5, | 13, | | | | 1, | 3, | | | 5.09 | 2½ | |
| Maxwell, Jesse, | | | | | | | | | 1, | | | | .40 | 5 | |

(Page 92) (1831)

| Persons Name | Acres Lnd. | Desc. Titl. | REMARKS (1907) | #of Ent.Rge. Sec.Dis.Lot | Town Poll | Free Sla. | Horse Sto. | Jac. | $.Cts. | M |
|---|---|---|---|---|---|---|---|---|---|---|
| Mosley, Robert, | 662, | | E. McIlhatton &Barnett, | 1, 5, 13, | 1, | 12, | | | 13.87 | 8 3/4 |
| Miller, George S., | | | | | 1, | 2, | | | 2.03 | |
| McIntosh, Charles, | | | | | 1, | | | | .40 | 5 |
| Miles, William, | 197, | | | 13, | | | | | 1.10 | 8 |
| Nailing, Nelson, | 106, | | | 1, 6, 13, 2, | | 4, | | | 5.84 | 6¼ |
| Nailing, John, R., | | | | | 1, | | | | .40 | 5 |
| Nailing, James, | | | | | 1, | | | | .40 | 5 |
| Nailing, Willis, | 50, | | John R. Nailing, | | 1, | 2, | | | 2.31 | 1¼ |
| Newton, James, | | | | 1, | | | | | 1.00 | |
| Nowland, Henry, | | | | | 1, | | | | .40 | 5 |
| Newton, James, | | | | | 1, | | | | .40 | 5 |
| Newland, Richard, | | | | | 1, | | | | .40 | 5 |
| Neil, William Hs. | | | | | | | | | | |
| Nell, William, Hs. | 660, | | Part of Andrew Nail, | | | | | | 3.71 | 2½ |
| Nelson, Robert, | 796½, | | 2 Tracts, | | | | | | 4.48 | 1 |
| Owens, Elisha, | | | | | | | | | .40 | 5 |
| Overton, John, | 3354½, | G., | 7 Tracts L. Carter, | 2&3, 9, 13, | 1, | | | | 15.28 | 0¼ |
| Overton & Wharton, | 630, | E, | | 25, 2, 9, 13, | | | | | 3.60 | |
| Owens, Daniel, | 47 3/4, | | Joel Penson, | 2, 7, 13, | | | | | .67 | 1¼ |
| Owen, Charles, | 67, | | Jas. Ward, | 2, 7, 13, | | | | | .37 | 6¼ |
| Owen James, | | | | | | 1, | | | 1.21 | 7½ |
| Oliver Stephen, | | | | | 1, | | | | .40 | 5 |
| Oliver, Isaacs, | 113, | | 2 Tracts | | 1, | | | | 1.04 | 1¼ |
| Oliver, Alexander | | | | | 1, | | | | .40 | 5 |
| Ore,William C. Hs., | 480, | | Hs. Isaac Burgess,640 | | | | | | 2.70 | |
| Outhouse, Israel F., | 28½, | | | 1, 6, 12, | 1, | | | | .56 | |
| Oneel, John, | 115, | | | | | | | | 1.04 | 1¼ |
| Parker & Bishop, | | | | 2, | | | | | 2.00 | |
| Parker, Lorenzo D., | | | | 1, | 1, | | | | 1.40 | 5 |
| Perry, Gideon, | | | | | 1, | | | | .40 | 5 |
| Parker, Gideon, | | | | 1, | 1, | | | | 1.40 | 5 |
| Pursell, Ausbourn, | | | | | 1. | | | | .40 | 5 |

(Page 93) (1831)

| Persons Name | Lnd. | Ttl., REMARKS | #of Ent. | Rge. | Sec. | Dis. | Town Lots | Free Poll | Sla. | Sto. | Horse or Jac. | $.Cts. | M. |
|---|---|---|---|---|---|---|---|---|---|---|---|---|---|
| Peck, John, | 402, | E. | 1353, | 1, | 6, | 12, | | | | | | 2.26 | 1½ |
| Parham, Amosa, | 16, | Abner Jones, | | 1, | 7, | 12, | | | | | | .40 | 5 |
| Payton Baley, | 285, | | | 1, | 8, | 13, | 1, | | | | | 1.60 | 3 |
| Polk, Thomas G., | 2000, | | 197, | 2, | 7 & 8, | 13, | | | | | | 11.25 | |
| Polk & Devereaux, | 2000, | 5 Tracts, | | | | | | | | | | 11.25 | |
| Polk, William, | 5000, | | 51, | 2, | 9, | 13, | | | | | | 28.12 | 5 |
| Polk, Thomas, Hs. | 300, | | 380, | 1, | 5, | 12, | | | | | | 1.68 | 7½ |
| Parker, Isaac, | 512, | | 615, | 2, | 6, | 13, | | | | | | 2.88 | |
| Parham, Thomas, | 200, | James Greer, | | 1, | 6 & 7, | 12, | | | | | | 1.12 | 5 |
| Prater, Josiah, | | | | | | | | 1, | | | | .40 | 5 |
| Prater, Martin, | | | | | | | | 1, | | | | .40 | 5 |
| Patterson, Robert, S., | | | | | | | | 1, | | | | .40 | 5 |
| Pope, John, W., | 160, | John Pope 500, | | | | 13, | | | | | | .90 | |
| Pope, John Heirs, | 180, | Part of same, | | | | 13, | | | | | | 1.00 | 1½ |
| Pope, Samuel, | 160, | | | | | 13, | | | | | | .90 | |
| Perry, John, | 57, | Joel Penson, | | 2, | 6, | 13, | | | | | | .72 | 5½ |
| Parrish, Henderson, | | | | | | | | 1, | | | | .40 | 5 |
| Price, William, | | | | | | | | 1, | | | | .40 | 5 |
| Parrish, John, | 400, | P. & Trustees N.C. | | 2, | 7, | 13, | | 1, | 5, | | | 6.71 | 7½ |
| Pearce, Abel, | | | | | | | | 1, | | | | .40 | 5 |
| Pearce, John, | | | | | | | | 1, | | | | .40 | 5 |
| Paschall, Jesse M., | | | | | | | | 1, | | | | .40 | 5 |
| Palmer, Paul, | 250, | Geo. Doherty Divis. 500, | 21, | 2, | 8, | 12, | | 1, | 10, | | | 9.93 | 7½ |
| Palmer, Smith, | 660, | D. Gillespie 2 tracts, | | | | | | 1, | | | | 3.72 | 2¼ |
| Palmer, Amosa, | | | | | | | | 1, | 1, | | | 1.21 | 7½ |
| Partle, Jesse, | | | | | | | | 1, | | | | .40 | 5 |
| Pettigrue, Ebenezer, | 3584, | G, 3 Tracts, J.G. & T. Blount, | | | | 13, | | | | | | 20.13 | 7¼ |
| Peeples, Samuel, | 200, | E, Shelton & Hamelin, | 1000, | 2, | 7, | 13, | | 1, | 1, | | | 2.34 | 2½ |
| Powel, John, | | | | | | | | 1, | | | | .40 | 5 |
| Powers, Charles, | | | | | | | | 1, | | | | .40 | 5 |
| Powers, Henny, | | | | | | | | 1, | | | | .40 | 5 |
| Pool, Jonathan, | | | | | | | | 1, | | | | .40 | 5 |
| Patton, John M., | | | | | | | | 1, | | | | .40 | 5 |
| Patton, William, | | | | | | | | 1, | | | | .40 | 5 |
| Patton, Thomas, | | | | | | | | 1, | | | | .40 | 5 |

(Page 94) (1831)

| Persons Name | Lnd. Titl. | REMARKS | #of Ent. | Rge. | Sec. | Dis. | Town Lots | Free Poll | Sla. | Sto. | Horse Jac. | $ | Cts. | M. |
|---|---|---|---|---|---|---|---|---|---|---|---|---|---|---|
| Parker, Tristun, | | | | | | | | | | | | .40 | 5 | |
| Penticost, William, | | | | | | | | 1, | | | | .40 | 5 | |
| Price, James, | | | | | | | | 1, | | | | .40 | 5 | |
| Penticost, Scarbrough, | | | | | | | | 1, | | | | .40 | 5 | |
| Price, Sampson, | | | | | | | | 1, | | | | .40 | 5 | |
| Pate, Stephen S., | 50, | E. | 77, | 2, | 6, | 12, | | 1, | 2, | | | 2.31 | 1½ | |
| Parker, William T., | | | | | | | | 1, | | | | .40 | 5 | |
| Parks, Fields, | | | | | | | | 1, | | | | .40 | 5 | |
| Powers, George, | | | | | | | | 1, | | | | .40 | 5 | |
| Pearce, Joseph, | 480, | Elias Smith, 640 | | 1, | 8, | 13, | | 1, | | | | 2.60 | | |
| Robertson, Edward, | | | | | | | | 1, | 1, | | | 1.21 | 7½ | |
| Roffe, Woodson, | | | | | | | | 1, | | | | .40 | 5 | |
| Rogers, Jonathan, T., | 200, | John Terrell, | | 1, | 7, | 13, | | 1, | 4, | | | 4.78 | | |
| Roulhac, George W., | | | | | | | | 1, | 3, | | | 2.84 | 2½ | |
| Revis, John H., | 100, | Wm. Qualls, | | 1, | 7, | 12, | | 1, | | | | .96 | 7½ | |
| Rogers, Jubilee, | 640, | John Terrell, | | 1, | 7, | 13, | 1, | 1, | 7, | | 1, | 15.69 | 2½ | |
| Ralston, Alexander, | 2750, | McLemore & Hopkins, | | | | 13, | | | | | | 15.46 | 8 | 3/4 |
| Rogers, Jubilee V., | | | | | | | | 1, | 1, | | | 1.21 | 7½ | |
| Riaal, Thomas | | | | | | | | 1, | | | | .40 | 5 | |
| Ray, Peters & Jenkins, | 640, | | | | | | | | | | | | | |
| Rogers, John W., | 356, | 2 Tracts, | | | | 13, | 2, | 1, | 6, | | | 3.60 | | |
| Ross, Joshua, | | | | | | | | 1, | | | | 9.28 | | |
| Ross, Lacie, | 40, | | | | | | | 1, | | | | .40 | 5 | |
| Rogers, Job, | 640, | John Jenkins, | | 1, | 8, | 13, | 1, | 1, | 1, | | | 1.44 | 2½ | |
| Ralls, William B., | | | | | | | | 1, | 7, | | | 10.28 | 7½ | |
| Roberds, William, | | | | | | | | 1, | | | | .40 | 5 | |
| Rogers, Thomas, | 119 3/4, | John Rogers, | | 2, | 9, | 12, | | 1, | 1, | | | 1.21 | 7½ | |
| Rogers, Jacob C., | | | | | | | | 1, | | | | 1.07 | 8 | |
| Rea, James N., | 100, | M. Carmichall, 5000, | | 2, | 9, | 12, | | 1, | | | | .40 | 5 | |
| Ridgway, James, | 350, | 2 Tracts, | | 2, | 8, | 12, | | | 4, | | | .56 | 2½ | |
| Ridgway, John, | | | | | | | | | 2, | | | 5.21 | 8 | 3/4 |
| Ridgway & Littlebury, | | | | | | | | 1, | | | | 2.03 | | |
| Ridgway, William, | | | | | | | | 1, | | | | .40 | 5 | |
| Ross, William G., | | | | | | | | 1, | | | | .40 | 5 | |

(Page 95,) (1831)

| Persons Name | Lnd. Titl. REMARKS | Ent. | Rge, | Sec. | Dis. | Lots, | Town Poll, | Free Sla. | Sto. | Horse Jac. | $ | Cts. | M. |
|---|---|---|---|---|---|---|---|---|---|---|---|---|---|
| Russell, George | Hs. 80, E., | 2, | 7, | 12, | | | | | | | .45 | | |
| Russell, Buckner Sr., | 50, Wm. Ralls, | 2, | 7, | 12, | | | | | | | .28 | 1½ |
| Russell, Buckner, Jr., | 3, Jas. Willoughby, | 2, | 7, | 12, | | | | | | | .41 | |
| Ralls, William, | | | | | | | 1, | | | | .40 | 5 |
| Rogers, Josiah, | | | | | | | 1, | | 2, | | 1.62 | 5 |
| Rogers, Thomas, | | | | | | | | | | | .40 | 5 |
| Richmond, Josiah A., | | | | | | | 1, | | 1, | | 1.21 | 7½ |
| Richmond, Ezekiel, | | | | | | | 1, | | | | .40 | 5 |
| Richie, James H., | | | | | | | 1, | | | | .40 | 5 |
| Rachels, William, | | | | | | | 1, | | | | .40 | 5 |
| Rachels, Valentine, | | | | | | | 1, | | | | .40 | 5 |
| Rogers, Jefferson, | 184, Jno. Terrell 640, | 1, | 6, | 13, | | | 1, | | 2, | | 3.06 | 5 |
| Rust, Vincent, | | | | | | | 1, | | | | .40 | 5 |
| Reynolds, Samuel B., | | | | | | | 1, | | | | .40 | 5 |
| Smith, Roddy, | 513, 2 Tracts, R Smith Hs., | | | 13, | | | | | | | 2.88 | 5¼ |
| Stovall, George, | | | | | | | | | 6, | | 4.87 | 5 |
| Smith, James W., | 3318 1/8, Abner Nash,4 Tracts, | | | 13, | | | | | | | 18.65 | 9 |
| Smith, William Hs., | 3431 1/8,Gr. 4 Tracts same, | | | 13, | | | | | | | 19.29 | 9 |
| Simmons, Thomas, | | | | | | | 1, | | | | .40 | 5 |
| Shutley, John M., | | | | | | | 1, | | | | .40 | 5 |
| Stone, Claibown, | | | | | | | 1, | | | | .40 | 5 |
| Spate, James, | | | | | | | 1, | | | | .40 | 5 |
| Ship Benton, | | | | | | | 1, | | | | .40 | 5 |
| Sommers, James, | | | | | | | 1, | | | | .40 | 5 |
| Smart, James H., | | | | | | | 1, | | | | .40 | 5 |
| Smart, Stephen, | 70, E., | 1, | 8, | 12, | | | 1, | | | | .39 | 3¼ |
| Smart, Phillip, | 220, Jas.Somers 3840, | 2, | 6, | 12, | | | 1, | | | | 1.22 | 5 |
| Shutley, Charles M., | | | | | | | 1, | | | | .40 | 5 |
| Shutley, Jacob, | | | | | | | 1, | | | | .40 | 5 |
| Shutley, Joseph, B., | | | | | | | 1, | | | | .40 | 5 |
| Shutley, David, | 80, | 1, | 9, | 13, | | | 1, | | | | .95 | 5 |
| Stephens, Lawrence, | | | | | | | 1, | | | | .40 | 5 |
| Smart, William C., | | | | | | | 1, | | | | .40 | 5 |
| Smart, Laleon, | | | | | | | 1, | | | | .40 | 5 |

(Page)96) (1831)

| Persons Name | Lnd. Titl. | REMARKS - #of Ent.Rge.Set.Dis.Lots,Poll,Sla.Sto. | Town Lots | Free Poll | Sla. | Horse Sto. Jac. | $ | .Cts. | M |
|---|---|---|---|---|---|---|---|---|---|
| Seagreaves, Willie, | | | | | | | | .40 | 5 |
| Siratt, John, | | | | 1, | | | | .40 | 5 |
| Siratt, Walter, | | | | 1, | | | | .40 | 5 |
| Stow, William A., | | | | 1, | | | | .40 | 5 |
| Stanley, Lewis, | | | | 1, | 1, | | | 1.21 | 7½ |
| Stunston, John, | 200,E., | 2, 9, 12, | | 1, | | | | .40 | 5 |
| Stunston, James, | | | | 1, | 4, | | | 4.37 | 5 |
| Stunston, Henry, | 218, | Joseph Cavitt 268, 2, 9, 12, | | 1, | | | | .40 | 5 |
| Summers, John, | | | | 1, | | | | 1.22 | 6¼ |
| Stuart, Samuel T., | | | | 1, | | | | .40 | 5 |
| Sprout, Alexander, | | | | 1, | | | | .40 | 5 |
| Stoker, Edmund, | | | | 1, | | | | .40 | 5 |
| Sommers, James, | 3000, | 3840, 2, 7, 12, | | | | | | 16.87 | 5 |
| Stanford, John, | | | | 1, | | | | .40 | 5 |
| Stanley, Elijah, | 106, | 2, 7, 12, | | 1, | | 1, | | 2.59 | 6¼ |
| Steel, John, | 40, | Porter & McDowel, 2, 7, 12, | | 1, | | | | .63 | |
| Steel, Samuel, | | | | 1, | | | | .40 | 5 |
| Shaw, Daniel, | | | | 1, | | | | .40 | 5 |
| Steel, George R., | 50, | Porter & McDowel, 2, 7, 12, | | 1, | | | | .68 | 6¼ |
| Stallings, John, | | | | 1, | | | | .40 | 5 |
| Shaw, Archibald, | 100, | Doherty & McCorkle, 2, 7, 12, | | 1, | | 2, | | 2.18 | 7½ |
| Sibley, Jacob, | 180, | 1, 7, 12, | | 1, | | 1, | | 2.23 | |
| Standley, Noah, | | | | 1, | | | | .40 | 5 |
| Shepherd, William B.,3100, | | G.,J.G.& T.Blount,3 Tracts, 13, | | 1, | | | | 17.43 | 7½ |
| Shepherd, Charles B.,3500, | | Same, 3 D, 13, | | | | | | 19.68 | 7¾ |
| Shepherd, James, B.,3572, | | Same 3 D. 13, | | | | | | 20.09 | 2½ |
| Shepherd, Richard M.,2754, | | Same 3 D., 13, | | | | | | 15.49 | 1¼ |
| Shepherd, John S., 2638, | | Same, 3 Tracts, 13, | | | | | | 14.83 | 8 3/4 |
| Shepherd, Penelope,S.,2550, | | Same 3 Do. 13, | | | | | | 14.34 | 3 3/4 |
| Smith, Hugh, D., | | | | 1, | | | | .40 | 5 |
| Smith, James, | 240,E., | 640, 1012,2, 6, 12, | | 1, | | | | 1.75 | 5 |
| Starks, Thomas, | 25, | 2, 6, 12, | | 1, | | | | .54 | 1¼ |
| Sneed, Israel, | | | | 1, | | 2, | | 2.03 | |
| Seal, William, | | | | 1, | | | | .40 | 5 |
| Stout, John E., | | | | 1, | | | | .40 | 5 |

(Page 97, 1831)

| Persons Name | Lnd. | Titl. | REMARKS - Ent., Rge. | Sec. | Town | Free/Dis.Lots | Poll | Sla. | Sto. | Horse | Pl. Jac. | Pl. Carg. $ | Cts. M |
|---|---|---|---|---|---|---|---|---|---|---|---|---|---|
| Seel, James B., | | | | | | | 1, | | | | | .40 | 5 |
| Sutten, Lemuel, | | | | | | | 1, | | | | | .40 | 5 |
| Spen, Moses T., | | | | | | | 1, | | | | | .40 | 5 |
| Stone, William, | | | | | | | 1, | | | | | .40 | 5 |
| Span, James, | | | | | | | 1, | | | | | .40 | 5 |
| Stanford, Thomas, | 25, | E., | | 1, | 6,13, | | 1, | | | | | .54 | 1 |
| Sample, Henry A., | | | | | | | 1, | | 1, | | | 5.40 | 5 |
| Sweany, James M., | 768, | | 2 Tracts, H. Belote, | | 13, | | 1, | | | | | 4.32 | 5 |
| Sneed, Samuel R., | | | | | | | 1, | | | | | .40 | 5 |
| Terrell, Peleg, | 327½, | | Jno. Terrell, 3840, | 1, | 6, 13, | | 1, | | | | | 2.24 | 7 |
| Terrell, John, | 3252, | | Different Tracts, 182 | 7, 13, | | | | 7, | | | | 30.98 | 5½ |
| Thomas, Joseph, | 220, | | 2 Tracts, | 1, | 7, 12, | | | 11, | | | | 10.17 | 5 |
| Taylor, Isaac, | 500, | | | 1, | 9, 12½, | | 1, | | | | | 2.81 | 2½ |
| Taylor, Jame P., | 552½, | G, | 3 Tracts L. Carter, | 3, | 9, 13, | | 1, | | | | | 3.2104 | 2½ |
| Terrell, Jepthah, | 500, | E, | Jno. Terrell 3840 | , | 9, 12, | | 1, | 2, | | | | 4.84 | 2½ |
| Thompson, Jacob, | 170, | | Jno. Terrell, 3840, | 1, | 6, 13 | | 1, | 4, | | | | 3.79 | 8 3/4 |
| Totten, Benjamin, | 892½, | | 2100 H & T | 475,3, | 7&8, 13, | | | | | | | 5.02 | 1 |
| Tansil, John, | 45, | | Joel Penson, | | 13, | | 1, | 1, | | | | 1.06 | 5½ |
| Terrell, Patrick, | 100, | | John Terrell, 3840, | | | | 1, | | | | | 1.37 | 5 |
| Tansil, Hiram W., | | | | | | | 1, | 1, | | | | 1.21 | 7½ |
| Thompson, Robert, | | | | | | | 1, | | | | | .40 | 5 |
| Travis, Moses B., | | | | | | 1, | 1, | 1, | | | | 2.21 | 7½ |
| Tucker, Alexander | | | | | | | 1, | | | | | .40 | 5 |
| Todd, William, | | | | | | | 1, | | | | | .40 | 5 |
| Todd, Willie, | | | | | | | 1, | | | | | .40 | 5 |
| Thompson, William, | | | | | | | 1, | | | | | .40 | 5 |
| Thomas, James D., | | | | | | | 1, | 2, | | | | 2.03 | 5 |
| Terrell, John, | 27 7/8, | | S. Majors 50 | 2, 9, | 13, | | 1, | | | | | .15 | 6¼ |
| Thompson, James, | | | | | | | 1, | | | | | .40 | 5 |
| Thompson, Jessee, | 365, | | Jas. Flack, | 470,3, | 9&10,13, | | 1, | 1, | | | | 3.26 | 9½ |
| Thornton, Sterling, | | | | | | | 1, | | | | | .40 | 5 |
| Thornton, Benjamin, | | | | | | | 1, | | | | | .40 | 5 |
| Thornton, Lemuel, | | | | | | | 1, | | | | | .40 | 5 |
| Taylor, Chapman, | 100, | | Jas. Winchester, | | | | 1, | | | | 1, | 3.96 | 7½ |
| Tansil, Edward, | 320, | | Hill 640, | 1, 6, | 13, | | 1, | 4, | | | | 5.05 | |

(Page 98 - 1831)

| Persons Name | Lnd. | Titl. | REMARKS - #of Ent, Rge, Sec. | Dis.Lots | Town Poll | Free Sla. | Sto. | Jac. | $ Cts. M. |
|---|---|---|---|---|---|---|---|---|---|
| Timmons, Joseph B., | | | | | | | | | .40 5 |
| Tucker, Daniel, | | | | | 1, | | | | .40 5 |
| Thomas, John, | 564, | E., | 5 Tracts, | | 1, | 11, | | | 12.11 |
| Travis, Fielding, | | | | 12, | | | | | .40 5 |
| Tate, Jane, | | | | | | | | | .40 5 |
| Tomlinson, Henry, | | | | | 1, | | | | .40 5 |
| Tompkins, Isaac, | | | | | 1, | | | | .40 5 |
| Trentham, Floyd, | | | | | 1, | | | | .40 5 |
| Thomas, William, | | | | | 1, | | | | .40 5 |
| Uhls, Frederick J., | | | | | 1, | | | | .40 5 |
| Ury, Robert, | 268, | | 2 Tracts, 82, | | 1, | 2, | | | 3.53 7½ |
| Vincent, Perry, | 100, | | Peter King, | | 1, | 2, | | | 3.59 4¼ 2½ |
| Vincent, Orrin, | | | | | | | | | 2.00 |
| Vincent, Abner, | 280, | | Jno. Terrell, 3840, | 13, | 1, | | | | 1.53 |
| Vincent, John M., | 100, | | Wm. G. Bowers, | 13, | 1, | 5, | | | 5.03 |
| Vincent, Joseph, | | | | | 1, | 1, | | | 1. 21 7½ |
| Warner, Mears, | 108, | | J. L. D. Smith, | 12, | 1, | 1, | | | 1. 82 2½ |
| Wilson, Alice S., | 27, | | Hs. of Jacob Bell 640,767, | 13, | | | | | .15 2 |
| Warren, John, | | | | | 1, | | | | .40 5 |
| Winston, Josiah, | | | | | 1, | | | | .40 5 |
| Wilson, Lewis, D., | 272, | | 495, | | | | | | 1.53 |
| Willingham, William, 30, | | | Richard Porter, | 12, 4, | 1, | 1, | | | 4.98 1¼ |
| Wilkins, Lewelin, | | | | | 1, | 1, | | | 1.21 7½ |
| Wharton, Jesse, | 1489½, | G, | L.Carter 3 Tracts, | 13, | | | | | 8.37 8¼ |
| Waterhouse, Richard, 797½, | | E, | Wm. Murfree 987½, 776, | 13, | | | | | 4.48 6¼ |
| Ward, Whitmore, J., 75, | | | | 13, | 1, | | | | .82 6¼ |
| Wilson, Joseph, | | | | | 1, | | | | 1.00 |
| White, Tyrel C. | | | | | | | | | |
| Wade, Kenchen, | | | | | 1, | | | | .40 5 |
| Ward, Elijah, | 150, | | Abner Roads, | | 1, | | | | .40 5 |
| Wilkerson, John, | | | | | 1, | | 1, | | 3.84 3 3/4 |
| Williams, Kinchen, | | | | | 1, | | | | .40 5 |
| Weinscot, Andrew, | | | | | 1, | | | | .40 5 |
| Wenston, George, | | | | | | 1, | | | .40 5 .81 2½ |

100

(Page 99, 1831)

| Persons Name | Acres Lnd. | Desc. Titl. | REMARKS #of -Ent.Rge. | Sec. | Dis.Lots | Town Poll | Free Sla. | Horse Sto. Jac. | $.Cts. M. |
|---|---|---|---|---|---|---|---|---|---|
| Winston, John, | | | | | | 1, | | | .40 5 |
| Wright, Jesse, | | | | | | 1, | | | .40 5 |
| Williams, Bartlett, | 100, | E., | Moses B. Travis, | | | 1, | | | 1.37 5 |
| Wood, James O.K., | 50, | | Wm. & Mary K. Roberts, | | | | | 1, | 3.18 6¼ |
| Williams, Allen, | 156, | | Peter Williams, 640, | 2, | 9, 12, | 1, | | | 1.29 2¾ |
| Williams, Ann., | 100, | | Part of same, | 2, | 9, 12, | | | | .56 2½ |
| Workman, Pleasant G., | | | | | | 1, | | | .40 5 |
| Whitus, Mark, | | | | | | 1, | | | .40 5 |
| Wall, Flemmin, | | | | | | 1, | | | .40 5 |
| Wester, William, | | | | | | 1, | | | .40 5 |
| Winsted, Johnston, | | | | | | 1, | | | .40 5 |
| Wilson, Joseph | 350, | | 2 Tracts, Jason Wilson, | 2, | 9, 12, | | 4, | | 5.21 8 3/4 |
| Webb, Nancy, | 228, | | Thos. Deloach | 2, | 8, 12, | | 3, | | 3.72 |
| Webb, Amosa, | | | | | | 1, | 1, | | 1.21 7½ |
| Wooten, Stephen, | | | | | | 1, | | 1, | 4.40 5 |
| Wooten, William, | | | | | | 1, | | | .40 5 |
| Ward, Messer, | 10, | | | 1, | 7, 12, | 1, | | | .40 8 3/4 |
| Willoughby, James, | 17, | | 2 Tracts, | 1, | 7, 12, | 1, | | | .41 7½ |
| Wells, Hayden, E., | 200, | | Shelta S. Hayden, | 2, | 7, 12, | 1, | 2, | | 3.15 5 |
| Williamson, Merideth, | | | | | | 1, | | | .40 5 |
| Ward, William, | | | | | | 1, | | | .40 5 |
| Williams, Newborn, | 27½, | | 640 | 1012, 2, 6, 12, | | 1, | | | .14 3¼ |
| Ward, William, | | | | | | 1, | | | .40 5 |
| Willis, Andrew, | | | | | | 1, | | | .40 5 |
| Wells, Sarah, | | | | | | | 1, | | .81 2½ |
| Williams, Briant, | | | | | | 1, | | | .40 5 |
| Ward, Britton, | | | | | | 1, | | | .40 5 |
| Winters, Aron, | 112, | | | 1, 10, | | 1, | 1, | | 1.44 2½ |
| Williams, Elisha, | 640, | | | | | 1, | | | 3.60 |
| Ward, John B., | | | | | | 1, | | | .40 5 |
| Welsh, John, | 28 3/4, | | | 1, 6, 12, | | 1, | | | .56 5 |
| Williams, Thomas, | | | | | | 1, | | | .40 5 |
| Williams, Allin S., | | | | | | 1, | | | .40 5 |
| Ward, George, | | | | | | 1, | | | .40 5 |
| Williams, Zachariah, | 240, | | Bexter Bolins &640, | 1, 6, 12, | | | 5, | | 5.36 2½ |

(Page 100)

| Persons Name | Land. Titl. | REMARKS - | #of Ent. | Rge. | Sec. | Dis. Lots, | Town Poll, | Free Sla. | Sto. | Horse Jac. | $ . Cts. M |
|---|---|---|---|---|---|---|---|---|---|---|---|
| Williams, Martin, | Hs. | | | | | | | | | | |
| Warren, Benjamin, | | | | | | | 1, | | | | .40 5 |
| Warren, Samuel, A., | 240, | By the Bells | 640, | 1, | 5, | 13, | 1, | | | | .40 5 |
| Yarbrough, Davis, | 715, | E. Geo. Doherty Divis., | 150, | 2, | 7, | 12, | 1, | 2 | | | 3.38 |
| Young, Henry J., | | | | | | | | | | | 4.02 2 |
| Young, Levi, | | | | | | | 1, | | | | .40 5 |
| Zimmerman, John, | | | | | | | 1, | | | | .40 5 |
| Dick N & G., | 1095, | E., 2560 Thos. Henderson, | | | | 13, | 1, | | | | .40 5 |
| Same, | 360, | Same, | | | | | | | | | 6.72 2 |
| Jones, Israel, | 640, | | | | | | | | | | 2.02 5 |
| Polk, Marshal T. Hs., | 200, | G., E. Patton | 500, | 28, | | 13, | 1, | 2, | | | 5.63 |
| Polk, Samuel, Hs. | 128, | E., P. Williams, | 640, | | | 12, | | | | | 1.12 5 |
| | | | | | | | | | | | .72 |

(P.101)    DANIEL DELANEYS LAST WILL & TESTAMENT RECORDED 16th August, 1831.

STATE OF TENNESSEE )
WEAKLEY COUNTY

In the name of God Amen. -

Tho being under much affliction of body yet believing myself to be in my right mind . Think proper to make this my last will & Testament for the purpose of disposing of my real and personal property in the way I think best for the benefit of my surviving family andin the first place wish to bequeath my soul unto God who gave it and secondly do give and bequeath unto my beloved wife Polly ll my possessions of land with house and plantation whereon Neal Delaney now lives with all the benefits arising there from during her widowhood or until such time as my youngest son Virgil shall become of age then the said premises to be equally divided between my two beloved sons, Sidney Clay and Virgil Delaney. Furthermore I give unto my wife Polly all and everyarticle of my household and kitchen furniture  also one axe, one hoe, one plow and set of Geers, one grubbing hoe, one cow & calf one colt, also one fifty dollar note that my brother Neal Delaney owes me Due first of April next. Two sows, thirty shoats, thirty barrels of corn and all the fodder I have  I have also cotton for family use, six hundred pounds of pork at killing time to have and to hold during her natural life time.   Also say that present crop of cotton shall be appropriated to the use of paying I. H. Moran my account for the present year and if any cotton left, it put to the use of buying salt and such articles as my family shall need for the pursuant year, also all the rest of my effects either in property cash or notes so managed by my executors as to pay all of my just debts accord-

(Page 101) Cont.

ing to contract and so much of the rest of said money detained in the hands of my Executors as shall be sufficient to clear my land out of the office whenever the same is opened and the balance if any so managed by my execu&shy;tors as it shall be put to the use of my family at any time when they need also for the purpose of schooling my children also do certify that
(Page 102) I have hereunto appointed Moses T. Spann and Neal Delaney as my lawful Executors for the purpose of executing this my last will and Testament given under my hand this 25th October 1830.

```
                                              his
Witnesses     )                       Daniel  X  Delaney, (Seal)
Thomas King,  )                              Mark
Archibald Jones )
```

STATE OF TENNESSEE WEAKLEY COUNTY COURT, January Term, 1831.

Then was the within will of Daniel Delaney produced in open court and the due execution thereof as the last will & Testament of said Delaney, proven by the oaths of Thomas King & Archibald Jones the sub&shy;scribing witnesses thereto and ordered to be recorded.

Wm. H. Johnson, Clerk.

---

COLLECTORS BOND 1831 RECORDED 16th August, 1831

STATE OF TENNESSEE )
WEAKLEY COUNTY     )

Know all men by these presents that we Alfred Gardner, John Jenkins, John Terrell, Benjamin Bondurant and John A. Gardner all of Weakley County and State of Tennessee are held and firmly bound unto William Carroll Governor of the state of Tennessee for the time being and his successors in office in the sum of one thousand five hundred dollars in which sum well and truly to be paid as aforesaid we bind ourselves our heirs &c Jointly and severally firmly by these presents sealed with our seals and dated the 13th Day of July, 1831.

The condition of the above obligation is such that whereas the above bound Alfred Gardner hath been appointed by the Justices of the county court of Weakley County - Sherriff & Collector of the public Taxes in the said county. Now if the said Alfred Gardner shall well & faithfully pay over to the treasurers of the state of Tennessee for the Western District all the taxes which he may be bound by law to collect & pay to t the said Treasurer of the state of Tennessee for the year 1831 within the
(Page 104) time prescribed by law for such payment of said state tax and according to the tenor thereof, Then the above obligation to be void else to remain in full force and virtue.

```
                                          Alfred Gardner, (Seal)
Signed sealed & acknowledged)             Jno. Terrell, (Seal)
in open court.              )             Benjm. Bondurant, (Seal)
Test. Wm. H. Johnson, Clerk )             John A. Gardner, (Seal)
```

(Page 104 ) Cont.
To Trustee:
### COLLECTORS BOND FOR 1831 RECORDED AUGUST 16th, 1831.

STATE OF TENNESSEE )
WEAKLEY COUNTY     )

Know all men by these presents that we Alfred Gardner, John Terrell, John Jenkins John A. Gardner & Benjamin Bondurant all of the County of Weakley & state of Tennessee are held and firmly bound unto Tyril C. White Chairman of the county court of Weakley County and his successors in office in the sum of five thousand dollars in the payment of which sum well and truly to be made we bind ourselves our heirs &c Jointly & severally firmly by these presents signed with our names & sealed with our seals and dated this the 13th day of July 1831.

The condition of the above obligation is such that whereas Alfred Gardner hath been appointed sheriff & collector of the taxes within said county by the Justices of the county. Now if said Alfred Gardner shall well & truly pay over to the Trustee of said county all moneys & taxes which by law he may be bound to collect and pay over to the said Trustee for the year 1831 within said county to wit: the county tax, Jury tax, and poor tax and public building tax laid by the county court for said year within the time and acording to the terms prescribed by law Then the above obligation to be void else to remain in full force & virtue.

Signed sealed and acknowledged )   Alfred Gardner, Seal,
in open court                  )   John Jenkins, Seal
Test. Wm. H. Johnson, Clk      )   Benjn. Bondurant, (Seal)
                                   Jno. Terrell, Seal
                                   Jno. A. Gardner, Seal

---

(Page 105)

Recorded March 8th, 1832.

Know all men by these presents that we Alfred Gardner, Joseph Thomas, John A. Gardner, Benjamin Bondurant & George Stovall all of the county of Weakley and State of Tennessee are held and firmly bound with William Carroll Esquire Governor of the state of Tennessee and his successors in office in the penal sum of six Thousand Dollars for the true and faithful payment of which we bind ourselves and Each of our heirs Executors and administrators Jointly and severally firmly by these presents sealed with our seals and dated the tenth Day of January, 1832.

The condition of the above obligation is such that whereas the above bound Alfred Gardner has been this Day duly elected and appointed sheriff in Deed for the county of Weakley for the ensuing two years. Therefore, should the said Alfred Gardner well & truly collect and pay over all fines forfeitures and Immersments and other sums of money that may become due and intrusted to him for collection during the time for which he the said Alfred Gardner shall be the incumbent of said office of sheriff then in that case the above obligation to be void otherwise to remain in full force and effect.

(Page 105) Cont.

```
Signed and acknowledged)          Alfred Gardner, Seal
   in open court          )       Jos. Thomas,    Seal
Wm. H. Johnson, Clk.      )       John M. Gardner, Seal
                                  Benjn. Bondurant, Seal
                                  George Stovall, Seal
```

---

(Page 106)

Recorded March the 8th, 1832.

Know all men by these presents that we Alfred Gardner, Benjamin Bondurant, Joseph Thomas, John A. Gardner & George Stovall all of the County of Weakley and state of Tennessee are held and firmly bound unto William Carroll, Esquire, Governor of the state of Tennessee for the time being and his successors in office in the penal sum of Ten Thousand Dollars and to secure the payment thereof we bind ourselves, our heirs, Executors and administrators Jointly and severally firmly by these presents sealed with our seals and dated the tenth Day of January, 1832.

The condition of the above obligation is such that whereas the above Alfred Gardner has been this day duly elected sheriff for Weakley County for the Insuing two years by the Justices of the court of pleas and quarter sessions for said county. Now if the said Alfred Gardner shall due return make upon all process & precepts to him Directed and pay and satisfy all fees and sums of money by him received or levied by virtue of any process unto the proper office by which the same by the tenor thereof ought to be paid or to the person or persons to whom it may be due his, her or their heirs Executors administrators attorneys or agents and in all other things well and truly and faithfully Executed the said office of sheriff according to law During his continuance in office then the above obligation to be void otherwise to remain in full force & virtue.

```
Signed, sealed and acknowledged  )    Alfred Gardner, (Seal)
in open court. Wm. H. Johnson Clk.)   Jos. Thomas, (Seal)
                                      John A. Gardner, (Seal)
                                      Benjn. Bondurant, (Seal)
                                      George Stovall, (Seal)
```

(Page 107)     Tax List for the year of 1832.

| Persons Name | Lnd. | Titl. R E M A R K S | #of Ent. | Rge. | Sec. | Dis. | Town Lots, | Free Poll, | Sla. | Sto. | Horse Jac. | $ .Cts. M. |
|---|---|---|---|---|---|---|---|---|---|---|---|---|
| Anderson Bailey Heirs, | 640, | E. | 603, | 1, | 9, | 13, | | | | | | 4.37 5 |
| Anderson, William, | 640, | | 805, | 2, | 7, | 12, | | | | | | 4.37 5 |
| Same, | 171, | | 829, | 1, | 10, | | | | | | | 1.16 7½ |
| Adams, Hardin S., | | | | | | | | 1, | | | | .53 |
| Adams, Charles, | | | | | | | | 1, | | | | .53 |
| Allen, Hugh, | | | | | | | | 1, | | | | .53 |
| Anderson, Burrell, | | | | | | | | 1, | | | | .53 |
| Adkison, William D., | | | | | | | | 1, | | | | .53 |
| Adkison, Welford, | | | | | | | | 1, | | | | .53 |
| Ashbrook, Moses, | | | | | | | | 1, | | | | .53 |
| Adkison, Edward, | 100, | Peter King, | 914, | 1, | 7, | 13, | | 1, | | | | 1.21 5 |
| Austin, Vincent, | | | | | | | | 1, | | | | .53 |
| Abernathy, Littleton F., | 81½ | | 1260, | 2, | 9, | 12, | | 1, | | | | 1.09 |
| Austin, Moses, Jr. | 100, | Peter Williams | 640, | 2, | 9, | | | 1, | | | | 1.21 5 |
| Austin, Moses Sr., | 156, | Same, | 327, | | | | | | | | | 1.07 2½ |
| Acre, Jesse, | | | | | | | | | | | | .53 |
| Adkins, Joseph R., | 30, | (1000) | | 2, | 7, | | | 1, | | | | .73 5 |
| Alexander, Augus, | 200, | Shelton &Haneline, | 1045, | 2, | 7, | | | 1, | 5, | | | 6.67 |
| Alexander Randolph, | | | | | | | | 1, | | | | .53 |
| Armstrong, John, | | | | | | | | 1, | 1, | | | 1.59 |
| Armstrong, Lynus, | | | | | | | | 1, | | | | .53 |
| Arnold, Furney, | 262½ | Thomas Hopkins, | 1173, | 2, | 6, | | | 1, | | | | 2.53 |
| Alexander, Adam, | 660, | | | 1, | 7, | 13, | | 1, | | | | 4.52 2½ |
| Adams, Abel Hs. | 88 | | | 1, | 5, | | | 1, | | | | .60 5 |
| Allen, James, | | | | | | | | 1, | 6, | | | 6.89 |
| Atkins, William, | 500, | Jno. W. Philpot, | | 3, | 6, | | | 1, | 6, | | | 9.78 |
| Allen, Nicholas, | 220, | Huntsman & Totten, | 2100, | 3, | 7&8, | 13, | | | | | | 1.50 5 |
| Brinkley, William, | 512, | Hs.Sion Williams, | 640, | 2, | 5 & 6, | 12, | | | | | | 3.50 7½ |
| Brehen, James G., | 800, | Part of 1000 | 109, | 3, | 7, | 13, | | | | | | 5.48 |
| Same, | 192, | Part of 240 | 601, | 1, | 9, | 12, | | | | | | 1.31 5 |
| Bredberry, James, | 258, | Hs. Richard Smith | 640, 715, | 3, | 5, | 13, | | | | | | 1.76 5 |
| Same, | 255, | Hs Richard Smith | 640, 602, | 1, | 8, | | | | | | | 1.74 |
| Butler, William E., | 352, | Robert Bitten, | 452, 693, | 1, | 7, | 13, | | | | | | 2.41 |
| Total | 6,218 | | | | | | | | | | 18 18 | |

(Page 108)

| Persons name | Lnd. Titl. REMARKS | #of Ent. | Rge. | Sec. | Town Dis. | Free Lots | Poll | Sla. | Horse Sto. | Jac. | $.Cts. M. |
|---|---|---|---|---|---|---|---|---|---|---|---|
| Bowers, Giles | | | | | | | | | | | .53 |
| Bondurant, Hillery H., | | | | | | 1, | | | | | |
| | 5 | | | | | (94) | | | | | 6.05 5 |
| Bondurant, Albert G., Jno. Terrell 640, | | 1,2 | 2, | 13, | 3(95,96),1, 2, | | | | | | |
| | 640, E.,Hs.Elijah Ward, | 348, 1, | 9, | 12, | 1,#23, 1, | 2 | | | | | 8.15 |
| Same 80, Three Tracts, | | | | 13, | | | | | | | .55 |
| Bayliss, Willie 1/8, John Terrells 640, | | 1, | 7, | 13, | | 1, | 2 | | | | 2.68 |
| Bayliss, Cullen, 2 5/8, Same, | | 1, | 7, | | | 1, | 4, | | | | 4.78 5 |
| Bayless, & Clements | | | | | | | | 1, | | | 5.00 |
| Bayless, C & W., | | | | | | | | | | | 3.37 5 |
| Berry, Presley,M. | | | | | | | | | | | .53 |
| Bondurant,Benjm. 145½ Ralph King, | | 1455, 1, | 6, | 12, | 3,(#16,17),1,<br>7,(36,48) | | | | | | 21.58 5 |
| Same, 226½, Jas. Winchester, | | 641 3, | 7, | 13, | (67,78,85) | 12, | | | | | 1.55 |
| Same, 109, Two Tracts, | | | | | | | | | | | .74 5 |
| Bell, Pulaski B., | | | | | | | 1, | | | | .53 |
| Baldridge, Daniel, 640, | | 725, 2, | 7, | | | | | | | | 4.37 5 |
| Bowling, Baxter, 160, Part of 640, | | 1082, 1, | 6, | 12, | | | | | | | 1.09 5 |
| Basley, John, 808, G, | | 309, | | | | | | | | | 5.53 5 |
| Same, 553, | | 313, | | | | | | | | | 3.78 7 ½ |
| Same, 300, | | 316, | | | | | | | | | 2.05 |
| Baldridge, Wm. 458, E., | | 2, | 7, | 13, | | | 1, | | | | 3. 12 5 |
| Baldridge, Andrew W.,65, | | 2, | 7, | | | | 1, | | | | .97 5 |
| Bradshaw, Thompson,30, | | 2, | 7, | | (775) | | 1, | | | | .75 5 |
| Bondurant,Robt.M.166 2/3,Hs. Jerome McClain, | | 2, | 7, | | | | 1, | | | | 2.73 |
| Barham, Benjamin, (3840) | | | | | | | 1, | | | | .53 |
| Bennit, George, | | | | | | | 1, | | | | .53 |
| Brain, Peter H., | | | | | | | 1, | | | | .53 |
| Bowers, Young P., | | | | | | | 1, | 2, | | | 2.65 |
| Bledsoe, Jacob, | | | | | | | 1, | 1, | | | 1.59 |
| Bynum, Thomas, | | | | | | | 1, | | | | .53 |
| Brand, James, 100, McLemore & Voulk, | | 2, | 9, | 12, | | | 1, | | 1, | | 1.21 5 |
| Buckley, James, | | | | | | | 1, | | 1, | | 1.06 |
| Buckley, Walter W., | | | | | | | 1, | | | | .53 |
| Buckley, Coleman, | | | | | | | 1, | | | | .53 |
| Brooks, William &Sebley,R. A.Love, ( 500,) | | 2, | 7, | | | | 1, | | | | 3.43 5 |

(Page 108) Cont.

| Persons Name, | Lnd., | Title. | REMARKS | #of Ent. | Rge. | Sec. | Dis.Lots | Town, Lot. | #of Poll | Free Sla. | Sto. | Horse Jac. | $.Cts. M |
|---|---|---|---|---|---|---|---|---|---|---|---|---|---|
| Boaz, Edmund, | | | | | | | | | 1, | | | | .53 |
| Barns, Solomon, | | | | | | | | | 1, | | | | .53 |
| | 4 993½ Acres | | | | | | | | | | | | |

(Page 109) (1832)

| | | | | | | | | | | | | | |
|---|---|---|---|---|---|---|---|---|---|---|---|---|---|
| Brooks, William, | | | | | | | 14, | | | 21,27, | 1, | | 3.18 |
| Brown, Conrad, | 50, | E, | | 1794, | 2, | 7, 12, | | | | 3, | | | 1.87, 2½ |
| Betts, Samuel, | D., | | | | | | | | 1, | | | | .53, 53 |
| Brewner, John, | | | | | | | | | 1, | | | | .53 |
| Busey, Susan, | | | | | | | | | | 4, | | | 4.24 |
| Barnard, George, | | | | | | | | | 1, | | | | .53 |
| Barnard, Pleasant, | 200, | | | | | 1, 5, 12, | | | 1, | | | | 1.90 |
| Barnard, William, | 300, | | | | | 1, 5, 12, | | | 1, | | | | 2.58  5 |
| Barnard, Caleb, | | | | | | | | | 1, | | | | .53 |
| Barnard, John, | | | | | | | | | 1, | | | | .53 |
| Billingsley, Bazel, | | | | | | | | | 1, | 1, | | | 1.59 |
| Bookout, Bradley, | | | | | | | | | 1, | | | | .53 |
| Blackley, James, | | | | | | | | | 1, | | | | .53 |
| Bradshaw, Henry, | | | | | | | | | 1, | 1, | | | 1.59 |
| Briges, Griffin, | | | | | | | | | 1, | | | | .53 |
| Bowers, William G., | 88½, | Two Tracts, | | 917, | 1, | 13, | | | 1, | 3, | | | 4.25 |
| Bourland, James, | 25, | | | | 1, | 6, | | | 1, | 3, | | | 3.88 |
| Brassfield, Caleb, | | | | | | | | | 1, | 5, | | | 5.83 |
| Baker, John, | | | | | | | | | 1, | | | | .53 |
| Bradshaw, John, | | | | | | | | | 1, | 2, | | | 2.65 |
| Bradshaw, Gideon T., | | | | | | | | | 1, | | | | .53 |
| Brown, James B., | | | | | | 2, | | 1, 28, | 1, | | | | 1.12  ½ |
| Byrd, Nazareth, | 53, | John Jenkins, | | | | 2, 6, | | | 1, | 1, | | | 1.95  2½ |
| Blakemore Willie B., | | | | | | | | 1, 54, | 1, | | | | .53 |
| Butt, John, | | | | | | | | | 1, | | | | .53 |
| Berger, Daniel, | D., | | | | | | | | 1, | | | | .53 |
| Byars, William, | 100, | Robert Butler, 452, | | 693, | 1, | 7, 13, | | | 1, | | | | .68  5 |
| Breedlove, Robert, | | | | | | | | | | 1, 1, | | | 1.59 |
| Cherry, Lawrence, | 640, | | | 52 | 2, | 9, 12, | | | | | | | 4.37  5 |
| Same, | 228, | | | 625, | 2, | 7, 13, | | | | | | | 1.36 |
| Same, | 213, | | | 1457, | 1, | 6, 12, | | | | | | | 1.45  5 |
| Cherry, Daniel, | 640, | Isaac Bateman, | | 676, | 1, | 8, 13, | | | | | | | 4.37  5 |
| Same, | 640, | | | 672, | | | | | | | | | 4.37  5 |
| | 3327½ | | | | | | 2, | | | 25, 25 | | | |

(Page 110)    Acres-Desc.                              Town  #of  Free                                    Horse
Persons  Name, Lnd.Titl. R E M A R K S - Ent. Rge.Sec.Dis. Lots, Lot, Poll,Sla. Sto. Jac.  $ .Cts. M

| Name | Remarks | Ent. | Rge. | Sec. | Dis. | Lots | Lot | Poll | Sla. | Sto. | Jac. | $ | .Cts. | M |
|---|---|---|---|---|---|---|---|---|---|---|---|---|---|---|
| Cherry, Darling,640,E# | | 769, | 2, | 9, | 12, | | | | | | | 4. | 37 | 5 |
| Claborn, Thomas,300,G. Landon Carter, | | 314, | 3, | 9, | 13, | | | | | | | 2. | 05 | 2½ |
| Same, 300, Same | | 324, | 3, | 9, | | | | | | | | 2. | 05 | 2½ |
| Same, 409, Same | | 322, | 3, | 9, | | | | | | | | 2. | 80 | 2½ |
| Clark, Levi, | | | | | | | | 1, | 1 | | | 1. | 59 | |
| Clark, James W.,3925,E, Part of 5000, | | 104, | 3 | 8, | 13, | | | | | | | 26. | 88 | 5 |
| Clark, Christopher,R., (1000) | | | | | | | | 1, | | | | | .53 | |
| Charlton, John, 178, Hs. Joseph Green | | 850 | 2, | 7, | | | | | | | | 1. | 21 | 7½ |
| Same, 209  2 tracts, | (858, 1,  7, 13,) 2, 10 &ll, 1, 2, | (1323, 2, 9, 12,) | | | | | | | | | | 6. | 32 | 7½ |
| Same, 190, Wm. Murphy,987½ | | 774, | | | | | | | | | | 1. | 30 | |
| Same, 370½, Hs; Jacob Bell 640, | | 767, | 1, | 7, | 13, | | | | | | | 2. | 53 | 5 |
| Same, 213 1/3, Thomas Dillon, | | 771, | 2, | 5, | | | | | | | | 1. | 45 | 6¼ |
| Same, 79, | | 1045, | 2, | 5, | | | | | | | | | .49 | 2½ |
| Chester, Henry W.,300, Jno. Terrell 3840,566, | | | 1, | 6, | | | | | 1, | 2 | | 4. | 70 | 2½ |
| Cotton, Charles, 640, | | 1366, | 1, | 5, | 12, | | | | | | | 4. | 37 | 5 |
| Cherry, Clemigle,520, | | 1043 | | | | | | | | | | 3. | 56 | 2½ |
| Catron, John, 1000, J.G. & Thos. Blount 258 | | | 1, | 6 | | | | | | | | 6. | 85 | |
| Childress, James,80, Elijah Robertson 500 | | 337, | 2, | 9, | 13 | | | | | | | | .54 | 7½ |
| Cowan, James, 640, E, | | 391, | 1, | 10, | | | | | | | | 4. | 37 | 5 |
| Same, 146, Dougherty &McCorkle, | | | 2, | 6, | 12, | | | | | | | 1. | | |
| Cooke, Willis, | | | | | | | | 1, | | | | | .53 | |
| Carmakel, Michael,3400, Part of 5000 | | 115, | 2, | 9&10, | 13, | | | | | | | 23. | 29 | |
| Campbell, Geo.W.,250, Thos. Jackson 1036,439, | | | 2&3, | 5, | | | | | | | | 1. | 71 | 2½ |
| Cochran, Dennis,160,  2 Tracts, | | | | | | 3,69,70,71,1, | 2, | | | | | 7. | 12 | |
| Clements, Robt.W., | | | | | | | | 1, | | | | | .53 | |
| Castle, John, | | | | | | | | 1, | | | | | .53 | |
| Claxton, James, 160, | | | | | | | | 1, | | | | 1. | 62 | 6¼ |
| Chambers, Greenbury, | | | | | | | | 1, | | | | | .53 | |
| Chambers, Willis, | | | | | | | | 1, | | | | | .53 | |
| Canada, Brethlem, | | | | | | | | 1, | 2, | | | 2. | 12 | |
| Crider, Wenston B., | | | | | | | | 1, | | | | | .53 | |
| Come, Amos T., | | | | | | | | 1, | | | | | .53 | |
| Casada, Jesse, | | | | | | | | 1, | | | | | .53 | |
| Clark, David, | | | | | | | | 1, | | 1, | 2.50, | 3. | 03 | |

(Page 110)

| Persons Name | Acres Lnd. | Titl. | REMARKS | #of Ent. | Rge. | Sec. | Dis. | Town Lots, | Lots, | #of Lot, | Free Poll, | Sla. | Horse Sto. | Jac. | $ | Cts. | M |
|---|---|---|---|---|---|---|---|---|---|---|---|---|---|---|---|---|---|
| Cavitt, John F., | 180, 14289 3/4 | | | 847, | 2, | 9, 2, | 12 | 5, | | | 1, 16, | 1, 10, | 1 | 12.50, | | 2.82 | 1/2 |

(Page 111) (1832)

| Persons Name | Acres | Titl. | REMARKS | Ent. | Rge. | Sec. | Dis. | Lots, | Lot, | Poll, | Sla. | Sto. | Jac. | $ Cts. | M |
|---|---|---|---|---|---|---|---|---|---|---|---|---|---|---|---|
| Cannon, John | | | | | | | | | | 1, | | | | .53 | |
| Cashen, Elam M. | | | | | | | | | | 1, | | | | .53 | |
| Clark, William, | | | | | | | | | | 1, | | | | .53 | |
| Cooke, Margaret, | 40, | E., | John Cooke, | 1747, | 2, | 10, | 12, | | | 1, | | | | .27 | 5 |
| Colman, John, | | | | | | | | | | 1, | | | | .53 | |
| Carsley, Seth T., | | | | | | | | | | 1, | | | | .53 | |
| Canada, Killebrew, | | | | | | | | | | 1, | | | | 1.59 | |
| Canada, Sampson, | 121, | | Swan | | 2, | 8, | | | | 1, | 1, | | | 1.88 | 5 |
| Clayton, John, | 270, | | Thomas Henderson | 640, | 2, | 7, | | | | 1, | 3, | | | 5.56 | 2½ |
| Clayton, Martin, | | | | | | | | | | 1, | 2, | | | 2.65 | |
| Cooper, Lewis, | | | | | | | | | | 1, | | | | .53 | |
| Croslin, James, | | | | | | | | | | 1, | | | | .53 | |
| Carler, Reubin, | | | | | | | | | | 1, | | | | .53 | |
| Christmas, Richard G., | | | | | | | | | | 1, | | | | .53 | |
| Casselman, Lazarus G., | | | | | | | | | | 1, | | | | .53 | |
| Cruse, Isaac, | 320, | | Joseph Alsap, | 640, | 1012, | 2, | 6, | | | 1, | | | | 2.71 | 7½ |
| Cotton, Solomon, | 800, | | Micajah, Thomas, | 1000, | 143, | 1, | 5 & 6, | | | 1, | | | | 5.48 | |
| Campbell, Daniel, | | | | | | | | | | 1, | 1, | | | 1.06 | |
| Cox, Edward M., | | | | | | | | | | 1, | | | | .53 | |
| Crow, Garland T., | | | | | | | | | | 1, | | | | .53 | |
| Cox, Henry B., | | | | | | | | | | 1, | | | | .53 | |
| Cox, Riley, | | | | | | | | | | 1, | | | | .53 | |
| Cantrell, Richard, | | | | | | | | | | 1, | | | | .53 | |
| Cantrell, Abraham, | | | | | | | | | | 1, | | | | .53 | |
| Cantrell, Joseph, | | | | | | | | | | 1, | | | | .53 | |
| Cantrell, Duke, | 135, | | | | | 1 & 2, | 5, | 13, | | 1, | | | | 1.45 | 5 |
| Crabtree, Anderson, | | | | | | | | | | 1, | | | | .53 | |
| Coley, George, | 70, | | Robert Watson | 140, | 455, | 2, | 5, | | | 1, | | | 1, | 2,3.01 | |
| Cravens, John, | | | | | | | | | | 1, | 1, | | | 1.06 | |
| Cravens, Joseph, | | | | | | | | | | 1, | 3, | | 1, | 2,5.18 | |
| Cooper, James, | | | | | | | | | | 1, | | | | .53 | |

(Page 110)Cont. Acres #of                          Town #of Free
Persons Name , Lnd. Titl. Ent. R E M A R K S *    Rge. Sec. Dis. Lots,Lot,Poll,Sla. Sto. Jac. $ Cts. M

| Persons Name | Acres Lnd. | Titl. Ent. | REMARKS | Rge. | Sec. | Dis. | Lots | Lot | Poll | Sla. | Sto. | Jac. | $ Cts. M |
|---|---|---|---|---|---|---|---|---|---|---|---|---|---|
| Chaplin, Moses, | | | | | | | | | | | | | .53 |
| Canada, James, | 170, | | | 1, | 5, | | | | 1, | | | | 1.69  5 |
| Curlin, Zacheus H., | 640, | 355, | Benjn. McCullock, | 3, | 9, | | | | 1, | | | | 4.90  5 |
| Chilton, William, | 300, | | | 2, | 5, | 12, | | | 1, | | | | 2.05  5 |
| | 2866, | | | | | | | 28, | 12, | 2, | 4, | | 30.82  5 |
| (Page 112) (1832) | | | | | | | | | | | | | |
| Craig, Ebenezer, | 40, | E. | Joel Penson, | 2, | 7, | 13, | | | 1, | | | | .80  5 |
| Cannon, Isham, | | | | | | | | | 1, | | | | .53 |
| Dent, Joseph E, | 7, | 767, | Hs. Joab Bell,640, | 1, | 7, | | | | 1, | | | | .57  5 |
| Devereaux, Thos.P. | 500, | 967, | | 1, | 5, | 12, | | | | | | | 3.42  5 |
| Dunnar Anthony Hs. | 640, | 1326, | | 2, | 9, | | | | | | | | 4.39  5 |
| Doherty, George, | 4500, | 98, | Part of 5000, | 3, | 9, | 13, | | | | | | | 30.82  5 |
| Same, | 862, | 937, | Part of 942, | 1 & 2, | 7, | 12, | | | | | | | 5.90  5 |
| Dickens, Samuel, | 364, | | | 1, | 5, | | | | | | | | 2.49  2½ |
| Same, | 200, | (set) | | 1, | 5, | | | | | | | | 1.37 |
| Same, | 605, | 631, | | 1, | 9 &10, | | | | | | | | 4.14  2½ |
| Dailey, Edward, | | | | | | | | | 1, | | | | .53 |
| Davis, Phenuel, | | | | | | | | | 1, | | | | .53 |
| Davis, Thomas, | | | | | | | | | 1, | | | | .53 |
| Davis, George, | | | | | | | | | 1, | | | | .53 |
| Drew, James H., | | | | | | | | | 1, | | | | .53 |
| Davis, Jonathan, | | | | | | | | | 1, | | | | .53 |
| Damron, Moses, | | | | | | | | | 1, | | | | .53 |
| Damron, John, | 35, | | | 1, | 8, | 12, | | | 1, | | | | .76  7½ |
| Damron, Constantine, | | | | | | | | | 1, | | | | .53 |
| Dawson, Isaac, | | | | | | | | | 1, | 1, | | | 1.59 |
| Damron, Charles, | | | | | | | | | 1, | | | | .53 |
| Damron, George, | 50, | 949, | | 1, 8, | 8, | 13, | | | 1, | | | | .96  5 |
| Damron, Samuel, | | | | | | | | | 1, | | | | .53 |
| Doherty, Dennis, | | | | | | | | | 1, | | | | .53 |
| Delaney, Elijah, | | | | | | | | | 1, | | | | .53 |
| Davis, Jesse B., | | | | | | | | | 1, | | | | .53 |
| Dotson, William, | | | | | | | | | 1, | | | | .53 |
| Danulson, Humphrey, | 180, | 392, | | 1, | 9, | 12, | | | 1, | | | | 1.23, 5 |
| Dunn, Mathew P., | | | | | | | | | 1, | | | | .53 |
| Davis, Isham S., | | | | | | | | | 1, | 1, | | | 1.59 |
| Davis, Jesse, | | | | | | | | | 1, | | | | .53 |
| Delaney, Niel, | | | | | | | | | 1, | | | | .53 |

(Page 112)Cont. Acr. Desc. #of                                    Town, #of Free

| Persons name | Lnd. | Titl. Ent. REMARKS - Rge., | Sec. | Dis. | Lots, | Lot, | Poll, | Sla. | Sto. | Jac. | $ .Cts. M |
|---|---|---|---|---|---|---|---|---|---|---|---|
| Dickson, Ephriam D., |  |  |  |  | 1, |  |  | 1, | 2, |  | 3.77 5 |
| Dickins, Samuel, | 500, | 1249, Henderson & Bras- | 2, | 6, |  |  |  |  |  |  | 3.42 5 |
| Darling, James S., |  | (field, 1000) |  |  |  |  |  | 1, | 1, |  | 1.59 |
| Eli Edwards, | 8543, |  |  |  |  |  |  |  |  |  |  |

(Page 113)

| | | (1832) (2560) | | | | | | | | | |
|---|---|---|---|---|---|---|---|---|---|---|---|
| Eley, Eli, | 200, | E, 735,Hs. Benjn.Coffield, 1, | 5, | 13, |  |  | 1, | 26, | 5, |  | 1.90 |
| Edwards, Thomas C., |  |  |  |  |  |  | 1, |  |  |  | .53 |
| Edwards, Thos. S., | 179, | two tracts Bursel Anderson | | | | | | | | | |
| | | & Hs. & Joseph Greer, | 2, | 6, |  | 1, | 30 |  |  |  | 2.87 |
| Eaves, Solomon, |  |  |  |  |  |  | 1, |  |  |  | .53 |
| Eaves, Robertson, |  |  |  |  |  |  | 1, |  |  |  | .33 |
| Eaves, Thomas J., |  |  |  |  |  |  | 1, |  |  |  | .53 |
| Eliott, George S., | 575, | 2 Tracts,525 Thomas Anderson, | 1, | 8, |  |  | 1, | 4, |  |  | 8.51 5 |
| Eaves, Bartlett, |  |  |  |  |  |  | 1, |  |  |  | .53 |
| Ethridge, Thomas, |  |  |  |  |  |  | 1, |  |  |  | .53 |
| Early Samuel, |  |  |  |  |  |  | 1, |  |  |  | .53 |
| Edmonston, Jesse,1, | 767, | Hs. Jacob Bell 640, | 1, | 7, | 13, | 1, | 1, 72, |  |  |  | 1.66 |
| Edmonston, Reubin, |  |  |  |  |  |  | 1, |  |  |  | .53 |
| Edmonston, James, |  |  |  |  |  |  | 1, |  |  |  | .53 |
| Fonville,John B. 5, |  | Jno. Terrills 640, | 1, | 7, |  | 1, | 1, 92, |  |  |  | 2.75 |
| Fuller, Joseph, |  |  |  |  |  |  | 1, |  |  |  | .53 |
| Fowler, William, |  |  |  |  |  |  | 1, |  |  |  | .53 |
| Fowler, Stephen, |  |  |  |  |  |  | 1, |  |  |  | .53 |
| Fowler, Thomas, |  |  |  |  |  |  | 1, | 3, |  |  | 3.71 |
| Forbis, Amarine M. |  |  |  |  |  |  | 1, |  |  |  | .53 |
| Freeman, John, |  |  |  |  |  |  | 1, |  |  |  | .53 |
| Freeman, Chas.A., | 100, | 963, James M. Long, | 1, | 7, |  |  | 1, |  |  |  | 1.21 5 |
| Farmer, Hewlitt, |  |  |  |  |  |  | 1, |  |  |  | .53 |
| Freeman, Richardson, |  |  |  |  |  |  | 1, |  |  |  | .53 |
| Fields, Absolom, |  |  |  |  |  |  | 1, |  |  |  | .53 |
| Fowler, John, |  |  |  |  |  |  | 1, | 2, |  |  | 2.12 |
| Fowler,Billard,A., |  |  |  |  |  |  | 1, | 1, |  |  | 1.59 |
| Farmer, Jesse, |  |  |  |  |  |  | 1, |  |  |  | .53 |
| Frizell, Jason, |  |  |  |  |  |  | 1, |  |  |  | .53 |

(Page 113) Cont. Acres Des.#of                                Town,#of Free           Horse
Persons Name,          Lnd.Title,Ent. R E M A R K S - Rge. Sec. Dis, Lots,Lot,Poll,Sla.Sto. Jac.  $ . Cts.  M.

| Persons Name | Acres | Des.#of Lnd. | Title,Ent. REMARKS | Rge. | Sec. | Dis | Lots | Lot | Poll | Sla. | Sto. | Jac. | $ | Cts. | M. |
|---|---|---|---|---|---|---|---|---|---|---|---|---|---|---|---|
| Fletcher, Jefferson, | | | | | | | | | 1, | | | | | .53 | |
| Fields, David, | | | | | | | | | 1, | | | | | .53 | |
| Farmer, Aron, | | | | | | | | | 1, | | | | | .53 | |
| Farmer, Hiram, | | | | | | | | | 1, | | | | | .53 | |
| Fike, John, | | | | | | | | | 1, | | | | | .53 | |
| Freeman, William, | | | | | | | | | 1, | 4, | | | | 4.77 | |
| Forbis, Lorenzo D., | 1060 | | | | | | 1, | 39, | 1, | 1, | | | 2, | 2.71 | 5 |
| | | | | | | | 4, | | 34, | 16, | | | | | |

(Page 114)

| Persons Name | Acres | Des.#of Lnd. | Title,Ent. REMARKS | Rge. | Sec. | Dis | Lots | Lot | Poll | Sla. | Sto. | Jac. | $ | Cts. | M. |
|---|---|---|---|---|---|---|---|---|---|---|---|---|---|---|---|
| Freeman, Evans, | 100,E, | 1542, | Porter & McGavock, | 2, (34&3/4) | 7, | 12, | | | 1, | 3, | | | | 4.39 | 5 |
| Frizell, Isaac, | 150, | | John H. Moore, | 2, | 7, | | | | 1, | 5, | | | | 6.33 | |
| Foley, Jesse, | | | | | | | | | 1, | | | | | .53 | |
| Finch, John W., | 25, | | | 1, | 6, | 13, | | | 1, | 2, | | | | 2.82 | 1¼ |
| Foree, William, | | | | | | | | | 1, | | | | | .53 | |
| Flemming, William, | 1664, | | 8 Tracts, | 2 & 3, | 5&6, | 12, | | | 1, | 8, | | | | 20.45 | |
| Fowler, Jason, | | | | | | | | | 1, | | | | | .53 | |
| Foley, Townsend, | | | | | | | | | 1, | | | | | .53 | |
| Furlong, Hudson, | | | | | | | | | 1, | | | | | .53 | |
| Fitzgerald, William, | 11, | | John Terrells 640, | 1, | 7, | 13, | | | 1, | 2, | | | | 2.72 | 5 |
| Guion, Alveh, | | | | | | | 1, | 26, | 1, | | | | | 1.12 | 5 |
| Glenn, Robert J., | | | | | | | | | 1, | 2, | | | | 2.65 | |
| Griffith, Abel, | | | | | | | | | 1, | | | | | .53 | |
| Griffith, Owen, | 10, | | Absolom Jones, | 1, | 6, | 12, | | | 1, | | | | | .59 | 7½ |
| Gleeson, Wm. W., | | | | | | | | | 1, | 2, | | | | 2.65 | |
| Glass, Dudley Jr., | | | | | | | | | 1, | | | | | .53 | |
| Gaston, William, | 640, | | | 3, | 7, | 13, | | | 1, | | | | | 4.37 | 5 |
| Gardner, John A., | 10, | | Jno. Terrells 640, | 1, | 7, | | 2, | 37,38, | 1, | 3, | | | | 6.02 | 7½ |
| Gardner, Alfred, | 69, | | Same, | 1, | 7, | | 3,18,19, | | 1, | | | | | 4.37 | 5 |
| Gordon, David, | 640, | | John C. McLemore, | 2, | 8, | | (51) | | 1, | | | | | 4.37 | 5 |
| Same, | 800, | | 671, Blakemore & Pat-terson, 867) | | | | | | | | | | | | |
| Same, | 120, | 674, | Henry Belotes 640, | 2¼, 2, | 7, 7 | 13, | | | 1, 1, | 5, | | | | 5.84 .82 | 1½ |
| Gardner, Jeptha, | | | | | | | | | 1, | | | | | 5.83 | |
| Garrett, Henry A., | | | | | | | 1, | 21, | | | | | | 1. 65 | 5 |
| Glass, Dudley,Sr., | | | | | | | | | 1, | 8, | | | | 8.48 | |
| Gardner, Jesse, | | | | | | | | | 1, | 3, | | | | 3.71 | |
| Greer, Aquilla P., | | | | | | | | | 1, | | | | | .53 | |

(Page 114) Cont. Acres Desc. #of　　　　　　　Town #of Free　　　　　　　Horse
Persons Name, Lnd., Titl. Ent. R E M A R K S - Rge. Sec. Dis. Lots, lot,Poll,Sla.Sto. Jac. $ . Cts M/

| Name | Acres | Desc. #of Titl. Ent. | REMARKS | Rge. | Sec. | Dis. | Town Lots | #of lot | Free Poll | Sla. | Sto. | Horse Jac. | $.Cts | M/ |
|---|---|---|---|---|---|---|---|---|---|---|---|---|---|---|
| Gains, Wilson, | 37, | | Daniel Baldridge, | 2, | 7, | | | | | | | | .78 | 2½ |
| Gillespie, William, | | | | | | | | | 1, | | | | .53 | |
| Galloway, Glidwell, | 0,150 | | 952,David Broadwell, | 640, 2, | 6, | | | | 1, | | | | 1.56 | |
| Galoway, Benjamin, | 150, | | 952, Same | 2, | 6, | | | | 1, | | | | 1.56 | |
| Gardner, Richard W., | | | | | | | | | 1, | | | | .53 | |
| Glover, Henry, | | | | | | | | | 1, | | | | .53 | |
| Gibbs, Jesse, | | | | | | | | | 1, | | | | .53 | |
| Garrett, Noah, | 100, | | 1985, Tavhere Wisdom, | 2, | 7, | 12, | | | 1, | | | | 1.21 | 5 |
| | 4676 | | | | | | 7, | | 28, | 43, | | | | |
| (Page 115) (1832) | | | (344 3/4) | | | | | | | | | | | |
| Gilliam, Henry, | 142, | | | | | | | | 1, | | | | .53 | |
| Gilliam, Grey, | 485, | | 1542,Porter & McGavock, | 2, | 7, | 12 | | | 1, | 1, | | | 2.03 | 5 |
| Greer, James, | 53, | | | | | | | | | | | | 3.33 | 2½ |
| Same, | | | | | | | | | | | | | .36 | 2½ |
| Gilbert, Jonathan M., | 91½ | | | | 2, | 7, | 13, | | 1, | 3, | | | 4.33 | 5 |
| Gilbert, Robert R., | 64, | | 767,Hs.Joab Bell | 640, 2, | 5, | 12, | | | 1, | 2, | | | 3.09 | |
| Gilbert, Randolph | | | | | | | | | 1, | 1, | | | 1.59 | |
| Goldsby, James, | | | | | | | | | 1, | 4, | | | 4.24 | |
| Goldsby, Stephen, | | | | | | | | | 1, | | | | .53 | |
| Green, Moses, Admr. | 60, | | E. Busby, | 2, | 5 | | | | | | | | .41 | 2½ |
| Gaily, Thomas, | | | | | | | | | 1, | | | | .53 | |
| Galley, Isaac, | | | | | | | | | 1, | | | | .53 | |
| Garner, John, | | | | | | | | | 1, | | | | .53 | |
| Garner, John, | | | | | | | | | 1, | | | | .53 | |
| Garner, Stephen, | | | | | | | | | 1, | | | | .53 | |
| Grooms, Stephen H., | 200 | | | 1, | 6, | | | | 1, | | | | 1.87 | |
| Geter, Robert, | 350, | | | 1& 2, | 5, | 13, | | | 1, | 9, | | | 11.94 | 5 |
| Geter, Samiel, | | | | | | | | | 1, | 5, | | | 5.83 | |
| Gailey, James, | | | | | | | | | 1, | | | | .53 | |
| Grooms, Bright, | | | | | | | | | 1, | | | | .53 | |
| Blasco, Isaac, | | | | | | | | | 1, | | | | .53 | |
| Guinn, Malcolm, | 124, | | Maxwell, | | | 12, | | | | | | | .85 | 2½ |
| Harbert, John, | 640, | 561 | Daniel Cherry, | 1, | 7, | 13, | 1, | 90, | 1, | 2, 1, | | | 13.15 | |
| Hopkins, Thomas | 3750, | 817 | McLemore & Hopkins, | 5000, 1 &2, | 7 &8, | | | | | | | | 25-68 | 7½ |
| Harris, Nathan, | | | | | | | | | | | | | .53 | |

(Page 115)Cont.

| Persons Name | Acres Lnd. | Desc. Tit. | #of Ent. | REMARKS | Rge. | Sec. | Town Dis. | #of Lots | Free Lot | Poll | Sla. | Sto. | Horse Jac. | $. | Cts. | M |
|---|---|---|---|---|---|---|---|---|---|---|---|---|---|---|---|---|
| Herd, Bailey, E., | 50, | | 930, | | | 1, 8, | 13, | 1, | 15, | 1, | 1, | | | 3.05 | 7½ | |
| Husky, Archibald, | 67, | | 671, | Blakemore & Patterson, | 2, | 7, | 13, | | | 1, | | | | .98 | 7½ | |
| Hendrix, Payton, | 50, | | | Daniel Baldridge, | 2, | 7, | | | | 1, | | | | .87 | 2½ | |
| Hornbock, William, | | | | | | | | | | 1, | | | | .53 | | |
| Hughes, Joseph, B., | 100, | | 931, | Archelous Hughes, | 1, | 7, | | | | | | | | .68 | 5 | |
| Hendrix, Jeremiah, | 228, | | 496, | | 2, | 8 &9, | | | | | | | | 1.56 | | |
| Harmon, Israel, | | | | | 2, | 14 &40, | 1, | | | | | | | 2.78 | | |
| Hill, Alfred, | | | | | | | | | | 1, | | | | .53 | | |
| Higgs, Alfred, | 150, | | 684, | Scarbrough &Sels 213 3/4, | 1, | 7, | | | | 1, | | | | 2.62 | | |
| Hill, James, | | | | | | | | | | 1, | 1, | | | 1.59 | | |
| Hungerford, Cullen, | | | | | | | | | | 1, | | | | .53 | | |
|  | 6604½ | | | | | | | 4, | 24, | 30, | 1, | | | | | |

(Page 116)

| Persons Name | Acres | Desc. Tit. | #of Ent. | REMARKS | Rge. | Sec. | Town Dis. | #of Lots | Free Lot | Poll | Sla. | Sto. | Horse Jac. | $. | Cts. | M |
|---|---|---|---|---|---|---|---|---|---|---|---|---|---|---|---|---|
| Herd, Martin, | | | | | | | | | | 1, | | | | .53 | | |
| Hughes & Gardner, | | | | | | | | | | 1, | 1, | | | 6.12 | 5 | |
| Hendrix, Alfred, | 119,E, | | 775, | Hs.Jerome McClain,5840, | 1 & 2, | 7, 13, | | 1, 46, | | 1, | | | | 1.34 | 5 | |
| Horton, John, | | | | | | | | | | 1, | | | | .53 | | |
| Horton, George, | | | | | | | | | | 1, | | | | .53 | | |
| Horton, James, | | | | | | | | | 1, | 1, | | | | 1.65 | 5 | |
| Horton, Archibald, | | | | | | | | | | 1, | | | | .53 | | |
| Horton, Robert, | | | | | | | | | | 1, | | | | .53 | | |
| Hall, James, | | | | | | | | | | 1, | | | | .53 | | |
| Hall, Samuel, | | | | | | | | | | 1, | | | | .53 | | |
| Hornsby, John, | | | | | | | | | | 1, | 1, | | | 1.06 | | |
| House, Isham, | | | | | | | | | | 1, | 3, | | | 3.18 | | |
| House, William F., | | | | | | | | | | 1, | | | | .53 | | |
| Houston, John, | | | | | | | | | | 1, | | | | .53 | | |
| Howard, Shedrick, | | | | | | | | | | 1, | 1, | | | 1.59 | | |
| Hays, David, | | | | | | | | | | 1, | 2, | | | 2.65 | | |
| Hamblin, Joel, | | | | | | | | | | 1, | | | | .53 | | |
| Huggins, Jerimah, | | | | | | | | | | 1, | | | | .53 | | |
| Huggins, Urbin, L., | | | | | | | | | | 1, | | | | .53 | | |
| Huggins, William, | | | | | | | | | | 1, | | | | .53 | | |
| Hernderson, Robert, | | | | | | | | | | 1, | | | | .53 | | |
| Henderson, John, | | | | | | | | | | 1, | | | | .53 | | |
| Howard, John, | | | | | | | | | | 1, | | | | .53 | | |

(Page 116) Cont. Acres, Desc. #of          Town,    #ofFree                              Horse
Persons Name,  Lnd., Titl, Ent. R E M A R K S - Rge., Sec. Dis., Lots, Lot, Poll, Sla. Sto. Jac $.Cts. M

| Persons Name | Acres | Desc/Titl/Ent | REMARKS - Rge., Sec.Dis., Lots | Lot | Poll | Sla. | Sto. | Horse Jac | $.Cts. | M |
|---|---|---|---|---|---|---|---|---|---|---|
| Howard, Geo. W., | 60, | | 2 Tracts, 2, 7, 12, | | 1, | | | | .94 | 2 |
| Honeycut, Heram, | | | | | 1, | | | | .53 | |
| Hall, Durham, | | | | | 1, | | | | .53 | |
| Hall, Thomas, | | | | | 1, | | | | .53 | |
| Holt, Benjamin, | 252, | | Two Tracts, | | 1, | 2, | | | 4.38 | |
| Hall, Abraham P., | 140, | | Hs. Isaac Bergers, 640, | | 1, | 1, | | | 2.55 | $2\frac{1}{2}$ |
| Henderson, John K., | 50, | | Part of 100, 2, 6, | | 1, | | | | .87 | 5 |
| Howard, Littleton, | | | | | 1, | 1, | | | 1.59 | |
| Henderson, Robert, | | | | | 1, | | | | .53 | |
| Hubert, William, | | | | | 1, | | | | .53 | |
| Hays, William, | 64, | | | | 1, | | | | .97 | |
| Howard, Enoch, | | | | | 1, | | | | .53 | |
|  | 685 | | | 2, | 32, | 11, | 1 | | | |

(Page 117, ) (1832)

| Persons Name | Acres | Desc/Titl/Ent | REMARKS | Lot | Poll | Sla. | Sto. | Horse Jac | $.Cts. | M |
|---|---|---|---|---|---|---|---|---|---|---|
| Hunter, William, | | | | | 1, | | | | .53 | |
| Hopper, Forester, | 100, | | 1, 5, 12, | | 1, | | | | 1.21 | 5 |
| Hoggard, Byers, | | | | | 1, | | | | .53 | |
| Hinton, Joseph, | | | | | 1, | | | | .53 | |
| Hisaw, Frederick, Sr., | | | | | 1, | | | | .53 | |
| Hisaw, Frederick, Jr., | | | | | 1, | | | | .53 | |
| Hughes, Archelous, M. | | | | | 1, | | | | .53 | |
| Josiah, Harmon, | | | | | 1, | | | | .53 | |
| Harmon, Jesse, | | | | | 1, | | | | .53 | |
| Hays, Moses, | | | | | 1, | | | | .53 | |
| Herrod, James, | | | | | 1, | | | | .53 | |
| Hamilton, William, | 50, E, | | 1, 5, 13, | | 1, | | | | .87 | $1\frac{1}{4}$ |
| Hornbeak, James, | 200, | | 4 Tracts, 1, 5, | | 1, | 2, | | | 3.49 | 5 |
| Hughes, Samuel, | 100, | | Abm. Charlton, 274, 2, 5, | | 1, | 1, | | | 2.27 | 5 |
| Hardin, | | | | | 1, | | | | .53 | |
| Huling, Frederick W. | 1000, | | G., J.G. & T. Blount, 1, 5, | | 1, | | | | 6.08 | 5 |
| Hopkins, Richard, | 30, | | 2, 5, | | | | | | .20 | 5 |
| Herrold, John, | | | (2100) | | 1, | | | | .53 | |
| Huntsman, Adem, | $787\frac{1}{2}$ | E.475, | Huntsman & Totten 3, 7 & 8 | | 1, | | | | 5.40 | |
| Henry, Moses, | | | | | 1, | | | | .53 | |
| Jinkins, Jesse, | 320, | 952, | David Broadwell, 640, 2, 6, | | 1, | 2, | | | 4.84 | $1\frac{1}{2}$ |

(Page 117) Cont. Acres, Desc.                #of              Town #of Free                              Horse
Persons Name,  Lnd. Titl. R E M A R K S     Ent. Rge. Sec. Dis.Lots,Lot,Poll,Sla. Sto. Jac. $ .Cts. M

| Persons Name | Lnd. | Titl. REMARKS | Ent. | Rge. | Sec. | Dis.Lots | Lots,Lot | Poll | Sla. | Sto. | Jac. | $ .Cts. | M |
|---|---|---|---|---|---|---|---|---|---|---|---|---|---|
| Julin, Richard O., | 1100, | | | | | | | | | | | .53 | |
| Jenkins, John, | 1920 | Terrell & Jenkins, | 1274, | 2, | 6, | | | 1, | | | 6, | 14.45 | 2½ |
| Same, | | James Terrell 2560 | 1360, | 1 &2, | 5&6,12, | | | 1, | | | | 13.15 | 2½ |
| Same, | 640, | James Hart, | | 2, | 6, | 13, | | | | | | 4.37 | 5 |
| Jackson, Robt. | 306, | Thomas Jackson 1036, | 439, | 2, | 5, | | | | | | | 2.09 | 5 |
| James, James W., | 200, | Part of Same, | 439 | 2, | 5, | | | | | | | 1.37 | |
| Jones, Gray, | | | | | | | | 1, | | | | .53 | |
| Jones, James K., | | | | | | | | 1, | | | | .53 | |
| James, Isaac, | | | | | | (83,84) | 1, | | | | | .53 | |
| Johnson, Wm. H., | 81½, | 2 Tracts, | | | | 13, | 4;12 | 82,1, | | | | 5.85 | 5 |
| Jones, Israel, | 640, | Robert Browder, | | 2, | 7, | | | 1, | | | 2, | 7.02 | 5 |
| Johnson, Wm. H., | 160, | A. B. Foree, | | 2, | 6, | | | | | | | 1.09 | 5 |
| Japlin, John, | | | | | | | | 1, | | | | .53 | |
| Jenkins, Thomas, | | | | | | | | 1, | | | | .53 | |
| | 7635 | | | | | | 4, | 26, | 13 | | | | |

(Page 118)

| Persons Name | Lnd. | Titl. REMARKS | Ent. | Rge. | Sec. | Dis.Lots | Lots,Lot | Poll | Sla. | Sto. | Jac. | $ .Cts. | M |
|---|---|---|---|---|---|---|---|---|---|---|---|---|---|
| Jones, William, | | | | | | | | 1, | | | | .53 | |
| Jones, Thornton, | | | | | | | | 1, | | | | .53 | |
| Jones, Willie, | 100, E., | | | 1, | 8, | 13, | | 1, | | | | .68 | 5 |
| Jolly, Reubin, | | | | | | | | 1, | | | | .53 | |
| Jones, William, | 100 | | | 1, | 8, | | 1, | 1, | | | 2, | 4.46 | |
| Johnston, John, | | | | | | | | 1, | | | | .53 | |
| Jones, Hiram, | | | | | | | | 1, | | | | .53 | |
| Jones, Jorden, | | | | | | | | 1, | | | | .53 | |
| Jones, Joshua, | | | | | | | | 1, | | | | .53 | |
| Jones, William, | | | | | | | | 1, | | | | .53 | |
| Jones, Bennit, | | | | | | | | 1, | | | | .53 | |
| Jzell, Urias, | | | | | | | | 1, | | | | .53 | |
| Jzell, James, | | | | | | | | 1, | | | | .53 | |
| Jones, Drury D., | | | | | | | | 1, | | | | .53 | |
| Jzalle Harison, | | | | | | | | 1, | | | | .53 | |
| Jorden, John, | | | | | | | | 1, | | | | .53 | |
| Jennings, Anderson H., | | | | | | | | 1, | 1, | | | 1.59 | |
| Jenkins, Marfield, | | | | | | | | 1, | | | | .53 | |
| Jones, Archibald, | | | | | | | | 1, | | | | .53 | |
| Jarvis, David, | | | | | | | | 1, | | | | .53 | |

Page 118)       Acres Desc.                    Town  #of Free
Persons Name,   Lnd.,Titl.- R E M A R K S - Ent.Rge.Sec. Dis.Lots, Lot,Poll, Sla. Sto. Jac.,$ .Cts. M

| Name | Acres | Remarks | Ent. | Rge. | Sec. | Dis.Lots | Lot | Poll | Sla. | Sto. | Jac. | $ | .Cts. | M |
|---|---|---|---|---|---|---|---|---|---|---|---|---|---|---|
| Jameson, Samuel | | | | | | | | 1 | | | | | .53 | |
| Julin, James J. | 9 3/4, | Jno. Terrell,640, | 1, | 7, | | | | 1, | | | | | .59 | 2½ |
| Jones, John, | | | | | | | | 1, | | | | | .53 | |
| Jenkins, James, | | | | | | | | 1, | 1, | | | | 1.59 | |
| Jones, Calvin, | 2560, | | 438, | 3, | 5, | | | | | | | | 17.60 | |
| King, Robert, | 150, | Part of 200, | 765, | 1, | 6 | | | | | | | | 1.02 | 7½ |
| Kirkpatrick, Jos. | 640, | | 1, | 7, | 12, | | | | | | | | 4.37 | 5 |
| Kindred, Elisha H., | | | | | | | | 1, | | | | | .53 | |
| Kemp, Joseph, | 175, | Thos. & John Jenkins, | 3, | 6, | | | | | | | | | 1.19 | 3 3/4 |
| Kelough, Isaac, | | | | | | | | 1, | | | | | .53 | |
| Killebrew, Elias, | | | | | | | | 1, | | | | | .53 | |
| Kyle, Barney C., | | | | | | | | 1, | | | | | .53 | |
| Kissel, Charles, | | | | | | | | 1, | | | | | .53 | |
| Ketchum, William, | | | | | | | | 1, | | | | | .53 | |
| Kemp, Frances, | 174, | Abram Charlton,274, | 2, | 5, | 13, | | | | | | | | 1.19 | 5 |
| | 3908 3/4 | | | | | | | 1, | 29, | 4, | | | | |

Page 119)

| Name | Acres | Remarks | Ent. | Rge. | Sec. | Dis.Lots | Lot | Poll | Sla. | Sto. | Jac. | $ | .Cts. | M |
|---|---|---|---|---|---|---|---|---|---|---|---|---|---|---|
| Love, Charles I. | 100, | E. Robert Wilson, | 242, | 2,8 & 9, | 13, | | | | | | | | .68 | 5 |
| Lytle, Archibald, | 236, | | 804, | 2, | 7, | 12, | | | | | | | 1.61 | 5 |
| Lindsey, Isaac, | 44, | | | 2, | 7, | 13, | | | | | | | .30 | |
| Lawler, Marlin, | 200, | 2 Tracts, | | 1, | 6 &7, | 12, | | | 1, | | | | 2.95 | 6¼ |
| Landrum, Thomas, | | | | | | | | 1, | | | | | .53 | |
| Long, James M. | | | | | | | | 1, | | | | | .53 | |
| Little, Wm. P., | 1825, | Part of 2500, | 82, | 1, | 5, | | | | | | | | 12.50 | |
| Landrum, Samuel, | | | | | | | | | 2, | | | | 2.12 | |
| Levister, Levi, | | | | | | | | 1, | | | | | .53 | |
| Lovin, James, | | | | | | | | 1, | | | | | .53 | |
| Lasswell, Peter, | | | | | | | | 1, | | | | | .53 | |
| Lasswell, Joseph, | 50, | | | 2, | 9, | 13, | | 1, | | | | | .87 | 2½ |
| Lasswell, Sarah, | 123, | 3 Tracts, | | 2, | 9, | | | 1, | | | | | .84 | 7½ |
| Lasswell, Jesse, | | | | | | | | 1, | | | | | 1.59 | |
| Lakey, William, | | | | | | | | 1, | | | | | .53 | |
| Laws, William, | | | | | | | | 1, | | | | | .53 | |
| Lawrence, Joseph, | 25, | | 1, | 8, | | | | 1, | | | | | .17 | 1¼ |
| Langley, Leonard S., | 250,E,Div. Geo. Doherty 500, | 21,2, | 8, | 12, | | | 1, | 8, | | | | 10.72 | 2½ |
| Lightner, David, | | | | | | | | 1, | | | | | .53 | |
| Langley, Jane J., | 1 4 wheel pleasure Carriage | | | | | | | 1, | 11, | | | | 16.66 | |

118

(Page 119)Cont. Acres Desc.                    Town, #of Free
Persons name,  Lnd. Titl.- R E M A R K S - Ent.Rge. Sec. Dis. Lots,Lot,Poll,Sla. Sto. Jac.,$ .Cts. M

| Persons name | Acres | Desc. Lnd. Titl. REMARKS | Ent. | Rge. | Sec. | Dis. | Lots | Lot | Poll | Sla. | Sto. | Jac. | $ | .Cts. | M |
|---|---|---|---|---|---|---|---|---|---|---|---|---|---|---|---|
| Lemmond, Thomas, | | | | | | | | | 1, | | | | | .53 | |
| Lawrence, Elias, | | | | | | | | | | 2, | | | | 2.12 | |
| Lovin, Joshua, | | | | | | | | | 1, | | | | | .53 | |
| Lemmond, David, | | | | | | | | | 1, | | | | | .53 | |
| McGavock, Francis, | 640, | Frances Lewis, | 268, | 1, | 9, 13, | | | | | | | | 4.37 | 5 | |
| Same, | 250, | Thomas Shark, | | 1, | 9, | | | | | | | | 1.71 | 2½ | |
| McLemore & Charlton, | 744, | | 775, | 1 &2, | 7, | | | | | | | | 5.09 | 8 3/4 | |
| Same & Same, | 146, | H's Jacob Bell, 640, | 767, | 1, | 7, | | | | | | | | 1.00 | | |
| McLemore & Blackfen, 1 | 50, | George Gritt, | 1065, | 2, | 9, 12, | | | | | | | | 1.03 | | |
| Same & Same, | 160, | Eldridge & Hill 640, | 1057, | 1, | 6,12, | | | | | | | | 1.09 | 5 | |
| McLemore, Jno. C., | 160, | Micajah Thomas,640, | 1362, | 2, | 5, 13, | | | | | | | | 1.09 | 5 | |
| Same, | 3 3/4, | | 816, | 1, | 8, 13, | | | | | | | | .02 | 1¼ | |
| Same, | 38, | | 828, | 3, | 7, | | | | | | | | .26 | | |
| Same, | 143½ | | 1071, | 2, | 9, 12, | | | | | | | | .97 | 2½ | |
| | 5288¾ | | | | | | | | | | | | | | |

(Page 120)(1832)     1-4 wheel Pleasure Carriage (555)

| Persons name | Acres | Desc. | Ent. | Rge. | Sec. | | | | | | | | $ | .Cts. | M |
|---|---|---|---|---|---|---|---|---|---|---|---|---|---|---|---|
| McLemore, John C., | 277½, | J.C.McLemore &R.T.Love,300, | 3, | 7, 13, | | | | | | | | | 1.90 | | |
| Same, | 1000, | Part of 2000, | 322, | 2, | 5, | | | | | | | | 6.85 | | |
| Same, | 1250, | McLemore & Hopkins 5000 | 817, | 1&2, | 7&8, | | | | | | | | 8.56 | 2½ | |
| Same, | 500, | John Willis 2500, | 240, | 2&3, | 7 &8, | | | | | | | | 3.42 | 5 | |
| Same, | 100, | | 795, | 2, | 5, | | | | | | | | .68 | 5 | |
| Same, | 542, | John McIver 4336, | 752, | 1, | 9 &10, | | | | | | | | 3.71 | | |
| McLemore & Vaulx, | 128, | H's ofSion Williams 640, | 351, | 2, | 5 & 6, 12, | | | 16, 25 | | | | | .87 | 5 | |
| Same & Same, | 1250, | John Rhea, 2500, | 302, | 3, | 6, 13, | | | | | | | | 8.56 | 2½ | |
| Same & S ame, | 48, | Jas. G. Brehon, 240, | 601, | 1, | 9, 12, | | | | | | | | .32 | 8½ | |
| Same & Same, | 128, | Hill & Collier 640, | 628, | 2, | 9, | | | | | | | | .87 | 5 | |
| Same & Same, | 330, | Andrew Nail, 1656, | 99, | 3, | 9, 13, | | | | | | | | 2.26 | 1¼ | |
| Same & Same, | 200, | James G. Brehem, 1000 | 109, | 3, | 7, | | | | | | | | 1.38 | | |
| Same & Same, | 420, | Huntsman & Totten, 2100, | 475, | 3, | 7 & 8, | | | | | | | | 2.87 | 7½ | |
| Same & Same, | 128, | John Evans H's 640, | 529, | 1, | 7, | | | | | | | | .87 | 5 | |
| Montgomery, John, | 500, | Wm. Montgomery, | 733, | 2, | 7, | | | | | | | | 3.43 | 5 | |
| Montgomery, Daniel, | 252, | | | 2, | 7, | | | | | | | | 1.72 | 7½ | |
| Murray, Robert, | 26, | H's.Jacob Bell 640, | 767, | 1, | 7, | | 1, 52, | | | | | | 1.30 | 2½ | |
| Moran, James H., | ½ | Same, | 767, | 1, | 7, | | 1, 24, | | 1, 2, 1, | | | | 8.77 | 7½ | |

(Page 120) Cont. Acres Desc.                                    Town,    # of Free,           Horse     120
Persons name,    Lnd.Titl. R E M A R K S - Ent.,Rge.,Sec. Dis. Lots, Lot, Poll,Sla, Sto.Jac.$. Cts. M.

| Persons name | Acres | Remarks | Ent. | Rge. | Sec. | Dis. Lots | Lot | Free Poll | Sla | Sto.Jac. | $ | Cts. | M. |
|---|---|---|---|---|---|---|---|---|---|---|---|---|---|
| McIver, John, | 227, | | 473, | 3, | 7, | | | | | | 1.55 | 5 | |
| Mitchell, Thomas, | | | | | | | | 1, | | | .53 | | |
| Same, | 372, | | 361, | 3, | 8, | | | | | | 2.55 | 1¼ | |
| Same, | 640, | | 131, | 2 &3, | 5, | | | | | | 4.37 | 5 | |
| Same, | 4336, | | 325, | 1 &2, | 5, | | | | | | 29.70 | 2½ | |
| Same, | 280, | | 327, | 3, | 7, | | | | | | 1.91 | 8 | 3/4 |
| Same, | 3252, | Part of 4336, | 752, | 1, | 9 & 10, | | | | | | 22.27 | 6¼ | 3/4 |
| McNeely, John, | | | | | | | | 1, | | | .53 | | |
| McGowan, John, | 175, | (640) | | | | | | 1, | 1, | | 2.79 | | |
| Malin, Benjamin, | 224, | Blakemore,Swaney &Ross,601, | 1 &2, | 7, | | | | | | | 2.04 | 8 | 3/4 |
| McClellan, Trigg, | | | | | | | | 1, | | | .53 | | |
| Mitchell, John, | | | | | | | | 1, | | | .53 | | |
| McIntosh, Charles, | | | | | | | | 1, | | | .53 | | |
| Melton, Thomas, | | | | | | | | 1, | | | .53 | | |
| Mathews, Samuel, | | | | | | | | 1, | 3, | | 3.71 | | |
| Marshall, Robert C., | | | | | | | | 1, | | | .53 | | |
| Majers, Samuel, | 16586 | | | | | | | 1, | | | .53 | | |
| | | | | | | | 2 | 12, 6, | 1, | | | | |
| (Page 121), (1832) | | | | | | | | | | | | | |
| Meredith, Daniel, | | | | | | | | 1, | | | .53 | | |
| McClain, Charles Sr.,50 E., | | | | | | | | 1, | | | .34 | 2½ | |
| McClain, John, | 50, | | | | | | | 1, | | | .57 | 5 | |
| Miles, William C., | | | | | | | | 1, | | | .53 | | |
| McDaniel, Moses, | | | | | | | | 1, | | | .53 | | |
| McClain, Charles Jr., | | | | | | | | 1, | | | .53 | | |
| McIntosh, Solomon, | | | | | | | | 1, | | | .53 | | |
| McClain, Charles younger, | | | | | | | | 1, | | | .53 | | |
| Mooney, Adam, | | | | | | | | 1, | | | .53 | | |
| McDaniel, Hiram, | | | | | | | | 1, | | | .53 | | |
| Moss, Bennit, | | | | | | | | 1, | 1, | | 1.59 | | |
| Mitchell, Ripley, | | | | | | | | 1, | 6, | | 6.36 | | |
| Moss, Geo. W. L. | 2035, | Thos. Henderson 2560, | 1, | 8, | 13, | | | | | | 13.93 | 7½ | |
| Same, | 640, | Same Name, | 1, | 8, | | | | | | | 4.37 | 5 | |
| Same, | 220, | H's.Elas Smith, 640, | 2, | 8, | | | | | | | 1.50 | 5 | |
| McClain, George, | 50, | | 1, | 10, | 12, | | | | | | .34 | 2½ | |
| Murrell, Benjamin, | | | | | | | | 3, | | | 3.18 | | |

(Page 121) Cont. Acres Desc.                Town,      # of Free        Horse
             # of        Ent.Rge. Sec., Dis.Lots,Lot,Poll,Sla. Sto.Jac.
Persons Name,    Lnd.Titl. R E M A R K S -                          $ . Cts.  M

| Name | Acres, Desc. | Ent. | Rge. | Sec. | Dis. Lots,Lot,Poll | Sla. | Sto. Jac. | Horse | $ | Cts. |
|---|---|---|---|---|---|---|---|---|---|---|
| Murrell, William, | | | | | 1, | | | | .53 | |
| Murrell, John L., | | | | | 1, | | | | .53 | |
| McCall, James | | | | | 1, | | | | .53 | |
| Moss, James, | | | | | 1, | | | | .53 | |
| Murrell, Lemuel, | | | | | 1, | | | | .53 | |
| McNeely, Michael, | 49, 3 tracts, | | 2, 9, | | 1, | | | | .86 | 5 |
| Mayo, William | 130, Samuel McCorkle, | | 2, 9, | | 1, | | | | 1.42 | 2½ |
| McWhorter, George, | | | | | 1, | | | | .53 | |
| McWhorter, John, | | | | | 1, | | | | .53 | |
| Mitchell, Standley, | | | | | 1, | | | | .53 | |
| Morgan, Samuel, | 370, Thos. Henderson,640, | | 2, 7, | 1, 55, | 1, | 6 | | | 10.55 | 2½ |
| Moore, John H., | | | | | 1, | 1, | | | 1.59 | |
| McFarland, Benj,M., | | | | | 1, | | | | .53 | |
| Moore, James, | | | | | 1, | | | | .53 | |
| Miller, George, | | | | | 1, | | | | .53 | |
| Moore, John, | 72, Part of 2500, | | 2, 5, | | 1, | | | | 1.02 | 5 |
| Miller, Andrew, | | | | | 1, | | | | .53 | |
| Mears, William, | 197,Deed, | | | | 1, | | | | 1.35 | |
| Mandy Thomas, | | | 3, | | 1, | | | | .53 | |
| | 3 666 | | | | | | | | | |
| | 3 863 | | | 1, | 28 | 17 | | | | |

(Page 122)

| Name | Acres, Desc. | Ent. | Rge. | Sec. | Dis. Lots,Lot,Poll | Sla. | Sto. Jac. | Horse | $ | Cts. |
|---|---|---|---|---|---|---|---|---|---|---|
| McElroy, Aquilla, | | | | | 1, | | | | .53 | |
| McElroy, William, | | | | | 1, | | | | .53 | |
| Mainard, Wm. W., | | | | | 1, | | | | .53 | |
| Mainard, John, | | | | | 1, | | | | .53 | |
| McCluskey, Wm. H. | | | | | 1, | | | | .53 | |
| Mobley, Ransom, | 100, E., Jno. Terrell 640, | | 1, 6, 12, | | 1, | 2, 1, | 4, | | 7.33 | 5 |
| Montgomery, William,100 | Same, | | 1, 6, | | 1, | | | | 1.21 | 5 |
| Montgomery, James, | | | | | 1, | | | | .53 | |
| Mathis, Daniel, | | | | | 1, | | | | .53 | |
| Moore, James, | | | | | 1, | | | | .53 | |
| Meadows, Spearman, | | | | | 1, | | | | .53 | |
| Moon, Vincent, | | | | | 1, | 1, | | | 1.59 | |
| Marcus, Phillip, | | | | | 1, | 2 | | | .53 | |
| Mosley, Edward, | 400, H's Bythel Bell 640, | | 1, 5, 13, | | | | | | 5.45 | |

Page 122) Cont. Acres Desc.            #of              Town  #of Free            Horse
Persons Name   Lnd. Titl.  R E M A R K S -  Ent.Rge.Sec. Dis. Lots, Lot,Poll,Sla.Sto.Jac.$ .Cts. M.
                                  (1907)

| Person | Acres | Title/Remarks | Ent. | Rge. | Sec. | Dis. | Town Lots | #of Lot | Poll | Sla. | Sto. | Free Jac. | Horse $ | .Cts. | M. |
|---|---|---|---|---|---|---|---|---|---|---|---|---|---|---|---|
| Mosley, Robert, | 927, | McIlhatton & Barnett, | | 1, | 5, | | | | 15, | | | | 22.26 | | |
| McLemore, Sugars | 700, | | | | | | | | | | | | 4.80 | | |
| McLemore & Vaulx | 390 | | | | | | | | | | | | 2.67 | | 5 |
| Maxwell, Jesse, | | | | | | | 1, | | | | | | .53 | | |
| Montgomery, Daniel, | 126½, | Henry Belote 640, | | | | | | | | | | | .86 | | 2½ |
| Michael Archelous, | 240, | | | | | | | | | | | | 4.40 | | |
| Moss Mason, | | | | | | | | | 2, | 1 | | | 1.59 | | |
| Maxwell, William, | | | | | | | | | 1, | | | | .53 | | |
| Nailing, Willis A, | 50, | J.R. Nailing, | | 1, | 7, | | | | 1, | 3, | | | 4.05 | | 2½ |
| Nailing, Nelson, | 166, | 2 Tracts, | | 1, | 6 & 7, | 1, | | | 2, | 5, | | | 8.62 | | 5 |
| Norvell, Nathan L., | | | | | | | | | 1, | | | | .53 | | |
| Nowland, Henry, | | | | | | | | | 1, | | | | .53 | | |
| Newton, James, | | | | | | | | | 1, | | | | .53 | | |
| Newmen, William, | | | | | | 1, | | | 1, | | | | 1.59 | | |
| Newton, James, | | | | | | | | | 1, | | | | 1.12 | | 5 |
| Oliver, Berry, | | | | | | | | | 1, | | | | .53 | | |
| Overton, John, | 488, | Gt., Landon Carter, | 319, | 3, | 9, | | | | | | | | 3.34 | | 6¼ |
| Same, | 232, | Same, | 322 | 3, | 9, | | | | | | | | 1.58 | | 8⅛ |
| Same | 488, | Same, | 317, | 3, | 9, | | | | | | | | 3.34 | | 6¼ |
| Same, | 622, | Same, | 323, | 2, | 10, | | | | | | | | 4.26 | | |
| Same, | 231, | Same, | 322 | 2 &3, g, | | 2, | | 26, 32, | 1, | | | | 1.58 | | |
|  | 5260½ | | | | | | | | | | | | | | |

(Page 123) (1832)

| Person | Acres | Title/Remarks | Ent. | Rge. | Sec. | Dis. | Town Lots | #of Lot | Poll | Sla. | Sto. | Free Jac. | Horse $ | .Cts. | M. |
|---|---|---|---|---|---|---|---|---|---|---|---|---|---|---|---|
| Overton, John, | 735, | Gt., Landon Carter, | | 2, | 9, | 13, | | | | | | | 5.03 | | |
| Same, | 98, | E, | | 2, | 9, | | | | | | | | .66 | | 7½ |
| Same, | 320, | Overton, & Wharton, | 25, | 2, | 9, | | | | | | | | 2.18 | | 7½ |
| Osteen, John, | | | | | | | | | 1, | | | | .53 | | |
| Oliver, Isaac, | 117, | 2 Tracts, | | 2, | 7, | 12, | | | 1, | | | | 1.33 | | 2½ |
| Oliver, Stephen, | | | | | | | | | 1, | | | | .53 | | |
| Ore, Wm.C. Heirs, | 640, | Isaac Burgess H's. | | 2, | 7, | | | | | | | | 4.37 | | 5 |
| Oneal, John, | 113, | | | 1, | 5, | 13, | | | 1, | | | | 1.30 | | 5 |
| Outhouse, Israel F., | 28½, | | | 1, | 6, | 12, | | | 1, | | | | .72 | | 5 |
| Owen, Daniel, | 97 3/4, | Joel Penson, | | 3, | 7, | 13, | | | 1, | | | | 1.20 | | |
| Owens, Elisha H., | | | | | | | | | 1, | | | | .53 | | |

(Page 123) Cont.           Town, #of Free                    Horse
Persons Name, Lnd.,Titl. REMARKS - Ent.Rge.Sec. Dis.Lots,Lot,Poll,Sla.Sto. Jac. $ .Cts. M

| Persons Name | Lnd. | Titl. REMARKS | Ent. | Rge. | Sec. | Dis.Lots | Lot | Poll | Sla. | Sto. | Jac. | $ | .Cts. | M |
|---|---|---|---|---|---|---|---|---|---|---|---|---|---|---|
| Parker, Lorenzo D., | | | | | | | 2, | | | | | 2.78 | | |
| Parker, Bishop, | | | | | | | 1, | 1, | | | | 1.65 | 5 | |
| Payton, John | 285, | | | | | | | 1, | | | | 1.95 | | |
| Peck, John, | 402, | | | 1, | 8, | | | | | | | 2.76 | 1¼ | |
| Pe<u>l</u>k, Thomas G., | 1850, | Part of 380, | 1353, | 1, | 6, | 12, | | | | | | 12.67 | 6¼ | |
| Parham, Amosa, | 16, | Part of 2000, | 197, | 2, | 7 &8, | 13, | | 1, | | | | .64 | | |
| Parker, Isaac, | 512, | Absolom Jones, | | 1, | 7, | 12, | | | | | | 3.50 | 7½ | |
| Parham, Thomas, | 200, | | | 2, | 6, | 13, | | | | | | 2.43 | | |
| Patterson, Robert S., | | Jas. Greer, | | 1, | 6 & 7,12, | | | | 1, | | | .53 | | |
| Parrish, John, | | | | | | | | 1, | | | | .53 | | |
| Phillips, Reagin D., | | | | | | | | 1, | | | | .53 | | |
| Polk & Devereaux, | 500, | | 289, | 1, | 5, | | | | | | | 3.43 | 5 | |
| Same & Same | 500, | | 59 | 1, | 9, | 13, | | | | | | 3.43 | 5 | |
| Same & Same, | 500, | | 119, | 1, | 9, | | | | | | | 3.43 | 5 | |
| Same & Same, | 305, | | 531, | 1, | 5, | 12, | | | | | | 2.08 | 7½ | |
| Same & Same, | 195, | | 732, | 1, | 5, | | | | | | | 1.33 | 2⅞ | |
| Polk William, | 500, | | 51, | 2, | 9, | 13, | | | | | | 3.43 | 5 | |
| Polk, Thomas H's, | 300, | | 82, | 1, | 5 & 6,12, | | | | | | | 2.05 | 5 | |
| Philpot, Edward, | 364, | | | 3, | 7, | 13, | | | | | | 2.49 | 2½ | |
| Parrish, Charles, | | | | | | | 1, | 1, | | | | 1.65 | 5 | |
| Parker, Gideon, | | | | | | | 1, | 1, | | | | 1.65 | 5 | |
| Prater, Josiah, | | | | | | | | 1, | | | | .53 | | |
| Prater, Martin, | | | | | | | | 1, | | | | .53 | | |
| Pope, John, | 180, | Part of 500, | | 2, | 8, | | | 1, | | | | 1.23 | 5 | |
| 8758½ | | | | | | | 5, | 17, | 1, | | | | | |

(Page 124, (1832)

| Persons Name | Lnd. | Titl. REMARKS | Ent. | Rge. | Sec. | Dis.Lots | Lot | Poll | Sla. | Sto. | Jac. | $ | .Cts. | M |
|---|---|---|---|---|---|---|---|---|---|---|---|---|---|---|
| Pope, John, | 160, | E., John Page 500, | | 2, | 8, | 13, | | 1, | | | | 1.09 | 5 | |
| Pope, Lemuel, | 160, | Same, | | 2, | 8, | | | 1, | | | | 1.09 | 5 | |
| Parrish, John, | 400, | J. W. Philpot, | | | | | 5, | | | | | 8.04 | | |
| Parrish, Henderson, | | | | | | | | 1, | | | | .53 | | |
| Paschall, Jesse M. | | | | | | | | 1, | | | | .53 | | |
| Payner, Jesse, | | | | | | | | 1, | | | | .53 | | |
| Pannel, William C., | | | | | | | | 1, | | | | .53 | | |
| Pearce, Joseph, | 420, | Eleas Smith 640, | | 2, | 8, | | (4W Car.) 12,(1) | 1, | | | | 21 .31 | 7½ | |
| Philpot, Bennit, | | | | | | | | 1, | | | | .53 | | |
| Pippin, Loftus | | | | | | | | 1, | | | | .53 | | |

123

(Page 124) Cont.          (1832)                    Town # of Free              124

| Persons Name | Lnd. | Titl. | REMARKS - Ent. | Rge. | Sec. | Dis. Lots | Lot | Poll | Sla. | Sto. | Jac. | $ | .Cts. | M |
|---|---|---|---|---|---|---|---|---|---|---|---|---|---|---|
| Pippin, Robert C., | | | | | | | | | | | | | .53 | |
| Palmer, Smith, | 765, | | 2 Tracts, | 2, | 9, | 12, | | 1, | | 9, | | 13.91 | 5 | |
| Palmer, Edmund, | | | | | | | | 1, | | | | | .53 | |
| Palmer, Paul, M., | 250, | | Div. Geo. Doherty 500, | 21, | 2, | 8, | | 1, | | 12, | | 14.96 | 7½ | |
| Purtle, Jesse, | | | | | | | | 1, | | | | | .53 | |
| Palmer, Amosa, | | | | | | | | 1, | | | | | .53 | |
| Powers, Charles, | | | | | | | | 1, | | | | | .53 | |
| Puples, Samuel, | 200, | | Shelton & Hanlines 1000, | 2, | 7, | | | 1, | | 1, | | 2.96 | | |
| Powell, John, | | | | | | | | 1, | | | | | .53 | |
| Powers, Henry, | | | | | | | | 1, | | | | | .53 | |
| Patton, John M., | | | | | | | | 1, | | | | | .53 | |
| Patton, Thomas, | 50, | | Part of 100, | 2, | 6, | | | 1, | | | | | .53 | |
| Pate, Stephen S., | 50, | | | 2, | 5, | | | 1, | | 2, | | 2.99 | 2½ | |
| Price, Sampson, | | | | | | | | 1, | | | | | .53 | |
| Pentecost, William, | | | | | | | | 1, | | | | | .53 | |
| Pentecost, Scarbrough, | | | | | | | | 1, | | | | | .53 | |
| Price, James, | | | | | | | | 1, | | | | | .53 | |
| Plaster, Samuel, | | | | | | | | 1, | | | | | .53 | |
| Price, John, | | | | | | | | 1, | | | | | .53 | |
| Parks, Fields, | | | | | | | | 1, | | | | | .53 | |
| Parker, Wm.G | | | | | | | | 1, | | | | | .53 | |
| Powers, George, | | | | | | | | 1, | | | | | .53 | |
| Perry, John, | 57, | | | | 13, | | | 1, | | | | | .92 | |
| Pearce, George, | | | | | | | | 1, | | | | | .53 | |
| Rhea, John, | 1250 | | Part of 2500, | 302, | 2 &3, | 6, | | | | | | 8.56 | 2½ | |
| | 3712 | | | | | | | 30, | 41 | 1 | | | | |

Page 125)

| | | | | | | | | | | | | | | |
|---|---|---|---|---|---|---|---|---|---|---|---|---|---|---|
| Russell, Price, H's. | 200, | E. | | | | | | | | | | | | |
| Roulhac, Geo. G., | 320, | Gt. | University of N. C., 1669, | 1, | 7 & 8, | 8, 12, | | 1, | | | | 1.37 | | |
| Rogers, Jubilee, | 840, | E, | 2 tracts, Jno. Ferrell, 2283, | 1, | 6, | 13, | | 1, | 3, | | | 5.89 | 7½ | |
| Rogers, Jonathan T., | 200, | | Same 3840, | 1, | 6 & 7, | 1, | 63 | 1, | 8, | 1, | 5, | 20.88 | | |
| Roffe, Woodson, | | | | 1, | 9, | | | 1, | 4, | | | 6.14 | | |
| Ross, Joshua, | | | | | | (97, 98,) | | 1, | | | | | .53 | |
| Reynolds, Seml B., | | | | | | 3, 99, | | 1, | | | | | .53 | |
| Revis, John H., | 100, | | Wm. Qualls, 1751, | 1, | 7, | 12, | | 1, | 1, | | | 3.90 | 5 | |
| | | | | | | | | | | | | 2.27 | 5 | |

(Page 125) Cont. Acres Desc.  #of   Town,  #of Free                              Horse    125

| Persons Name | Lnd.Title. R E M A R K S - | #of Ent.Rge. | Sec. | Dis. Lots, Lot, Poll, Sla. Sto. Jac. | $. Cts.M |
|---|---|---|---|---|---|
| Russell, George Heirs, 80 Acres | | 2 | 7 | | .55 |
| Rust, Vincent, | | | | 1, | .53 |
| Rogers, Jubilee, V., | | | | 1, 1, | 1.59 |
| Ralston, Alexander, 2750, H's Jerome McClain, | 1 & 2, 7, | 13, 3, | 1, 2, | 24.33 |
| (3840 Acres) | | | | | |
| Royal, Thomas, | | | | 1, | .53 |
| Rogers, John W., | 357, 2 Tracts, | 2, 6, | 2, | 1, 6, | 11.58 5 |
| Ralls, Wm. P., | | | | 1, | .53 |
| Rogers, Job, | 770, 2 Tracts, | 1, 8, | | 1, 9, | 14.94 5 |
| Ross, Lacie, | 40, | 1, 9, | 12, | 1, 1, | 1.86 5 |
| Ross, John, | | | | 1, | .53 |
| Right, Jesse, | | | | 1, | .53 |
| Rogers, Jacob C., | | | | 1, | .53 |
| Rogers, Thomas, | | | | 1, | .53 |
| Rogers, Richard, | | | | 1, | .53 |
| Rea, James, W., | 100, Carmicles 5000, | | | 1, | .68 5 |
| Ross, William G., | | | | 1, 1, | 1.59 |
| Ridgway, William, | | | | 1, | .53 |
| Ridgway, John, | | | | 1, 2, | 2.65 |
| Ridgway, Littlebury E., | | | | 1, | .53 |
| Ridgway, James, | 349, 2 Tracts, | 2, 8, | | 1, 4, | 6.63 7½ |
| Russell, Buckner, Sr., 50, William, Ralls, | | 2, 7, | | 1, | .34 2½ |
| Russell, Buckner Jr., 3, Jas. Willoughby, | | 2, 7, | | 1, | .55 |
| Rhoads, Littlebury A., | | | | 1, | .53 |
| Rogers, Jefferson | 184, Jno. Terrell 640, | 1, 6, | 13, | 1, 2, | 2.91 2½ |
| Rachels, Voulline, | | | | 1, | .53 |
| Ragsdale, Mathew, | | | | 1, | .53 |
| Redick, David, | 6343 | | | 1, | .53 |
| (Page 126) | | | 10 | 28 44 1, 5, | |
| Smith, Rody, | 258, E., H's. Richard Smith, 115, 3, | 5, | 13, | | 1.76 5 |
| | (640) | | | | |
| Same, | 255, Same name | 602, 1, 8, | | | 1.74 |
| Smith, James W/. | 653, Gt. Abner Nash 1000, | 133, 3, 8, | | | 4.74 |
| Same, 1000, | Same, | 132, 3, 8, | | | 6.85 |
| Same, 500, | Same, | 134, 3, 8, | | | 3.43 5 |
| Same, 1175 | Same, | 149, 3, 8, | | | 8.05 |

(Page 126) Cont. Acres Desc. | Town, #of Free Horse
Persons Name, Lnd., Titl. R E M A R K S - #of Ent. Rge., Sec., Dis.Lots, Lot, Poll, Sla. Sto. Jac. $ Cts. M

| Persons Name | Acres | Desc. Lnd., Titl. REMARKS | #of Ent. | Rge. | Sec. | Dis.Lots | Lot | Poll | Sla. | Sto. | Horse Jac. | $ | Cts. | M |
|---|---|---|---|---|---|---|---|---|---|---|---|---|---|---|
| Speight, | 320, | E., Speight &McGavock, | 828, | 1, | 12, | 12, | | | | | | 2.18 | | 2½ |
| Spate, James, | | (640) | | | | | | | | | | | .53 | |
| Ship, Benton, | | | | | | | 1, | | | | | | .53 | |
| Slawter, John, | | | | | | | 1, | | | | | | .53 | |
| Stanley, Lewis, | | | | | | | 1, | | | | | | .53 | |
| Smart, Phillip, | 230, | Jas. Somers 3840, | | 2, | 6, | 12, | 1, | | | | | 1.57 | | 2½ |
| Smart, Labon, | | | | | | | 1, | | | | | | .53 | |
| Smart, James H., | | | | | | | 1, | | | | | | .53 | |
| Smart, William J., | | | | | | | 1, | 1, | | | | | 1.59 | |
| Shutty, John M., | | | | | | | 1, | | | | | | .53 | |
| Segraves, Willie, | | | | | | | 1, | | | | | | .53 | |
| Somers, James, | | | | | | | 1, | | | | | | .53 | |
| Stephen, Lawrence, | | | | | | | 1, | | | | | | .53 | |
| Shutty, Charles M., | | | | | | | 1, | | | | | | .53 | |
| Shutty, David, | 80, | | | 1, | 9, | 13, | 1, | | | | | 1.08 | | |
| Serett, John, | | | | | | | 1, | 1, | | | | | 1.59 | |
| Stow, William, | | | | | | | 1, | | | | | | .53 | |
| Stow, Joel W., | | | | | | | 1, | | | | | | .53 | |
| Sims, John, | | | | | | | 1, | 2, | | | | | 2.65 | |
| Somers, John, | | | | | | | 1, | | | | | | .53 | |
| Somers, Richard, | | | | | | | 1, | | | | | | .53 | |
| Stunston, James, | | | | | | | 1, | | | | | | .53 | |
| Smith, David, | | | | | | | 1, | | | | | | .53 | |
| Stewart, Samuel T., | | | | | | | 1, | | | | | | .53 | |
| Sprout, Alexander, | | | | | | | 1, | | | | | | .53 | |
| Sharp, Spencer, | | | | | | | 1, | | | | | | .53 | |
| Stoker, Edmund, | | | | | | | 1, | | | | | | .53 | |
| Steele, Samuel, | | | | | | | 1, | | | | | | .53 | |
| Sanford, John, | | | | | | | 1, | | | | | | .53 | |
| | 4471 | | | | | | 27, | 4 | | | | | | |
| (Page 127) | | | | | | | | | | | | | | |
| Stanley, Elijah, | 106, | E., | 1406, | 2, | 7, | 12, | 1, | | | | | 1.25 | | 7½ |
| Stanley, Noah, | | | | | | | 1, | | | | | | .53 | |
| Simpson, John, | | | | | | | 1, | | | | | | .53 | |
| Stallings, John, | | | | | | | 1, | 1, | 1, | | | | 1.53 | |
| Sommers, James, | 3505, | Part of 3840, | | 2, | 7, | | 1, | | | | | 24.01 | | 5 |

(Page 127) Cont.

| Persons name | Lnd. Acres | Titl. | REMARKS Desc. | #of Acres | Ent.Rge. | Sec. | Dis. | Town. Lots | #of Lots | Poll | Sla. | Sto. | Jac. | Free $.Cts. | M |
|---|---|---|---|---|---|---|---|---|---|---|---|---|---|---|---|
| Sommers & McFarland, | | | | | | | | | | | | | | 5.00 | |
| Sibley, Jacob, | | | | | | | | | | | | 1, | | 1.59 | |
| Steele, George R., | 50, | | Porter &McGavock 344¼, | | 2, | 7, | | | | 1, | | | | .87 | 2½ |
| Steele, John, | 40, | | Same, | | 2, | 7, | | | | 1, | | | | .80 | 5 |
| Shaw, Archibald, | 100, | | Daugherty &McCorkle, | | 2, | 7, | | | | | | 2, | | 2.80 | 5 |
| Stark, Thomas, | 25, | | | | 2, | 6, | | | | | | | | .70 | |
| Smith, Richey, | | | | | | | | | | 1, | | | | .53 | |
| Smith, Alfred, | | | | | | | | | | 1, | | | | .53 | |
| Smith, Hugh D., | | | | | | | | | | 1, | | | | .53 | |
| Smith, James, | 242½, | | | 1012, | 2, | 6, | | | | 1, | | | | 2.19 | |
| Shaw, Deniel B., | | | | | | | | | | 1, | | | | .53 | |
| Seal, William, | | | | | | | | | | 1, | | | | .53 | |
| Span, Moses, T., | 80, | | John Terrell's 640, | | 1, | 6, | | | | 1, | 1, | | | 2.14 | |
| Span, Jeremiah, | 100, | | Jas. Greer, | | 1, | 6, | | | | 1, | 1, | | | 1.74 | |
| Span, John T., | | | | | | | | | | 1, | | | | .53 | |
| Span, James, | | | | | | | | | | 1, | | | | .53 | |
| Swim, Jeremiah W., | | | | | | | | | | 1, | | | | .53 | |
| Stanford, Thomas, | 25, | | | | 1, | 6, | 13, | | | 1, | | | | .70 | 1½ |
| Styers, John, H., | | | | | | | | | | 1, | | | | .53 | |
| Stone, Claborn, | | | | | | | | | | 1, | | | | .53 | |
| Spragg, James, | | | | | | | | | | 1, | | | | .53 | |
| Stovall, George | 220, | | | | 1, | 7, | 12, | | | 1, | | 5, | | 6.66 | 2½ |
| Sample, Henry A., | | | | | | | | 1, | | 1, | | | | 1.65 | 5 |
| Span, Willis, | | | | | | | | | | 1, | | | | .53 | |
| Stunston, John, | 200, | | | | | | 12, | | | | | 5, | | 6.67 | |
| Shepherd, Charles B., | 1250, | Gt., | J.G. & T. Blount, | | | | 13, | | | | | | | 8.56 | 2½ |
| Same, | 1250, | | Same & Same, | | | | | | | | | | | 8.56 | 2½ |
| Same, | 1000, | | Same & Same, | | | | | | | | | | | 6.85 | 5 |
| Stunston, Henry, | 218, | E., | Joseph Cavit, | | 2, | 9, | 12, | | | | | | | 1.49 | 7½ |
| Shepherd, Richard M., | 1125, | Gt., | J.G. & T. Blount, | | | | 13, | | | | | | | 7.75 | |
| | 9536½ | | | | | | | 1, | | 24, | 15, | 1, | 1, | 1, | |

(Page 128)

| Persons name | Lnd. Acres | Titl. | REMARKS Desc. | #of Acres | Ent.Rge. | Sec. | Dis. | Town. Lots | #of Lots | Poll | Sla. | Sto. | Jac. | Free $.Cts. | M |
|---|---|---|---|---|---|---|---|---|---|---|---|---|---|---|---|
| Shepherd, Richard M., | 1362, | Gt., | J.G. & T. Blount, | | | | 13, | | | | | | | 9.34 | |
| Same, | 267, | | Same, | | | | | | | 1, | | | | 1.82 | 5 |
| Thomas, Mathew, | | | | | | | | | | | | | | .53 | |

Page 128) Cont. Acres Desc.                    #of Rng.         Town,      #of Free                    Horse
Persons Name   Lnd.   Titl. R E M A R K S  -   Ent./Sec. Dis.,Lots,Lot,Poll, Sla. Sto. Jac. / ¢.Cts. M.

Terrell, Peleg,    327½,  E., Jno. Terrell 3840,   1, 6,          1,                        2.78
Tailor, Isaac,     500,                            1, 9,  12,                               3.43   5
Thomas, William,                                                                            1.06
Thompson, Joseph,  220,       John Terrell,        1, 7,          1,  9,   1,        $4., 14.69    5
Thompson, Jacob,   170,       John Terrell, 3840,  1, 7,  13,     1,  4,                    5.93   5
Thorp, William,A., 326,       H's John Evans 640,  1, 7,                                    2.23   5
Terrell, Jeptha,   500,       Jno. Terrell 3840,   1, 7,          1,  2,                    6.08   5
Terrell, John,     640,       Jno. Jenkins,        1, 6,   4,        5,                    14.17   5
Same,             1581,       4 Tracts,          1 &2,6 & 7,                               10.84  2½
Same,              108,       John H. Revis,       1, 8,                                     .73  7½
Same,              240,       Baxter Boling,       1, 6,  12,                               1.64  3 3/4
Terrell, Patrick,  100,       Jno. Terrell 3840,   1, 6,  13,     1,                        1.74   5
Tansil, Edward,    320,       Eldridge & Hill,640,                3,                        5.36
Tansil, Hiram,W.,                                                                            .53
Traywick,Gibson,   100,       Ju.Philpot,          2, 7,          1,                         .68   5
Thomas, James D.,                                                 2,                        2.65
Thornton, Benjamin,                                               1,                         .53
Thornton, Sterling,                                               1,                         .53
Thompson, Jesse,                                                  1,                         .53
Terrell, John,      27,       Samuel Majors, 50,   2, 9,          1,                         .18  2½
Thompson, William,                                                1,                         .53
Todd, William,      50,                            1, 7,  12,     1,                         .96  2½
Todd, Willie,                                                     1,                         .53
Tucker, Alexander,                                                1,                         .53
Thompson, Robert,                                                 1,                         .53
Travis, Moses B.,                                                 1,         1,             1.59
Taylor, Edmund,                                                   1,                         .53
Taylor, William,                                                  1,                         .53
Temmons, Joseph B.,                                               1,                         .53
Taylor, Chapman,                                                  1,                         .53
Tucker, Daniel,                                                   1,                         .53
Travis, Fielding,                                                 1,                         .53
                  6838½                                       4, 21, 28¼,

(Page 129)(Year 1832)
Thomas, John,      564, E,                        12,            10,                       14.47
Tomlinson, Henry,                                                 1,                         .53

(Page 129) Cont. Acres-Titl.                                    Town  #Of  Free                Horse
Persons Name,    Lnd.Desc.,    R E M A R K S    Ent.Rge.,Sec. Dis. Lots,Lot,Poll,Sla. Sto. Jac. $. Cts. M

Tompkins, Isaac,                                                         1,                       .53
Trantham, Floyd,                                                         1,                       .53
Thompson, James,                                                         1,                       .53
Tansil, John,       40,    Joel Pison,                          13,                         1333  5
Turner, John,                                                            1,                       .53
Totten, Benjamin, 672½,   Huntsman & Totten, 2100, 3, 7 &8,                                  4.62
Ury, Joseph,                                                             1,                       .53
Uhls, Frederick J.,                                                      1,                       .53
Ury, Robert,                                                             1,                       .53
Vincent, Perry,    100  Jno. Terrell 3840       1, 7,       1, 31,   1,  2,                  2.65
Vincent, Abner,    200,   Same,                 1, 7,                1,  2,                  4.43
Vincent, Orin,                                              2,79,80, 1,  2,                  4.02
Vincent, John M., 100,    Allen Williams,       1, 7,                1,                      2.78
Vincent, JosephL.,52½,                          1, 5,                1,  7,                  8.63  5
Valentine, Thomas 160,    Robt. Cartright,                           1,  2,                  3.01
Wharton, Jesse,   200,Gt.Landon Carter,  243, 3, 9,    12,                                   1.10
Same,             595½,   Same,          310, 3, 10,   14,                                   1.37
Same,             730,    Same,          325, 3, 9,                                          4.08  2½
Waterhouse, Richard,797½,E,Wm. Murphy,987½,776  2, 7,                                        4.55  2½
Willis, John,    2000,    Part of 2500,  204, 2&3, 7&8,                                      5.47
Ward, Whitmore J., 75,    Jas. Greer,           1, 7,  12,                                   13.70
Williams, Allen S.,50,                          1, 7,  13,           1,                      1.04  2½
Williams, Joseph G.,                                                 1,                       .87  2½
Warren, John,                                                        1,                      1.59
Warner, Meers,    107 3/4, J.L. D. Smith, 274,  1, 7,  12,           1,                       .53
Wilson, Lewis D.,1000,Bowers & Wilson,      29, 1,1 &2, 7, 13,       1,  1,                  2.32  5
Wills, Hayden,E., 250,    2 Tracts, M. Farson,  1, 7,  12,           1,                      6.85
Wilson, George W., 23, H's Joab Bell 640,       1, 7,  13,           1,  2,                  4.36  2½
Winston, Josiah,                                                     1,                       .68  5
Wiggins, Benjamin,                                                   1,                       .53
White, Tysel,C.,                            1, 20,                   1,                       .53
Wade, Kinchen,                              1                        1,                      1.65  5
Williams, Kinchen,                                                   1,                      1.65  5
                                                                                              .53
                                                            ─────────────────────────────────────
                                                            5,   25,   30,
                                    ──────
                                    8 717 3/4

P. 130)

| Person's Name | Acres Lnd. | Desc. Witl. | REMARKS | # of Ent. | Rge., | Sec. | Town Dis. Lots,Lot | #of Poll, | Free Sla. | Horse Sto. Jac.$ | Cts. M. |
|---|---|---|---|---|---|---|---|---|---|---|---|
| Ward, Isaac, | | | | | | | | | | .53 | |
| Whitley, Benjamin, | | | | | | | | 1, | | .53 | |
| Whitley, John, | | | | | | | | 1, | | .53 | |
| Wood, Wilson, | | | | | | | | 1, | | .53 | |
| Willingham, William, | 30, | E. | Richard Porter, | | 1, | 7, | 12, | 1, | 2, | 8.48 | |
| Whitsil, Peter, | | | | | | | | 1, | | .53 | |
| Williams, Bartlett, | 100, | | Moses B. Travis, | | 1, | 8, | 13, | 1, | 1, | 2.27 | 5 |
| Wester, William, | | | | | | | | 1, | | .53 | |
| Williams, Allen, | 156, | | Peter Williams 640, | | 2, | 9, | 12, | | | 1.07 | 2½ |
| Williams, Ann, | 100, | | Same, | | 2, | 9, | | | | .68 | 5 |
| Walls, Fleming, | | | | | | | | | | .53 | |
| Workman, Pleasant G., | | | | | | | | 1, | | .53 | |
| Winsted, Johnston, | 228, | | Cave Johnston, | | 1, | 9, | | 1, | | 2.09 | 2½ |
| Wilson, Joseph, | | | | | | | | | 4, | 4.24 | |
| Webb, Amosa, | 350, | | 2 Tracts Jason Wilson, | | 2, | 9, | | 1, | 1, | 3.99 | 5 |
| Webb, Nancy, | | | | | | | | | 3, | 3.18 | |
| Wooten, Stephen, | | | | | | | | | | .53 | |
| Willoughby, James, | 58, | | 3 Tracts, | | 2, | 7, | | 1, | | .92 | 7⅛ |
| Ward, Messer, | 10, | | Peter McGavock,344 3/4 | | 2, | 7, | | 1, | | .59 | 7⅞ |
| Willbanks, Gardner, | | | | | | | | 1, | | .53 | |
| Williamson, Meredith, | | | | | | | | 1, | | .53 | |
| Watts, Marvel, | | | | | | | | 1, | | .53 | |
| Wooten, William, | | | | | | | | 1, | | .53 | |
| Woolbanks, Hiram, | | | | | | | | 1, | | .53 | |
| Williams, Newborn, | 27½, | | | 640, | 1012, 2, | 6, | | 1, | | .18 | 7½ |
| Wallace, Andrew, | | | | | | | | 1, | | .53 | |
| Ward, William, | | | | | | | | 1, | | .53 | |
| Ward, Britton, | | | | | | | | 1, | | .53 | |
| Williams, Thomas, | | | | | | | 12 | 1, | | .53 | |
| Welsh, John, | 28½, | | | | 1, | 6, | | 1, | | .72 | 5 |
| Ward, George, | | | | | | | | 1, | | .53 | |
| Ward, John B., | | | | | | | | 1, | | .53 | |
| White, James, H., | | | | | | | | 1, | | .53 | |
| Williams, Zacheriah, | 240, | | Baxter Boling, | | 1, | 5, | | 1, | 5, | 6.94 | 5 |
| Williams, Bennett B., | | | | | | | | 1, | | .53 | |
| | 1328 | | | | | | | 5, 29, | 16 | | |

(Page 131)

| Persons Name | Acres Lnd. | Desc. Titl. | REMARKS | #of Ent.Rge., | Sec. | Dis.Lots, | Town, Lot, | #of Free Poll, | Sla.Sto.Jac. | Horse $ .Cts. | 131 M |
|---|---|---|---|---|---|---|---|---|---|---|---|
| Warner, Samuel A., | | | | | | | | | | 2.71 | |
| Ward, John, | | | | | | | | 1, | 2, | .53 | |
| Williams, Martin H. S., | | | | | | | | 1, | | .53 | |
| Wolf, Jonathan, | | | | | | | | 1, | | .53 | |
| Williams, Arthur, | | | | | | | | 1, | | .53 | |
| Willis, George W., | | | | | | | | 1, | | .53 | |
| Ward, Roberson, | | | | | | | | 1, | | .53 | |
| Winters, Aron, | 112, | E. | Doherty & McCorkle, | 2 | | 5, | 12, | | | .77 | |
| White, Lemuel, | | | | | | | | 1, | | .53 | |
| Yarbrough, David, | 715, | | Divis.Geo.Doherty, | 150, | 2, | | 7 | 1, | | 4.90 | |
| Young, Harris, | | | | | | | | 1, | | .53 | |
| Young, Levi, | | | | | | | | 1, | | .53 | |
| Young, Abraham, | 40, | | | | | 1, | 7, | | | .27 5 | |
| Young, Henry J., | 867, | | | | | | | 1, | 11,2, | | |

There is 146376½ acres of land @ 68½ cts. per 100 acres is .......................... $1001.48
  "   "  79 Town Lots @ $112½ per lot is ..................................................  88.87½
  "   "  579 Free Polls @ 53 cents per poll is ............................................ 
  "   "  474 Slaves @ $1.06 cts. per poll is .............................................. 
  "   "  5 Retail stores at $5.00 per store is ............................................ 
  "   "  6 Stud Horses @ various prices is ................................................ 
  "   "  2 Carriages of pleasure with 4 wheels each is .................................... 

(Note: Total of above not given)

(Page 132)

## THOMAS JONES LAST WILL & TESTAMENT

A Will: In the name of God Amen. I, Thomas Jones, of the County of Weakley and State of Tennessee, (being in sound mind and memory) calling to mind the mortality of my body and knowing that it is appointed unto all men once to die, do make this my last will and testament in form and words as followeth:

First of all I give and bequeath my Soul unto the hands of that God who gave it, and my body to be consigned to its mother dust - and as to those worldly concerns wherewith it has pleased God to bless me I give and bequeath them in the following manner (to wit)

Item 1, I give and demise unto my loving wife Frances Jones during her natural life, the tract of land whereon I now live and all my farming utensils. I also give her my stock of horses, cattle, hogs and sheep together with the household and kitchen furniture.

Item 2. Should my daughter Frances alter her situation in life by marriage, it is my wish that she should have of the personal property (above demised) a share equal in value to the part already given to my daughter Rebecca.

Item 3. It is my wish that my said wife Frances Jones make a will at her decease, but in case she should not, it is my will that the stock of every description, farming utensils and furniture of all kinds be sold on a credit of nine months and the proceeds equally divided among my several children.

Item 4. - It is my wish that the children of my sons or daughters who may have deceased, have the share to which their deceased parent would have been entitled.

Thomas Jones (seal)

Item 5. It is my wish and request that my two sons, John and Thomas Jones stay with their mother and assist her to take care of the plantation stock and everything pertaining to it and if they do so it is my will that they have the land on which I now live, and I do hereby appoint my said sons John and Thomas Jones Executors to this my last will and Testament; hereby revoking all former wills by me made.

(Page 133)
In witness I have hereunto set my hand and seal this Day of -------- in the year of our Lord, 1832.

Thomas Jones (Seal)

Signed sealed published and Declared by )
the said Thomas Jones as his last will )
and testament in the presence of us whose)
names are hereunto subscribed )
Test. John H. Reaves )
     Vincent Rust )

Page 133) Cont.

STATE OF TENNESSEE )
WEAKLEY COUNTY ) COURT OF PLEAS & QUARTER SESSIONS JULY TERM, 1832.

There was the due execution of the foregoing will freely proven in open court by the oaths of John H. Reaves and Vincent Rust, the subscribing witnesses and ordered to be recorded.

Wm. H. Johnson Clk.

---

COLLECTORS BOND FOR 1833 RECORDED 12th AUGUST, 1833.

STATE OF TENNESSEE )
WEAKLEY COUNTY )

Know all men by these presents that we Alfred Gardner, John A. Gardner, S. A. Warner, A.G. Bondurant and John Terrell all of the County of Weakley and State of Tennessee are held and firmly bound unto William Carroll Governor of the State of Tennessee for the time being and his successors in office in the sum of one thousand five hundred dollars which sum well & truly to be made we bind ourselves, our heirs, Execurots and administrators Jointly and severally firmly by these presents sealed with our seals and dated the 11th day of July 1833.

The condition of the above obligation is such that whereas the above bound Alfred Gardner has been appointed by the Justice of the county court for Weakley County Sheriff & Collector of the public taxes in the said county of Weakley. Now if the said Alfred Gardner shall well and faithfully pay over to the treasurer of the State of Tennessee for the Western District all the taxes which he may be bound by law to collect and (Page 134) pay to the said treasurer of the State of Tennessee for the year 1833 within the time prescribed by law for such payment of the state taxes and according to the tenor thereof then the above obligation to be void else to remain in full force & virtue.

Signed and acknowledged )        Alfred Gardner (Seal)
in open court              )        A. G. Bondurant, (Seal )
Test. Wm. H. Johnson Clk.  )        S. A. Warner, (Seal)
                                    Jno. A. Gardner, (Seal)
                                    Jno. Terrell, (Seal)

---

COLLECTORS BOND FOR 1833 RECORDED 17th AUGUST, 1833.

STATE OF TENNESSEE )
WEAKLEY COUNTY )

Know all men by these presents that we Alfred Gardner, A. G. Bondurant, S. A. Warner, John A. Gardner and George Stovall all of the County of Weakley & state of Tennessee are held and firmly bound unto Perry Vincent Chairman of the County Court of Weakley County and his successors in office in the penal sum of five thousand dollars the payment of which well and truly to be made we bind ourselves our heirs Executors and administrators Jointly & severally firmly by these presents sealed with our seals & dated the 11th day of July, 1833.

(Page 134) Cont.

    The condition of the above obligation is such that whereas the above bound Alfred Gardner hath been appointed sheriff & collector of the taxes within said county of Weakley by the Justices of said county court. Now if the said Alfred Gardner shall well and truly pay over to the trustee of said county all the moneys & taxes which by law he may be bound to collect & pay over to the said trustee for the year 1833 within said county, to wit, the county tax, Jury tax, Poor tax, public building tax laid by the county court for said year within the time and according to the terms prescribed by law, then the above obligation to be void otherwise to remain in full force & virtue.

(Page 135)

Signed and Acknowledged    )
in open court.    )
Test. Wm. H. Johnson, Clk.  )

Alfred Gardner, (Seal)
A. G. Bondurant, (Seal)
S. A. Warner, (Seal)
Jno. A. Gardner, (Seal)
Geo. Stovall, (Seal)

---

Stephen H. Grooms Last Will & Testament Recorded 24th of August, 1833.

STATE OF TENNESSEE )
WEAKLEY COUNTY    )

    In the name of God, Amen. Taking into consideration the shortness of life and the certainty of Death also being much Debilitated in body yet of sound mind think fit for the benefit of my creditors also my wife and surviving children to make this as my last will and testament. 1st, I would bequeath my soul unto God who gave it me. 2nd I do constitute and appoint Brite Grooms as my lawful Executor to attend to the said annexed.

    3rd, I further order that one hundred acres of my land whereon I now live shall be laid off on the East boundry of the same by running a north & south line through the center of said tract and immediately after my decease my said executor shall be authorized to advertise and sell the same for ready money for the purpose of paying certain Judgments and Executions that are now and will be due against my said estate and he is hereby authorized in as full and ample manner as I myself would be to make the purchaser a title in fee simple.

    4th I do further will that my said Executor shall so manage all the rest of my said estate either in goods and chattels, lands or tenements that he shall pay all my just debts as the law directs and whatever there may be left of the effects of said estate I do bequeath unto my beloved wife, Winiford for to enable her to support and raise our children during her natural life or widowhood and if any there be at her death or marriage, the same shall be equally divided amongst all our children.

    5th - I do further will that my said wife, Winiford he and she is hereby vested with full authority at any time she may think fit to sell and make a title in fee simple to the remaining hundred acres (Page 136) of land whereon I now live and the effects to be appropriated as above.

(Page 136) Cont.

    Given under my hand and seal this the 3rd May, 1833.

                                                   Stephen H. Grooms, (Seal)

Test.      )
M.T.Spann, )
David Redick )

---

STATE OF TENNESSEE )  Court of Pleas & quarter sessions July Term, 1833.
WEAKLEY COUNTY     )

    Then was the due Execution of the within last will & testament proven in open court by the oaths of Moses T. Spann and David Redick, the subscribing witnesses thereto and ordered to be recorded.

                                                   Wm. H. Johnson, Clerk.

---

SHERIFF BOND $10,000  GIVEN JANUARY, 1834;  RECORDED FEB'Y., 1834.

    Know all men by these presents that we Alfred Gardner, John Terrell, George Stovall, Jonathan M. Gilbert and Jubilee Rogers all of the County of Weakley and State of Tennessee are held and firmly bound unto William Carroll Esquire, Governor in and for the State of Tennessee and his successors in office in the penal sum of Ten Thousand dollars for which payment well and truly to be made we bind ourselves, our heirs, executors, and administrators Jointly & severally firmly by these presents sealed with our seals & dated the 14th Day of January, 1834 -

    The condition of the above obligation is such that whereas the above bound Alfred Gardner is this day duly Elected constituted and appointed sheriff of Weakley County by the worshipful, the county court of the county aforesaid, if therefore the said Alfred Gardner shall well and truly Execute and duly return make of all process and precepts to him directed and pay and satisfy all fees and sums of money by him received or levied by virtue of any process into the proper office by which the same by the tenor thereof ought to be paid or to the person or persons to whom the same shall be due his, her or their Executors, administrators attorneys or agents and in all other things well truly and faithfully Execute the said office  (Page 137)  of sheriff during his continuance therein then the above obligation to be void otherwise to remain in full force and virtue.

    Witness our hands and seals the day and date above written.

Signed and acknowledged )
in open court.                )
Test. Wm. Johnson, Clk. )

                                                    Alfred Gardner, (Seal)
                                                    Jno. Terrell,(Seal)
                                                    George Stovall ( Seal)
                                                    J. Rogers, (Seal)
                                                    J.M.Gilbert, (Seal)

(Page 137) Cont.

SHERIFF'S BOND OF $6000 RECORDED THE 18th FEB'Y., 1834.

Know all men by these presents that we, Alfred Gardner, John Terrell, George Stovall, Jonathan M. Gilbert and Jubilee Rogers all of the County of Weakley and State of Tennessee are held and firmly bound unto William Carroll Esquire, Governor of the State of Tennessee and his successors in office in the penal sum of six thousand dollars for the true and faithful payment of which we bind ourselves, our heirs, Executors and administrators jointly and severally firmly by these presents.

The condition of the above obligation is such that whereas the above bound Alfred Gardner has this day been duly constituted and appointed sheriff in Deed for the County of Weakley therefore should the said Alfred Gardner well and truly collect & Pay over all fines and county taxes that may become due during the time for which the said Alfred Gardner may be the incumbent of said office then & in that case the above obligation to be nul and void otherwise to remain in full force and virtue. Witness our hands and seals the 14th Day of January, 1834.

Signed and acknowledged in open court .
Test.
Wm. H. Johnson, Clk.

Alfred Gardner, (Seal)
Jno. Terrell, (Seal)
George Stovall, (Seal)
J. Rogers, (Seal)
J. M. Gilbert, (Seal)

---

(Page 138)

NICHOLASS W. SHRUMS LAST WILL & TESTAMENT-

In the name of God, Amen. I, Nicholas W. Shrum of the County of Weakley in the State of Tennessee being at present weak in body but of sound mind, memory and understanding do make and publish this my last will and testament in manner form following to wit, I recommend my soul to God the Lord and giver of life in hope of a glorious resurection in and through the merits of our blessed Redeemer and my body I recommend to a christian burial, and after the payment of all my Just debts it is my desire that my Worldly estate should be disposed in the following manner.

I desire that my filly and saddle and one cow and one fur hat should be sold and my land and all I possess and the remainder of the amount of the sale after my just debts are paid out of it I give to my wife and children. This the 24th of September, 1833.

Nicholas W. Shrum.

Test.
Martin Richie P. )
John P. Johnson )
   his )
William X Elder P. )
   mark. )

(Page 138)

STATE OF TENNESSEE )
WEAKLEY COUNTY    )    October Term.

Then was the due Execution of the within will and testimony duly proven by the oaths of Martin Richie and William Elder the subscribing witnesses thereto and ordered to be recorded.

Wm. H. Johnson, Clerk.

---

(Page 139)

JESSE STROUD'S LAST WILL & TESTAMENT
RECORDED THE 17th DAY OF JULY, 1834.

I, Jesse Stroud of the County of Weakley and State of Tennessee. Planter, being weak in body but sound in mind and memory. Calling to mind the mortality of the body and that it is appointed for all men once to die and from the common cause of nature, feel and know that I am not long for this world, consequently do this the 24th day of May one thousand Eight hundred and thirty four make and order this my last will and testament in the manner and form following that is to say-

First - I give and bequeath to my wife Tabitha and her six children (viz.) Elizabeth, Deniza, Obedience, Margaret, Jane, James & Richard my two tracts of land lying in Obion County and State of Tennessee one of which was deeded to me by Rice Williams. It being part of 1000 acre tract in the name of Nathan and Joel Pinson on the waters of Davidson Creek. Also one tract of land on the Clover Creek fork of Obion River being part of a seven hundred acre tract conveyed by Edward Harris to Sam'l Love and by him conveyed to John Hunter by will and by him to John Hoyter and from John J. Hoyter to me , Jesse Stroud. Also all of my stock of horses, cattle, hogs & sheep, my farming tools Household & Kitchen furniture the above property to be under the guidance control & full management of my wife Tabitha, to be used discretionary with her as she considers right for the raising and educating those six named children during her natural lifetime or until the youngest surviving child shall arrive at the age of twenty one years then the above specified property is to be equally divided between those six named children with the exception of my daughter Deniza who is and may have the amount allotted for her during her life, at her death to belong to the heirs of her body and shall not in any wise have the disposal of same.

(Page 140)

Secondly, I give and bequeath unto my son Howell an occupant claim lying in the county of Weakley purchased by me from Thos. M. Buchanon entered on the General plan and in the name of William B. Rolls also one hundred dollars to be furnished or such part thereof as would be sufficient to purchase a good valid title to the above occupant which is to be done in due time by warrant or otherwise , the remainder if any to be paid to him when he arrives to the age of twenty one years.

Thirdly, I give and bequeath to my son Silas an occupant claim

Page 140) Cont.

lying in Weakley County purchased by me from Sterling Parker entered on the General plan by and in the name of Mary Baker, also one hundred dollars to be furnished or such part there off as will be sufficient to purchase a good and valid title to the above named occupant claim which is to be done in due time by warrant or otherwise the remainder if any to be paid to the said Silas whenever he arrives to the age of Twenty one years. The benefits arising from rents & c from each or either of those occupant claims to be applied to the education of my two sons, Howell and Silas and improving the same.

Fourthly, having had eleven children by my first wife Naoma and having heretofore contributed to each liberally, I do therefore give to each one dollar (viz.) Echolds, Isaac, Jesse, John, Thomas, Nancy, Rebecca, Polly, Sally, William & Peter, if called to be paid by my wife Tabitha. I do hereby anull all former wills & testaments and declare this to be my last will & testament. In witness whereof I have hereunto set my hand and seal this day & date above written.

Signed sealed and delivered in the presence of these witnesses.
                                    his
                        Jesse R. Stroud, Seal)
                                    mark.

Harden S. Adams,  p )
Samuel Hall         )
Thornton Jones      )

---

STATE OF TENNESSEE WEAKLEY COUNTY COURT   JULY TERM 1834.

Then was the within last will & testament of James Stroud, Deceased produced in open court and the due Execution thereof was proven by the oaths of Hardin S. Adams & Samuel Hall two of the subscribing witness thereto. It was thereupon ordered by the court that it be admitted of record.
                                    Wm. H. Johnson, Clk.

---

(Page 141)

SHERIFF & COLLECTOR'S BOND FOR 1834 - $1500.

STATE OF TENNESSEE )
WEAKLEY COUNTY     )

Know all men by these presents that we Alfred Gardner, George Stovall, Jubilee Rogers and Samuel A. Warner, all of the County of Weakley and State of Tennessee are held and firmly bound unto William Carroll, Esquire, Governor of the State of Tennessee for the time being and his successors in office in the penal sum of one thousand five hundred dollars, and to secure the payment thereof we bind ourselves, our heirs, executors and administrators jointly and severally firmly by these presents.

(Page 141) Cont.

The condition of the above obligation is such that whereas the above bound alfred Gardner hath appointed by the justice of the county court of Weakley County, Sheriff and collector of the public taxes in said county. Now if the said Alfred Gardner shall well & faithfully pay over to the State of Tennessee for the Western district all the taxes which he may be bound by law to collect and pay over to the said Treasurer of the State of Tennessee for the year 1834 within the time prescribed by law for which payment of said Taxes and according to the terms thereof, then this obligation to be void otherwise to remain in full force & virtue.

In testamony whereof we have hereunto set our names and affixed our seals the 14th day of July, 1834.

Signed, sealed and acknowledged )
in open court. )
Test. Wm. H. Johnson, Clk. )

Alfred Gardner, (Seal)
S. A. Warner, (Seal)
George Stovall, (Seal)
J. Rogers, (Seal)

---

(Page 142)

COLLECTORS BOND FOR 1834, $5000.

STATE OF TENNESSEE )
WEALKEY COUNTY )

Know all men by these presents that we Alfred Gardner, Jubilee -- George Stovall and Samuel A Warner, all of the County of Weakley and State of Tennessee are held & firmly bound unto Perry Vincent, Chairman of the Court of Pleas & quarter sessions for Weakley County or his successors in office in the penal sum of five thousand dollars the payment of which well and truly to be made we bind ourselves, our heirs, Executors or administrators Jointly & severally firmly by these presents signed with our names & sealed with our seals & dated the 14th day of July, 1834.

The condition of the above obligation is such that whereas the above bound Alfred Gardner has been appointed sheriff and collector of the public taxes within the said county of Weakley by the justices of said county court. Now if the said Alfred Gardner shall well and truly pay over to the trustee of said county all moneys and taxes which by law he may be bound to collect and pay over to said Trustee for the year 1834 within said county, to wit, the county tax, Jury Tax, Poor Tax, Public building tax, and taxes laid to furnish weights and measures for said county (which taxes are all laid by the said county for said year) within the time and according to the terms prescribed by law.

Then the above obligation to be void otherwise to remain in full force and virtue.

Signed & acknowledged in open court )
Wm. H. Johnson, Clk. )

Alfred Gardner, (Seal)
S. A. Warner, Seal)
Geo. Stovall, (Seal)
J. Rogers, (Seal

## JOHN PARRISH'S LAST WILL & TESTAMENT
### Recorded October 24th, 1834.

In the name of God Amen - I, John Parrish of the County of Weakley & State of Tennessee considering the uncertainty this mortal life and being of sound mind & memory blessed by God for the same. Do make & Publish this my last will & testament in manner & Form following that is to -wit:

First - I give & Bequeath to my beloved wife Beedy Parish during her natural life or widowhood. Two hundred acres of land, it being part of the tract of land where I now live & fore negros, Charles, Nelson, Aggy & Molly my household & kitchen furniture my stock of horses, cattle & hogs, My meaning is only for my wife to have a sufficient quantity of the above named stock as will sute her conveneacy and comfort also my farming tools.

Item 2nd, I give & bequeath to my son, Mathew Parish, the property that I have heretofore given him and no more.

Item 3, I give and bequeath to my son Henderson Parish one hundred acres of land where he now lives the West part of the track where I now live together with all the property that I have given him heretofore.

Item 4, I give & bequeath to my son John Parish one hundred acres of land where he now lives the north part of my tract of land where I now live to him & his heirs & assigns forever with all the property that I have heretofore given him.

Itom 5. I give & bequeath to my son Charles Parish the proceeds of sale sale of my stock provided the amount so raised from the sale of my surperlous property and stock should excede two hundred & twenty five dollars for the balance to be divided among my other children.

Itom 6, I give and bequeath to my youngest son, Isom Parish, two hundred acres of land at the death of my wife or if she should mary for the land to be his, his heirs and assigns forever also one horse & saddle one feather bed and necessary clothing one cow & calf when he arives to twenty one years of age.

7, I give and bequeath to my eldest daughter Elizabeth one negro boy by the name of Ned together with the property that I have heretofore given her to her & her heirs & assigns forever.

8, I give and bequeath to my dauter Liddy a negro boy name Mansor to her & her heirs & assigns forever also the property that I have heretofore given her.

9. I give & bequeath to my dauter Mary, now a single a negro girl by the name of Sarah one feather bed with usual clothing & one cow & calf to her and her heirs & assigns forever.

Page 144) Cont.

    10 - Give & Bequeath to my daughter Eliza a negro boy by the name of Heardy  one feather bed & clothing one cow and calf to her, her heirs & assigns forever -

    11 - As may be better understood my will is that part of my stock be sold and all my just Debts be paid & the balance go to my son Charles as far as the amount as I have before stated. My will is that my eight youngest children shall share equally in my property or its value -

    Therefore at the death of my wife that all the balance of my property that is left for the benefit of my wife be equally divided at the death of my wife in order that it may be better understood and my will further known that all the property that I have willd in support of my wife during her life ,that at her death be sold and the money divided in the following manner:  my three sons in order to make them equal for them to have one hundred & thirty seven Dollars a peace  that is my sons, Henderson, John & Isom, also my two Dauters  Mary and Eliza to have one hundred and seventy fournty dollars to to be divided between them in the dollowing manner. Mary to have sixty two Dollars & Eliza to have one hundred & twelve Dollars.

    My will is further that my son Charles Parish may be Equal with the rest of my children at the Death of his Mother.  I give him a sufficency to make up for hundred & fifty two dollars counting in ninety dollars which he has received from me & the amount which he may receive from the sale of stock as I have above  Directed.

    (Page 145)  Then the balance of my Estate to be Equally Divided among all my children - and lastly I hereby appoint my son Henderson Parish & my friend & my son Charles Parish my Executors to this my last will & testament and hereby revoking all former wills by me made.  In witness whereof I have hereunto set my hand & seal this the 19th day of June in the year of our Lord, 1834.

                                                John Parish, (Seal)

Signed sealed published and Declared   )
by the above named John Parish to be  )
his last will and testament in the     )    Interlined before signed
presence of a us all who have hereunto )  at the word seventy & We.
subscribed our names as witnesses      )
in the presence of the testator.       )

Test.
Benja. Barham
Hatwell Parrish

---

(146)      SHERIFF'S BOND FOR $12500.  RECORDED .
               Recorded 18th September, 1835.

    Know all men by these presents that we Peleg Terrell, John Terrell Jeptha Terrell, Jubilee Rogers, Caleb Brasfield and Hillry H. Bondurant

(Page 146) Cont.

All of the County of Weakley and State of Tennessee are held and firmly bound unto William Carroll Governor of the State of Tennessee for the time being and his successors in office in the penal sum of twelve thousand five hundred dollars and to secure the payment thereof we bind ourselves our heirs, executors and administrators jointly and severally firmly by these presents sealed with our seals and dated this 14th day of July, 1835.

The condition of the above obligation is such that whereas the above bound Peleg Terrell is constituted and appointed sheriff of Weakley County by the Justices of the court of pleas & quarter sessions of said county. Now if the said Peleg Terrell shall well and truly execute and due return make upon all process and precepts to him directed and pay and satisfy all fees and sums of money by him received or levied by virtue of any process into the proper office by which the same by the tenor thereof ought to be paid his, her or their executors administrators agents or attorneys and in all things well and truly and faithfully execute the said office of sheriff during his conteneance therein then the above obligation to be void, otherwise to remain in full force and effect.

              Peleg Terrell, (Seal)
              John Terrell, (Seal)
              Jeptha Terrell, (Seal)
              J. Rogers, (Seal)
              C. Brasfield, (Seal)
              H. H. Bondurant. (Seal)

---

(147)  SHERIFF AND COLLECTORS BOND FOR 1835.

Know all men by these presents that Peleg Terrell John Terrell Jubilee Rogers and Jeptha Terrell all of the County of Weakley and State of Tennessee are held and firmly bound unto Perry Vincent Chairman of the Court of Pleas & quarter Sessions for Weakley County or his successors in office in the penal sum of five thousand Dollars the payment of which well and truly to be made we bind ourselves our heirs Executors and administrators Jointly Severally firmly by these presents sealed with our seals and dated the 14th Day of July, 1835.

The condition of the above obligation is such that whereof the above bound Peleg Terrell has been appointed sheriff and collector of the taxes within said county of Weakley by the Trustees of said county court. Now if the said Peleg Terrell shall well and truly pay over to the Trustee of said county all money and taxes which by law he may be bound to cllect and pay over to said Trustee for the year 1835 within said county to wit. The county taxes, Jury tax, Poor tax and Public building Tax which Taxes are all laid by the said county court for said year within the time and according to the time prescribed by the law then this obligation to be void otherwise to remain in full force and effect.

              Peleg Terrell, (Seal)
              John Terrell, (Seal)
              J. Rogers, (Seal)
              Jeptha Terrell, (Seal)

(Page 147) Cont.

Know all men by these preasants that we Peleg Terrell John Terrell Jubilee Rogers and Jeptha Terrell all of the County of Weakley and State of Tennessee are held and firmly bound unto William Carroll Esquire, Governor of the State of Tennessee for the time being in the penal sum of twelve hundred Dollars to be paid to the said governor or his successors in office the payment of which well and truly to be made. We bind ourselves our heirs Executors administrators Truly and firmly by these presents sealed with our seals and dated this the 14th of July, 1835.

(148) The condition of the above obligation is such that where as the above bounden Peleg Terrell has been appointed by the Justice of Weakley County court sheriff and collector of the publick taxes in said county now if the said Peleg Terrell shall well and truly pay over to the trustees of the state of Tennessee for the western District all the taxes which he may be bound by law to collect and pay over to the said Trustees of the State of Tennessee for the year, 1835 within the time prescribed by law for such payment of said taxes and according to the tenor thereof then the above obligation to be void otherwise to remain in effect.

                                                          Peleg Terrell, (Seal)
                                                          John Terrell, (Seal)
                                                          Jubilee Rogers, (Seal)
                                                          Jeptha Terrell, (Seal)

---

### BENJAMIN MERRILL'S WILL

In the name of God Amen. I Benjamin Merrill of the County of Weakley and state of Tennessee being weak in boddy but of sound mind and memory blessed be the Almity God for the same do make and publish this my last will and testimony in manner and form following that is to say first I Give and bequeath unto my beloved wife Mary Merrell after paying all my Just Debts unpaid, all my estate both real and personal during her natural life time for her only purposes and support after the Death of my beloved (149) wife Mary Merrill. I also give and bequeath unto the heirs of James Slauter & Joseph Ruth one Dollar each. I also give and bequeath unto my three Daughters Chas. H Merrill Jemima Hide & Lucy Cunningham the sum of fifty Dollars each clear and above and equalportion with the ballance of my children. I also give and bequeath an equal portion after the death of my beloved wife Mary Merrill of all the property amongst all my children including the three Daughters above mentioned I hereby leave Daniel Smith Lemuel Merrell and William Merrell Executors of this last will and testament hereby revoking all former wills by me made in witness whereof I have hear unto set my hand and seal this the 10th of May one thousand Eight hundred and thirty five. Signed and sealed published by the above named Benjamin Merrell to be his last will and testament in the presants of us.

                                                          Benjamin Merrill, (Seal)

William Western
J. M. Fennel

(P.149) Cont.
Proven in open court at October term 1835 by William Wester & J. M. Fennell subscribing witnesses.

---

### ELIAS KILLEBREWS WILL

The Eleventh of April one thousand Eight hundred and thirty five I Elias Killebrew being in a low state of heth but of a sound mind and memory and knowing that it is appointed for all men to Die and being Desirous to have my business in an orderly way have ordered constituted and appointed this Instrument of writing as my last will and testament in manner and form following. first I wish all my Just Debts to be paid out of my property the balance to my beloved wife Matilda Killebrew during her life or widowhood at which time I wish all my property to be sold and Divided amongst my children as the law Directs   Also I with to appoint my beloved friend Thomas Killebrew Jr. and Killebrew Kennedy Executors to this my last will and testament.

      bloted out before assigned in presant of us -
                                        Elias Killebrew (Seal)

James Paris    )
James W. Buckley )
William Martin   )

---

STATE OF TENNESSEE )
WEAKLEY COUNTY     )   July term, 1835

The within will proven in open court by the oaths of James W. Buckley & William Martin subscribing witnesses thereto and ordered to be recorded.
                                  W. H. Johnson   Clk.

---

(150)       WILLIAM ROBERTS LAST WILL & TESTAMENT
               Recorded January 20th, 1838.

I William Roberts of the county of Weakley and State of Tennessee being sick and weak of Body but of sound mind & understanding, calling to mind the mortality of my body and knowing that it is appointed for all men once to die have thought proper to make & ordain this my last will & testament.

First I recommend my soul to God who gave it and my body to the dust to be buried in christian like manner & to dispose of my worldly goods in the following manner, viz. I give & bequeath to my beloved wife Martha during her natural life, one fourth of the tract of land whereon I now live to be in the middle thereof. I give & bequeath to her on the same terms my negroes Davy, Thaddy, Bob & Anica all of my stock consisting of horses cows and hogs, also

(P.150) Cont.

cows and hogs. My waggon, also all of household and kitchen furniture and plantation utensils. I give & bequeath to my son Henry Roberts one dollar having advanced him his full portion already. I give and bequeath to my son William C. Roberts' children two hundred dollars to be equally divided amongst them. I loan to my daughter Winifred Gordon one quarter section of land lying and being in Graves County, Kentucky known as the Davidson place and at her death I give and bequeath it to her children to be equally divided among them. I give and bequeath to Frances Roberts as trustee for the lawful heirs of the body of my son (P. 151) John Roberts one negro girl named Eliza and her increase which is now in the possession of said John Roberts and so to remain during her natural life and at her death to be equally divided among the lawful heirs of the body of said John Roberts also to my son John Roberts ninety five dollars which I have loaned him, I give & bequeath unto my son Francis Roberts sixty dollars. I give and bequeath to my son Richard Roberts my negro man called big Matt also two hundred dollars. I give & bequeath to my son Thomas Roberts one fourth part of the land whereon I live lying in the southeast corner of the tract subject to one fourth of my wife's dower, my negro man Curd and my negro girl Mickey. I give and bequeath to my daughter Rebecca Ann Farmer my negro man named little Matt also one hundred dollars. I give and bequeath to my son David Watthall Roberts one fourth part of the tract of land whereon I now live subject to my wife's dower and my negroes Joe and Silas. I give and bequeath to my son Martin U Roberts one fourth part of the tract of land whereon I now live to be in the north west corner of said tract subject to my wife's dower my negroes Roda & Peter. I give & bequeath to my son James R. Roberts one fourth part of my land whereon I now live to be in the northeast corner of said tract subject to my wife's dower my negroes Will, Vincent and Catharine. I loan to Elizabeth Bailey nine acres of land on the state line west of the pond during her natural life which is a part left to my son James R. Roberts. I further will and direct that the property left to my two youngest sons remain with that willed to my wife until James R. Roberts arrives to the age of Eighteen (152) years and that they be supported and Educated without any charge. I further will & direct that at the decease of my wife or if that should be before my son James R. Roberts arrives to the age of Eighteen years that then and not till then, that the money by acirs named before be paid and the ballance if any remaining be equally divided amongst the children of my present wife Martha Roberts, And lastly I constituted ordain and appoint my beloved sons Francis Roberts, Richard Roberts and Thomas Roberts my Executors of this my last will & Testament. Hereby annull all other wills and disclaiming this to be my last will & testament in witness I have hereunto set my hand and seal this ninth day of May in the year of our Lord one thousand Eight hundred and thirty five.

William Roberts (Seal)

Signed & sealed in the presence of)
J. A. Roberts )
Jacob G. Gates )
Wm. Taylor )
Wm. V. Boatwright )

STATE OF TENNESSEE )
WEAKLEY COUNTY ) County court January Term 1836.

(P.152) Cont.

Then was the Due Execution of the within will Duly proven in open court by the oaths of Jacob G. Gates William Taylor and William V. Boatwright subscribing witnesses thereto and ordered to be recorded.

Wm. H. Johnson Clk.

---

(153) BUCKNER RUSSELS LAST WILL & TESTAMENT,
Rendered January 21st, 1836.

I Buckner Russel assigned, being weak in body but of sound perfect mind & memory blessed by Almighty God for the same do make and publish this my last will & testament in the manner & form following that is to say First, I give & bequeath unto my beloved Rachel Russel one carriage and harness and all my household & Kitchen furniture & one cow and one heifer and my Bible and books. I do also give and bequeath unto my daughter Margaret Russel wife of Aaron Russel one cow named pud. I do also give & bequeath unto my son Buckner Russel three head of cattle two sows & thirteen shoats two horses and all my tools of every description - I do also give & bequeath unto my grandson William Russel son of Buckner Russel two steers which said several species of property or legacies I will & order shall be paid and delivered over to the said legatees within six months after my decease. I further give and advise to my wife Rachel Russel her heirs and assigns all that tract of land lying and being in the County of Weakley in 12th surveyors district 2nd Range and 7th section on Thomas Creek granted to me the 1st day of January, 1835 by grant No. 2619 containing 34½ acres of Land and lastly I do hereby appoint my beloved wife Rachel Russel/sole Executrix of this my last will & testament hereby re- (154) voking all former wills by me made in witness whereof I have hereunto set my hand and seal this 8th day of April in the year of our Lord one thousand Eight hundred & thirty five.

Signed sealed published & declared by the above named Buckner Russel to be his last will & testament in the presents of us who have here unto subscribed our names as witnesses in the presents of the testator.

JOHN HENRY MOON )              his
Boaz Thizzell     )       Buckner X Russel, (Seal)
                              mark

---

JAMES BUCKLEYS LAST WILL & TESTAMENT
Recorded 12th of April, 1836.

STATE OF TENNESSEE )
WEAKLEY COUNTY      )

One thousand Eight hundred & thirty five September 1st Day, I James Buckley being in perfect health and sound mind and memory, but knowing that it is appointed for all men to Die and being desirous to have my Business Settled in a Lawful manner have this day constituted and appointed this writing as my last will and Testament in manner & form following (viz.) first of all my property I lend to my beloved wife, Mary Buckley during her

(P. 154) Cont.

life or widowhood, Except the stock got too large for her to support, then for to sell of such as she could spair & and divide among our children. She keeping a sufficiency for her own support while she lives or during widowhood and as her Death or marriage, it is my will that all the property be Equally Divided among all my children, and I appoint my beloved son Coleman Buckley as my Executor to settle my business according to law, and this my last will and Testament, also when the occupant that we live on at this time, when it comes into market, I want my son Coleman Buckley to raise money and ( 155 ) save the same and at the death or widowhood of said Mary Buckley to be sold & equally divided as above mentioned.

In Testimony of the above I have subscribed my seal and name the day and year above written.

Interlined in fifteenth line before signed. Signed sealed & acknowledged in presence of us.

James Buckley, (Seal)

James Parrish )
John Ridgway )

---

### JOHN STUNSTONS LAST WILL & TESTAMENT
Recorded 8th June, 1836.

This is to certify that I John Stunston of the County of Weakley & State of Tennessee being of sound & perfect mind and memory do make and publish this my last will and testament in manner and form following. First, I give and bequeath unto my son James Stunston one malatto boy Martin and one hundred acres of land which I now live on & one half of an occupant adjoining the same tract, one sorrel mare to him and his heirs at my death. I do also give and bequeath unto my son Levi Stunston one boy named Isom one hundred acres of land apart of the above named tract and one half of the ocipint adjoining to it also one sorrel colt at my death. I also give to my daughter Rebeca Stunston one negro Girl Succa to her and her heirs. I also give to Sally Summers one negro Girl named Martha to her and her heirs. I also give and bequeath to my Daughter Elizabeth Somers one negro girl named Betsy at my death. I also wish my stock of hogs and cattle and sheep and three horses to be gathered together and sold and my Debts and my son James Stunston to be paid out of the above named stock and the balance of it may be equally divided amongst my children William Stunston and Nancy Dunn to have an equal part of all the perishable property (156) and money also my negro girl named Sally that is now in law to be sold and equally divided among all the above named children one negro Girl named Jane I wish to be set free at my Death induren her natural life.

This my last will and Testament hereby revoking all former wills by me made in witness whereof I have here unto set hand and offered my seal this eight day of April in the year of our Lord one thousand eight hundred thirty six.

Attest )
George Bussell )
Henry his X Stunston )
     mark

John Stunston

(P.156) Cont.

Know all men by these presents that we William H. Johnson, Mears Warner, Richard C. Williams & James H. Moran all of the County of Weakley and State of Tennessee are held and firmly bound unto Newton Cannon Governor of the State of Tennessee and his successors in office in the sum of five thousand dollars to which payment well and truly to be made. We bind ourselves heirs executors and administrators Jointly and severally firmly by these presents sealed with our seals and Dated this second day of May, 1836.

The condition of the above obligation is such that whereas the above bound William H. Johnson is constituted and appointed clerk of the county court of Weakley County by the citizens of said county. Now if the said William H. Johnson do well and truly faithfully and impartially execute the Duties of the said office of clerk of the county court of said county during his continuance therein according to law and reserve and take care of the records of said court then the above obligation to be void Else to remain in full force and virtue. In testamony where of we have hereunto set our hand & seal the day first above written.

Signed & acknowledged )
in open court -  )
    Test.  )

Wm. H. Johnson, (Seal)
Mears Warner, (Seal)
R. C. Williams, (Seal)
J. H. Moran, (Seal)

---

(157) Know all men by these presents that we William H. Johnson, Mears Warner, Richard C. Williams all of the county of Weakley and State of Tennessee are held and firmly bound unto Newton Cannon Governor of the State of Tennessee and his successors in office in the penal sum of five hundred dollars to which payment well and truly to be made we bind ourselves our heirs Executors and administrators Jointly and severally firmly by these presents sealed with our seals and dated this second day of May 1836.

The condition of the above obligation is such that whereas the above bound William H. Johnson shall well & truly collect and pay over all fines forfeitures and state tax which he may by virture of his office be bound to collect according to the true intent and meaning of the acts of assembly in such cases made and provided. Then the above obligation to be void. Otherwise to remain in full force and virtue.

Wm. H. Johnson, (Seal)
Mears Warner, (Seal)
R. C. Williams, (Seal)

---

STATE OF TENNESSEE )
WEAKLEY COUNTY    )

Know all men by these presents that we William S. Scott, James H. Moran, Isaac Killough, Beverly J. Milner, William Thompson William L. Cochrum & Littleton C. Duke all of the County of Weakley and State of Tennessee are held and firmly bound unto Newton Cannon Esquire Governor

(P.157) Cont.

in and for the State of Tennessee or his successors in office in the penal sum twelve thousand five hundred dollars the payment of which well and truly to be made. We bind ourselves our heirs Executors and Administrators Jointly and severally firmly by these presents sealed with our seals and dated this 2nd day of May 1836.

The condition of the above bounden William S. Scott is constituted and appointed sheriff of Weakley County (158) by the citizens of said county. If therefore the said William S. Scott shall well and truly Execute and due return make of all process and precepts to him directed and pay and satisfy all fees and sums of money by him received or levied by virtue of any process into the proper office by which the same by the tenor thereof ought to be paid or to the person or persons to whom the same shall be due his her or their Executors administrators attorneys or agents and in all other things well, truly and faithfully execute the said office of sheriff during his continuance therein then the above obligation to be void otherwise to remain in full force and effect. In testimony whereof we have hereunto set our hands & seals the Day and year first above writen. (158)
Signed sealed and acknowledged in open court Test.
Wm. H. Johnson, Clerk.

W. S. Scott, (Seal)
J. H. Moran, (Seal)
Isaac Killough, (Seal)
Wm. Thompson, (Seal)
B. J. Milner, (Seal)
William T. Cockrum, (Sea)
L. C. Duke, (Seal)

---

COLLECTORS BOND FOR 1836.

STATE OF TENNESSEE )
WEAKLEY COUNTY    )

Know all men by these presents that we William S. Scott, Ephriam D. Dickson, Richard C. Williams & Isaac Killough all of the county of Weakley and State of Tennessee are held and firmly bound unto Newton Cannon Esquire Governor of the State of Tennessee for the time being or his successors in office in the penal sum of one thousand Dollars and to secure the payment thereof we bind ourselves our heirs Executors and administrators Jointly & severally firmly by these presents sealed with our seals & Dated this 5th Day of September, 1836.

The condition of the above obligation is such that whereas the above bound William S. Scott hath been by the citizens of Weakley County Duly Elected Sheriff (159) and collector of the public taxes for Weakley County. Now if the said William S. Scott shall well and truly pay over to the treasurer of the State of Tennessee all the taxes which he may be bound by law to collect and pay over to said Treasurer for the year 1836 within the time prescribed by law for such payment of said taxes and according to the tenor thereof then the above obligation to be void otherwise to remain in full force and virtue. In testimony whereof we have here-

(P.159) Cont.
unto set our hands and seals the Day and Date above written.

| | |
|---|---|
| Signed & acknowledged ) | W. S. Scott, (Seal) |
| in open court. ) | E. D. Dickson, (Seal) |
| Wm. H. Johnson, Clk. ) | R.C. Williams, (Seal) |
| | Isaac Killough, (Seal) |

---

## COLLECTORS BOND TO TRUSTEE FOR 1836.

STATE OF TENNESSEE )
WEAKLEY COUNTY )

Know all men by these presents that we William S. Scott, Ephriam D. Dickson, Richard C. Williams & Isaac Killough all of the county of Weakley & State of Tennessee are held and firmly bound unto Caleb Brasfield Chairman of the county court of said county court of said county of Weakley or his successors in office in the penal sum of Two thousand five hundred Dollars the payment of which well and truly to be made we bind ourselves our heirs Executors Administrators Jointly & severally firmly by these presents  Sealed with our seals & Dated this 5th Day of September, 1836.

The condition of the above obligation is such that whereas the above bound William S. Scott has been by the citizens of said county of Weakley Duly elected sheriff and collector of the public taxes for said county of Weakley and within the same.  Now if the said William (160) S. Scott shall well and truly pay over to the trustee of said county all moneys and taxes which by law he may be bound to collect and pay over to the said trustee for the year of 1836. (towit, the county tax, Jury tax, Poor tax, public Building tax and Bridge tax which taxes are all laid by the court) within the time prescribed by law then the above obligation to be void Else to remain in full force and virtue . In testimony whereof we have hereunto set our hands & seals this Day & Date above written.

| | |
|---|---|
| Signed & acknowledged ) | W. S. Scott, (Seal) |
| in open court ) | E. D. Dickson, (Seal) |
| Wm. H. Johnson, Clk. ) | R. C. Williams, (Seal) |
| | Isaac Killough, (Seal) |

---

## THE LAST WILL & TESTAMENT OF JOHN P. JOHNSON

In the name of God Amen  I John P. Johnson of Weakley County Tennssee sick and weak of body but of sound mind  memory and understanding and considering the certainty of Death and the uncertainty of the time thereof, and to the end I may be the better prepared to leave this world whenever it shall please God to call me hence do therefore make (and) declare this my last will and Testament in manner folowing. That all my Just debts as shall be by me owing at my death Shall be fully paid and satisfied and from and after payment thereof and subject thereunto .  Then my will is that all the residue of my property Shall remain in the hands of my wife during her lifetime or widowhood for the support of my children  and then to be equally parted and divided them Share & share alike  and I do appoint my said dear wife shall have the guardianship and tuition of them
so long a

(P.160) Cont.
so long as she shall continue to be sole    In witness whereof I the testator have to this my last will consisting of one sheet of paper set my hand and seal this the 18 of December, 1836.

                                    John P. Johnson

Test.                         Proven by Herroll & graham
T. S. Parry                Feby term, 1837
John Harroll             Wm. Johnson, Clk.
E. L. Graham

---

(P.161)
STATE OF TENNESSEE )
WEAKLEY COUNTY    )

    Know all men by these presents that we William S. Scott  Richard C. Williams Zephariah Harris  Edward P Lathem & James H  Moran - All of the County of Weakley and State of Tennessee are held and openly bound unto Caleb Brasfield chairman of this County Court of said county in the sum of six Thousand Two Hundred Dollars  to be paid to said chairman or his successors in office the payment of which well & truly to be made we bind ourselves, our heirs, Executors & administrators Jointly & severally firmly by these presents  Sealed with our seals and dated this 1st day of May 1837  the condition of the above obligation is such that whereas the above bounded William S. Scott this day recovered the tax list of said county from the clerk of said county court to be collected for the year 1837  Now if the said William S. Scott collect or cause to collected all county taxes which he may be bound to collect for said year and pay the same over to the county trustee within the time prescribed by law then the above obligation to be void otherwise to remain in full force and virtue.

                                  William S. Scott, (Seal)
                                  Z. H. Harris, (Seal)
                                  R. C. Williams, (Seal)
                                  James H. Moran, (Seal)

---

(Page 162)
STATE OF TENNESSEE )
WEAKLEY COUNTY     )

    Know all men by these presents that we William S. Scott James H. Moran  Richard E. Williams Edward P. Latham Zaphariah H. Harris  all of this county and state aforesaid are held and firmly bound unto Newton Cannon Esquire Governor of the State of Tennessee or his successors in office in the penal sum of one thousand two hundred Dollars the payment of which well and truly to be made we bind ourselves our heirs Executors and administrators jointly severally firmly by these presents - The condition of the above obligation is such that whereas the above bounded William S. Scott has this day received the tax list from the clerk of the said county court to be collected for the year 1837  Now if the said William S. Scott shall collect or cause to be collected all the tax which he may be bound to collect for said year and pay the same over to the comptroller of the State of Tennssee within the time prescribed by law then the above obligation to be void otherwise to remain in full force and virtue -
In testimony whereof we have hereunto set our hands and seals.

(P.162) Cont.
This 1st day of May 1837.

W. S. Scott, (Seal)
Z. H. Harris, (Seal)
J. H. Moran, (Seal)
R. C. Williams, (Seal)

---

(P.163)
STATE OF TENNESSEE )
WEAKLEY COUNTY     )

Know all men by these presents that we Kinchen Williams Dennis Cochran John A. Gardner J. P. G Roulhac  Isaac Killough  John Tansil William W. Gleeson Thomas S Edwards  A. B. Foree all of the County of Weakley and State of Tennessee are held and firmly bound unto Caleb Brasfield chairman of the county court of said county in the penal sum of Five Thousand Dollars for the payment of which well and truly to be made we bind ourselves our heirs Executors administrators and assigns firmly Jointly severally  sealed with our seals and dated the 7th of August 1837.

The condition of the above obligation is such that the above bound Kinchin Williams was this day Elected by the county court of the said County of Weakley at the August term of said court  Clerk of said court in conformity to the statute in such case made and provided to fill the vacancy in said office occasioned by the resignation of William H. Johnson Now if the said Kinchin Williams shall well and truly do and  perform the several duties injoined upon him by virtue of the office of clerk of Weakley to the best of his Judgment and ability then this obligation to be void Else to remain in full force and effect.

K. Williams, (Seal)
John A. Gardner, (Seal)
J. P. G. Roulhac, (Seal)
Dennis Cochran, (Seal)
Wm. W. Gleeson, (Seal)
A. B. Foree, (Seal)
Isaac Killough, (Seal)
John Tansil, (Seal)
Thomas S. Edwards, (Seal)

---

(P.164)    THE LAST WILL & TESTAMENT OF W  BAYLESS

I Willie Bayless of the County of Weakley and State of Tennessee being of Sound and disposing mind do hearby make and publish this my last will and Testament hereby revoking all former and other wills or codicils by me at any time heretofore made and published  And 1st I wish my funeral expenses and all my just debts of whatsoever kind first paid and Satisfied out of Estate which I Desire shall be done by my Executors as far as possible by the collection of the debts due me.

And 2nd I give and bequeath to my beloved wife Virginia Ann Bayless as her absolute property to be disposed of as she thinks proper.  My negro Girl Eliza aged about Seventeen years , two feather Beds  Bedsteads and furniture  of her own selection also two good Substantial farm horses

(P.164) Cont.
my goald watch and an Eight day metal clock and one yoke of work oxen
and my wagon and yok   Also two milch cows &(P.165) cal&ethere calves to
be selected by her out of my stock of cattle and all of my stock of hogs
that I may own and possess at my death - and also the necessary farming
utensils to cultivate and carry on the farm and all suitable and necessary
House hold and kitchen furniture, provided she continues to keep house
and carry on the farm after my death and if she should not choose to do
Either then latter articles  from the words and also I wish sold by my
Executors  The proceeds of such sale applied to my wife's use and benefit.

3 , It is my will and wish and I do order and direct that should my
wife choose to keep house and carry on a farm after my death that she
have the use of the farm where I now live should I die Seized and possessed of the same free from rent or charge of any kind so long as she wishes
to cultivate the same or until she marries but should my wife not choose
to cultivate the farm or should die or marry before my son Thomas Cullin
arrives at lawful age, then and in that case or in the happening of Either
of said three/events  I wish my Executor to rent out said farm or sell the same
as they may think most to the Interest of my Estate  and the proceeds of
the rent or sale to apply to the Education Surport and maintenance of my
sonThomas Cullin & the ballance to be given to him on his arrival at the
age of Twenty one, all moneys belonging to my estate to be placed at Interest
that is not wanted to Execute some provision in this my last will & Testament.

4th I further Give and bequeath nto my wife one Hundred Dollars in
money out of my Estate to be raised and paid to her by my Executors as
soon after my Death as possible and also on the stock of provisions on
hand at my death of every kind but the foregoing bequests bequests &
provisions in favor of my wife are expressly made on condition that she
relinquishes right of Dower out of my real estate in favor of our son
Thomas Cullin Bayliss.

5th It is my will and desire  and I specially request George Smith
of whom I purchased one half of the horse  Bertrand  In to return to my
Estate the one hundred Dollars I paid him for said horse and the note he
holds of mine for nine hundred Dollars the ballance of the purchis money
but should said Smith refuse to recind said contract then and in that case I
hereby authorize and empower my Executors to advertise and sell my interest
in said horse to the highest  on a credit of Twelve months.

6th  The use possession and enjoyment of all the rest and residue of
my Estate not herein already disposed of  I give to my beloved wife
Virginia Ann Bayless during her natural life or widowhood or until my
Son Thomas Cullen arrives at the age of twenty one  one the happening of
either of which events the whole of my property both real and pursonal
& effects of any and every kind whatsoever not herein before disposed of
otherwise.   I give bequeath and devise to my son Thomas Cullin Bayless
and should he die before he  (P.166) arrives at the age of Twenty oneyears
and at his death my wife should still be living in that event I give and
devise the whole of my estate to my wife Virginia Ann Bayless out of the use
and profits of my estate it is my wish and desire that my wife or Executors
or  both should suitably cloth support and educate my son Thomas Cullin.

(P.166) Cont.

7th If my wife should not continue to keep house and carry on the farm after my death in that case it is my will and desire that my Executors should sell all my perishable property Except negroes & such other articles as I have already given my wife on a credit of Twelve months & that they hire out the negroes except the one given to my wife and place the proceeds of such sale and hire on interest for the benefit of my Estate the Interest to be used for the joint support of my wife and our son Thomas Cullin until she dies or marries or he arrives at full age in either of which events the whole    (P.167) of the interest and principal of such funds shall go to Thomas C. Bayliss.

8th It is my will and wish that my Executors as soon after my death as convenient shall sell on a credit of Twelve months all my perishable property my negroes excepted herein specially given and bequeath to my wife - and lastly I hereby constitute and appoint my esteamed friend James H. Moran & John A. Gardner execturos of this my last will & Testament and my beloved and affectionate wife Virginia Ann Bayliss Guardian of our infant and minor son Thomas Cullen Bayliss hearby again revoking all former and other wills by me at any time heretofore made and published. In testimony of this solemn act and in witness of this my last will & t testament I have hereunto subscribed my name and affixed my seal this the 7th day of January in the year of our Lord one thousand Eight Hundred & thirty eight.

                Willie Bayliss (Seal)

Signed sealed and Executed in presence of us the date above written both of whom have witnessed the same at the request and in the presence of the testator.

Benjn. Bondurant  )
Jas. E. Bondurant  )

  Proven in open court 5th day of February  1838.

---

(P.168)
STATE OF TENNESSEE )
WEAKLEY COUNTY  )

  Know all men by these presents that we Wm. S. Scott Jas H. Moran Wm. Jones & D. P. Calowell all of the state and County aforesaid are held and firmly bound unto Newton Cannon Governor of the State of Tennessee for the time being and his successors in office for the use of the said State in the sum of Twelve Thousand five Hundred dollars to the payment of which well and truly to be made we bind ourselves our heirs executors and administrators Jointly and severally firmly by these presents sealed with our seals and dated the 2nd day of April, 1838.

  The condition of the above obligation as these that whereas the above bound William S. Scott has been duly and consitutionally elected sheriff and collector of the Public Taxes of said county of Weakley for two years from the first Saturday in March 1838.    Now if the said William S. Scott

(P.168) Cont.
shall well and truly collect all State Taxes and also all taxes on school lands within said county which by law he ought to collect and well and truly account for and pay over all taxes by him collected or which ought to be collected on the first day of December in the years 1838 and 1839 respectively then the above obligation to be void otherwise to remain in full force and virtue.

Attest
K. Williams Clerk,

W. S. Scott, (Seal)
Jas. H. Moran, (Seal)
William Jones, (Seal)
D. P. Calowell, (Seal)

---

(P.169)
STATE OF TENNESSEE )
Weakley County )

Know all men by these presents that we Wm. S. Scott Jas. H. Moran Wm. Jones & D. P. Caldwell all of the state and county aforesaid are held and firmly bound unto Newton Cannon Governor of the State of Tennessee for the time being and his successors in office for the use of the said State in the sum of Twelve thousand five hundred dollars to the payment of which well and truly to be made we bind ourselves our heirs Executors and administrators jointly and severally firmly by these presents - sealed with our seals and dated the 2nd day of April 1838.

The condition of the above obligation as these whereas the above bound William S. Scott has been duly and constitutionally elected Sheriff and collector of the Public Taxes of said County of Weakley for two years from the first Saturday in March 1838. Now if the said William S. Scott shall well and truly collect all state Taxes and also all Taxes on school lands within said county which by law he ought to collect and well and truly account for and pay over all taxes by him collected or which ought to be collected on the first day of December in the years 1838 and 1839 respectively then the above obligation to be void otherwise to remain in full force and virtue.

Attest
K. Williams Clerk

Wm. S. Scott (Sl.)
Jas. H. Moran (Sl.)
William Jones (Sl.)
D. P. Caldwell (Sl.)

---

STATE OF TENNESSEE )
WEAKLEY COUNTY )
(P.170)

Know all men by these presents that we Kinchin Williams Jas H. Moran D. P. Caldwell William W. Gleason Isaac Killough all of the County of Weakley and State of Tennessee are held and firmly bound unto Newton Cannon Governor of the State of Tennessee and successors in office in the sum of Five thousand Dollars to which payments well and truly to be made we bind ourselves our heirs Executors and administrators jointly and severally firmly by these presents sealed with our seals and dated this 2nd day of April 1838.

The condition of the above obligation is such that whereas the above

(P.170) Cont.

bound Kinchen Williams is constitutionally Elected clerk of the county court of Weakley County by the citizens of said county. Now if the said Kinchin Williams does well and Truly faithfully and impartially execute the duties of the said office of clerk of the county court of said county during his continuance therein according to law and take care of the records of said court, then the above obligation to be void else to remain in full force and virtue. In testimoney whereof we have hereunto set our hands & seals this the 2nd day of April, 1838.

Signed & acknowledged )    K. Williams, (Seal)
in open court            )    J. H. Moran, (Seal)
                              D. P. Caldwell, (Seal)
                              W. W. Gleeson, (Seal)
                              Isaac Killough, (Seal)

---

(P.171)
STATE OF TENNESSEE )
WEAKLEY COUNTY     )

Know all men by these presents that we Kinchin Williams Jas H Moran D. P. Caldwell William W. Gleeson Isaac Killough all of the County of Wealkey and State of Tennessee are held and firmly bound unto Newton Cannon Governor of the State of Tennessee and successor in office in hhe sum of Five THousand Dollars to which payment well and truly to be made we bind ourselves our heirs Executors and administrators jointly and severally firmly by these presents sealed with our seals and dated this 2nd day of April 1838.

The condition of the above obligation is such that whereas the above bound Kinchin Williams is constitutionally Elected clerk of the County Court of Weakley County by the citizens of said county. Now if the said Kinchin Williams does well and truly faithfully and impartially execute the duties of the said office of Clerk of the County Court of said county during his continuance therein according to law and take care of the records of said court then the above obligation is void else to remain in full force and virtue.

In testimony whereof we have hereunto set our hands & seals this the 2nd day of April, 1838.

Signed & acknowledged)    K Willims (Seal)
in open court         )    J. H. Moran, (Seal)
                           D. P. Caldwell, (Seal)
                           W. W. Gleeson, (Seal)
                           Isaac Killough, (Seal)

---

(P.172)

In the name of God Amen - I Sarah Williams of the County of Weakley & State of Tennessee being old & infirm but of sound mind and disposing memory and knowing that it is appointed for all the Human family once to

(P. 172) Cont.
die, do make & Publish this my last will & Testament in manner & form following (towit)

Item 1, I give to my three youngest Grand children the children of the late Jenny Bowers the former wife of Young P. Bowers namely Athonatious Bowers William G. Bowers & Panther Matildy Bowers one negro boy by the name of Henry which said boy Henry I wish to be hired out untill the youngest of my said Grand children becomes of lawful age then I desire the said Boy Henry should be sold & the money arising from both the hire & sale shall be equally Divided between them & their heirs forever giving one fourth part of said money to the heirs & children Sarah Bowers the wife of James Bowers the other three fourths to be Divided them as stated above.

I further give the said three Grand children one iron pot one skillet one pot rack one bed and furniture to I also wish should be sold & the amount Divided Equally between them.

Item 2nd I give to grand Daughter Panther Matildy Bowers one trunk & its contents consisting of my worn clothes & C.

Item 3 I give to my two Grand sons Athonatious & William G. Bowers two white counterpins, one for each one of them.

(P.173)
Item 4, I give to my grandchildren the lawful heirs of Joseph G. Williams which he now has or may hereafter have one negro woman named Betty all of my stock of cattle Crock to be Equally Divided between them to them & there Heirs forever.

Item 5, I give to Nancy Bowers wife of William G. Bowers Flos Hachel & Iron spice mortar.

In witness whereof I have hereunto set my hand and affixed my seal this 13th day of January 1836 signed sealed & acknowledged to be her last will & Testament.

|  |  |
|---|---|
| in Presents us ) | her |
| Joseph Pearce ) | Sarah X Williams ,(Seal) |
| Orren Vincent ) | mark |

---

(P.174)
In the name of God Amen. I Robert Jeter of the County of Weakley & State of Tennessee being of sound mind and desposing memory but feable in in health wishing to provide against the uncertainty of life do make and ordain this as my last will and Testament in manner as follows (viz.)

First my will and desire is that all my Just debts shall be paid by my Executors hearin after named out of my estate as early as can conveniently be made.

2nd my will and desire is that my wife Susannah live with any of my children or move from one to the other at her pleasure as she may think proper and that they be paid a fee and reasonable price for the same in proportionable to the time and trouble they may be at for keeping her the

(P.174) Cont.

money to be paid out of any money arising from the sale of my property. I also lend her one negro her choice of all my family of negroes her choice of one of my best bed & bedstead & what clothing she may think proper to take for the use of the bed  something to be provided to keep her clothing plentifully & decent out of my estate and any other small articles she may want and that she and the negro be kept in a Decent manner and the negroes taxes to be paid  in case my wife or her servant may become sick and require medical aid and any occasional expenses may accrue then it will be the duty of all my legatees to pay back their proportionable parts of all Expenses and for trouble: this property above mentioned which I lone to my wife during hur natural life at her Death I desire it sold and the proceeds be Equally divided amongst    (P.175) my four Daughters Katharine Brasfield Condon Winston Mary Rogers & Frances Rogers also the children of Samuel Jeter Deceased that is Elizabeth, William, Maryann, Robert Allen, George, John & Samuel Jeter they are to have one fifth part to be Equally divided between them.  My wish is that some one of my legatees buy the negro-

   3rd I lend to my grand som James Allen the following Property(to wit) the tract of land I bot of James Hill containing one hundred acres more of less also the forty Eight acres I bot of F. W.Huling joining the Hill tract lying due South of the above named tract adjoining the whole containing one hundred and forty eight acres be the same more or less also three negroes George Grace and her child   choice of my bay or  Albert Sorrel Filly  one good bed bed stead & furniture one good cow & calf  two ewes & lambs my rifle gun choice of one Cary plough  & shovel & cotter the ax called his  1 good hilling hoe or weading hoe one trunk all my shaving tools his school books 3 plates 1 dish 3 chairs to have the benefit of the above property until he arrives to lawful age provided he will then in a reasonable time after he becoming of age convey and make over all the right title & interest he has in right of his mother Elizabeth Allen deed to a pease of land I give to my son Allen Jeter  Deed lying in North Carolina  Granville County on the Ready Branch by Deed otherwise then and in that case they are to give up all the above named property and not before  Should he die without an heir or heirs then the above named property is to be Equally divided amongst my four (P.176) Daughters & Samuel Jeter's Dec'd  Eight children as named in Item the 2nd the children to have one fifth part of the same.

   4th I give to my grand son William B. Jeter the tract of land which I bot of F. W. Huling containing ninety three acres more or less lying on the East side of where his mother Ann Jeter now lives bounded by his lines on the West Joseph Cravens  on the North the tract I bot of Hill on the East which Bounds will show by reference to the Deed received of F. W. Huling which was Executed and dated 5th January 1836 which tract or parcel of land I hereby will and direct the said William B. Jeter shall pay the sum of $1.50 per acre with interest from date of Huling deed to me as will show 5th January, 1836 which will amount to $139.50 with interest as aforesaid which is to be deducted out of legacy or any part therefore which may be coming or due him from my estate after that to divide Equal with the rest of my son's Samuel Jeters Decd children.

   5th Item my will is that all my negroes except those I give to my

(P.176) Cont.
Grandson James Allen and the one my wife Susannah Jeter may make choice for her use & benefit during her natural life to be equally divided in four parts so as to make four equal lots and divide among my four Daughters as heretofore named if they can agree amongst themselves if they cannot in the division of the negroe they must get men to value the same equally and draw for them & those that get the most valuable lots is to pay to those of less value to make all of equal value as near as possible.

(P.177) Item 6 My will and desire is that the children of my som Samuel Jeter Deceased as named above have in money amongst them all equally in amount one of my other legatees which will be one fifth part of the value of all my negroes except those allowed to my Grand son James Allen & the one for my wife afore mentioned which money is to be taken from the proceeds of the sales of my land not otherwise willed & perishable property stock & the money to be put out at interest until they respecfully arrives of age at which time each of them are to draw on there guardian for there equal part of the money due them from my estate

Item 7 My will is that my executors sell my land unwilled as they may think most advisable that is to altogether or divide as they may think best either for cash or upon what credit they may think most advisable all the rest of my property (not willed) to be sold on a credit of twelve months .

Item 8 - My will is that the money arising from the sale of my land and other property together with all money on hand & moneys received on all debts due my estate(if any left) after given to Samuel Jeters children one share equal to one one of my other legatees to be equally divided amongst my four Daughters reserving one fifth part of the same for the eight children of Samuel Jeter & to be equally divided as before.

Itam 9 - I will that a graveyard be received out of my land where my son Samuel Jeter & Jefferson Rogers little daughter was buried including the ground where Joseph Cravins Daughter is buried some as land to the west of the (P.178) other Beginning at a stake James Allen line with white oak & shugar tree pinters thence north seventy five feet to a white oak thence west one hundred sixty feet thence south seventy five feet to a stake James Allen line thence East along said Allens line one hundred & sixty feet to the beginning to be kept & recovered for a burying ground for my family of children and their posterity after them.

Item 10, If either of my Executors shall refuse to qualify the one who shall do so is fully authorised to Execute this will.

Lastly I hereby nominate constitute and appoint my sons in law David Winston Jefferson Rogers Executors to this my last will and testament in witness whereof I hereunto subscribed my name and affixed my seal this fourteenth day of July A. D. Eighteen Hundred and thirty Eight.

Subscribed sealed by the )
Testator in our presents )        Robert Jeter (Seal)
who in the presents of Each )
other witness the same - )
Jonathan Higgs Sr. )
James Allen )

(P.179)

In the name of God Amen. I Job Rogers of the County of Weakley & State of Tennessee Being infirm in Boddy but of sound mind and memory Thanks be unto God for the same and calling to mind the mortality of the Boddy & knowing that it is appointed for all men once to die, do make and ordain this my last will & Testament for the purpose of Disposing of such worldly estate as it has Pleased God to bless me with & pointing out the manner in which I wish it Divided after Death & other things. I Recommend my soul unto God that gave it me & my boddy to the Earch from whence it came to be Buried in a Decent manner christian like at the Discression of my Executors hereafter named nothing Doubting But at the Resurection I shall Receive such a one as it shall please God to give. & as to my Estate I give & devise in the following manner.

Itom - My will and desire is that all my just and lawful Debts & funeral Expenses be paid-

Itom - I gave and devise unto my loving wife Agnes Rogers one negro girl named Mariah one horse the choice of my stock of horses one saddle & bridle one yoke of oxen two cows & calves five head of sheep four sows & pigs one feather bed & furniture one chaney press and its contents one half Dozzen sitting chairs one half Dozzen knives & forks one chest one coffe kittle one pair of fire dogs 2 spinning wheels 2 pair of cards one loom & kitchen furniture sufficient for her use one Dining table Two ploughs & Geer & one years provision for herself and family at her own Desposal to do as she pleases with- (

(180) Itam - I lend unto my Beloved wife Agnes Rogers one negro man named Lewis one negro woman Eliza one careall & geer one pair cart wheels during the time she Remains my widow & no longer then to revert to my estate & be disposed of as I shall hereafter Direct I also lone her one hundred acres of land to be laid off in the following manner to-wit Beginning at the mouth of Owl Branch & Running up the meanders of the same far enough to inclose my dwelling House & and one third part of my Plantation & timber & fire wood sufficient for her and I lend the same to her during the time she remains my widow & no longer then to revert to my Estate to be Disposed of as I shall hereafter direct. None of the property above loaned is to be removed out of Weakley County if such an attempt is made it is no longer to be a lone but immediately to revert to my estate -

Itam - I give and devise unto my two young Daughters Sarah Jane Benjamin Rogers and Druseller Allen Rogers three hundred acres of land to be Equally Devided Between them to be laid of in the following manner (viz.) Beginning at the mouth of Owl Branch & running up the nearest course of the same sufficiently for so as to Just include the Hundred acres loaned to my wife Agnes Roger their mother and so continue on & include two hundred acres more than I loaned my wife Agnes & so include the plantation & timber & fire wood sufficient to support the plantation & to be passed with the two hundred acres . When either of them marrys or arrives at the age of Eighteen years old to be equally Divided between them and the other hundred (181) acres when my wife may marry or decease also to be Equally Devided between them which I give to them & their heirs Begotten of their Boddy forever. I also give them the nine following negroes to wit one negro man named Lewis and one negro woman named Eliza & her child named Catherine

(P.181) Cont.

one negro Girl named Emeline one negro boy named Henry one negro girl named Grace  one negro boy named Freeman  one negro girl named Mary one negro girl named Martha to be possessed with Lewis & Eliza at the marriage or Decease of my wife  Agnes & the others when Either of them marrys or Either of them arives to the age of Eighteen years old to be Equally divided between them except one of the negroes loaned to my wife Agnes ther mother should die or become infirm if so my will is my Executors hereafter named shall put my wife in possession of one other of the negroes I have given to my two youngest Daughters  such a one as they may think proper which negro she shall hold so long as she remains my widow & keeps the same in this county & at her marriage or decease I give the whole of the above named negroes to them & the heirs begotten of ther Boddy But if either of them should die without heirs begotten of there Boddy & in that case the whole of the property alloted to the one or both of them so doing shall be Divided among the rest of my children  which I give to them and their heirs forever-

I also give unto my two youngest Daughters one Feather Bed & furniture (182) a peace  one horse Briddle & saddle a peace  two cows & calves apeace two sows and pigs apeace two ewes & lambs apeace one plough and Geer apeace one years provision for themselves and their family of negros alloted to them  It is also my will thay & ther  property shall remain with my wife Agnes  untill they shall marry or arrive  of the age of Eighteen years old Except my Executors shall think proper to send them to some female institution to receive their education or some other reasonable cause & in that case my will is that my Executors here after named shall act at their own Discression to the best advantage for my infant daughters-

Itom - I gave & Devine unto my Beloved son John W. Rogers seventy acres of land lying in Dyer County it being part of a six Hundred & forty acre tract of land Deeded from Richard Smith & Jesse Gill to Jubilee Rogers I also gave him one negro man named Daniel  one negro girl named Mima one negro girl named Gilla also one horse Bridle & saddle one feather Bed & furniture now in his possession to him and his heirs forever-

Itom- I gave and Devise unto Beloved son Jubilee V. Rogers the five following negroes (towit)  one negro man named Henderson one negro boy named Mcklin one negro Boy named Pleasant and one negro woman named Sarah & her child named Lawson also one mare Bridle & saddle  one feather Bead & furniture now inhis possession to him & his heirs forever-

Itom - I gave & devise unto my son in law Jacob Thompson that married my Daughter Mary P. Rogers seventy acres of land  (183)  lying in Dyer County  & Being part of the same tract of land given to my son John W. Rogers  I also gave him one negro man named Alfred & one negro woman named Winny & all the children the said Winny now has & one negro girl named Caroline one Horse Bridle & saddle one feather bed & furniture now inhis possession to him and his heirs forever.

Item - I gave & Devise unto Whimeal H. Cooper that married my daughter Elizabeth Allen Rogers one note of  hand I hold against him being about Seven Hundred Dollars to him & his heirs forever.

(183) Cont.

Itom- I gave & Devise unto the children of Whitmeal H. Cooper Born of the Boddy of Daughter Elizabeth Allen Cooper one negro man named Charles one negro woman named Nelley & said Nelleys children Being negroes I have heretofore made a Deed in Trust to which Deed in Trust my will is shall continue in full force & virtue untill the said children shall recover them in full possession agreeable to the full meaning & interest of the same.

Itom - I gave & Devise unto my grand son Job Calvin Rogers son of John W Rogers one negro Boy named Coy to him and his heirs forever-

Itom - I gave & Devise unto my grand son John Chesley Thompson son of Jacob Thompson one negro boy named Simon to him and his heirs forever.

Itom- I gave & Devise unto John W. Rogers & Jubilee V., Rogers & Jacob Thompson & the children that is now Born & may hereafter Be born of the boddy of my Daughter (184) Elizabeth Allen Cooper all negroes & perishable property I may decease possest with that is not above named except one negro girl named Candis which negro I gave more than the other children to the children of my Daughter Elizabeth Allen Cooper which is now born or may hereafter be Born of her Boddy & also said negro Candis child & her further increase to be possesed with as I shall hereafter Direct- I also gave unto John W. Rogers Jacob Thompson & the children that is now born or may hereafter be born of the boddy of my Daughter Elizabeth Allen Cooper all the lands I may deceased possessed of or any claim thereto that is not above named & particular specified - My will is that all the property that is above given to my children that is of age they shall Be possessed with at my Deceased  But the property given to my the children of my Daughter Elizabeth Allen Cooper shall be in the hands of my Executors hereafter named as Trustees & my will is they shall have full power to hire out said negroes or keep them on a farm as they in their Descression may think proper & the profits ariving therefrom shall be converted to the support of my Daughter Elizabeth Allen Cooper & family so long as she may live and at her Decease the whole of the property to be Equally Divided among her children Except my Executors may Believe or conseave in process of time that the said property may Increase or so accumulate that there may be more than what may be necessary for the support of (P.185) my Daughter Elizabeth Allen & family then & in that case my will is that my Executors shall have full power to gave of to any of her children that may marry or arrive of age one or more negroes not exceeding a childs part to such of her children so marrying or becoming of age & at her Decase when all the property is to be Devided the child so re - ceiving property shall only account for the value of said property when they arrived the same in possession-

I constitute & appoint my Brother Jubilee Rogers & my two Nephews Caleb Brasfield  Pelig Terrell & my son John W. Rogers Executors of this my will & testament Ratifying & confirming this & no other to be my last will & Textament .

Signed sealed and Delivered by the Testator to be his last will & Testament in the presents of us that is presant at the time of signing & sealing of the same in Testamony whereof I have hereunto set my seal hand and seal this 10th day of February A. D. 1837.

(P.185) Cont.
Attest )
E. P. Lathum )
Spencerd Wilbanks )                 Job Rogers, (Seal)
J. P. Rust, )
John D. Jones )
H. W. Crosser )
Alexander Tucker )
Clemmons Shanklin )
Isaac Dawson, )

---

(P.186)
STATE OF TENNESSEE )
WEAKLEY COUNTY )

    Know all men by these presents that I Caleb Brasfield in right of my wife Katharine Brasfield I David Winston in right of my wife Condon Winston & I Jefferson Rogers in right of my wife Mary Rogers & I Jonathan T. Rogers in right of my wife Frances Rogers all being the lawful heirs of Robert Jeter Decd to Inherit & possess the slaves belonging to said Estate as named and Directed in the 5 Item of the last will and testament of said Decd hath this day mutually and voluntary consented and agreed that we believe it will not be possible for us for us to divide the slaves as named in 5 Item of said Deceased will without the assistance of men appointed for that purpose & we believing it was the said Deceased intention that we should divide the slaves ourselves as named in 5 Item of his will if we could agree & believing cannot agree we therefore all agree that the county court of Weakley now in session shall appoint five good and lawful men to meet on some convenient day and assess the value of the property and Divide the same and report to the next term of county court and state that we abide by & stand to the decision of the same given under our hands & seals this 6th day of August A. D. 1838-

                                       C. Brasfield, (Seal)
                                       David Winston, (Seal)
                                       Jefferson Rogers, (Seal)
                                       Jonathan T. Rogers, (Seal)

---

(P. 187)
STATE OF TENNESSEE )
WEAKLEY COUNTY ) We the undersigned commissioners agreeably to an order made at the county court of weakley & state aforesaid on the first Monday in August 1838 to divide & value the slaves belonging to the Estate of Robert Jeter Deceased amongst his four daughters as named in his last will and testament (towit) Katherine Brasfield, Candon Winston, Mary Rogers & Frances Rogers all meet at the house of the said Robert Jeter Deceased on the 10th day of August A. D. 1838 and after being duly sworn according to law that we would without partiality or reward value and report to the best of our skill & ability after having all the slaves brot before us there being twenty five in number of various sexes sorts & ages say from sixty five years to small suckling children we say upon oath that the negroes are worth in cash seven Thousand Seven Hundred Dollars which will show below both the names and

(P.187) Cont.
valuation of the Different slaves in the division there being four legatees (to wit) Caleb Brasfield in right of his wife Katharine, David Winston in right of his wife Candon, Jefferson Rogers in right of his wife Mary & Jonathan T. Rogers in right of his wife Frances, we report that the Devision & valuation as following (towit)

first Caleb Brasfield in right of his wife Katharine Received in the Devision the following named slaves and at the following valuations Caty and her Boy child Eaton $600. Mary $250. Washington $200. Susan $300. Anica and her child Sally Ann $350. Abram $200. whole amount $1900.00

David Winston in right of his wife Candon received the following negroes and at the following valuation- Stephen $600. (P.188) Littleton $400. Viney $300. Eloy $200. Rose and her child Squire $350. whole amount of D. Winston $1850.00

Jefferson Rogers in right of his wife Mary received the following negroes at the following valuation John $500. Sam 600. Willis $350. Ransom $150. Hilliard $200.00 Frank $150. Whole amount of Jefferson Rogers $1950.00

Jonathan T. Rogers in right of his wife Frances received the following negroes at the following valuation Cherry & Boy child Haywood $600. Lewis $550. Anthony $550. Lucy $300. Whole amount of Jonathan T. Rogers $2000.00.

The above sum Brot down & aded the whole amount of valuation $7700. The above sum of $7700 Divided in four Equal parts will make the sum of nineteen Hundred and seventy five Dollars due Each Legatee from the valuation & Devision of the slaves which (P.188) will leave Jonathan T. Rogers to pay back $75. with interest from the date and Jefferson Rogers to pay back $25./from the date David Winston will be entitled to receive from those sums $75. with interest from the date Caleb Brasfield will be entitled to receive $25. from those sums at Interest from the day which will make all Equal.

All of which we report to the worshipful County court of Weakley under our hands & seals this 10th day of August A. D. 1838 -

        Nelson Nailing, (Seal)
        James Hornbeak, (Seal)
        Robert Moseley, (Seal)
        John Peck, (Seal)
        John K. Jones, (Seal)

---

(P.189)
I Hillary H. Bondurant of the County of Weakley and the State of Tennessee being of sound and disposing mind do hereby make ordain and publish this my last will and Testament hereby revoking all former wills and codicils by me at any time heretofore made and published.

And first it is my will and desire that my executors herein after named as soon after my death as they may think proper, shall advertise and sell all my real estate lying within the corporation of the town of

(P.189) Cont.
Dresden consisting of family residence and the lot of ground opposite thereunto on the west side of the road, also all my real estate in the town of Christmasville Carroll County consisting of an interest in a Tavern House there and a gin & the ground appertaining thereto on such credit of credits as they may think best for the interest of my estate. I also wish my Executors to sell all the rest & residue of my personal and perishable property (except my negroes) on such a credit as they may think advisable and out of the proceeds of the sale of the above mentioned property to pay off and discharge all my just debts of whatsoever kind-

And Secondly - It is my will and desire that after all my Just debts are paid by my executors that they cause all the rest and residue of my estate remaining of whatsoever kind to equally divide between my beloved wife Harriedt E. C. Bondurent and my two little daughters Sarah Elizabeth and Martha Emaline Bondurent and that my executors choose three disinterested persons to make said division -

And Thirdly - I hereby constitute and appoint the two Grandfathers of my two little daughters namely Benjamin Bondurant & Jno. Terrell Guardians of my (P.190) minor children during thur minority to attend to thur rearing, education and support and manage their Estate and their persons I commit especially to the keeping of Grandfather Jno. Terrell during his natural life.

And lastly - I do hereby constitute and appoint my esteemed & trusty friend John A. Gardner and David P. Caldwell Executors of this my last will and Testament. In testimony of this solemn act - I have herewith set my hand & affixed my seal this the 29th day of November A. D. 1838.

                                            H. H. Bondurant, (Seal)

Signed sealed executed & published in presence of us each of whom have witnessed they same at the request and in the presence of the Testator.

Jno. B. Fonville )
Rob Moseley    )

---

Know all men by these presents that we William S. Scott, William Jones, E. T. Latham & Sand S. A. Warner all of the County of Weakley & State of Tennessee are held and firmly bound unto John H. Moore Chairman of the County Court of said County in the sum of five thousand dollars to be paid to said chairman or his successors in office to the payment whereof well and truly to be made we do bind ourselves our heirs executors or administrators jointly and severally promptly by these presents sealed with our seals and dated this 6th day of May, 1839.

The condition of the above obligation is such that whereas the above bounden William S. Scott collector of the public revenue has this day received the tax list for said county from the clerk of said county to be collected for the year 1839. Now if the said William S. Scott shall collect or cause to be collected all county taxes which he may be bound to collect for said year and pay the same over to the county trustee

(P.191)
within the time prescribed by law then the above obligation to be void otherwise to remain in full force and virtue of law-

                              W.S. Scott, (Seal)
                              E. P. Latham, (Seal)
                              William Jones, (Seal)
                              S. A.Warner, (Seal)

---

(P.192)
    I Solomon Sedewick do make and publish this my last will and Testament hereby revoking and making void all other wills by me at any time made -

    First, I direct that so much of my perishable property as may be sufficient be sold and that my just debts be paid out of the proceeds thereof.

    Secondly, I give and bequeath all the remainder of my property of every description to my beloved wife Faney Penelope during her natural life and at her death to be equally divided among my children -

    Secondly, Should John Messick think proper he is at liberty to clear land, build houses and make such other improvements on any part of my unimproved land as he may think proper and remain on and cultivate the same during the lifetime of my sister Sophiah Messick free of rent or charges of any description whatever -

    Lastly, I do hereby nominate and appoint John Dewey my Executor and Faney Penelope Sedwick my Executrix in witness whereof I do to this my will set my hand and seal This 29th day of June, 1839.

                              Solomon Sedwick, (Seal)

Signed sealed and published in our presents and we have subscribed our names hereto in the presents of the testator this 29th day of June, 1839.

J.W.Cochran, )
Wm. R.Stone )

---

(P.193)    LAST WILL & TESTAMENT OF W. JOHNSON

    I, Willis Johnson do make and publish this my last will and Testament hereby revoking and making void all other wills by me at any time made.

    First, I desire that my just debts be paid as soon after my death as possible out of any monies that I may die possessed of or if there be none that a sufficiency of perishable property be sold for that purpose -

    Secondly, I give unto my wife Mary after paying all my just debts as above directed the whole of my estate to have and to hold during her widowhood. If she shall marry I wish her to draw an equal portion of my estate with my children and at her death such portion as she shall have drawn to equally divided amongth my four children Caroline William Cemantha and Mary Eliza -

(P.193) Cont.

I also desire that should either of my children become of age or marry during her widowhood that she shall lend to him or her such property as she mad deem proper - not exceeding his or her proportionable estate -

Lastly- I do hereby nominate and appoint William Higgs and Kinchin White my Executors and wish them to act in that capacity untill my son arrives at the age of twenty one at which time should the court consider him capable of acting in the capacity of executor it is my desire that he take charge of the estate.

In witness whereof I do to this my will set my hand and seal this 21st day of May, 1838.

W. Johnson, (Seal)

Signed sealed and published in our presents and we have subscribed our names hereto in the presents of the testator this 21st day of May, 1838.

Sam Irvin )
John B. Dent )

---

(P. 194) I, Solomon Sedwick do make and publish this as my last will and testament hereby revoking and making void all other wills by me at any time made.

First I desire that so much of my perishable property as may be sufficient be sold and that my just debts be paid out of the proceeds thereof-

Secondly I give and bequeath all the remainder of my property of every description to my beloved wife Fany Penelope during her natural life and at her death to be divided equally between my children

Secondly, Should John Murfrees think proper and make such other improvements on any part of my unimproved land as he may think proper and remain on cultivate the same during the lifetime of my sister Sophiah Messick free of rent or charges of any description whatever -

Lastly I do hereby nominate and appoint John Drewry my executor and Fanny Penelope Sedwick my Executors to in witness whereof I do to this my last wills set my hand and seal this 29th day of June 1839.

Solomon Sedwick, (Seal)

Signed sealed and published in our presents and we have subscribed our names hereto in the presents of the Testator this 29th of June 1839.
J. W. Cochran )
Wm. B. Stone )

---

(P.195) SMITH PALMER LAST WILL & TESTAMENT -

In the name of God Amen. I Smith Palmer of Weakley County and State of Tennessee being of perfect mind and memory thanks be given unto God calling unto mind the mortality of my body and knowing that it is ap-

(P.195) Cont.

pointed for all men once to die do make and ordain this my last will and Testament and as touching such worldly estate wherewith it has pleased God to bless me in this life I give devise and dispose of the same in the following manner and form:

Item first, As I have heretofore given to William A. Palmer my eldest son to the amount of one thousand and seventy dollars. And to James A. Palmer my second son one negro man named Gilbert valued at one thousand dollars and a certain tract of one hundred acres of land valued at three hundred dollars.

And to Emily M. A. Cavett my eldest daughter one negro girl named Margaret valued at seven hundred dollars and one negro boy named Doctor valued at six hundred dollars.

Item 2nd As the above named William A. Palmer, James A. Palmer & Emily M. A. Cavitt have received each of them the above named sums I now proceed to give and bequeath John W. Palmer my third son Henry O. Palmer my fourth son, Mary R. Palmer my second daughter, Elizabeth C. Palmer my third daughter all these last four four jointly and severally the number of eight negroes viz. I give unto John W. Palmer Henry O. Palmer Mary R. A. Palmer & Elizabeth C. Palmer Reuben, Isham, Henderson, Manuel Ralph Ailsey Ann & Reeny which last mentioned eight negroes to be equeally divided between John W. Palmer Henry O. Palmer Mary R. A. Palmer & Elizabeth C. Palmer as each become of age.

Item 3rd I also give and bequeath unto James A. Palmer Emily M. A. Cavett (P.196) John W. Palmer Henry O. Palmer Mary R. A. Palmer & Elizabeth C. Palmer the number of five negroes viz. Amy, Cuida Willis Thomas Jim jointly and severally to be equally divided between them after my decease.

Item 4th, I give and bequeath unto my beloved wife Elizabeth Palmer and Amanda M. F. Palmer Tennessee Palmer Virginia Palmer and Edward H. Palmer a certain number of negroes viz. Nick Nancy Wat Charles Washington Susan Phil Isaac to be jointly and severally and equally divided between Elizabeth Palmer my beloved wife and Amanda M. F. Palmer Virginia Palmer Tennessee Palmer and Edward H. Palmer.

Item 5 - I give and bequeath unto my beloved wife Elizabeth Palmer the manner negroes viz. Nick, Nancy Wat, Charles, Washington Susan Phil and Isaac to have and to hold the same and the use of them while she the Elizabeth Palmer my beloved wife remains a widow.

Item 6th, I do and it is my wish that all my lands household furniture and perishable property shall be sold after my decease and the money equally divided between Elizabeth Palmer my beloved wife, James A. Palmer William A. Palmer Emily M. A. Cavett John W. Palmer Henry O. Palmer Mary R. A. Palmer Elizabeth C. Palmer Amanda M. F. Palmer Virginia Palmer Tennessee Palmer and Edward H. Palmer.

Item 7th It is my wish that John W. Palmer shall act and be executor of my estate and it is further my wish that the court do not demand and bond and security from the said John W. Palmer for the same. It is

(p.196) Cont.

further my wish that John W. Palmer my Executor should sell all my lands either Publicly or privately on a credit of one two and (P.197) three years and all my perishable Property and household furniture &c to be sold at public sale on a twelve months credit.

Item 8th - It is my wish that Leonard S. Langley shall take care of my daughter Mary R. A. Palmer and act as guardian for her, Also for Paul Palmer to take my daughter Elizabeth C. Palmer and act as guardian for her.

And I the said Smith Palmer do hereby utterly disallow revoke and annul all and every other former testament and will legacies bequests and executors by me in anywise before named willed and bequeathed ratifying and confirming this and no other to be my last will and testament. In witness whereof I have hereunto set my hand and seal this sixth day of September in the year of our Lord one thousand eight hundred and thirty nine.

Smith Palmer (Seal)

Signed sealed published/pronounced and declared by the said )
Smith Palmer as his last will and testament in )
the presence of us who in his presence of each other )
have herewith subscribed our names. )
George W. McWhorter )
Hiram Jones )
James Brann )

STATE OF TENNESSEE )
WEAKLEY COUNTY ) April term 1840.

This was the Execution of the foregoing last will & testament of Smith Palmer proven in open court by the oaths of Geo. W. McWhorter Hiram Jones and James Brann subscribing witnesses thereunto and ordered to be recorded. Jno. C. Dodds Jr., Clk.

---

(P.198)
STATE OF TENNESSEE )
WEAKLEY COUNTY )

To John W. Palmer a citizen of Weakley County

It appearing to the court that Smith Palmer died leaving a written will in which you are appointed executor which has been duly proved in open court and you being qualified according to law and it having been ordered by said court that letters testimintary issue to you.

These are therefore to impower you to enter upon the execution of said will and take unto your possession all the property and to make to the next court a perfect inventory thereof and make due collection of all debts and after paying all just demands against the testator and settling up the business of said estate agreeable to law you will pay over and deliver the property and effects that may remain in your hands and do all other things that may be required according to the provisions of said will and the laws of the land.

(P.198) Cont.

Given under my hand at office this 7th day of April 1840.

fees 50¢        J. C. Dodds, Clk.

---

(P.199)
STATE OF TENNESSEE )
WEAKLEY COUNTY    )

Know all men by these presents that we William S. Scott, William Jones Samuel Irvin John A. Gardner James H. Moran, all of the county of Weakley and state aforesaid are held and firmly bound unto James K. Polk Governor of the State of Tennessee for the time being and his successors in office for the use of the said state in the sum of Twelve Thousand Dollars the payment of which well and truly to be made we bind ourselves our heirs Executors and administrators Jointly severally firmly by these presents sealed with our seals and dated this the 6th day of April, 1840.

The conditions of the above obligation are these whereas the above bound William S. Scott has been duly and constitutionally Elected sheriff and collector of the Public Taxes of said County of Weakley for two years from the first Saturday in March 1840. Now if the said Wm. S. Scott shall well and truly collect all the state taxes and also all Taxes on school land within said county which by law he ought to collect and well and truly account for and pay over all taxes him so collected or which ought to be collected on the first day of December in the year 1840 & 1841 respectively then the above obligation to be void otherwise to remain in full force and virtue. Attest.

W. S. Scott, (Seal)
William Jones (Seal)
Samuel Irvin, (Seal)
James H. Moran, (Seal)
Jno. A. Gardner, (Seal)

---

(P.200)
This Indenture made this 27th day of March 1841 between William Mosley of Weakley County, Tennessee of the one part and Thomas E. Mosley Elizabeth Cole wife of Moses E. Cole and her children John W. Rogers and Thos. L. Cole & George B. Mosley William Mosley Green Mosley Rebecca I Ausburn wife of William Ausburn Hillery Mosley & William T. Mosley Mary A. Mosley Moses Mosley Martha Mosley Hillery Mosley the last five are children of Arthur Mosley all of the County of Weakley except the children of Arthur Mosley those of Gibson County Tennessee of the second part.

Witnesseth that for the natural love and affection I bear to my children and grandchildren above named and the consideration that they support me and their mother and grandmother during our natural life. I have this day bargained sold and delivered to them and their heirs and a assignees the following property to wit- one tract of land lying in Weakley County containing six hundred and forty acres it being the tract of land whereon I live granted to Henry A. Coleman one negro man named Washington one negro man by the name of Christopher one negro boy John one negro boy Hagen one negro boy named Daniel negro woman named Betsy one negro woman named Betty one negro woman named Mary one negro girl

(P.200) Cont.

named Joanna also three head of horses also Eight head of (P.201) cattle also one waggon and three yoke of oxen about fifty head of hogs also fifteen head of sheep also a second tract of land lying in the County of Gibson Tennessee containing six hundred & forty acres where Arthur C. Mosly now lives purchased of the said Henry A. Coleman, to have and to hold the aforesaid property to them the sd. Thos. E. Mosley, Elizabeth Cole, John W. Rogers, Thos. L. Cole, George B. Mosley, William Mosley, Green Mosley, Rebecca J. Ausburn, Hillery Mosly, William T. Mosly, Mary A. Mosley, Moses Mosley, Martha Mosly & Hillery Mosley their heirs and assigns and the said William Mosley covenanting with the aforesaid parties that he warrants and defends the titles to them of the aforesaid property against the claim of all and every person whatever.

Witness my hand and seal &c

William Mosley (Seal)

Witness )
R. P. Raines )
A. C. Nimmo )

---

(P.202)
STATE OF TENNESSEE )
WEAKLEY COUNTY )

Know all men by these presents that we John C. Dodd, Saml Taylor Thomas Parham and William S. Scott all of the county and state aforesaid are firmly bound unto Jas C. Jones Governor of the State of Tennessee for the time being and his successors in office in the sum of one thousand dollars which payment well and truly to be made we each of us bind ourselves our heirs executors and administrators Jointly and severally and firmly by these presents sealed with our seals and dated the 4th day of April, 1842.

The condition of the above obligation is such that whereas the above bound John C. Dodds was on the 1st Saturday in March last elected clerk of the county court of Weakley County for a term of four years. Now should he the said Dodds Clerk aforesaid well and truly collect all the County and state Revenue which may be due which by the tenor of his office is his duty to collect and pay the same over to the proper authority according to law then this obligation to be null and void otherwise to remain in full force and virtue.

John C. Dodds, (Seal)
Saml. Taylor, (Seal)
Thos. Parham, (Seal)
W. S. Scott, (Seal)

---

(P.203)
STATE OF TENNESSEE )
WEAKLEY COUNTY )    SHERIFF BOND 1842.

Know all men by these presents that we The. Hall, Jeptha Gardner, Robert Thompson, and Jesse Leigh all of the County of Weakley and State of Tennessee are bound unto James C. Jones Governor of the State of Tennessee for the time being and his successors in office in the sum of two thousand dollars which payment well and truly to be made we and each of us bind ours

(P.203) Cont.

of us bind ourselves our heirs executors and administrators jointly and severally and firmly by these presents sealed with our seals and dated this the 6th day of June 1842.

The condition of the above obligation is such that whereas the above bound The. Hall sheriff and collec or of public taxes for Weakley County having this day received of the court the tax book for 1842.

Now should he well and truly collect and pay over to the proper authorities authorized to receive the same all the state revenue due and ai owing the state of Tennessee from Weakley County as set forth in said tax book made out by the clerk of the county court and received by him this day then this obligation to be void otherwise to remain in full force and virtue.

                                        The.Hall (Seal)
                                        Jeptha Gardner, (Seal)
                                        Robt. Thompson, (Seal)
                                        J. Leigh, (Seal)

Attest
John Henry Moore       )
Chairman and presiding )
Justice for said County )

---

THE END

AARON, negro, 80
ABBOTH, Spencer, 28
ABBOTT, Spencer, 55
ABERNATHY, Littleton, 55
ABERNATHY, Littleton, 81
ABERNATHY, Littleton F., 106
ABERNATHY, Littleton F., 2
ABERNATHY, Littleton F., 28
ABNER, Nash, 10
ABOTT, Spencer, 2
ABRAM, slave, 164
ABSOLOM?, Jim, 12
ACRE, Jesee, 2
ACRE, Jesse, 106
ACRE, Jesse, 28
ACRE, Jesse, 55
ACRE, Jesse, 81
ADAIR, John, 3
ADAMS, Abel, 106
ADAMS, Abel, 28
ADAMS, Abel, 3
ADAMS, Abel, 55
ADAMS, Abel (heirs), 81
ADAMS, Charles, 106
ADAMS, Harden S., 138
ADAMS, Harden S., 81
ADAMS, Hardin S., 106
ADAMS, Hardin S., 138
ADAMS, Thomas, 2
ADAMS, Thomas, 55
ADAMS, Thos., 28
ADKERSON, James, 28
ADKERSON, Wm., 28
ADKINS, Joseph B., 28
ADKINS, Joseph R., 106
ADKINS, Joseph R., 2
ADKINS, Joseph R., 55
ADKINS, Josiah R., 81
ADKINSON, James, 3
ADKINSON, John, 3
ADKINSON, Wm., 3
ADKISON, Edward, 106
ADKISON, Edward, 81
ADKISON, James, 55
ADKISON, Welford, 106
ADKISON, Welford, 81
ADKISON, Williford, 55
ADKISON, Wm., 55
ADKISON, Wm. D., 106
ADKISON, Wm. P., 81
AGGY, negro, 140
AILSEY, negro, 168
ALEXANDER, Adam, 106
ALEXANDER, Adam R., 28
ALEXANDER, Adam R., 55
ALEXANDER, Adam R., 81
ALEXANDER, Augus, 106
ALEXANDER, Randolph, 106
ALFRED, negro, 161
ALLEN, Hugh, 106
ALLEN, James, 106
ALLEN, James, 158
ALLEN, James, 159
ALLEN, Nicholas, 106
ALSAP, Jos., 13
ALSAP, Joseph, 110
ALSOP, Jos., 32
ALSOP, Joseph, 7
AMY, negro, 168
ANDERSON, B., 63
ANDERSON, Bailey, 2

ANDERSON, Bailey, 81
ANDERSON, Bailey (heirs), 106
ANDERSON, Bailey (heirs), 55
ANDERSON, Bailie, 28
ANDERSON, Burrel, 86
ANDERSON, Burrell, 106
ANDERSON, Burrell, 2
ANDERSON, Bursel, 112
ANDERSON, Thomas, 112
ANDERSON, Wm., 106
ANDERSON, Wm., 25
ANDERSON, Wm. E., 28
ANDERSON, Wm. E., 55
ANDERSON, Wm. E., 81
ANDERSON, heirs, 28
ANDREWS, Culen, 19
ANDREWS, Cullen, 78
ANDREWS, Cullin, 2
ANICA, negro, 144
ANICA, slave, 164
ANN, negro, 168
ANTHONY, negro, 164
ARMSTRONG, John, 106
ARMSTRONG, John, 81
ARMSTRONG, Lynus, 106
ARMSTRONG, Thomas, 2
ARMSTRONG, Thomas, 28
ARMSTRONG, Thomas, 55
ARMSTRONG, Thomas, 81
ARNOLD, F., 3
ARNOLD, Farney, 75
ARNOLD, Furney, 106
ARNOLD, Kerney, 81
ASHBROOK, Moses, 106
ASHBROOKS, Moses, 81
ASHER, Sam'l, 55
ASHER, Samuel, 2
ATCHISON, John, 44
ATCHISON, John, 88
ATCHISON, Willis, 2
ATKINS, Wm., 106
AULD, Callin, 25
AUSBURN, Rebecca I., 170
AUSBURN, Rebecca J., 171
AUSBURN, Wm., 170
AUSTIN, Moses, 81
AUSTIN, Moses jr., 106
AUSTIN, Moses jr., 2
AUSTIN, Moses jr., 28
AUSTIN, Moses jr., 55
AUSTIN, Moses sr., 106
AUSTIN, Moses sr., 2
AUSTIN, Moses sr., 28
AUSTIN, Moses sr., 55
AUSTIN, Moses sr., 81
AUSTIN, Samel F., 55
AUSTIN, Samuel, 81
AUSTIN, Samuel F., 2
AUSTIN, Samuel F., 28
AUSTIN, Vincent, 106
AUSTIN, Vincent, 2
AUSTIN, Vincent, 28
AUSTIN, Vincent, 55
AUSTIN, Vincent, 81
BAILEY, Elizabeth, 145
BAKER, James, 31
BAKER, James, 57
BAKER, Jas., 91
BAKER, John, 108
BAKER, John, 30

BAKER, John, 56
BAKER, John, 6
BAKER, John, 83
BAKER, Mary, 138
BALDRIDGE, Andrew W., 107
BALDRIDGE, Andrew W., 56
BALDRIDGE, Andrew W., 82
BALDRIDGE, D., 82
BALDRIDGE, Daniel, 107
BALDRIDGE, Daniel, 114
BALDRIDGE, Daniel, 115
BALDRIDGE, Daniel, 29
BALDRIDGE, Daniel, 3
BALDRIDGE, Daniel, 56
BALDRIDGE, Daniel, 56
BALDRIDGE, Daniel, 82
BALDRIDGE, Walker, 6
BALDRIDGE, Wm., 107
BALDRIDGE, Wm., 29
BALDRIDGE, Wm., 54
BALDRIDGE, Wm., 82
BALDRIDGE, Wm. sr., 1
BALDRIDGE, Wm. sr., 6
BARGER, Daniel, 30
BARGER, Daniel D., 108
BARGER, Daniel D., 82
BARHAM, Benja., 141
BARHAM, Benjamin, 107
BARHAM, Benjamin, 30
BARLEY, John, 25
BARLEY, John, 56
BARLEY, John, 81
BARNARD, Caleb, 108
BARNARD, George, 108
BARNARD, George, 57
BARNARD, John, 108
BARNARD, John, 30
BARNARD, John, 5
BARNARD, John, 56
BARNARD, John, 83
BARNARD, Pleasant, 108
BARNARD, W., 83
BARNARD, Wm., 108
BARNARD, Wm., 30
BARNARD, Wm., 5
BARNARD, Wm., 56
BARNARD, Zadock, 30
BARNARD, Zadock, 5
BARNES, John, 5
BARNES, Samuel, 5
BARNES, Solomon, 29
BARNES, Solomon, 56
BARNES, Solomon, 83
BARNES, Stephen, 25
BARNET, ____, 16
BARNETT, Andrew, 78
BARNS, John, 30
BARNS, Solomon, 108
BASLEY, John, 107
BATEMAN, Isaac, 108
BATEMAN, Isaac, 58
BATEMAN, Isaac, 8
BATEMAN, J., 31
BATTS, Geraldin, 3
BAXTER, negro, 80
BAYLES, C., 82
BAYLES, W., 82
BAYLESS, C & W, 29
BAYLESS, C., 107
BAYLESS, Cullen, 82
BAYLESS, Thomas Cullen, 154

BAYLESS, Virginia Ann, 152
BAYLESS, Virginia Ann, 153
BAYLESS, Virginia Ann, 154
BAYLESS, W., 107
BAYLESS, W., 152
BAYLESS, Wiley, 4
BAYLESS, Wiley, 82
BAYLESS, Wilie, 29
BAYLESS & CLEMENTS, , 107
BAYLISS, C., 55
BAYLISS, Cullen, 107
BAYLISS, Cullin, 55
BAYLISS, Thomas Cullin, 153
BAYLISS, W., 55
BAYLISS, Willie, 107
BAYLISS, Willie, 55
BEADLES, Bassel A., 30
BEADLES, Bassit A., 56
BEADLES, Bassit?, 82
BEADLES, Duke, 82
BEADLES, Wm., 30
BEADLES, Wm., 4
BEADLES, Wm., 56
BEADLES, Wm., 82
BEAUCHAMP, Thomas D., 31
BELL, Byhel, 34
BELL, Byhel, 60
BELL, Bythel, 121
BELL, Jacob, 100
BELL, Jacob, 109
BELL, Jacob, 119
BELL, Jacob, 119
BELL, Jacob, 15
BELL, Jacob, 87
BELL, Jacob, 88
BELL, Jacob (heirs), 15
BELL, Joab, 111
BELL, Joab, 114
BELL, Joab, 129
BELL, Joab, 36
BELL, Joab, 40
BELL, Joab, 62
BELL, Joab, 85
BELL, John, 56
BELL, John, 82
BELL, Pulaski B., 107
BELL, Pulaski B., 29
BELL, Pulaski B., 4
BELL, Pulaski B., 55
BELL, Pulaski B., 83
BELL & TERRELL, , 36
BELL?, Bethel, 9
BELLS, Joab, 11
BELLS, Joab, 73
BELLS, ____, 41
BELOTE, H., 99
BELOTE, Henry, 122
BELOTE, Henry, 21
BELOTE, Henry, 29
BELOTE, Henry, 30
BELOTE, Henry, 45
BELOTE, Henry, 5
BELOTE, Henry, 56
BELOTE, Henry, 83
BELOTE, Henry A., 29
BELOTE, Henry A., 5
BELOTES, Henry, 113
BENNET, George, 30
BENNIT, George, 107
BERRY, Martha, 78
BERRY, Martha, 82

BERRY, Preseley M., 29
BERRY, Presley M., 107
BERRY, Wm., 30
BERY, Presley M., 4
BETSY, negro, 147
BETSY, negro, 170
BETTS, Samuel D., 108
BETTS, Samuel D., 83
BETTY, negro, 157
BETTY, negro, 170
BEVARD, James H., 29
BILLINGLY, aset, 83
BILLINGSBY, Bazil, 30
BILLINGSLEY, Bazel, 108
BILLINGSLY, Bazel, 56
BISHOP, Richard, 29
BITTEN, Robert, 106
BLACKLEY, James, 108
BLACKLEY, James, 57
BLAGG, James, 83
BLAKEMORE, Benjn., 83
BLAKEMORE, James, 29
BLAKEMORE, James, 4
BLAKEMORE, James, 75
BLAKEMORE, James, 82
BLAKEMORE, Willie, 83
BLAKEMORE, Willie B., 108
BLAKEMORE & PATTERSON, , 113
BLAKEMORE & PATTERSON, , 115
BLAKEMORE & PATTERSON, , 29
BLAKEMORE & PATTERSON, , 4
BLAKEMORE & PATTERSON, , 75
BLAKEMORE & PATTERSON, , 82
BLAKEMORE & ROSS, , 21
BLAKEMORE SWANEY & ROSS, , 120
BLAKEMORE SWANEY & ROSS, , 83
BLAKEMORE SWANEY & ROSS, , 92
BLASSINGAME, , 25
BLASSINGAME, Jas., 6
BLEDSOE, Jacob, 107
BLEDSOE, Jacob, 6
BLEDSOE, Jacob, 82
BLOUNT, G., 116
BLOUNT, J., 90
BLOUNT, J. G, 109
BLOUNT, J. G, 116
BLOUNT, J. G, 127
BLOUNT, J. G, 15
BLOUNT, J. G, 27
BLOUNT, J. G, 27
BLOUNT, J. G, 30
BLOUNT, J. G, 42
BLOUNT, J. G, 44
BLOUNT, J. G, 45
BLOUNT, J. G, 83
BLOUNT, J. G, 83
BLOUNT, J. G, 95
BLOUNT, John G, 29
BLOUNT, John G, 4
BLOUNT, John G, 55
BLOUNT, John G, 82
BLOUNT, T., 116

BLOUNT, T., 127
BLOUNT, T., 42
BLOUNT, T., 44
BLOUNT, T., 45
BLOUNT, T., 83
BLOUNT, T., 90
BLOUNT, T., 95
BLOUNT, Thomas, 4
BLOUNT, Thomas, 66
BLOUNT, Thos., 109
BLOUNT, Thos., 15
BLOUNT, Thos., 25
BLOUNT, Thos., 27
BLOUNT, Thos., 27
BLOUNT, Thos., 30
BLOUNT, Thos., 83
BLOUNTS, J. G, 40
BLOUNTS, Thos., 40
BOATWRIGHT, Wm. V., 145
BOATWRIGHT, Wm. V., 146
BOAZ, Edmund, 108
BOB, negro, 144
BOLEING, Baxter, 82
BOLING, Baxter, 128
BOLING, Baxter, 130
BOLING, Baxter, 29
BOLING, Baxter, 75
BOLING, Boxter, 47
BOLINGS, Barder, 33
BOLINS, Baxter, 101
BONDERANT, Hillary H., 55
BONDURANT, A. G., 133
BONDURANT, A. G., 134
BONDURANT, Albert G., 107
BONDURANT, Albert G., 29
BONDURANT, Albert G., 3
BONDURANT, Albert G., 52
BONDURANT, Albert G., 55
BONDURANT, Albert G., 81
BONDURANT, Benj., 81
BONDURANT, Benjamin, 103
BONDURANT, Benjamin, 104
BONDURANT, Benjamin, 3
BONDURANT, Benjamin, 76
BONDURANT, Benjm., 107
BONDURANT, Benjm., 29
BONDURANT, Benjn., 105
BONDURANT, Benjn., 154
BONDURANT, Benjn., 55
BONDURANT, Benjn., 77
BONDURANT, H. H., 142
BONDURANT, H. H., 165
BONDURANT, Hilary H., 4
BONDURANT, Hillary H., 164
BONDURANT, Hillery H., 107
BONDURANT, Hillery H., 29
BONDURANT, Hillery H., 81
BONDURANT, Hillry H., 141
BONDURANT, Jas. E., 154
BONDURANT, Robert M., 30
BONDURANT, Robert M., 5
BONDURANT, Robert M., 56
BONDURANT, Robert M., 82
BONDURENT, Benjamin, 165
BONDURENT, Harriet E. C., 165
BONDURENT, Martha Emaline, 165
BONDURENT, Robt. M., 107
BONDURENT, Sarah Elizabeth, 165

BONDURNT, Benjn., 75
BOOKOUT, Bradley, 108
BOOKOUT, Bradley, 29
BOOKOUT, Bradley, 5
BOOKOUT, Bradley, 55
BOOKOUT, Bradley, 83
BOSLY, John, 29
BOURLAND, James, 108
BOURLAND, James, 31
BOURLAND, James, 57
BOURLAND, James, 6
BOURLAND, James, 83
BOWERS, Athonatious, 157
BOWERS, E., 47
BOWERS, Elbert J., 29
BOWERS, Giles, 107
BOWERS, Giles, 29
BOWERS, Giles, 83
BOWERS, James, 157
BOWERS, Jenny, 157
BOWERS, John, 29
BOWERS, John, 3
BOWERS, John, 56
BOWERS, John, 81
BOWERS, Nancy, 157
BOWERS, Panther Matildy, 157
BOWERS, Wm. G, 100
BOWERS, Wm. G, 108
BOWERS, Wm. G, 157
BOWERS, Wm. G, 25
BOWERS, Wm. G, 30
BOWERS, Wm. G, 4
BOWERS, Wm. G, 57
BOWERS, Young P., 107
BOWERS, Young P., 157
BOWERS, Young P., 30
BOWERS, Young P., 4
BOWERS, Young P., 56
BOWERS, Young P., 82
BOWERS & WILSON, , 129
BOWERS & WILSON, , 3
BOWERS & WILSON, , 73
BOWERS & WILSON, , 82
BOWLING, Baxter, 107
BRACKIN, James, 56
BRACKING, James, 29
BRADBERRY, James, 106
BRADBURY, James, 82
BRADLEY, James, 56
BRADSHAW, Charles, 1
BRADSHAW, Charles, 5
BRADSHAW, Gideon, 57
BRADSHAW, Gideon, 6
BRADSHAW, Gideon T., 1
BRADSHAW, Gideon T., 108
BRADSHAW, Gideon T., 83
BRADSHAW, Henry, 108
BRADSHAW, Henry, 83
BRADSHAW, John, 1
BRADSHAW, John, 108
BRADSHAW, John, 31
BRADSHAW, John, 57
BRADSHAW, John, 6
BRADSHAW, John, 83
BRADSHAW, Lucretia, 1
BRADSHAW, Polly, 1
BRADSHAW, Rebecca, 1
BRADSHAW, Susanna, 1
BRADSHAW, Thompson, 107
BRADSHAW, Thompson, 30
BRADSHAW, Thompson, 5

BRADSHAW, Thompson, 56
BRADSHAW, Thompson, 82
BRAIM, Peter H., 75
BRAIN, Peter H., 107
BRAIN, Peter H., 82
BRAM, James, 30
BRAND, James, 107
BRAND, James, 4
BRAND, James, 56
BRAND, James, 83
BRANDER, D., 63
BRANDON, John W., 5
BRANN, James, 169
BRASEL, Edward, 30
BRASFIELD, C., 142
BRASFIELD, C., 163
BRASFIELD, Caleb, 141
BRASFIELD, Caleb, 162
BRASFIELD, Caleb, 163
BRASFIELD, Caleb, 164
BRASFIELD, Caleb, 164
BRASFIELD, Caleb, 82
BRASFIELD, Katharine, 163
BRASFIELD, Katharine, 163
BRASFIELD, Katharine, 164
BRASIEL, Edward M., 57
BRASSFIELD, Caleb, 108
BRAWNER, John, 108
BRAWNER, John, 5
BRAWNER, John, 51
BRAWNER, John, 56
BRAWNER, John, 83
BREEDLOVE, Robert, 108
BREEDLOVE, Robert H., 83
BREHEM, James G., 119
BREHEN, James G, 106
BREHON, Jas. G., 119
BREKEN, James G., 25
BREKEN, James G., 29
BREKEN, James G., 55
BRIDGES, Griffin, 30
BRIDGES, Griffin, 5
BRIDGES, Griffin, 56
BRIDGES, Griffin, 83
BRIGES, Griffin, 108
BRINKLEY, Wm., 106
BRINKLEY, Wm., 82
BROADWELL, D., 61
BROADWELL, David, 114
BROADWELL, David, 116
BROADWELL, David, 19
BROADWELL, David, 44
BROADWELL, David, 88
BROADWELL, David, 90
BROCKEN, James, 82
BROOKS, Sebley, 107
BROOKS, Wm., 107
BROOKS, Wm., 108
BROOKS, Wm., 83
BROWDER, John, 56
BROWDER, R., 56
BROWDER, Robert, 117
BROWDER, Robert, 28
BROWDER, Robt., 14
BROWN, Conrad, 4
BROWN, Coonrad, 108
BROWN, Coonrad, 29
BROWN, Coonrad, 56
BROWN, Coonrad, 83
BROWN, Eli, 108
BROWN, Eli, 30

BROWN, James B., 108
BROWN, Levi, 31
BROWN, Levi, 5
BROWN, Nathaniel, 75
BROWN, Nathaniel, 82
BROWN, Wm. K., 82
BROWN, Wm. R., 56
BRYANT, Jno. H., 25
BRYANT, John H., 30
BRYANT, John H., 83
BUCHANON, Thos. M., 137
BUCKLEY, Coleman, 107
BUCKLEY, Coleman, 147
BUCKLEY, James, 107
BUCKLEY, James, 146
BUCKLEY, James, 147
BUCKLEY, James, 30
BUCKLEY, James, 4
BUCKLEY, James, 56
BUCKLEY, James, 83
BUCKLEY, James W., 144
BUCKLEY, Mary, 147
BUCKLEY, Nathaniel H., 30
BUCKLEY, Nathaniel H., 6
BUCKLEY, Walter W., 107
BUCKLY, Walter W., 4
BULLOCK, A. M., 56
BUNTON, Wm., 5
BUNTON, Wm., 56
BURGER, Isaac, 22
BURGESS, Isaac, 122
BURGESS, Isaac, 17
BURGESS, Isaac, 89
BURGESS, Isaac, 94
BURGIN, Abner, 57
BURNIT, George, 82
BURTON, Charles, 56
BUSEY, Edward, 30
BUSEY, Edward, 5
BUSEY, Lucy, 83
BUSEY, Susan, 108
BUSSELL, George, 147
BUTLER, Robert, 108
BUTLER, Robert, 25
BUTLER, Robert, 82
BUTLER, Robt., 82
BUTLER, Wm. E., 106
BUTLER, Wm. E., 82
BUTT, John, 108
BYARS, Wm., 108
BYARS, Wm., 56
BYARS, Wm., 82
BYHEL, ____, 41
BYNHAM, Thomas, 82
BYNUM, Thomas, 107
BYNUM, Thomas, 30
BYNUM, Thomas, 56
BYRD, Bryan, 31
BYRD, Bryan, 6
BYRD, Nazareth, 108
BYRD, Nazareth, 30
BYRD, Nazareth, 56
BYRD, Nazareth, 82
BYRON, Harvey J., 6
CABLE, Henry, 8
CAGE, Wilson, 51
CAGE, Wilson, 6
CAIN, James C., 33
CAIN, James C., 8
CAIN & CHARLTON, , 41
CALDWELL, D. P., 155

CALDWELL, D. P., 156
CALDWELL, David P., 165
CALDWELL, David P., 31
CALOWELL, D. P., 154
CALVERT, John D., 7
CALVERT, Joseph W., 31
CALVERT, Joseph W., 7
CALVERT, Levi, 7
CAMPBELL, Daniel, 110
CAMPBELL, Daniel, 32
CAMPBELL, Daniel, 58
CAMPBELL, Daniel, 7
CAMPBELL, Daniel, 84
CAMPBELL, Geo. W., 109
CAMPBELL, Geo. W., 7
CAMPBELL, George W., 84
CANADA, Behethlum, 7
CANADA, Brethlam, 109
CANADA, James, 111
CANADA, Killebrew, 110
CANADA, Sampson, 110
CANADY, Behithalum?, 57
CANDIS, negro, 162
CANNON, Isha, 111
CANNON, John, 110
CANNON, Newton, 148
CANTRELL, Abraham, 110
CANTRELL, Abraham P., 33
CANTRELL, Abraham P., 85
CANTRELL, Abraham S., 59
CANTRELL, Abron P., 8
CANTRELL, Duke, 110
CANTRELL, Duke, 33
CANTRELL, Duke, 58
CANTRELL, Duke, 8
CANTRELL, Duke, 85
CANTRELL, Joseph, 110
CANTRELL, Joseph, 33
CANTRELL, Joseph, 59
CANTRELL, Joseph, 8
CANTRELL, Joseph, 85
CANTRELL, Richard, 110
CANTRELL, Richard, 85
CARLER, Reubin, 110
CARMAKEL, Michael, 109
CARMICHAEL, Michael, 6
CARMICHAEL, Michael, 85
CARMICHALL, M., 96
CARMICHEL, Michael, 57
CAROLINE, negro, 161
CAROLINE, negro, 80
CARR, Silas, 57
CARR, Silas, 84
CARR, Thompson, 32
CARROLL, Wm., 103
CARROLL, Wm., 51
CARROLL, Wm., 52
CARROLL, Wm., 76
CARSBY, Seth T., 33
CARSLEY, Seth L., 58
CARSLEY, Seth T., 110
CARSLEY, Seth T., 8
CARSLEY, Seth T., 84
CARTER, B., 68
CARTER, G. L., 100
CARTER, G. L., 47
CARTER, L., 31
CARTER, L., 42
CARTER, L., 6
CARTER, L., 68
CARTER, L., 73

CARTER, L., 83
CARTER, L., 94
CARTER, L., 99
CARTER, Landon, 109
CARTER, Landon, 122
CARTER, Landon, 129
CARTER, Landon, 17
CARTER, Landon, 19
CARTER, Landon, 26
CARTER, Landon, 31
CARTER, Landon, 57
CARTER, Landon, 57
CARTER, Reubin, 32
CARTER, Reubin, 58
CARTER, Reubin, 7
CARTER, Rubin, 84
CARTRIGHT, Robert, 32
CARTRIGHT, Robt., 129
CARTWRIGHT, Elizabeth, 50
CARTWRIGHT, Elizabeth, 78
CARTWRIGHT, Elizabeth, 84
CARTWRIGHT, Evalina, 50
CARTWRIGHT, Penney, 50
CARTWRIGHT, Robert, 50
CARTWRIGHT, Robt., 7
CARTWRIGHT, Thomas N., 84
CASADA, Jesse, 109
CASHEM, Martin, 7
CASHEN, Elam M., 110
CASHEN, Elum M., 58
CASHER, Elam M., 84
CASHIN, Martin, 32
CASSEL, John, 84
CASSELMAN, Lazarus, 32
CASSELMAN, Lazarus, 84
CASSELMAN, Lazarus G., 110
CASSELS, John, 33
CASSLMAN, Lazarus, 26
CASTLE, John, 109
CASTLES, John, 8
CATHARINE, negro, 145
CATHARINE, negro, 160
CATHEY, A. J. W., 58
CATHEY, A. J. W., 84
CATHEY, J. W., 32
CATHEY, Thomas, 58
CATHEY, Thomas, 84
CATHEY, Thos. D., 32
CATRON, John, 109
CATRON, John, 83
CATY, slave, 164
CATY (CATHARINE), negro girl, 1
CAVETT, Emily M. A., 168
CAVETT, Emily M. A., 168
CAVETT, Emily M. A., 168
CAVIT, John F., 32
CAVIT, John F., 58
CAVIT, Joseph, 127
CAVITT, John F., 110
CAVITT, John F., 84
CAVITT, Joseph, 98
CESSEL?, John, 22
CHAMBERS, Greenberry, 84
CHAMBERS, Greenbury, 109
CHAMBERS, Willis, 109
CHANEY, negro (f), 50
CHAPLIN, Moses, 111
CHAPLIN, Moses, 59
CHAPLIN, Moses, 7
CHARLES, negro, 140

CHARLES, negro, 162
CHARLES, negro, 168
CHARLES, negro, 168
CHARLESTON, A., 64
CHARLETON & WILLINGHAM, , 84
CHARLTON, Abm., 116
CHARLTON, Abram, 118
CHARLTON, Jno., 38
CHARLTON, Jno., 8
CHARLTON, John, 109
CHARLTON, John, 31
CHARLTON, John, 31
CHARLTON, John, 57
CHARLTON, John, 6
CHARLTON, John, 83
CHARLTON, John, 84
CHARLTON, John, 91
CHARMBERS?, Greenbury, 8
CHARRY, Jesse, 32
CHARTON, John, 33
CHERRY, Clemigle, 109
CHERRY, Clemigle, 31
CHERRY, Clemigle, 48
CHERRY, Clemigle, 84
CHERRY, Clenigle, 19
CHERRY, Clermigle, 57
CHERRY, Daniel, 108
CHERRY, Daniel, 114
CHERRY, Daniel, 31
CHERRY, Daniel, 58
CHERRY, Daniel, 84
CHERRY, Darling, 109
CHERRY, Darling, 32
CHERRY, Darling, 58
CHERRY, Darling, 8
CHERRY, Darling, 84
CHERRY, Jesse, 114
CHERRY, Jesse, 78
CHERRY, Jesse, 8
CHERRY, Laurence, 84
CHERRY, Lawrence, 108
CHERRY, Lawrence, 32
CHERRY, Lawrence, 57
CHERRY, Lawrence, 8
CHERRY, negro, 164
CHESTER, Henry W., 109
CHESTER, Henry W., 83
CHILDRESS, James, 109
CHILDRESS, James, 33
CHILDRESS, James, 84
CHILDRESS, Jas., 25
CHILTON, Wm., 111
CHILTON, Wm., 32
CHILTON, Wm., 75
CHILTON, Wm., 85
CHRISTIAN, G., 35
CHRISTIAN, G. (heirs of), 10
CHRISTMAN, Richard, 32
CHRISTMAN, Richard, 7
CHRISTMAN, Richard, 84
CHRISTMAS, Richard, 58
CHRISTMAS, Richard G., 110
CHRISTOPHER, negro, 170
CIMBRELL, Joseph, 32
CLABORN, Thomas, 109
CLABOURNE, Thomas, 83
CLAIBORN, Thomas, 31
CLAIBOURN, Thomas, 57
CLARK, Christopher, 83
CLARK, Christopher R., 109

CLARK, Christopher R., 32
CLARK, Christopher R., 57
CLARK, Christopher R., 7
CLARK, David, 109
CLARK, David, 32
CLARK, David, 58
CLARK, David, 7
CLARK, David, 84
CLARK, James W., 109
CLARK, James W., 31
CLARK, James W., 57
CLARK, James W., 7
CLARK, James W., 84
CLARK, Levi, 109
CLARK, Levi, 31
CLARK, Levi, 57
CLARK, Levi, 7
CLARK, Levi, 83
CLARK, Wm., 110
CLARK, Wm., 32
CLARK, Wm., 58
CLARK, Wm., 7
CLARK, Wm., 84
CLARK, Wm. H., 75
CLARK, Wm. H., 84
CLAXTON, James, 109
CLAXTON, James, 32
CLAXTON, James, 58
CLAXTON, James, 83
CLAYBOURN, Thos., 26
CLAYTON, John, 110
CLAYTON, John, 32
CLAYTON, John, 58
CLAYTON, John, 7
CLAYTON, John, 84
CLAYTON, Martin, 110
CLAYTON, Martin, 84
CLEMENTS, Robt. W., 109
CLIFTON, Eldridge, 32
CLIFTON, John M., 32
COCHRAN, Dennis, 109
COCHRAN, Dennis, 152
COCHRAN, Dennis, 31
COCHRAN, Dennis, 57
COCHRAN, Dennis, 6
COCHRAN, Dennis, 84
COCHRAN, J. W., 166
COCHRAN, J. W., 167
COCHRUM, Wm. L., 148
COCKE, Benjamin, 84
COCKRUM, Wm. T., 149
COCKS, Edward M., 32
COFFIELD, B. B., 34
COFFIELD, Benj., 48
COFFIELD, Benj., 85
COFFIELD, Benj., 86
COFFIELD, Benjn., 60
COFFIELDS, Benjn., 78
COFIELD, Benjm., 19
COLE, Elizabeth, 170
COLE, Elizabeth, 171
COLE, Moses E., 170
COLE, Thomas L., 170
COLE, Thos. L., 171
COLEMAN, Henry A., 170
COLEMAN, John, 32
COLEMAN, John, 58
COLEMAN, John, 84
COLEY, George, 110
COLLIER, Wm., 63
COLMAN, John, 110

COME, Amos T., 109
CONDON, Katharine Brasfield, 158
CONNER, Isham, 32
CONNER, Isham, 58
CONNER, Isham, 8
CONNER, Isham, 84
CONRAD, George, 75
CONRAD, George C., 57
CONRAD, N., 75
COOK, John, 32
COOK, John, 58
COOK, Richard, 75
COOKE, John, 110
COOKE, John, 25
COOKE, John, 84
COOKE, Margarett, 110
COOKE, Margarett, 84
COOKE, Willis, 109
COOKE, Willis, 57
COOKS, John, 10
COOLEY, George, 33
COOLEY, George, 58
COOLEY, George, 8
COOLEY, George, 85
COONS, John, 35
COOPER, Elizabeth Allen, 162
COOPER, Henry, 32
COOPER, Henry, 7
COOPER, James, 110
COOPER, James, 59
COOPER, James, 85
COOPER, John, 33
COOPER, John, 8
COOPER, Lewis, 110
COOPER, Whimeal H., 161
COOPER, Whitmeal H., 162
COOPER, Whitnell, 6
COOPER, Whitnil, 31
CORDEL, Mark B., 32
CORTEN, Landen, 15
COSTEN, L., 23
COSTEN, L., 41
COTTON, Charles, 109
COTTON, Charles, 31
COTTON, Charles, 57
COTTON, Charles, 6
COTTON, Charles, 62
COTTON, Charles, 83
COTTON, Solomon, 110
COVET, John F., 7
COWAN, James, 109
COWAN, James, 32
COWAN, James, 78
COX, Edward M., 110
COX, Edward M., 58
COX, Edward M., 85
COX, Henry B., 110
COX, Henry B., 58
COX, Henry B., 85
COX, Riley, 110
COX, Robert, 85
COX, Robert T., 58
COY, negro (m), 162
CRABTREE, Anderson, 110
CRABTREE, Anderson, 33
CRABTREE, Anderson, 59
CRABTREE, Anderson, 85
CRAGLEY, Loyd, 8
CRAIG, Ebenezer, 111
CRAIG, Ebenezer, 58

CRAIG, Ebenezer, 84
CRAIG, Hugh, 58
CRAIG, Hugh, 7
CRAIG, Samuel, 58
CRAIG, Wm., 58
CRAIG, Wm., 7
CRAIG, Wm. D., 58
CRAVEN, Joseph, 158
CRAVENS, John, 110
CRAVENS, John, 33
CRAVENS, John, 58
CRAVENS, John, 8
CRAVENS, John, 85
CRAVENS, Joseph, 110
CRAVENS, Joseph, 33
CRAVENS, Joseph, 58
CRAVENS, Joseph, 8
CRAVENS, Joseph, 85
CRAVIN, Joseph, 159
CRAW, Benjm. B., 32
CRIDER, David, 58
CRIDER, David, 8
CRIDER, David, 84
CRIDER, David, 90
CRIDER, Wenston B., 109
CRIDER, winston B., 84
CROCKETT, D., 70
CROCKETT, David, 20
CROCKETT, David, 59
CROFFORD, Thomas, 6
CROLEY, Wm., 8
CROSLIN, James, 110
CROSSER, H. W., 163
CROW, Benjamin B., 8
CROW, Garland T., 110
CROWLEY, Jesse, 85
CRUICE, Isaac, 7
CRUISE, Isaac, 32
CRUISE, Isaac, 58
CRUM, Peter, 32
CRUM, Peter, 58
CRUM, Peter, 7
CRUSE, Isaac, 110
CRUSE, Isaac, 84
CUDER, David, 33
CUIDA, negro, 168
CULER, Alonzo D., 78
CUMMINS, Sally, 53
CUNNINGHAM, Lucy, 143
CURD, negro, 145
CURLIN, Lemuel, 33
CURLIN, Samuel, 8
CURLIN, Zachariah H.?, 8
CURLIN, Zacheus H., 111
CURLIN, Zacheus H., 33
CURLIN, Zacheus H., 58
CURLIN, Zacheus H., 84
CYNTA, negro, 1
D, John, 57
DAILEY, Edward, 111
DALTON, E. T., 67
DALTON, T., 16
DALTON, Tracts, 40
DAMRON, Charles, 111
DAMRON, Charles, 34
DAMRON, Charles, 59
DAMRON, Charles, 85
DAMRON, Charles, 9
DAMRON, Constantine, 111
DAMRON, Constantine, 59
DAMRON, Constantine, 85

DAMRON, George, 111
DAMRON, George, 34
DAMRON, George, 59
DAMRON, George, 85
DAMRON, George, 9
DAMRON, Isaac, 59
DAMRON, John, 111
DAMRON, John, 34
DAMRON, John, 59
DAMRON, John, 85
DAMRON, John, 9
DAMRON, John T., 34
DAMRON, John T., 59
DAMRON, John T., 9
DAMRON, Moses, 111
DAMRON, Moses, 34
DAMRON, Moses, 59
DAMRON, Moses, 9
DAMRON, Moses L., 85
DAMRON, Nobel L., 85
DAMRON, Noble L., 9
DAMRON, Samuel, 111
DAMRON, Samuel, 85
DANIEL, Delaney, 34
DANIEL, negro, 161
DANIEL, negro, 170
DANULSON, Humphrey, 111
DARLING, James S., 112
DARLING, James S., 85
DAUGHERTY, Geo., 24
DAUGHERTY, Geo., 34
DAUGHERTY, Geo., 49
DAUGHERTY, Geo., 69
DAUGHERTY, George, 59
DAUGHERTY, R. E. (C.?), 43
DAUGHERTY & MCCORKLE, , 11
DAUGHERTY & MCCORKLE, , 12
DAUGHERTY & MCCORKLE, , 127
DAUGHERTY & MCCORKLE, , 24
DAVIS, David W., 33
DAVIS, David W., 9
DAVIS, Fennel, 59
DAVIS, Fennel, 85
DAVIS, Fenuel, 9
DAVIS, George, 111
DAVIS, George, 86
DAVIS, Isham L., 34
DAVIS, Isham L., 59
DAVIS, Isham L., 86
DAVIS, Isham L., 9
DAVIS, Isham S., 111
DAVIS, Jess B., 59
DAVIS, Jesse, 111
DAVIS, Jesse, 33
DAVIS, Jesse, 34
DAVIS, Jesse, 59
DAVIS, Jesse, 86
DAVIS, Jesse, 9
DAVIS, Jesse, 9
DAVIS, Jesse B., 111
DAVIS, Jesse B., 86
DAVIS, Jonathan, 111
DAVIS, Mary, 80
DAVIS, Newel, 34
DAVIS, Nicholas, 9
DAVIS, Phenuel, 111
DAVIS, Terrell, 33

DAVIS, Thomas, 111
DAVY, negro, 144
DAWSON, Isaac, 111
DAWSON, Isaac, 163
DAWSON, Isaac, 33
DAWSON, Isaac, 86
DAWSON, Isaac, 9
DECK, Daniel, 34
DECK, Daniel, 60
DECOACH, Thomas, 23
DELANEY, Daniel, 102
DELANEY, Daniel, 103
DELANEY, Daniel, 41
DELANEY, Daniel, 60
DELANEY, Danl., 55
DELANEY, David, 15
DELANEY, Elijah, 111
DELANEY, Elijah, 59
DELANEY, Elijah, 85
DELANEY, Elijah, 9
DELANEY, Neal, 102
DELANEY, Neal, 103
DELANEY, Neil, 86
DELANEY, Neill, 34
DELANEY, Nell, 9
DELANEY, Niel, 111
DELANEY, Polly, 102
DELANEY, Sidney, 102
DELANEY, Virgil, 102
DELANEY, Will, 59
DELANY, Daniel, 9
DELANY, Elijah, 51
DELANY, Wm., 9
DELL, Joseph, 59
DELL, Zebulon, 59
DELOACH, Thomas, 33
DELOACH, Thomas, 73
DELOACH, Thos., 101
DEMING, A., 32
DEMING, A., 78
DENNING, Adr., 7
DENNING, Thomas, 33
DENT, John B., 167
DENT, Jos. E., 85
DENT, Joseph, 9
DENT, Joseph E., 111
DENT, Joseph E., 33
DENT, Joseph E., 59
DEVEREAUX, Thos. P., 111
DEVEREAUX, Thos. P., 33
DEVEREAUX, Thos. P., 59
DEVEREAUX, Thos. R., 85
DEVEROUGH, Thos. D., 8
DEWEY, John, 166
DICK?, G., 102
DICK?, N., 102
DICKENS, Samuel, 111
DICKENS, Samuel, 33
DICKENS, Samuel, 59
DICKENS, Wm., 9
DICKINS, Samuel, 112
DICKINS, Samuel, 8
DICKINS, Samuel, 85
DICKINS, Wm., 8
DICKSON, E. D., 150
DICKSON, Ephram D., 34
DICKSON, Ephriam D., 112
DICKSON, Ephriam D., 149
DICKSON, Ephriam D., 60
DICKSON, Ephriam D., 86
DICKSON, Ephriam D., 9

DICKSON, Jourden, 33
DICKSON, Matton, 85
DICKSON, Tilman, 29
DILL, Joseph, 86
DILL, Zebulon, 86
DILLON, Thomas, 109
DILLON, Thomas, 31
DILLON, Thomas, 9
DOCTOR, negro, 168
DODD, John C., 171
DODDS, Jno. C. jr., 169
DOHERTY, Dennis, 111
DOHERTY, Dennis, 34
DOHERTY, Dennis, 59
DOHERTY, E. Geo., 102
DOHERTY, G., 91
DOHERTY, Geo., 118
DOHERTY, Geo., 124
DOHERTY, Geo., 131
DOHERTY, Geo., 65
DOHERTY, Geo., 75
DOHERTY, Geo., 95
DOHERTY, George, 111
DOHERTY, George, 85
DOHERTY & MCCORKLE, , 131
DOHERTY & MCCORKLE, , 48
DOHERTY & MCCORKLE, , 71
DOHERTY & MCCORKLE, , 98
DONELSON, Humphrey, 33
DONELSON, Humphrey, 59
DONELSON, Humphrey, 86
DONELSON, Humphrey Drew, 9
DOTEY, James, 26
DOTSON, Wm., 111
DOTY, James, 34
DOUGHERTY, Dennis, 85
DOUGHERTY, Dennis, 9
DOUGHERTY, George, 33
DOUGHERTY, George, 8
DOUGHERTY, George, 9
DOUGHERTY & MCCORK, Daniel, 7
DOUGHERTY & MCCORKLE, , 109
DOUGHERTY & MCCORKLE, , 14
DOUGLASS, Elmore, 33
DOUGLASS, Elmore, 75
DOUGLASS, Elmore, 85
DOUGLASS, Emore, 9
DREW, James, 9
DREW, James H., 111
DREW, James H., 34
DREW, James H., 59
DREW, James H., 86
DREWRY, John, 167
DUAGHERTY, Jonathan M., 36
DUAGHERTY, R. E. C., 36
DUKE, L. C., 149
DUKE, Littleton C., 148
DUNHAM, Wm., 33
DUNHAM, Wm., 86
DUNLAP, John H., 33
DUNN, John, 33
DUNN, John, 59
DUNN, John, 85

DUNN, John, 9
DUNN, John P., 34
DUNN, John P., 9
DUNN, Mathew, 34
DUNN, Mathew P., 111
DUNN, Mathew P., 59
DUNN, Mathew P., 86
DUNN, Mathew P., 9
DUNN, Nancy, 147
DUNN, Nathaniel, 86
DUNN, Thomas, 33
DUNN, Thomas, 9
DUNNAR, Anthony, 111
DUNNAR, Anthony, 59
DUNNAR, Anthony, 85
DUNNAR, Anthony H., 33
DUNNAS, Anthony, 8
DUNNELBARGER, Daniel, 59
DUNNING, George W., 60
DURHAM, Wm., 60
EARLY, Samuel, 112
EAST, John, 10
EAST, John, 34
EASTAS, John H., 10
EASTER, negro woman, 1
EATON, John R., 10
EATON, slave, 164
EAVES, Bartlett, 112
EAVES, Robertson, 112
EAVES, Solomon, 112
EAVES, Solomon jr., 86
EAVES, Thomas J., 112
EAVES, Thomas J., 86
EDMONSTON, James, 112
EDMONSTON, James, 60
EDMONSTON, James, 86
EDMONSTON, Jesse, 112
EDMONSTON, Jesse, 34
EDMONSTON, Jesse, 60
EDMONSTON, Jesse, 60
EDMONSTON, Jesse, 86
EDMONSTON, Jesse, 9
EDMONSTON, Reuben, 34
EDMONSTON, Reubin, 10
EDMONSTON, Reubin, 112
EDMONSTON, Reubins, 86
EDMONSTON, Robert, 86
EDMONSTON, Wm., 60
EDMONTSON, James, 10
EDWARDS, Eleas, 60
EDWARDS, Eli, 112
EDWARDS, Eli, 60
EDWARDS, Eli, 86
EDWARDS, Thomas C., 112
EDWARDS, Thomas C., 34
EDWARDS, Thomas C., 9
EDWARDS, Thomas S., 152
EDWARDS, Thomas S., 86
EDWARDS, Thos. C., 60
EDWARDS, Thos. C., 86
EDWARDS, Thos. S., 112
EHTRIDGE, Thomas, 86
ELDER, Wm., 136
ELDER, Wm., 137
ELDRIDGE & HILL, , 119
ELDRIDGE & HILL, , 128
ELDRIDGE & HILL, , 30
ELDRIDGE & HILL, , 35
ELDRIDGE & HILLS, , 10
ELESON, Ingram, 86
ELEY, Eli, 112

ELEY, Eli, 60
ELEY, Eli, 86
ELI, Eley, 9
ELI, Ely, 34
ELIOTT, G. S., 77
ELIOTT, George S., 112
ELIOTT, George S., 34
ELIOTT, George S., 60
ELIOTT, George S., 76
ELIOTT, George S., 86
ELLIOTT, George S., 10
ELIZA, negro, 145
ELIZA, negro, 152
ELIZA, negro, 160
ELIZA, negro, 160
ELZEY, Wm., 60
EMELINE, negro, 161
ENGLAND, David, 60
ENGLISH, Asa, 60
ETHRIDGE, Thomas, 112
ETHRIDGE, Thomas, 60
EVANS, J., 63
EVANS, Jno., 22
EVANS, John, 119
EVANS, John, 128
EVANS, John, 47
EVANS, John, 90
EZZELL, Hanson, 60
EZZELL, Harison, 10
EZZELL, Harison, 86
EZZELL, Urias, 60
FANNY, negro, 1
FARBIS, Almarine M., 34
FARBIS, Lorenzo D., 34
FAREL, Albert B., 87
FARLEY, Thomas M., 60
FARMER, Aron, 10
FARMER, Aron, 113
FARMER, Aron, 35
FARMER, Aron, 61
FARMER, Aron, 87
FARMER, Hewlitt, 112
FARMER, Hiram, 10
FARMER, Hiram, 113
FARMER, Hiram, 35
FARMER, Hiram, 61
FARMER, Hiram, 87
FARMER, Hulitt, 87
FARMER, Jesse, 112
FARMER, Jesse, 87
FARMER, Rebecca Ann, 145
FARR, George, 35
FARSON, M., 129
FENNEL?, J. M., 143
FENNELL, J. M., 144
FERRELL, Jno., 22
FICH, John W., 10
FIELDS, Absolom, 112
FIELDS, David, 113
FIELDS, David, 87
FIKE, John, 113
FILPOT, Bennet, 60
FINCH, John W., 113
FINCH, John W., 35
FINCH, John W., 61
FINCH, John W., 87
FISH, Moses, 35
FISK, Moses, 10
FITZGERALD, Wm., 10
FITZGERALD, Wm., 113
FITZGERALD, Wm., 34

177

| | | | |
|---|---|---|---|
| FITZGERALD, Wm., 60 | FOWLER, Wm., 112 | GARDNER, Alfred, 133 | GETER, Robert, 114 |
| FITZGERALD, Wm., 87 | FOWLER, Wm., 15 | GARDNER, Alfred, 134 | GETER, Samuel, 114 |
| FLACK, James, 10 | FOWLER, Wm., 34 | GARDNER, Alfred, 135 | GIBBS, Jesse, 114 |
| FLACK, Jas., 99 | FOWLER, Wm., 40 | GARDNER, Alfred, 136 | GIBBS, Jesse, 88 |
| FLEMING, Wm., 75 | FOWLER, Wm. A., 86 | GARDNER, Alfred, 138 | GILBERT, Jonathan, 11 |
| FLEMMING, Wm., 10 | FOWLER, Wm. H., 60 | GARDNER, Alfred, 139 | GILBERT, Jonathan M., 114 |
| FLEMMING, Wm., 113 | FOWLER, Wm. H., 86 | GARDNER, Alfred, 35 | GILBERT, Jonathan M., 135 |
| FLEMMING, Wm., 35 | FRANCES, old negro woman, 1 | GARDNER, Alfred, 51 | GILBERT, Jonathan M., 136 |
| FLEMMING, Wm., 50 | FRANK, negro, 164 | GARDNER, Alfred, 52 | GILBERT, Jonathan M., 62 |
| FLEMMING, Wm., 51 | FRANKLING, Barnard, 10 | GARDNER, Alfred, 76 | GILBERT, Jonathan M., 88 |
| FLEMMING, Wm., 87 | FREELS, David, 10 | GARDNER, Alfred, 77 | GILBERT, Randolph, 11 |
| FLETCHER, Jefferson, 113 | FREELS, David, 35 | GARDNER, Alfred, 87 | GILBERT, Randolph, 114 |
| FOLEY, Jesse, 113 | FREELS, David, 60 | GARDNER, Jeptha, 11 | GILBERT, Randolph, 36 |
| FOLEY, Jesse, 35 | FREELS, Garritt, 60 | GARDNER, Jeptha, 113 | GILBERT, Randolph, 62 |
| FOLEY, Jesse, 61 | FREEMAN, Charles, 26 | GARDNER, Jeptha, 171 | GILBERT, Randolph, 88 |
| FOLEY, Townsend, 113 | FREEMAN, Charles, 35 | GARDNER, Jeptha, 172 | GILBERT, Robert, 11 |
| FOLEY, Townsend, 61 | FREEMAN, Charles A., 10 | GARDNER, Jeptha, 51 | GILBERT, Robert, 36 |
| FOLEY, Townsend, 87 | FREEMAN, Charles A., 34 | GARDNER, Jeptha, 52 | GILBERT, Robert, 88 |
| FOLKS, Shearward, 10 | FREEMAN, Charles A., 60 | GARDNER, Jeptha, 61 | GILBERT, Robert R., 114 |
| FOLKS, Shearwood, 34 | FREEMAN, Charles A., 86 | GARDNER, Jeptha, 88 | GILBERT, Robert R., 62 |
| FOLKS, Shearwood, 87 | FREEMAN, Chas. A., 112 | GARDNER, Jepthah, 36 | GILBERT, negro, 168 |
| FONVILLE, Jno. B., 165 | FREEMAN, Evans, 113 | GARDNER, Jesse, 113 | GILBERT?, Robert, 12 |
| FONVILLE, John B., 112 | FREEMAN, Evans, 34 | GARDNER, Jesse, 87 | GILL, Jesse, 161 |
| FONVILLE, John B., 86 | FREEMAN, Evans, 61 | GARDNER, Jiptha, 87 | GILLA, negro, 161 |
| FORBIS, Almerick M., 60 | FREEMAN, Evans, 87 | GARDNER, Jno. A., 134 | GILLESPIE, D., 95 |
| FORBIS, Amarine M., 112 | FREEMAN, James, 10 | GARDNER, Jno. A., 52 | GILLESPIE, David, 36 |
| FORBIS, Amarine M., 87 | FREEMAN, John, 10 | GARDNER, John, 61 | GILLESPIE, Wm., 114 |
| FORBIS, Lorenzo D., 113 | FREEMAN, John, 112 | GARDNER, John A., 103 | GILLIAM, Gray, 114 |
| FORBIS, Lorenzo D., 60 | FREEMAN, John, 34 | GARDNER, John A., 104 | GILLIAM, Gray, 62 |
| FORBIS, Lorenzo D., 87 | FREEMAN, John, 86 | GARDNER, John A., 104 | GILLIAM, Gray, 88 |
| FORCE, Albert B., 11 | FREEMAN, Richardson, 11 | GARDNER, John A., 113 | GILLIAM, Henry, 114 |
| FORCE, Albert B., 60 | FREEMAN, Richardson, 112 | GARDNER, John A., 133 | GILLIAM, Henry, 62 |
| FORCE, Wm., 10 | FREEMAN, Richardson, 35 | GARDNER, John A., 152 | GILLIAM, Henry, 88 |
| FORCE, Wm., 61 | FREEMAN, Richardson, 60 | GARDNER, John A., 154 | GLACO, Isaac, 61 |
| FOREE, A. B., 117 | FREEMAN, Richardson, 87 | GARDNER, John A., 165 | GLASCO, Isaac, 11 |
| FOREE, A. B., 152 | FREEMAN, Wm., 113 | GARDNER, John A., 170 | GLASCO, Isaac, 114 |
| FOREE, Wm., 113 | FREEMAN, Wm., 87 | GARDNER, John A., 36 | GLASCO, Isaac, 36 |
| FORLE, Albert B., 35 | FREEMAN, negro, 161 | GARDNER, John A., 51 | GLASCO, Isaac, 75 |
| FORREST, Elisha, 10 | FRIZELL, Isaac, 113 | GARDNER, John A., 61 | GLASCO, Isaac, 87 |
| FOSTER, Clabourn, 11 | FRIZELL, Jason, 112 | GARDNER, John A., 87 | GLASS, Dudley, 36 |
| FOSTER, Clabourn, 78 | FRIZZELL, Israel, 87 | GARDNER, John M., 105 | GLASS, Dudley jr., 113 |
| FOSTER, Clabourn, 87 | FRIZZELL, Jason, 87 | GARDNER, Richard W., 114 | GLASS, Dudley jr., 61 |
| FOSTER, George, 11 | FULLER, Joseph, 112 | GARDNER, Richard W., 36 | GLASS, Dudley jr., 87 |
| FOSTER, George M., 51 | FULLER, Joseph, 86 | GARDNER, Richard W., 61 | GLASS, Dudley sr., 113 |
| FOSTER, James, 61 | FURLONG, Hudson, 11 | GARDNER, Richard W., 88 | GLASS, Dudley sr., 61 |
| FOSTER, James C., 10 | FURLONG, Hudson, 113 | GARDNER, Wm. H., 75 | GLASS, Dudley sr., 87 |
| FOSTER, James C., 35 | FURLONG, Hudson, 35 | GARISON, Edward, 36 | GLASS, Elisha W., 11 |
| FOSTER, Nathaniel H., 87 | FURLONG, Hudson, 87 | GARISON, Isham, 11 | GLASS, Elisha W., 36 |
| FOWLER, Billard A., 112 | GAIBY, James, 88 | GARISON, Isham, 62 | GLEESON, W. W., 156 |
| FOWLER, Bullard A., 60 | GAILEY, Isaac, 114 | GARNER, John, 114 | GLEESON, Wm. W., 113 |
| FOWLER, Bullard A., 87 | GAILEY, James, 114 | GARNER, John, 61 | GLEESON, Wm. W., 152 |
| FOWLER, James, 35 | GAILEY, James, 12 | GARNER, John, 88 | GLEESON, Wm. W., 61 |
| FOWLER, James jr., 11 | GAILEY, James, 36 | GARNER, Stephen, 114 | GLEESON, Wm. W., 87 |
| FOWLER, James sr., 11 | GAILEY, James, 62 | GARRETT, Henry A., 11 | GLEN, Phillip B., 61 |
| FOWLER, Jason, 113 | GAILY, Thomas, 114 | GARRETT, Henry A., 113 | GLEN, Robert J., 61 |
| FOWLER, John, 112 | GAINS, James, 88 | GARRETT, Henry A., 35 | GLENN, Phillip B., 36 |
| FOWLER, John, 34 | GAINS, Wilson, 114 | GARRETT, Henry A., 61 | GLENN, Robert J., 113 |
| FOWLER, John, 35 | GALLOWAY, Benjn., 61 | GARRETT, Henry A., 88 | GLENN, Robert J., 88 |
| FOWLER, John, 60 | GALLOWAY, Glidwell, 114 | GARRETT, Noah, 114 | GLOVER, Henry, 114 |
| FOWLER, John, 87 | GALLOWAY, Glidwell, 61 | GARRISON, Edward, 11 | GOING, Henry J., 61 |
| FOWLER, Samuel, 11 | GALOWAY, Benjamin, 114 | GARTER, Wm., 11 | GOING, Levi, 61 |
| FOWLER, Samuel, 35 | GALOWAY, Benjn., 88 | GASTON, Wm., 113 | GOLDSBY, James, 11 |
| FOWLER, Samuel, 61 | GALOWAY, Glidwells, 88 | GASTON, Wm., 36 | GOLDSBY, James, 114 |
| FOWLER, Samuel, 87 | GARDEN, David, 88 | GASTON, Wm., 87 | GOLDSBY, James, 36 |
| FOWLER, Stephen, 112 | GARDNER, A., 52 | GATES, Jacob G., 145 | GOLDSBY, James, 62 |
| FOWLER, Stephen, 34 | GARDNER, Alford, 61 | GATES, Jacob G., 146 | GOLDSBY, James, 88 |
| FOWLER, Stephen, 86 | GARDNER, Alfred, 103 | GELLESPIE, Geo. T., 87 | GOLDSBY, Stephen, 11 |
| FOWLER, Thomas, 112 | GARDNER, Alfred, 104 | GEORGE, Solomon, 18 | GOLDSBY, Stephen, 114 |
| FOWLER, Thomas, 34 | GARDNER, Alfred, 105 | GEORGE, Solomon, 51 | GOLDSBY, Stephen, 36 |
| FOWLER, Thomas, 60 | GARDNER, Alfred, 11 | GERTNER, John, 36 | GOLDSBY, Stephen, 88 |
| FOWLER, Thomas, 86 | GARDNER, Alfred, 113 | GESTER, John, 26 | GOLDSBY, Stephen H., 62 |

GOODMAN, Samuel, 88
GORDON, David, 113
GORDON, Winifred, 145
GRACE, negro, 161
GRAHAM, E. L., 151
GRAHAM, Elijah, 62
GREEN, Alvah, 87
GREEN, Caswell, 36
GREEN, Jas., 18
GREEN, Jos. H., 11
GREEN, Joseph, 109
GREEN, Joseph heirs, 36
GREEN, Moses, 114
GREEN, S. Brackin, 11
GREER, Aquilla P., 113
GREER, David, 35
GREER, David S., 11
GREER, James, 11
GREER, James, 114
GREER, James, 35
GREER, James, 60
GREER, James, 61
GREER, James, 68
GREER, James, 87
GREER, James, 87
GREER, Jas., 127
GREER, Jas., 129
GREER, Jas., 42
GREER, Jas., 43
GREER, Jos., 85
GREER, Joseph, 112
GREER, Joseph, 84
GREER & MCCORKLE, , 11
GREER & MCCORKLE, , 35
GRENDER, ____, 41
GRIFFITH, Abel, 113
GRIFFITH, Abel, 35
GRIFFITH, Abel, 88
GRIFFITH, Owen, 113
GRIFFITH, Owen, 35
GRIFFITH, Owen, 88
GRIGGS, Thos. H., 11
GRIGGS, Wm. A., 11
GRITT, George, 119
GROOM, Bright, 11
GROOM, Bright, 36
GROOM, Stephen H., 12
GROOMS, Bright, 114
GROOMS, Bright, 62
GROOMS, Bright, 88
GROOMS, Stephen H., 114
GROOMS, Stephen H., 134
GROOMS, Stephen H., 135
GROOMS, Stephen H., 62
GROOMS, Winiford, 134
GUEST, George, 36
GUEST, George, 61
GUIN, James, 36
GUINN, Malcolm, 114
GUINN, Wm., 12
GUION, Alvah, 113
GUION, Alvah, 36
GUNTER, Frances, 88
GWEN, Malcolm, 36
GWION, Avah, 61
HABERT, John, 114
HAGEN, negro, 170
HAIL, Wilson, 37
HAINES, Samuel, 51
HAINS, Andrew, 12
HAINS, Andrew, 12

HALL, Abraham P., 116
HALL, Abraham P., 63
HALL, Abraham P., 89
HALL, Britton, 88
HALL, Durham, 116
HALL, Durham, 63
HALL, Durham, 89
HALL, James, 115
HALL, Samuel, 115
HALL, Samuel, 138
HALL, Samuel, 138
HALL, The., 172
HALL, Thomas, 116
HALL, Thomas, 63
HALL, Thomas, 89
HAMBLIN, Joel, 115
HAMBLIN, Joel, 62
HAMBLY, Joel, 89
HAMILTON, Wm., 116
HAMILTON, Wm., 26
HAMILTON, Wm., 37
HAMILTON, Wm., 63
HAMILTON, Wm., 89
HANELINE, Shelton, 74
HANING, Samuel, 78
HARDIN, ____, 116
HARMON, Abram, 13
HARMON, Israel, 115
HARMON, Israel, 12
HARMON, Israel, 36
HARMON, Israel, 62
HARMON, Israel, 88
HARMON, Jesse, 116
HARMON, Jesse, 12
HARMON, Jesse, 37
HARMON, Jesse, 62
HARMON, Jesse, 90
HARMON, Josiah, 116
HARMON, Samuel, 13
HARMON, Wm., 63
HARPER, Forester, 13
HARPINS, Thomas, 62
HARPOLE, Moses, 62
HARPOLE, Moses, 88
HARREL, John, 37
HARREL, John, 90
HARRIETT, negro, 53
HARRIS, Ed, 6
HARRIS, Edward, 137
HARRIS, Edward, 31
HARRIS, Nathan, 114
HARRIS, Z. H., 152
HARRIS, Zephariah, 151
HARROD, James, 37
HARROLD, John, 116
HARROLD, John, 26
HARROLL, John, 151
HARROLL, John, 63
HART, James, 117
HART, James, 12
HART, James, 36
HART, James, 39
HART, James, 66
HART, James, 78
HARTS, James, 48
HASKY, Archibald, 12
HATLER, James, 12
HATTEN, James, 63
HAYDEN, Shelta S., 101
HAYNOR, Samuel, 37
HAYS, David, 115

HAYS, Moses, 116
HAYS, Wm., 116
HAYS, Wm., 37
HAYS, Wm., 89
HAYSE, Williams, 63
HAYSE, Wm., 12
HAYWOOD, negro, 164
HEALT, Benjamin, 63
HEARDY, negro, 141
HENDERSON, Jno. R., 12
HENDERSON, John, 115
HENDERSON, John, 63
HENDERSON, John K., 116
HENDERSON, John K., 37
HENDERSON, John K., 89
HENDERSON, Robert, 116
HENDERSON, Robert, 12
HENDERSON, Robert, 12
HENDERSON, Robert, 63
HENDERSON, Robert, 89
HENDERSON, Robt., 13
HENDERSON, Thomas, 110
HENDERSON, Thomas, 16
HENDERSON, Thomas, 26
HENDERSON, Thomas, 51
HENDERSON, Thomas, 7
HENDERSON, Thos., 102
HENDERSON, Thos., 12
HENDERSON, Thos., 120
HENDERSON, Thos., 121
HENDERSON, Thos., 32
HENDERSON, Thos., 37
HENDERSON, Thos., 58
HENDERSON, Thos., 86
HENDERSON, negro, 161
HENDERSON, negro, 168
HENDRICKS, Alford, 53
HENDRICKS, Alford, 54
HENDRICKS, Cary, 53
HENDRICKS, Elizabeth, 53
HENDRICKS, Henry, 53
HENDRICKS, Paden, 53
HENDRICKS, Pinkney, 53
HENDRICKS, Polly Ann, 53
HENDRICKS, Sally, 53
HENDRICKS, Washington, 53
HENDRICKS, Wm., 53
HENDRIX, Alfred, 115
HENDRIX, Alfred, 13
HENDRIX, Alfred, 62
HENDRIX, Alfred, 88
HENDRIX, Henry, 13
HENDRIX, Jeremiah, 115
HENDRIX, Jeremiah, 26
HENDRIX, Payton, 115
HENERSON, John K., 63
HENLEBERT, Wm., 12
HENRY, Hendrix, 37
HENRY, John H., 12
HENRY, Moses, 116
HENRY, Moses, 13
HENRY, Moses, 37
HENRY, Moses, 62
HENRY, Moses, 89
HENRY, negro, 157
HENRY, negro, 161
HERD, Bailey E., 115
HERD, Bailey E., 36
HERD, Bailey E., 62
HERD, Bailey E., 88
HERD, Baley E., 13

HERD, George D., 12
HERD, George D., 36
HERD, George D., 62
HERD, Martin, 115
HERNDERSON, Robert, 115
HERNDON, Benj., 82
HERROD, James, 116
HERROD, James, 13
HERROD, James, 63
HERROD, James, 90
HERROLL & GRAHAM, , 151
HERRON, James, 13
HERRON, Wm., 13
HIDE, Jemima, 143
HIGGS, Alfred, 115
HIGGS, Alfred, 62
HIGGS, Jonathan sr., 159
HIGGS, Wm., 167
HIGHSAW, Frederick, 89
HIGNIGHT, John, 13
HILL, Alfred, 115
HILL, Dilila, 12
HILL, Henry M., 12
HILL, Henry M., 37
HILL, Henry M., 89
HILL, James, 115
HILL, James, 158
HILL, James, 88
HILL, Wm., 12
HILL, Wm., 6
HILL & COLIER, , 89
HILL & COLLIER, , 119
HILL & COLLIER, , 63
HILLIARD, negro, 164
HINDERSON, Thomas, 26
HINTON, Joseph, 116
HINTON, Joseph, 89
HISAW, Frederick jr., 116
HISAW, Frederick sr., 116
HOCKNEY, Isaac S., 12
HOGGARD, Byars, 13
HOGGARD, Byars, 37
HOGGARD, Byars, 89
HOGGARD, Byas, 63
HOGGARD, Byers, 116
HOLLEY, Hazel, 89
HOLLIS, M. J., 16
HOLLY, Hazel, 37
HOLLY, Hazell, 13
HOLLY, Hazell, 63
HOLT, Benjamin, 116
HOLT, Benjamin, 37
HOLT, Benjamin, 89
HONEYCUT, Heram, 116
HONEYCUT, Hiram, 89
HOOD, John, 89
HOPKINS, Richard, 116
HOPKINS, Thomas, 106
HOPKINS, Thomas, 114
HOPKINS, Thomas, 12
HOPKINS, Thomas, 21
HOPKINS, Thomas, 36
HOPKINS, Thomas, 46
HOPKINS, Thos., 66
HOPPER, Elizabeth, 53
HOPPER, Forester, 116
HOPPER, Forester, 53
HOPPER, Forester, 54
HOPPER, Forester, 88
HOPPER, Forister, 62
HORNBACK, James, 37

HORNBEAK, James, 116
HORNBEAK, James, 12
HORNBEAK, James, 62
HORNBEAK, James, 90
HORNBEAK, Wm., 62
HORNBEAK, Wm., 89
HORNBOCK, Wm., 115
HORNSBY, John, 115
HORNSBY, John, 88
HORTON, Archibald, 115
HORTON, Archibald, 13
HORTON, Archibald, 36
HORTON, Archibald, 62
HORTON, Archibald, 89
HORTON, George, 115
HORTON, George, 13
HORTON, George, 37
HORTON, George, 62
HORTON, George, 89
HORTON, James, 115
HORTON, James, 13
HORTON, James, 36
HORTON, James, 62
HORTON, James, 89
HORTON, John, 115
HORTON, John, 13
HORTON, John, 37
HORTON, John, 62
HORTON, John, 89
HORTON, Robert, 115
HORTON, Robert, 13
HORTON, Robert, 37
HORTON, Robert, 62
HORTON, Robert, 89
HOUSE, Isham, 115
HOUSE, Isham, 37
HOUSE, Isham, 88
HOUSE, John, 12
HOUSE, John, 37
HOUSE, Wilbourn, 37
HOUSE, Wm., 88
HOUSE, Wm. F., 115
HOUSE?, Bethel Bells, 9
HOUSTON, John, 115
HOWARD, Enoch, 116
HOWARD, Geo. W., 116
HOWARD, Geo. W., 12
HOWARD, Geo. W., 63
HOWARD, George W., 37
HOWARD, George W., 89
HOWARD, John, 115
HOWARD, John, 63
HOWARD, John, 89
HOWARD, Littleton, 116
HOWARD, Littleton, 37
HOWARD, Littleton, 63
HOWARD, Littleton F., 89
HOWARD, M. H., 12
HOWARD, Shedrck, 115
HOYTER, John, 137
HUBBARD, Williams, 63
HUBBARD, Wm., 89
HUBBERT, Wm., 37
HUBERT, Wm., 116
HUEY, John, 13
HUGGINS, James, 37
HUGGINS, James, 89
HUGGINS, Jeremiah, 12
HUGGINS, Jeremiah, 37
HUGGINS, Jeremiah, 63
HUGGINS, Jeremiah, 89

HUGGINS, Jerimah, 115
HUGGINS, Robert, 37
HUGGINS, Robert, 63
HUGGINS, Robt., 12
HUGGINS, Urbin L., 115
HUGGINS, Urbin L., 89
HUGGINS, Wm., 115
HUGGINS, Wm., 12
HUGGINS, Wm., 12
HUGGINS, Wm., 37
HUGGINS, Wm., 63
HUGGINS, Wm., 89
HUGHES, Archelous, 115
HUGHES, Archelous, 27
HUGHES, Archelous, 90
HUGHES, Archelous M., 116
HUGHES, Archelous M., 12
HUGHES, Archelous M., 62
HUGHES, Archelsus? M., 36
HUGHES, John, 26
HUGHES, John, 37
HUGHES, Joseph B., 115
HUGHES, Joseph B., 62
HUGHES, Samuel, 116
HUGHES, Samuel, 90
HUGHES & GARDNER, , 115
HULETH, Thomas P., 37
HULETT, Thomas P., 78
HULING, F. W., 158
HULING, F. W., 158
HULING, Frederick W., 116
HULITH, Thoas P., 13
HULITT, Austin, 13
HUNEYCUT, Herman, 63
HUNGERFORD, Cullen, 115
HUNGERFORD, Cullin, 62
HUNGERFORD, Cullin, 88
HUNSTMAN & TOTTEN, , 51
HUNTER, John, 137
HUNTER, John, 89
HUNTER, Wm., 116
HUNTER, Wm., 12
HUNTER, Wm., 37
HUNTER, Wm., 78
HUNTSMAN, Adam, 116
HUNTSMAN, Adam, 89
HUNTSMAN & TATTEN, , 26
HUNTSMAN & TOTTEN, , 106
HUNTSMAN & TOTTEN, , 116
HUNTSMAN & TOTTEN, , 119
HUNTSMAN & TOTTEN, , 129
HUNTSMAN & TOTTEN, , 62
HUNTSMAN & TOTTON, , 65
HURT, Samuel, 37
HUSKEY, Archibald, 62
HUSKEY, Archibald, 89
HUSKEY, Isam, 36
HUSKY, Archibald, 115
IRVIN, Sam, 167
IRVIN, Samuel, 170
ISAAC, negro, 168
ISAAC, negro, 168
ISHAM, negro, 168
ISRAEL, Michael, 64
ISRAEL, Urias, 38
IZALLE?, Harison, 117
IZELL?, James, 117

IZELL?, Urias, 117
IZZELL, Uriah, 13
JACKSON, Newton, 90
JACKSON, Robt., 117
JACKSON, Thomas, 117
JACKSON, Thomas, 26
JACKSON, Thos., 109
JAMES, Archibald, 90
JAMES, Gray, 13
JAMES, Hosea, 13
JAMES, Hosea, 38
JAMES, Hosea, 64
JAMES, Hosea, 90
JAMES, Isaac, 117
JAMES, Isaac, 64
JAMES, James W., 117
JAMES, Wm., 90
JAMES, negro, 1
JAMESON, Samuel, 118
JAMESON, Samuel, 38
JAMESON, Samuel, 90
JANE, negro, 147
JAPLIN, John, 117
JARVIS, David, 117
JEFFRIES, David, 48
JEFFRIES, David, 78
JEMISON, Samuel, 64
JENKINS, James, 118
JENKINS, James, 38
JENKINS, James, 64
JENKINS, James, 90
JENKINS, Jesse, 13
JENKINS, Jesse, 38
JENKINS, Jesse, 63
JENKINS, Jesse, 64
JENKINS, Jesse, 90
JENKINS, Jno., 12
JENKINS, Jno., 128
JENKINS, John, 103
JENKINS, John, 104
JENKINS, John, 108
JENKINS, John, 117
JENKINS, John, 118
JENKINS, John, 13
JENKINS, John, 20
JENKINS, John, 38
JENKINS, John, 40
JENKINS, John, 44
JENKINS, John, 51
JENKINS, John, 52
JENKINS, John, 63
JENKINS, John, 70
JENKINS, John, 76
JENKINS, John, 77
JENKINS, John, 90
JENKINS, John, 96
JENKINS, Mansfield, 13
JENKINS, Mansfield, 38
JENKINS, Mansfield, 64
JENKINS, Mansfield, 90
JENKINS, Marfield, 117
JENKINS, Thomas, 117
JENKINS, Thomas, 13
JENKINS, Thomas, 38
JENKINS, Thomas, 38
JENKINS, Thomas, 64
JENKINS, Thomas, 90
JENKINS, Thos., 118
JENKINS, ____, 96
JENKINS & THARP, , 63
JENKINS & THORP, , 90

JENNINGS, Anderson, 64
JENNINGS, Anderson, 90
JENNINGS, Anderson H., 117
JENNINGS, Andrew, 38
JENNY, negro, 53
JETER, Allen, 158
JETER, Ann, 158
JETER, Elizabeth, 158
JETER, Frances, 158
JETER, George, 158
JETER, John, 158
JETER, Katharine Brasfield, 158
JETER, Mary, 158
JETER, Maryann, 158
JETER, Robert, 157
JETER, Robert, 159
JETER, Robert, 163
JETER, Robert, 163
JETER, Robert, 90
JETER, Robert Allen, 158
JETER, Samuel, 158
JETER, Samuel, 158
JETER, Samuel, 158
JETER, Samuel, 159
JETER, Susannah, 157
JETER, Susannah, 159
JETER, Wm., 158
JETER, Wm. B., 158
JETER, Wm. B., 158
JIM, negro, 168
JINKINS, Jesse, 116
JINNY, negro girl, 1
JOANNA, negro, 171
JOE, negro, 145
JOHN, negro, 164
JOHN, negro, 170
JOHNSON, Caroline, 166
JOHNSON, Cave, 48
JOHNSON, Cemantha, 166
JOHNSON, Gray, 13
JOHNSON, John, 13
JOHNSON, John, 38
JOHNSON, John, 38
JOHNSON, John, 64
JOHNSON, John P., 136
JOHNSON, John P., 150
JOHNSON, Mary, 166
JOHNSON, Mary Eliza, 166
JOHNSON, W., 166
JOHNSON, W., 167
JOHNSON, Wm., 166
JOHNSON, Wm., 90
JOHNSON, Wm. H., 1
JOHNSON, Wm. H., 117
JOHNSON, Wm. H., 13
JOHNSON, Wm. H., 148
JOHNSON, Wm. H., 148
JOHNSON, Wm. H., 38
JOHNSON, Wm. H., 49
JOHNSON, Wm. H., 51
JOHNSON, Wm. H., 52
JOHNSON, Wm. H., 54
JOHNSON, Wm. H., 63
JOHNSON, Wm. H., 76
JOHNSON, Wm. H., 79
JOHNSTON, Cane, 12
JOHNSTON, Cave, 130
JOHNSTON, Cave, 78
JOHNSTON, John, 117
JOLLY, Henry, 14

JOLLY, Henry, 64
JOLLY, Henry, 90
JOLLY, Reuben, 90
JOLLY, Reuben M., 64
JOLLY, Reubin, 117
JONES, Absolom, 113
JONES, Absolom, 123
JONES, Absolom, 23
JONES, Absolom, 36
JONES, Adonijah, 38
JONES, Archibald, 103
JONES, Archibald, 117
JONES, Bennet, 90
JONES, Bennit, 117
JONES, Bennit, 64
JONES, Calvin, 118
JONES, Calvin, 63
JONES, D. A., 68
JONES, Drury, 13
JONES, Drury D., 117
JONES, Frances, 132
JONES, Gray, 117
JONES, Gray, 38
JONES, Gray, 63
JONES, Gray, 90
JONES, Hiram, 117
JONES, Hiram, 169
JONES, Isaac, 90
JONES, Israel, 102
JONES, Israel, 117
JONES, Israel, 14
JONES, Israel, 38
JONES, Israel, 63
JONES, James, 13
JONES, James K., 117
JONES, James K., 90
JONES, John, 118
JONES, John, 132
JONES, John D., 163
JONES, John K., 37
JONES, Jorden, 117
JONES, Joshia, 13
JONES, Joshua, 117
JONES, Joshua, 64
JONES, Joshua, 90
JONES, Josiah, 38
JONES, Rebecca, 132
JONES, Thomas, 132
JONES, Thomas, 132
JONES, Thornton, 117
JONES, Thornton, 138
JONES, Thornton, 14
JONES, Thornton, 38
JONES, Thornton, 38
JONES, Thornton, 63
JONES, Wilie, 38
JONES, Wilie, 38
JONES, Wilie, 90
JONES, Williams, 38
JONES, Williams, 38
JONES, Willie, 117
JONES, Willie, 14
JONES, Willie, 64
JONES, Wm, 90
JONES, Wm., 117
JONES, Wm., 117
JONES, Wm., 117
JONES, Wm., 13
JONES, Wm., 14
JONES, Wm., 14
JONES, Wm., 154

JONES, Wm., 155
JONES, Wm., 165
JONES, Wm., 166
JONES, Wm., 170
JONES, Wm., 38
JONES, Wm., 63
JONES, Wm., 64
JONES, Wm., 64
JOPLEN, John, 37
JORDAN, John, 64
JORDEN, John, 117
JOURDEN, John, 90
JOWDEN, John, 13
JULEN, James J., 90
JULEN, Richard O., 90
JULIAN, James, 13
JULIAN, James J., 38
JULIAN, James J., 63
JULIN, James J., 118
JULIN, Richard O., 117
KAIN, John, 14
KAIN, John, 64
KAMP, Frances, 14
KEATH, John, 64
KECHUM, Solomon, 91
KECHUM, Solomon, 91
KECHUM, Wm., 91
KELE, Barney C., 38
KELOUGH, Isaac, 118
KELOUGH, Isaac, 91
KEMP, Frances, 118
KEMP, Frances A., 64
KEMP, Francis, 38
KEMP, Francis A., 91
KEMP, Joseph, 118
KEMP, Joseph B., 91
KENEDY, Betholam, 38
KENEDY, James, 14
KENEDY, James, 38
KENEDY, Killebrew, 91
KENEDY, Sampson, 91
KENNEDY, James, 64
KENNEDY, Killebrew, 144
KETCHUM, Wm., 118
KILE, Barney C., 78
KILE, Barney C., 91
KILE, Barney C., 91
KILLBREW, Elias, 14
KILLEBREW, Elias, 118
KILLEBREW, Elias, 144
KILLEBREW, Elias, 38
KILLEBREW, Elias, 75
KILLEBREW, Elias, 91
KILLEBREW, Matilda, 144
KILLEBREW, Thomas jr., 144
KILLOUGH, Isaac, 148
KILLOUGH, Isaac, 149
KILLOUGH, Isaac, 149
KILLOUGH, Isaac, 150
KILLOUGH, Isaac, 152
KILLOUGH, Isaac, 156
KIMBRELL, Joseph, 64
KINDRED, Elisha H., 118
KINDRED, Elisha H., 38
KINDRED, Elisha H., 64
KINDRED, Elisha H., 91
KINDRED, Jos. C., 14
KINDRED, Joseph C., 38
KINDRED, Joseph C., 64
KING, P., 47
KING, Peter, 100

KING, Peter, 106
KING, Peter, 23
KING, Ralph, 107
KING, Ralph, 29
KING, Randolph, 3
KING, Robert, 118
KING, Robert, 91
KING, Thomas, 103
KINGSTON, Simeon, 91
KIRK, George D., 14
KIRK, George D., 38
KIRK, George D., 64
KIRK, Wm., 38
KIRK, Wm., 64
KIRKPATRICK, Jos., 118
KIRKPATRICK, Joseph, 27
KIRKPATRICK, Joseph, 38
KIRKPATRICK, Joseph, 64
KIRKPATRICK, Joseph, 91
KIRKSEY, John, 38
KIRKSEY, John C., 64
KIRKSEY, John C., 91
KISSEE, Charles, 91
KISSEE, Charles, 91
KISSEL, Charles, 118
KIZZEE, Charles, 64
KOEN, John, 38
KOPLIN?, John, 63
KUYKENDALL, Jesse, 64
KYLE, Barney c., 118
LAAMORE, Charles J., 65
LAKEY, Wm., 118
LAKEY, Wm., 91
LANDRUM, James, 39
LANDRUM, James, 65
LANDRUM, Samuel, 118
LANDRUM, Samuel, 14
LANDRUM, Samuel, 38
LANDRUM, Samuel, 64
LANDRUM, Samuel, 91
LANDRUM, Thomas, 118
LANDRUM, Thomas, 65
LANDRUM, Thos., 91
LANGLEY, James T., 91
LANGLEY, Jane J., 118
LANGLEY, Jane J., 65
LANGLEY, Leonard, 65
LANGLEY, Leonard, 91
LANGLEY, Leonard S., 118
LANGLEY, Leonard S., 169
LASSWELL, D., 65
LASSWELL, Daniel, 91
LASSWELL, Donnie, 39
LASSWELL, Gilliam, 65
LASSWELL, Gilliam, 91
LASSWELL, Jesse, 118
LASSWELL, Jesse, 65
LASSWELL, Joseph, 118
LASSWELL, Joseph, 39
LASSWELL, Joseph, 65
LASSWELL, Joseph, 91
LASSWELL, Peter, 118
LASSWELL, Peter, 39
LASSWELL, Peter, 65
LASSWELL, Peter, 91
LASSWELL, Robert, 39
LASSWELL, Sarah, 118
LASSWELL, Sarah, 39
LASSWELL, Sarah, 65
LASSWELL, Sarah, 91
LASSWELL, Wm., 65

LASWELL, Joseph, 14
LASWELL, Peter, 14
LASWELL, Sarah, 14
LATHAM, E. P., 166
LATHAM, E. T., 165
LATHEM, Edward P., 151
LATHUM, E.? P., 163
LAULER, Martin, 14
LAWLER, Marlin, 118
LAWLER, Martin, 38
LAWLER, Martin, 65
LAWLER, Martin, 91
LAWRENCE, Charles J., 92
LAWRENCE, Elias, 119
LAWRENCE, Joseph, 118
LAWRENCE, Joseph, 39
LAWRENCE, Joseph, 65
LAWRENCE, Joseph, 91
LAWRENCE, Wm., 65
LAWRENCE, Wm., 92
LAWS, Thomas, 91
LAWS, Wm., 118
LAWSON, Jas., 3
LAWSON, negro, 161
LAXON, Jno., 14
LAXON, Wm., 14
LEA, Henry, 14
LEA, John, 14
LEDBETTER, Lewis, 14
LEE, Jeremiah, 14
LEIGH, J., 172
LEIGH, Jesse, 171
LEMMOND, David, 119
LEMMOND, David, 39
LEMMOND, David, 92
LEMMOND, Robert, 39
LEMMOND, Robt., 14
LEMMOND, Thomas, 119
LEMMOND, Thomas, 92
LEMOND, David, 65
LEVI, Levister, 39
LEVISTER, Levi, 118
LEVISTER, Levi, 64
LEVISTER, Levi, 91
LEWIS, Frances, 119
LEWIS, Frances, 40
LEWIS, James, 14
LEWIS, James, 39
LEWIS, Wiley, 14
LEWIS, negro, 160
LEWIS, negro, 160
LEWIS, negro, 164
LIDDLE, Frances, 65
LIDDLE, Francis, 14
LIDDLE, Francis, 39
LIDDLE, Francis, 92
LIGHTNER, Daniel, 91
LIGHTNER, David, 118
LIGHTNER, David, 14
LILLA, negro, 53
LINDSEY, Isaac, 118
LINDSEY, Isaac, 26
LINDSEY, Isaac, 65
LINDSEY, Isaac, 91
LITTLE, Wm. P., 118
LONG, James, 26
LONG, James, 34
LONG, James, 60
LONG, James M., 112
LONG, James M., 118
LONG, Jas., 86

LONG, John, 60
LOONEY, Joseph, 14
LOVE, Charles I., 118
LOVE, R. A., 107
LOVE, R. T., 119
LOVE, Robert, 65
LOVE, Robert J., 91
LOVE, Robt., 26
LOVE, Robt., 65
LOVE, Sam'l, 137
LOVE, T., 39
LOVE, Thomas, 26
LOVE, Thos., 65
LOVELADY, Mars., 14
LOVEN, James, 39
LOVEN, Joshua, 14
LOVEN, Joshua, 39
LOVIN, James, 118
LOVIN, James, 14
LOVIN, James, 65
LOVIN, Joshua, 119
LOVIN, Joshua, 65
LOYD, Thomas, 14
LOYD, Thomas, 39
LOYD, Thomas, 91
LOZETTE, negro, 80
LUCY, negro, 164
LUSTER?, Zadock, 15
LYLE, Archibald, 64
LYNN, Elam, 39
LYNN, Elum, 14
LYNN, Wm., 14
LYNN, Wm., 39
LYNN, Wm., 64
LYTLE, Archibald, 118
LYTLE, Archibald, 14
LYTLE, Archibald, 39
LYTLE, Archibald, 91
LYTLE, wm. P., 91
MAINARD, Jas., 40
MAINARD, John, 121
MAINARD, John, 93
MAINARD, Wm. H., 40
MAINARD, Wm. W., 121
MAJERS, Samuel, 120
MAJORS, Samuel, 128
MAJORS, Samuel, 17
MAJORS, Samuel, 41
MAJORS, Samuel, 66
MAJORS, Samuel, 92
MALIN, Benjamin, 1
MALIN, Benjamin, 120
MALIN, Benjamin, 54
MANARD, Wm. W., 93
MANDY, Thomas, 121
MANDY, Thomas, 16
MANDY, Thomas, 93
MANDY, Thos., 40
MANSOR, negro, 140
MANUEL, negro, 168
MAR, George W. L., 51
MARCUS, Phillip, 121
MARCUS, Phillip, 41
MARCUS, Phillips, 16
MARCUS, Phillips, 67
MARGARET, negro, 168
MARIA, negro girl, 1
MARIAH, negro, 160
MARPHAY, Wm., 15
MARR, George W. L., 27
MARR, Peter, 67

MARSHALL, Joseph, 16
MARSHALL, Joseph, 41
MARSHALL, Joseph, 92
MARSHALL, Joseph S., 66
MARSHALL, Robert, 41
MARSHALL, Robert, 66
MARSHALL, Robert, 92
MARSHALL, Robert C., 120
MARTHA, negro, 161
MARTHA, negro girl, 147
MARTIN, Andrew L., 92
MARTIN, Wm., 144
MARTIN, mulatto boy, 147
MARY, negro, 161
MARY, negro, 170
MATHEW, F. Michel, 40
MATHEWS, Samuel, 120
MATHIS, Daniel, 121
MATHIS, Daniel, 67
MATHIS, Daniel, 93
MATHIS, John, 16
MATT, negro, 145
MAXWELL, Jesse, 122
MAXWELL, Jesse, 67
MAXWELL, Jesse, 93
MAXWELL, Wm., 122
MAXWELL, Wm., 93
MAXWELL, _____, 114
MAYFIELD, Martin, 14
MAYNARD, James, 16
MAYNARD, Mandy, 67
MAYNARD, Thomas, 67
MAYNARD, Wm. W., 16
MAYNARD, Wm. W., 67
MAYO, Frederick, 16
MAYO, Wm., 121
MAYO, Wm., 17
MAYO, Wm., 41
MAYO, Wm., 67
MAYO, Wm., 93
MCBRIDE, Wm., 93
MCCALL, James, 121
MCCARTER, Isiah, 66
MCCLAIN, Charles, 17
MCCLAIN, Charles, 26
MCCLAIN, Charles, 66
MCCLAIN, Charles, 92
MCCLAIN, Charles jr., 120
MCCLAIN, Charles sr., 120
MCCLAIN, Charles sr., 41
MCCLAIN, Charles younger, 120
MCCLAIN, Chas. jr., 41
MCCLAIN, Christiana, 66
MCCLAIN, George, 120
MCCLAIN, George, 40
MCCLAIN, George, 66
MCCLAIN, George, 93
MCCLAIN, Jerome, 107
MCCLAIN, Jerome, 115
MCCLAIN, Jerome, 125
MCCLAIN, Jerome, 15
MCCLAIN, Jerome, 37
MCCLAIN, Jerome, 40
MCCLAIN, Jerome, 5
MCCLAIN, Jerome, 6
MCCLAIN, Jerome, 82
MCCLAIN, Jerome, 88
MCCLAIN, John, 120
MCCLAIN, John, 17
MCCLAIN, John, 26

MCCLAIN, John, 41
MCCLAIN, John, 66
MCCLAINES, Jerome, 56
MCCLELLAN, Trigg, 120
MCCLELLAN, Trigg, 92
MCCLESKY, John, 16
MCCLUSKEY, John, 93
MCCLUSKEY, Wm. H., 121
MCCLUSKY, John, 40
MCCLUSKY, Wm., 67
MCCONNELS, Philip H., 26
MCCORKLE, S., 88
MCCORKLE, Samuel, 121
MCCORKLE, Samuel, 93
MCCORMACK, Charles, 16
MCCORMACK, Charles, 66
MCCRAY, Wm., 16
MCCULLOCH, Benjn., 78
MCCULLOCK, Benjm., 26
MCCULLOCK, Benjm., 84
MCCULLOCK, Benjn., 111
MCCULLOCK, Benjn., 58
MCCULOCK, Janja., 39
MCCULOCKS, Benjn., 48
MCDANEL, Wm., 17
MCDANIEL, Hiram, 120
MCDANIEL, Hiram, 66
MCDANIEL, John, 16
MCDANIEL, John, 26
MCDANIEL, John, 40
MCDANIEL, John, 66
MCDANIEL, Moses, 120
MCDANIEL, Moses, 17
MCDANIEL, Moses, 66
MCDANIEL, Moses, 92
MCELROY, Aquilla, 121
MCELROY, Equilla, 93
MCELROY, Isham H. S., 16
MCELROY, Wm., 121
MCELROY, Wm. T., 67
MCELROY, Wm. T., 93
MCFARLAND, Benj. M., 121
MCGAVOCK, Frances, 26
MCGAVOCK, Francis, 119
MCGAVOCK, Francis, 92
MCGAVOCK, Peter, 130
MCGAVOCK & WILSON, , 40
MCGOWAN, John, 120
MCILATTON & BARNETT, , 94
MCILHATTON & BANDY, , 26
MCILHATTON & BARNETT, , 122
MCINTOSH, Charles, 120
MCINTOSH, Charles, 94
MCINTOSH, Solomon, 120
MCINTOSH, Solomon, 17
MCINTOSH, Solomon, 41
MCINTOSH, Solomon, 92
MCITOSH, Charles, 39
MCIVER, John, 119
MCIVER, John, 120
MCIVER, John, 15
MCIVER, John, 39
MCIVER, John, 92
MCIVERS, J., 78
MCIVERS, Jno., 19
MCIVERS, John, 48
MCIVERS, John, 66
MCIVERS, _____, 15

MCKLIN, negro, 161
MCLEMORE, Chas., 15
MCLEMORE, J. C., 39
MCLEMORE, J. C., 40
MCLEMORE, J. C., 78
MCLEMORE, J. C., 88
MCLEMORE, Jno. C., 119
MCLEMORE, Jno. C., 15
MCLEMORE, John C., 113
MCLEMORE, John C., 119
MCLEMORE, John C., 26
MCLEMORE, John C., 39
MCLEMORE, John C., 65
MCLEMORE, John C., 66
MCLEMORE, John C., 92
MCLEMORE, R., 39
MCLEMORE, Sugars, 122
MCLEMORE, Sugars, 15
MCLEMORE, Sugars, 40
MCLEMORE, Sugars, 66
MCLEMORE & BLACKFAN, , 119
MCLEMORE & CHARLTON, , 119
MCLEMORE & CHARLTON, , 15
MCLEMORE & CHARLTON, , 40
MCLEMORE & CHARLTON, , 65
MCLEMORE & CHARTTON, , 92
MCLEMORE & GREER, , 92
MCLEMORE & HOPKINS, , 114
MCLEMORE & HOPKINS, , 119
MCLEMORE & HOPKINS, , 96
MCLEMORE & HOPKISS, , 39
MCLEMORE & LOVE, , 66
MCLEMORE & VAULX, , 119
MCLEMORE & VAULX, , 122
MCLEMORE & VAULX, , 26
MCLEMORE & VAULX, , 92
MCLEMORE & VAULX, Wm., 65
MCLEMORE & VOULK, , 107
MCLEMORE BLACKFAN ELDRIDGE & HILL, , 92
MCLUSKEY, Wm. H., 93
MCLUSTER?, Zadock, 15
MCMILLAN, John, 92
MCMULLAN, John, 41
MCMULLAN, St. John, 15
MCMULLAN, St. John, 15
MCNEEL, Wm. S., 15
MCNEELEY, John, 39
MCNEELY, John, 120
MCNEELY, John, 15
MCNEELY, John, 66
MCNEELY, John, 92
MCNEELY, Michael, 121
MCNEELY, Michael, 16
MCNEELY, Michael, 40
MCNEELY, Michael, 67
MCNEELY, Michael, 93
MCNEILL, Wm. L., 1
MCWHARTER & BARNETT, , 41
MCWHERTER, George, 67
MCWHERTER, John, 67

MCWHORTER, Frankling, 93
MCWHORTER, George, 121
MCWHORTER, George, 93
MCWHORTER, George W., 169
MCWHORTER, John, 121
MCWHORTER, John, 93
MEADOWS, Spearman, 121
MEADOWS, Spearman, 16
MEADOWS, Spearman, 67
MEADOWS, Spearman, 93
MEADOWS, Spearson, 40
MEARS, Wm., 121
MELTON, Thomas, 120
MEREDITH, Daniel, 120
MEREDITH, Daniel, 16
MEREDITH, Daniel, 92
MERIDETH, Moses, 16
MERRELL, Lemuel, 143
MERRELL, Wm., 143
MERRILL, Benjamin, 143
MERRILL, Chas., 143
MERRILL, Jemima, 143
MERRILL, Lucy, 143
MERRILL, Mary, 143
MERRILL, Mary, 143
MESSICK, John, 166
MESSICK, Sophiah, 166
MESSICK, Sophiah, 167
MICAJAH, Thomas, 110
MICAYAH, Thomas, 35
MICHAEL, Archelous, 122
MICHAEL, Archelous, 67
MICHAEL, Thomas, 92
MICHEL, Kisiah, 40
MICHEL, Standly, 15
MICHEL, Thomas, 39
MICKEY, negro (f), 145
MILES, Wm., 16
MILES, Wm., 16
MILES, Wm., 41
MILES, Wm., 78
MILES, Wm., 94
MILES, Wm. C., 120
MILES, Wm. C., 66
MILES, Wm. C., 92
MILLER, Andrew, 121
MILLER, Andrew, 16
MILLER, Andrew, 41
MILLER, Andrew, 67
MILLER, Andrew, 93
MILLER, George, 121
MILLER, George, 16
MILLER, George, 51
MILLER, George, 67
MILLER, George, 93
MILLER, George S., 67
MILLER, George S., 94
MILLER, Iaac?, 67
MILLER, Isaac, 16
MILLER, Isaac, 93
MILLER, John, 16
MILLIGHLEY, Jas., 70
MILNER, B. J., 149
MILNER, Beverly J., 148
MIMA, negro, 161
MITCHAEL, Archelous, 93
MITCHEL, Archelous, 51
MITCHEL, John, 92
MITCHELL, John, 120
MITCHELL, John, 75
MITCHELL, Kissey, 66

MITCHELL, Ripley, 120
MITCHELL, Standley, 121
MITCHELL, Standley, 67
MITCHELL, Thomas, 120
MIZELL, John, 15
MIZELLE, Williams, 40
MIZELLE, Wm., 16
MIZELLE, Wm., 67
MIZELLE, Wm., 93
MOBLEY, Ransom, 121
MOBLY, Ransom, 93
MOFFIT, John, 93
MOLIN, Benja., 39
MOLIN, Benjamin, 15
MOLIN, Benjamin, 66
MOLIN, Benjamin, 92
MOLLY, negro, 140
MONTGOMERY, A., 67
MONTGOMERY, Daniel, 119
MONTGOMERY, Daniel, 122
MONTGOMERY, Daniel, 26
MONTGOMERY, Daniel, 65
MONTGOMERY, Daniel, 92
MONTGOMERY, James, 121
MONTGOMERY, James, 93
MONTGOMERY, John, 26
MONTGOMERY, John, 65
MONTGOMERY, John, 92
MONTGOMERY, Wm., 119
MONTGOMERY, Wm., 121
MONTGOMERY, Wm., 26
MONTGOMERY, Wm., 65
MONTGOMERY, Wm., 92
MONTGOMERY, Wm., 93
MOON, John Henry, 146
MOON, Vincent, 121
MOON, Wm., 16
MOON, Wm., 39
MOON, Wm., 65
MOON, Wm. R., 15
MOONEY, Adam, 120
MOONEY, Henry, 17
MOONEY, Henry, 66
MOONEY, Kenny, 92
MOONY, Henry, 51
MOORE, James, 121
MOORE, James, 121
MOORE, James, 16
MOORE, James, 40
MOORE, James, 67
MOORE, James, 93
MOORE, Jno. H., 16
MOORE, Jno. H., 87
MOORE, John, 121
MOORE, John, 16
MOORE, John, 40
MOORE, John, 67
MOORE, John, 93
MOORE, John H., 113
MOORE, John H., 121
MOORE, John H., 165
MOORE, John H., 40
MOORE, John H., 51
MOORE, John H., 67
MOORE, John Henry, 172
MOORE, Somerset, 15
MOORE, Somerset, 39
MORAN, I. H., 102
MORAN, J. H., 149
MORAN, J. H., 152
MORAN, J. H., 156

MORAN, James H., 119
MORAN, James H., 148
MORAN, James H., 148
MORAN, James H., 151
MORAN, James H., 154
MORAN, James H., 170
MORAN, James H., 40
MORAN, James H., 66
MORAN, James H., 92
MORAN, Jas. H., 154
MORAN, Jas. H., 155
MORE, John H., 93
MORGAN, Samuel, 121
MORGAN, Samuel, 16
MORGAN, Samuel, 40
MORGAN, Samuel, 67
MORGAN, Samuel, 93
MORRIS, Francis, 40
MORRIS, Mathew J., 92
MORRIS, Thomas, 17
MOSELEY, Rob, 165
MOSES?, E., 101
MOSLEY, Arthur, 170
MOSLEY, Edward, 121
MOSLEY, Edward, 16
MOSLEY, Edward, 41
MOSLEY, Edward, 67
MOSLEY, Edward, 93
MOSLEY, George B., 170
MOSLEY, George B., 171
MOSLEY, Green, 170
MOSLEY, Green, 171
MOSLEY, Hillery, 170
MOSLEY, Martha, 170
MOSLEY, Mary A., 170
MOSLEY, Moses, 170
MOSLEY, Robert, 122
MOSLEY, Robert, 41
MOSLEY, Robert, 67
MOSLEY, Robert, 94
MOSLEY, Robt., 16
MOSLEY, Thomas E., 170
MOSLEY, Thos. E., 171
MOSLEY, Wm., 170
MOSLEY, Wm., 170
MOSLEY, Wm., 171
MOSLEY, Wm. T., 170
MOSLY, Hillery, 171
MOSLY, Martha, 171
MOSLY, Mary A., 171
MOSLY, Moses, 171
MOSLY, Wm. T., 171
MOSS, Bennet, 41
MOSS, Bennit, 120
MOSS, Bennit, 66
MOSS, Bennit, 92
MOSS, Geo. W. L., 120
MOSS, James, 121
MOSS, James, 93
MOSS, Mason, 122
MOSS, Mason, 92
MULLION, Jackson, 17
MURFEES, John, 167
MURFREE, Wm., 100
MURFREE, Wm., 31
MURHPY, Wm., 109
MURPHY, Wm., 129
MURPHY, Wm., 40
MURPHY, Wm., 66
MURRAY, John, 41
MURRAY, Robert, 119

MURREL, John S., 67
MURRELL, Benjamin, 120
MURRELL, Benjamin, 93
MURRELL, John, 93
MURRELL, John L., 121
MURRELL, Lemuel, 121
MURRELL, Wm., 121
NAIL, Andrew, 119
NAIL, Andrew, 26
NAIL, Andrew, 94
NAILING, J. R., 122
NAILING, J. R., 17
NAILING, J. R., 41
NAILING, James, 41
NAILING, James, 94
NAILING, John R., 41
NAILING, John R., 94
NAILING, John R., 94
NAILING, Jones, 17
NAILING, Nelson, 122
NAILING, Nelson, 17
NAILING, Nelson, 67
NAILING, Nelson, 94
NAILING, Willis, 17
NAILING, Willis, 94
NAILING, Willis A., 122
NAILING, willis, 67
NAKES, Evalina, 50
NALIN, Willis, 41
NALL, Andrew, 41
NANCY, negro, 168
NANCY WAT, negro, 168
NASH, A., 20
NASH, A., 20
NASH, Abner, 125
NASH, Abner, 97
NED, negro, 140
NEIL, Wm., 94
NEILL, Alexander, 74
NEILLS, Andrew, 74
NELLEY, negro, 162
NELSON, H., 79
NELSON, John, 39
NELSON, Nailing, 41
NELSON, Robert, 74
NELSON, Robert, 94
NELSON, negro, 140
NETTLES, John A., 17
NETTLES, John A., 50
NETTLES, Penney, 50
NETTLES, Shedrick, 17
NEWLAND, Richard, 94
NEWMAN, Wm., 122
NEWMAN, Wm., 17
NEWMAN, Wm., 41
NEWTON, Abram, 12
NEWTON, James, 122
NEWTON, James, 122
NEWTON, James, 17
NEWTON, James, 17
NEWTON, James, 67
NEWTON, James, 94
NEWTON, James, 94
NEWTON, James W., 41
NEWTON, James W., 67
NICHOLAS, John, 41
NICHOLS, James, 67
NICHOLS, John, 17
NICHOLS, Joseph, 17
NICK, negro, 168
NICK, negro, 168

183

| | | | |
|---|---|---|---|
| NIMMO, A. C., 171 | PALMER, Amanda M. F., 168 | PARKER, Lorenzo D., 68 | PATTON, John M., 95 |
| NOLEN, Henry, 17 | PALMER, Amanda M. F., 168 | PARKER, Lorenzo D., 94 | PATTON, Thomas, 124 |
| NOLEN, Henry, 41 | PALMER, Amos A., 69 | PARKER, Sterling, 138 | PATTON, Thomas, 18 |
| NOLIN, Henry, 67 | PALMER, Amosa, 124 | PARKER, Tristun, 96 | PATTON, Thomas, 43 |
| NORVELL, Nathan L., 122 | PALMER, Amosa, 95 | PARKER, Wm. F., 18 | PATTON, Thomas, 69 |
| NOWLAND, Henry, 122 | PALMER, Edmund, 124 | PARKER, Wm. G., 124 | PATTON, Thomas, 95 |
| NOWLAND, Henry, 94 | PALMER, Edward H., 168 | PARKER, Wm. T., 43 | PATTON, Wm., 95 |
| OAN, Wm. C., 42 | PALMER, Edward H., 168 | PARKER, Wm. T., 69 | PAYNER, Jesse, 123 |
| OAR, Wm. C., 68 | PALMER, Elizabeth, 168 | PARKER, Wm. T., 69 | PAYTON, Bailey, 18 |
| OLIVER, Alexander, 68 | PALMER, Elizabeth C., 168 | PARKER, Wm. T., 96 | PAYTON, Bailey, 42 |
| OLIVER, Alexander, 94 | PALMER, Elizabeth C., 168 | PARKER & BISHOP, , 68 | PAYTON, Baley, 95 |
| OLIVER, Berry, 122 | PALMER, Elizabeth C., 169 | PARKER & BISHOP, , 94 | PAYTON, Bayley, 68 |
| OLIVER, Isaac, 122 | PALMER, Emily M. A., 168 | PARKS, Fields, 124 | PAYTON, John, 123 |
| OLIVER, Isaac, 42 | PALMER, Henry O., 168 | PARKS, Fields, 18 | PEARCE, Abel, 95 |
| OLIVER, Isaac, 68 | PALMER, Henry O., 168 | PARKS, Fields, 42 | PEARCE, George, 124 |
| OLIVER, Isac, 94 | PALMER, Henry O., 168 | PARKS, Fields, 78 | PEARCE, John, 95 |
| OLIVER, Stephen, 122 | PALMER, James A., 168 | PARKS, Fields, 96 | PEARCE, Joseph, 123 |
| OLIVER, Stephen, 94 | PALMER, James A., 168 | PARKS, Isaac, 26 | PEARCE, Joseph, 157 |
| OLIVER, Stephin, 42 | PALMER, James A., 168 | PARRISH, Beedy, 140 | PEARCE, Joseph, 96 |
| ONEAL, John, 122 | PALMER, John W., 168 | PARRISH, Charles, 123 | PECK, John, 123 |
| ONEAL, John, 17 | PALMER, John W., 168 | PARRISH, Charles, 140 | PECK, John, 18 |
| ONEAL, John, 18 | PALMER, John W., 168 | PARRISH, Charles, 141 | PECK, John, 42 |
| ONEAL, John, 42 | PALMER, John W., 169 | PARRISH, Eliza, 141 | PECK, John, 68 |
| ONEAL, John, 68 | PALMER, John W., 169 | PARRISH, Eliza, 141 | PECK, John, 95 |
| ONEAL, John, 94 | PALMER, Mary R., 168 | PARRISH, Elizabeth, 140 | PEEPLES, Samuel, 95 |
| OOPER, Henry, 85 | PALMER, Mary R. A., 168 | PARRISH, Hartwell, 141 | PENSON, Jack, 78 |
| ORE, Wm. C., 17 | PALMER, Mary R. A., 168 | PARRISH, Henderson, 123 | PENSON, Joel, 111 |
| ORE, Wm. C., 94 | PALMER, Mary R. A., 169 | PARRISH, Henderson, 140 | PENSON, Joel, 122 |
| ORE, Wm. C. (heirs), 122 | PALMER, Paul, 169 | PARRISH, Henderson, 141 | PENSON, Joel, 42 |
| OSTEEN, John, 122 | PALMER, Paul, 69 | PARRISH, Henderson, 69 | PENSON, Joel, 72 |
| OSTEEN, John, 17 | PALMER, Paul, 95 | PARRISH, Henderson, 95 | PENSON, Joel, 75 |
| OSTEEN, John, 42 | PALMER, Paul M., 124 | PARRISH, Isom, 140 | PENSON, Joel, 94 |
| OSTEEN, John, 68 | PALMER, Smith, 124 | PARRISH, Isom, 141 | PENTECOST, Scarbrough, 124 |
| OUTHOUSE, Israel, 18 | PALMER, Smith, 167 | PARRISH, James, 147 | PENTECOST, Searbrough, 69 |
| OUTHOUSE, Israel F., 122 | PALMER, Smith, 169 | PARRISH, Jesse, 43 | PENTECOST, Wm., 124 |
| OUTHOUSE, Israel F., 42 | PALMER, Smith, 95 | PARRISH, John, 123 | PENTECOST, Wm., 18 |
| OUTHOUSE, Israel F., 68 | PALMER, Tennessee, 168 | PARRISH, John, 123 | PENTECOST, Wm., 69 |
| OUTHOUSE, Israel F., 94 | PALMER, Virginia, 168 | PARRISH, John, 140 | PENTEOST, Wm., 43 |
| OVERBY, Thos. P., 68 | PALMER, Virginia, 168 | PARRISH, John, 140 | PENTICOST, Scarbrough, 96 |
| OVERLY, Thomas, 42 | PALMER, Wm. A., 168 | PARRISH, John, 141 | PENTICOST, Wm., 96 |
| OVERLY, Thos., 17 | PALMER, Wm. A., 168 | PARRISH, John, 141 | PEOPLES, Samuel, 18 |
| OVERTON, John, 122 | PALMER, Wm. A., 168 | PARRISH, John, 43 | PEOPLES, Samuel, 43 |
| OVERTON, John, 122 | PANNEL, Wm. C., 123 | PARRISH, John, 69 | PEOPLES, Samuel, 69 |
| OVERTON, John, 17 | PANNEL, Wm. C., 19 | PARRISH, John, 95 | PEPIPIN, Loftis, 43 |
| OVERTON, John, 41 | PANNEL, Wm. C., 43 | PARRISH, Lidy, 140 | PERRY, Gideon, 69 |
| OVERTON, John, 68 | PARCH, Israel, 68 | PARRISH, Mary, 140 | PERRY, Gideon, 94 |
| OVERTON, John, 94 | PARHAM, Amosa, 123 | PARRISH, Mary, 141 | PERRY, John, 124 |
| OVERTON & WHARTON, , 122 | PARHAM, Amosa, 18 | PARRY, T. S., 151 | PERRY, John, 18 |
| | PARHAM, Amosa, 42 | PARTEE, Jesse, 43 | PERRY, John, 43 |
| OVERTON & WHARTON, , 17 | PARHAM, Amosa, 68 | PARTER & MCDANIEL, , 87 | PERRY, John, 69 |
| OVERTON & WHARTON, , 42 | PARHAM, Amosa, 95 | PARTLE, Jesse, 95 | PERRY, John, 95 |
| OVERTON & WHARTON, , 94 | PARHAM, Thomas, 123 | PASCHALL, Elisha, 27 | PERRY, Solomon, 43 |
| OVERTON & WHORTON, , 67 | PARHAM, Thomas, 171 | PASCHALL, Jess M., 95 | PERRY, Solomon, 69 |
| OWEN, Charles, 18 | PARHAM, Thomas, 18 | PASCHALL, Jesse M., 123 | PERSONS, Thomas, 48 |
| OWEN, Charles, 94 | PARHAM, Thomas, 42 | PASCHALL, Jesse M., 19 | PERSONS, Thomas, 78 |
| OWEN, Charles M., 42 | PARHAM, Thomas, 68 | PASCHALL, Jesse M., 43 | PETER, negro, 145 |
| OWEN, Daniel, 122 | PARHAM, Thomas, 95 | PASCHALL, Jesse M., 68 | PETER, negro, 50 |
| OWEN, Daniel, 18 | PARIS, James, 144 | PASCHELL, Alexander, 19 | PETTIGREW, Ebenezer, 42 |
| OWEN, Daniel, 42 | PARISH, Jesse, 18 | PATE, Stephen, 43 | PETTIGRUE, Ebenezer, 95 |
| OWEN, Daniel, 75 | PARKER, Bishop, 123 | PATE, Stephen S., 124 | PETTYGREW, Ebenezer, 27 |
| OWEN, James, 94 | PARKER, Gedeon?, 68 | PATE, Stephen S., 69 | PHARLEY, Thos. M., 19 |
| OWEN, Sarah, 18 | PARKER, Gideon, 123 | PATE, Stephen S., 96 | PHARR, James, 18 |
| OWEN, Sarah, 42 | PARKER, Gideon, 43 | PATTERSON, Robert, 95 | PHIL, negro, 168 |
| OWEN, Solomon H., 18 | PARKER, Gideon, 94 | PATTERSON, Robert S., 123 | PHIL, negro, 168 |
| OWENS, Charles M., 68 | PARKER, Isaac, 123 | PATTON, Elijah, 84 | PHILLIPS, Burrell, 19 |
| OWENS, Daniel, 94 | PARKER, Isaac, 26 | PATTON, Elijah, 92 | PHILLIPS, Bursell, 69 |
| OWENS, Elisha, 94 | PARKER, Isaac, 43 | PATTON, G.? E., 102 | PHILLIPS, David, 43 |
| OWENS, Elisha H., 122 | PARKER, Isaac, 68 | PATTON, John M., 124 | PHILLIPS, Reagin D., 123 |
| OWENS, Solmon H., 68 | PARKER, Isaac, 95 | PATTON, John M., 43 | PHILLIPS, Thos. H., 18 |
| OWENS, Solomon H., 51 | PARKER, Lorenzo, 43 | PATTON, John M., 69 | PHILPOT, Bennit, 123 |
| PAGE, John, 123 | PARKER, Lorenzo D., 123 | | PHILPOT, Edward, 123 |

PHILPOT, J. W., 123
PHILPOT, Jno. W., 106
PHILPOT, Jno. W., 18
PHILPOT, Ju., 128
PIERCE, Abel, 78
PIERCE, John, 78
PILARS, Henry, 20
PINSON, Jel, 37
PINSON, Joel, 137
PINSON, Joel, 24
PINSON, Joel, 84
PINSON, Nathan, 137
PIPKIN, Wm. C., 19
PIPPIN, Joplin, 19
PIPPIN, Loftis, 69
PIPPIN, Loftus, 123
PIPPIN, Robert C., 124
PISON, Joel, 129
PLASTER, Samuel, 124
PLEASANT, negro, 161
POINDEXTER, Sam I., 18
POINDEXTER, Samuel, 43
POLK, A. Devereaux, 18
POLK, Marshal T., 102
POLK, Samuel, 102
POLK, Thomas, 123
POLK, Thomas, 95
POLK, Thomas G., 123
POLK, Thomas G., 95
POLK, Thomas H., 68
POLK, Thos. H., 18
POLK, Thos. heirs, 42
POLK, Wm., 123
POLK, Wm., 18
POLK, Wm., 42
POLK, Wm., 68
POLK, Wm., 95
POLK & DEVERAUX, , 68
POLK & DEVEREAUX, , 123
POLK & DEVEREAUX, , 42
POLK & DEVEREAUX, , 95
POOL, Asa, 19
POOL, Asa, 69
POOL, Jonathan, 95
POOL, Wm., 19
POPE, John, 123
POPE, John, 123
POPE, John, 19
POPE, John, 42
POPE, John, 69
POPE, John (heirs), 95
POPE, John W., 19
POPE, John W., 42
POPE, John W., 69
POPE, John W., 95
POPE, Lemuel, 123
POPE, Lemuel, 69
POPE, Samuel, 19
POPE, Samuel, 42
POPE, Samuel, 95
PORTER, John, 18
PORTER, R., 24
PORTER, R., 73
PORTER, Richard, 100
PORTER, Richard, 130
PORTER & MCDOWEL, , 98
PORTER & MCGAVOCK, , 113
PORTER & MCGAVOCK, , 114
PORTER & MCGAVOCK, , 127
PORTER & MCGAVOCK, , 21
PORTER & MCGAVOCK, , 23

PORTER & MCGAVOCK, , 47
PORTER & MCGAVOCK, , 61
POTTER?, R., 47
POUND, Hiram, 18
POWEL, John, 95
POWELL, John, 124
POWELL, Robert, 18
POWELL, Robert, 42
POWERS, Charles, 124
POWERS, Charles, 43
POWERS, Charles, 69
POWERS, Charles, 95
POWERS, George, 124
POWERS, George, 43
POWERS, George, 69
POWERS, George, 96
POWERS, Henny, 95
POWERS, Henry, 124
POWERS, Henry, 43
POWERS, Henry, 69
POWERS, Joseph, 69
PRATE, Josiah, 18
PRATER, Josiah, 123
PRATER, Josiah, 42
PRATER, Josiah, 68
PRATER, Josiah, 95
PRATER, Martin, 123
PRATER, Martin, 95
PREAN, John, 19
PRICE, James, 124
PRICE, James, 43
PRICE, James, 96
PRICE, James W., 18
PRICE, John, 124
PRICE, Sampson, 124
PRICE, Sampson, 96
PRICE, Thomas, 69
PRICE, Wm., 43
PRICE, Wm., 69
PRICE, Wm., 69
PRICE, Wm., 95
PUPLES, Samuel, 124
PURCEL, Abel, 78
PURSEL, Abel, 68
PURSEL, Auburn, 43
PURSELL, Ausbourn, 94
PURTLE, Jesse, 124
PURTLE, Jesse, 18
PURTLE, Jesse, 69
QUALLS, Wm., 124
QUALLS, Wm., 19
QUALLS, Wm., 43
QUALLS, Wm., 69
QUALLS, Wm., 96
RACHELS, Valentine, 70
RACHELS, Valentine, 97
RACHELS, Voulline, 125
RACHELS, Wm., 44
RACHELS, Wm., 70
RACHELS, Wm., 97
RAGSDALE, Joel, 19
RAGSDALE, Joel, 43
RAGSDALE, Joel, 69
RAGSDALE, Mathew, 125
RAINES, R. P., 171
RALLS, William, 125
RALLS, Wm., 20
RALLS, Wm., 20
RALLS, Wm., 44
RALLS, Wm., 70
RALLS, Wm., 97

RALLS, Wm., 97
RALLS, Wm. B., 20
RALLS, Wm. B., 44
RALLS, Wm. B., 70
RALLS, Wm. B., 96
RALLS, Wm. P., 125
RALPH, negro, 168
RALSTON, Alexander, 125
RALSTON, Alexander, 96
RANDEL, Wm., 19
RANSOM, negro, 164
RATTEN, Tatton, 44
RAY, Jno. & Co., 19
RAY, John, 44
RAY, Peters, 96
RAY & PETERS, , 48
RAY JOHN & CO., , 48
RAY JOHN & CO., , 78
REA, James, 20
REA, James N., 96
REA, James W., 125
REA, James W., 70
REAVES, John H., 132
REAVES, John H., 133
REDICK, David, 125
REDICK, David, 135
REECE, Yarnel, 20
REENY, negro, 168
REN, John, 20
REN, John, 44
REN, John, 70
REUBEN, negro, 168
REVICE, John H., 43
REVICE?, John, 19
REVIS, John H., 124
REVIS, John H., 128
REVIS, John H., 96
REYNOLDS, Saml. B., 124
REYNOLDS, Samuel B., 97
RHEA, John, 119
RHEA, John, 124
RHEA, John, 19
RHEA, John, 40
RHEA, John, 43
RHEA, John, 65
RHEA, John, 69
RHEA, John W., 44
RHOADS, John A. C., 44
RHOADS, Littlebury A., 125
RHODES, Elisha, 19
RHODES, Henry (heirs), 51
RHODES, Henry H., 27
RHODES, Jno. A. C., 19
RIAAL, Thomas, 96
RICHIE, James H., 44
RICHIE, James H., 97
RICHIE, Martin, 137
RICHIE, Martin P., 136
RICHMOND, Ezekiel, 97
RICHMOND, Josiah A., 97
RIDGWAY, James, 125
RIDGWAY, James, 20
RIDGWAY, James, 44
RIDGWAY, James, 70
RIDGWAY, James, 96
RIDGWAY, John, 125
RIDGWAY, John, 147
RIDGWAY, John, 20
RIDGWAY, John, 44
RIDGWAY, John, 70
RIDGWAY, John, 81

RIDGWAY, John, 96
RIDGWAY, Littlebury E., 125
RIDGWAY, Richard, 20
RIDGWAY, Richard, 44
RIDGWAY, Thomas, 20
RIDGWAY, Thomas, 44
RIDGWAY, Thomas, 70
RIDGWAY, Wm., 125
RIDGWAY, Wm., 70
RIDGWAY, Wm., 96
RIDGWAY & LITTLEBURY, , 96
RIGHT, Jesse, 125
RIGHTNER, Wm., 20
RIVES, John H., 69
ROADES, Abner, 20
ROADS, Abner, 100
ROADS, Abner, 43
ROADS, Abner, 70
ROBERDS, Wm., 96
ROBERDS, Wm. C., 70
ROBERTS, David Watthall, 145
ROBERTS, Frances, 145
ROBERTS, Francis, 145
ROBERTS, Henry, 145
ROBERTS, J. A., 145
ROBERTS, James R., 145
ROBERTS, John, 145
ROBERTS, Martha, 144
ROBERTS, Martha, 145
ROBERTS, Martin U., 145
ROBERTS, Mary K., 101
ROBERTS, Mary K., 39
ROBERTS, Nathaniel, 48
ROBERTS, Rebecca Ann, 145
ROBERTS, Richard, 145
ROBERTS, Thomas, 145
ROBERTS, Winifred, 145
ROBERTS, Wm., 101
ROBERTS, Wm., 144
ROBERTS, Wm., 145
ROBERTS, Wm., 20
ROBERTS, Wm., 39
ROBERTS, Wm. C., 145
ROBERTSON, Edward, 19
ROBERTSON, Edward, 43
ROBERTSON, Edward, 69
ROBERTSON, Edward, 96
ROBERTSON, Elijah, 109
ROBERTSON, Elijah, 25
ROBERTSON, Elijah, 33
ROBERTSON, Elijah, 82
ROBERTSON, Jno. L., 20
RODA, negro, 145
ROFFE, Woodson, 124
ROFFE, Woodson, 19
ROFFE, Woodson, 69
ROFFE, Woodson, 96
ROFFE, Woson, 43
ROGERS, Agnes, 160
ROGERS, Agnes, 160
ROGERS, Daniel L., 19
ROGERS, Druseller Allen, 160
ROGERS, Elizabeth Allen, 161
ROGERS, Frances, 158
ROGERS, Frances, 163
ROGERS, Frances, 163
ROGERS, Frances, 164
ROGERS, Isabelle, 69
ROGERS, J., 139
ROGERS, J., 142

185

ROGERS, Jacob, 20
ROGERS, Jacob, 44
ROGERS, Jacob C., 125
ROGERS, Jacob C., 70
ROGERS, Jacob C., 96
ROGERS, Jefferson, 125
ROGERS, Jefferson, 159
ROGERS, Jefferson, 163
ROGERS, Jefferson, 163
ROGERS, Jefferson, 164
ROGERS, Jefferson, 97
ROGERS, Jno., 70
ROGERS, Job, 125
ROGERS, Job, 160
ROGERS, Job, 163
ROGERS, Job, 20
ROGERS, Job, 44
ROGERS, Job, 70
ROGERS, Job, 96
ROGERS, Job Calvin, 162
ROGERS, Joel, 70
ROGERS, John, 19
ROGERS, John, 44
ROGERS, John, 96
ROGERS, John W., 125
ROGERS, John W., 161
ROGERS, John W., 161
ROGERS, John W., 162
ROGERS, John W., 170
ROGERS, John W., 171
ROGERS, John W., 20
ROGERS, John W., 43
ROGERS, John W., 70
ROGERS, John W., 96
ROGERS, Jonathan, 96
ROGERS, Jonathan T., 124
ROGERS, Jonathan T., 163
ROGERS, Jonathan T., 163
ROGERS, Jonathan T., 164
ROGERS, Josiah, 97
ROGERS, Jubile V., 70
ROGERS, Jubilee, 124
ROGERS, Jubilee, 135
ROGERS, Jubilee, 136
ROGERS, Jubilee, 138
ROGERS, Jubilee, 141
ROGERS, Jubilee, 143
ROGERS, Jubilee, 161
ROGERS, Jubilee, 162
ROGERS, Jubilee, 19
ROGERS, Jubilee, 43
ROGERS, Jubilee, 96
ROGERS, Jubilee V., 125
ROGERS, Jubilee V., 161
ROGERS, Jubilee V., 162
ROGERS, Jubilee V., 96
ROGERS, Mary, 158
ROGERS, Mary, 163
ROGERS, Mary, 163
ROGERS, Mary, 164
ROGERS, Mary P., 161
ROGERS, Richard, 125
ROGERS, Sarah Jane Benjamin, 160
ROGERS, Thomas, 125
ROGERS, Thomas, 44
ROGERS, Thomas, 70
ROGERS, Thomas, 96
ROGERS, Thomas, 97
ROGERS, Thos., 19
ROLEN, Tarlton, 20

ROLLS, Wm. B., 137
RORIE, Reubin, 20
ROSS, John, 125
ROSS, John, 20
ROSS, Joshua, 124
ROSS, Joshua, 20
ROSS, Joshua, 44
ROSS, Joshua, 70
ROSS, Joshua, 96
ROSS, Lacie, 125
ROSS, Lacie, 44
ROSS, Lacie, 75
ROSS, Lacie, 96
ROSS, Lacy, 20
ROSS, Reubin, 20
ROSS, Reubin, 44
ROSS, Thomas, 20
ROSS, Wm., 44
ROSS, Wm. G, 125
ROSS, Wm. G, 20
ROSS, Wm. G, 70
ROSS, Wm. G, 96
ROULHAC, Geo. G, 124
ROULHAC, Geo. G, 52
ROULHAC, George G, 51
ROULHAC, George G, 69
ROULHAC, George W., 96
ROULHAC, J. P. G, 152
ROYAL, Thomas, 125
RUSE, Yarnel, 70
RUSH, John, 61
RUSSEL, Aaron, 146
RUSSEL, Buckner, 146
RUSSEL, Margaret, 146
RUSSEL, Rachel, 146
RUSSEL, Wm., 146
RUSSELL, Buckner, 70
RUSSELL, Buckner jr., 125
RUSSELL, Buckner jr., 20
RUSSELL, Buckner jr., 44
RUSSELL, Buckner jr., 97
RUSSELL, Buckner sr., 125
RUSSELL, Buckner sr., 20
RUSSELL, Buckner sr., 44
RUSSELL, Buckner sr., 97
RUSSELL, George, 20
RUSSELL, George, 97
RUSSELL, George (heirs), 125
RUSSELL, George (heirs), 70
RUSSELL, Price, 124
RUST, J. P., 163
RUST, Vincent, 125
RUST, Vincent, 132
RUST, Vincent, 133
RUST, Vincent, 97
RUTH, Joseph, 143
SALLY, negro, 147
SALLY ANN, slave, 164
SAM, negro, 164
SAMDERS, Saml., 44
SAMPLE, Henry A., 127
SAMPLE, Henry A., 21
SAMPLE, Henry A., 44
SAMPLE, Henry A., 70
SAMPLE, Henry A., 99
SANDERS, James, 44
SANDERS, James, 70
SANDERS, Samuel, 20
SANFORD, John, 126
SANFORD, John, 45
SANFORD, John, 71

SARAH, negro, 140
SARAH, negro, 161
SARAH, negro, 50
SCARBEROUGH & SELLS, , 25
SCARBROUGH & SELLS, , 30
SCARBROUGH & SELS, , 115
SCOTT, Vaughn, 21
SCOTT, W. S., 152
SCOTT, W. S., 155
SCOTT, W. S., 166
SCOTT, Wm. S., 148
SCOTT, Wm. S., 149
SCOTT, Wm. S., 149
SCOTT, Wm. S., 150
SCOTT, Wm. S., 151
SCOTT, Wm. S., 154
SCOTT, Wm. S., 155
SCOTT, Wm. S., 165
SCOTT, Wm. S., 170
SCOTT, Wm. S., 171
SEAGRAVES, Willie, 98
SEAL, James B., 99
SEAL, Wm., 127
SEAL, Wm., 72
SEAL, Wm., 98
SEARCY, Isaac, 71
SEATH, Wiley, 21
SEDEWICK, Faney Penelope, 166
SEDEWICK, Solomon, 166
SEDWICK, Fany Penelope, 167
SEDWICK, Solomon, 167
SEDWICK, Solomon, 167
SEGRAVES, Wilie, 46
SEGRAVES, Wilie, 71
SEGRAVES, Willie, 126
SEGRAVES & TERRELL, , 55
SELF, John, 46
SERATT, John, 126
SHANKLIN, Clemmons, 163
SHANKLIN, David, 21
SHARK, Thomas, 119
SHARP, Spencer, 126
SHARP, Thomas, 21
SHARP, Thomas, 40
SHARP, Wm., 15
SHARP, Wm., 40
SHARP, Wm., 66
SHARPE, Thos., 21
SHAW, Archbald, 71
SHAW, Archibald, 127
SHAW, Archibald, 98
SHAW, Daniel, 98
SHAW, Daniel B., 127
SHAW, Daniel B., 45
SHAW, Daniel B., 72
SHELTON, Abraham, 70
SHELTON & HAMELIN, , 95
SHELTON & HANELINE, , 106
SHELTON & HANLINE, , 69
SHELTON & HANLINES, , 124
SHELTON & HINELINE, , 18
SHELTON & LOVELACE, , 24
SHEPHERD, Abraham, 27
SHEPHERD, Charles, 45
SHEPHERD, Charles B., 127
SHEPHERD, Charles B., 27
SHEPHERD, Charles B., 98
SHEPHERD, Fred'k B., 45
SHEPHERD, Frederick B., 27

SHEPHERD, James B., 27
SHEPHERD, James B., 45
SHEPHERD, James B., 98
SHEPHERD, John S., 28
SHEPHERD, John S., 45
SHEPHERD, John S., 98
SHEPHERD, Penelope S., 27
SHEPHERD, Penelope S., 45
SHEPHERD, Penelope S., 98
SHEPHERD, Rich'd M., 45
SHEPHERD, Richard M., 127
SHEPHERD, Richard M., 27
SHEPHERD, Richard M., 98
SHEPHERD, T., 98
SHEPHERD, Wm. B., 27
SHEPHERD, Wm. B., 44
SHEPHERD, Wm. B., 98
SHIP, Bennet, 46
SHIP, Benton, 126
SHIP, Benton, 71
SHIP, Benton, 97
SHORT, Epes, 46
SHRUMS, Nicholass W., 136
SHULTEY, Charles, 46
SHULTEY, Charles M., 71
SHULTEY, Jacob, 71
SHULTEY, John R., 71
SHULTY, David, 71
SHULTY, Jacob, 46
SHULTY, John M., 44
SHULTY, John M., 71
SHULTY, John R., 44
SHULTZ, David, 46
SHUTLEY, Charles M., 97
SHUTLEY, Chas., 21
SHUTLEY, David, 21
SHUTLEY, David, 97
SHUTLEY, Jacob, 21
SHUTLEY, Jacob, 97
SHUTLEY, Jno. M., 21
SHUTLEY, Jno. R., 21
SHUTLEY, John M., 97
SHUTLEY, Joseph B., 97
SHUTTY, Charles M., 126
SHUTTY, David, 126
SHUTTY, John M., 126
SIBLEY, Jacob, 127
SIBLEY, Jacob, 98
SILAS, negro, 145
SILVIA, negro, 53
SIMMONS, Charles, 21
SIMMONS, Charles, 78
SIMMONS, Thomas, 71
SIMMONS, Thomas, 97
SIMON, negro, 162
SIMPSON, John, 126
SIMS, John, 126
SIRATT, John, 98
SIRATT, Walter, 98
SKAGGS, James, 21
SKAGGS, James, 46
SKAGGS, James, 71
SKAGGS, Martin, 21
SKAGGS, Martin, 71
SLAUTER, James, 143
SLAWTER, John, 126
SMART, James H., 126
SMART, James H., 46
SMART, James H., 71
SMART, James H., 97
SMART, Joseph, 21

SMART, Labon, 126
SMART, Laleon, 97
SMART, Philip, 21
SMART, Phillip, 126
SMART, Phillip, 46
SMART, Phillip, 71
SMART, Phillip, 97
SMART, Stephen, 21
SMART, Stephen, 46
SMART, Stephen, 97
SMART, Stephens, 71
SMART, Wm., 21
SMART, Wm. C., 97
SMART, Wm. J., 126
SMART, Wm. J., 71
SMART, Wm. S., 46
SMITH, Alfred, 127
SMITH, Daniel, 143
SMITH, David, 126
SMITH, Elas, 120
SMITH, Eleas, 123
SMITH, Elias, 96
SMITH, George, 153
SMITH, Hugh D., 127
SMITH, Hugh D., 21
SMITH, Hugh D., 72
SMITH, Hugh D., 98
SMITH, J. L. D., 100
SMITH, J. L. D., 129
SMITH, J. L. D., 47
SMITH, J. L. D., 62
SMITH, J. L. D., 73
SMITH, James, 127
SMITH, James, 21
SMITH, James, 72
SMITH, James, 98
SMITH, James W., 125
SMITH, James W., 70
SMITH, James W., 97
SMITH, Jas. W., 20
SMITH, Jas. W., 20
SMITH, Joseph, 70
SMITH, L. D., 23
SMITH, R., 75
SMITH, R., 82
SMITH, Richard, 106
SMITH, Richard, 125
SMITH, Richard, 161
SMITH, Richard, 44
SMITH, Richard, 78
SMITH, Richd. (heirs of), 29
SMITH, Richey, 127
SMITH, Richey, 72
SMITH, Roddy, 97
SMITH, Rody, 125
SMITH, Wm., 70
SMITH, Wm., 97
SMITH, Wm. H., 20
SMYTH, Hugh D., 46
SMYTH, James, 45
SNEED, Israel, 45
SNEED, Israel, 98
SNEED, Samuel R., 44
SNEED, Samuel R., 70
SNEED, Samuel R., 99
SNELL, Israel, 72
SOMERS, Elizabeth, 147
SOMERS, James, 126
SOMERS, James, 21
SOMERS, Jas., 126
SOMERS, Jas., 21

SOMERS, Jas., 97
SOMERS, John, 126
SOMERS, Richard, 126
SOMERS, Wm., 19
SOMMERRS, James, 98
SOMMERS, Charles, 46
SOMMERS, James, 126
SOMMERS, James, 27
SOMMERS, James, 45
SOMMERS, James, 46
SOMMERS, James, 71
SOMMERS, James, 71
SOMMERS, James, 97
SOMMERS, Jas., 46
SOMMERS, Jas., 71
SOMMERS & MCFARLAND, , 127
SORREL, Albert, 158
SPAN, James, 127
SPAN, James, 99
SPAN, Jeremiah, 127
SPAN, John T., 127
SPAN, Moses T., 127
SPAN, Moses T., 72
SPAN, Moses T., 99
SPAN, Willis, 127
SPANN, Moses T., 103
SPANN, Moses T., 135
SPARKS, Hardy, 45
SPATE, James, 126
SPATE, James, 71
SPATE, James, 97
SPEIGHT, ____, 126
SPEIGHT & MCGAVOCK, , 126
SPEIGHT & MCGAVOCK, , 27
SPEIGHT & MCGAVOCK, , 44
SPEIGHT & MCGAVOCK, , 70
SPRAGG, James, 127
SPROUNT, Elexander, 45
SPROUT, Alexander, 126
SPROUT, Alexander, 21
SPROUT, Alexander, 71
SPROUT, Alexander, 98
STALLINGS, John, 126
STALLINGS, John, 27
STALLINGS, John, 44
STALLINGS, John, 71
STALLINGS, John, 98
STANDFOR, Jno., 21
STANDLEY, Elijah, 21
STANDLEY, Elijah, 71
STANDLEY, Lewis, 22
STANDLEY, Lewis, 71
STANDLEY, Noah, 21
STANDLEY, Noah, 45
STANDLEY, Noah, 71
STANDLEY, Noah, 98
STANDLY, Elijah, 45
STANFORD, Hiram, 21
STANFORD, Hiram, 45
STANFORD, Hiram, 72
STANFORD, John, 98
STANFORD, Thomas, 127
STANFORD, Thomas, 21
STANFORD, Thomas, 72
STANFORD, Thomas, 99
STANFORD, Thos., 46
STANLEY, Elijah, 126
STANLEY, Elijah, 98
STANLEY, Lewis, 126

STANLEY, Lewis, 98
STANLEY, Noah, 126
STANTON, Henry, 71
STARK, Thomas, 127
STARK, Thomas, 45
STARK, Thos., 21
STARKS, Thomas, 72
STARKS, Thomas, 98
STEEL, George R., 45
STEEL, George R., 98
STEEL, John, 45
STEEL, John, 98
STEEL, Samuel, 98
STEELE, Geo. R., 21
STEELE, George R., 127
STEELE, George R., 71
STEELE, John, 127
STEELE, John, 71
STEELE, Samuel, 126
STEPHEN, Lawrence, 126
STEPHENS, Lawrence, 97
STEWARD, Samuel, 71
STEWART, Samuel T., 126
STOKER, Edmund, 126
STOKER, Edmund, 71
STOKER, Edmund, 98
STONE, Claborn, 127
STONE, Claibourn, 70
STONE, Claibown, 97
STONE, Wm., 46
STONE, Wm., 72
STONE, Wm., 99
STONE, Wm. B., 167
STONE, Wm. R., 166
STOUT, John E., 98
STOVALL, Geo., 134
STOVALL, George, 104
STOVALL, George, 105
STOVALL, George, 127
STOVALL, George, 133
STOVALL, George, 135
STOVALL, George, 136
STOVALL, George, 138
STOVALL, George, 139
STOVALL, George, 70
STOVALL, George, 97
STOW, Joel W., 126
STOW, Wm., 126
STOW, Wm. A., 98
STROUD, Deniza, 137
STROUD, Echolds, 138
STROUD, Elizabeth, 137
STROUD, Howell, 137
STROUD, Howell, 138
STROUD, Isaac, 138
STROUD, James, 137
STROUD, James, 138
STROUD, Jane, 137
STROUD, Jesse, 137
STROUD, Jesse, 138
STROUD, Jesse R., 138
STROUD, John, 138
STROUD, Margaret, 137
STROUD, Nancy, 138
STROUD, Naoma, 138
STROUD, Obedience, 137
STROUD, Peter, 138
STROUD, Polly, 138
STROUD, Rebecca, 138
STROUD, Richard, 137
STROUD, Sally, 138

STROUD, Silas, 137
STROUD, Silas, 138
STROUD, Tabitha, 137
STROUD, Tabitha, 138
STROUD, Thomas, 138
STROUD, Wm., 138
STUART, Samuel T., 98
STUFF, Henry, 44
STUNSON, Henry, 78
STUNSON, John, 45
STUNSTON, Elizabeth, 147
STUNSTON, Henry, 127
STUNSTON, Henry, 147
STUNSTON, Henry, 45
STUNSTON, Henry, 98
STUNSTON, Henry sr., 71
STUNSTON, James, 126
STUNSTON, James, 147
STUNSTON, James, 147
STUNSTON, James, 71
STUNSTON, James, 98
STUNSTON, Joh, 21
STUNSTON, John, 127
STUNSTON, John, 147
STUNSTON, John, 147
STUNSTON, John, 71
STUNSTON, John, 98
STUNSTON, Levi, 21
STUNSTON, Rebeca, 147
STUNSTON, Wm., 147
STUNSTON, Wm., 21
STYERS, John H., 127
SUCCA, negro girl, 147
SUMMERS, John, 98
SUMMERS, Richard, 71
SUMMERS, Sally, 147
SUNNEYS, John, 71
SURSEY, Isaac, 46
SUSAN, negro, 168
SUSAN, negro, 168
SUSAN, slave, 164
SUTHERN, Benny, 21
SUTTON, Lemuel, 72
SUTTON, Lemuel, 99
SUTTON, Samuel, 21
SWANEY, James M., 45
SWANEY, James M., 70
SWANEY, James M., 99
SWANEY, John L., 45
SWANEY, John L., 70
SWANEY & ROSS, , 66
SWEENEY, Jno. L., 20
SWENY, Jas. M., 20
SWIM, Jeremiah W., 127
SYLVIA, negro, 50
TAILOR, Isaac, 128
TANSIL, Edward, 128
TANSIL, Edward, 22
TANSIL, Edward, 78
TANSIL, Edward, 99
TANSIL, Hiram W., 128
TANSIL, Hiram W., 99
TANSIL, John, 129
TANSIL, John, 152
TANSIL, John, 99
TANSIL, John sr., 22
TATE, Jame, 100
TATE, James, 72
TATE, Wm., 72
TAUSIL, Edward, 47
TAUSIL, John, 47

TAUSIL, John, 72
TAYLOR, Caleb, 72
TAYLOR, Caleb heirs, 46
TAYLOR, Chapman, 128
TAYLOR, Chapman, 72
TAYLOR, Chapman, 99
TAYLOR, Edmund, 128
TAYLOR, Edmund, 72
TAYLOR, Isaac, 22
TAYLOR, Isaac, 46
TAYLOR, Isaac, 61
TAYLOR, Isaac, 72
TAYLOR, Isaac, 72
TAYLOR, Isaac, 99
TAYLOR, Jame P., 99
TAYLOR, Saml., 171
TAYLOR, Thomas, 22
TAYLOR, Wm., 128
TAYLOR, Wm., 145
TAYLOR, Wm., 146
TEMMONS, Joseph B., 128
TERRELL, D. J., 47
TERRELL, J., 46
TERRELL, J., 47
TERRELL, J., 58
TERRELL, J., 61
TERRELL, J., 63
TERRELL, J., 69
TERRELL, J., 72
TERRELL, J., 73
TERRELL, James, 117
TERRELL, James, 16
TERRELL, Jeptha, 128
TERRELL, Jeptha, 141
TERRELL, Jeptha, 142
TERRELL, Jeptha, 143
TERRELL, Jeptha, 22
TERRELL, Jeptha, 46
TERRELL, Jeptha, 72
TERRELL, Jepthah, 99
TERRELL, Jno., 100
TERRELL, Jno., 107
TERRELL, Jno., 109
TERRELL, Jno., 113
TERRELL, Jno., 118
TERRELL, Jno., 121
TERRELL, Jno., 125
TERRELL, Jno., 128
TERRELL, Jno., 129
TERRELL, Jno., 165
TERRELL, Jno., 77
TERRELL, Jno., 87
TERRELL, Jno., 97
TERRELL, John, 103
TERRELL, John, 104
TERRELL, John, 107
TERRELL, John, 113
TERRELL, John, 127
TERRELL, John, 128
TERRELL, John, 133
TERRELL, John, 135
TERRELL, John, 136
TERRELL, John, 141
TERRELL, John, 142
TERRELL, John, 143
TERRELL, John, 18
TERRELL, John, 22
TERRELL, John, 22
TERRELL, John, 28
TERRELL, John, 29
TERRELL, John, 3

TERRELL, John, 34
TERRELL, John, 43
TERRELL, John, 46
TERRELL, John, 51
TERRELL, John, 52
TERRELL, John, 55
TERRELL, John, 55
TERRELL, John, 60
TERRELL, John, 72
TERRELL, John, 76
TERRELL, John, 81
TERRELL, John, 82
TERRELL, John, 83
TERRELL, John, 88
TERRELL, John, 96
TERRELL, John, 96
TERRELL, John, 99
TERRELL, John, 99
TERRELL, Patrick, 128
TERRELL, Patrick, 22
TERRELL, Patrick, 72
TERRELL, Patrick, 99
TERRELL, Peleg, 128
TERRELL, Peleg, 141
TERRELL, Peleg, 142
TERRELL, Peleg, 143
TERRELL, Peleg, 22
TERRELL, Peleg, 46
TERRELL, Peleg, 99
TERRELL, Pelig, 162
TERRELL & CHARLTON, , 46
TERRELL & JENKINS, , 117
TERRELL & LAWRENCE, , 29
TERRILL, John, 112
THADDY, negro, 144
THARP, Wm. A., 15
THARP, Wm. A., 22
THARP, Wm. A., 40
THARP, Wm. A., 47
THARP & JENKINS, , 22
THIZZELL, Boaz, 146
THOMAS, G., 27
THOMAS, J., 27
THOMAS, James D., 128
THOMAS, James D., 22
THOMAS, James D., 46
THOMAS, James D., 72
THOMAS, James D., 99
THOMAS, John, 100
THOMAS, John, 128
THOMAS, John, 22
THOMAS, John, 46
THOMAS, John jr., 72
THOMAS, Jos., 105
THOMAS, Joseph, 104
THOMAS, Joseph, 128
THOMAS, Joseph, 22
THOMAS, Joseph, 46
THOMAS, Joseph, 72
THOMAS, Joseph, 99
THOMAS, M., 10
THOMAS, M., 10
THOMAS, Mathew, 127
THOMAS, Mathew, 46
THOMAS, Mathew, 72
THOMAS, Micajah, 119
THOMAS, Micajah, 46
THOMAS, Micajah, 75
THOMAS, Tristrum H., 22
THOMAS, Wm., 100
THOMAS, Wm., 128

THOMAS, negro, 168
THOMAS CREEK, , 146
THOMASON, Pheneas, 22
THOMPSON, Benjm. G., 22
THOMPSON, Jacob, 128
THOMPSON, Jacob, 161
THOMPSON, Jacob, 162
THOMPSON, Jacob, 22
THOMPSON, Jacob, 46
THOMPSON, Jacob, 72
THOMPSON, Jacob, 99
THOMPSON, James, 129
THOMPSON, James, 47
THOMPSON, James, 72
THOMPSON, James, 99
THOMPSON, Jesse, 128
THOMPSON, Jesse, 22
THOMPSON, Jesse, 47
THOMPSON, Jessee, 99
THOMPSON, John Chesley, 162
THOMPSON, Robert, 128
THOMPSON, Robert, 171
THOMPSON, Robert, 22
THOMPSON, Robert, 47
THOMPSON, Robert, 75
THOMPSON, Robert, 99
THOMPSON, Robt., 172
THOMPSON, Wm., 148
THOMPSON, Wm., 149
THOMPSON, Wm., 22
THOMPSON, Wm., 47
THOMPSON, Wm., 72
THOMPSON, Wm., 99
THORNTON, Benjamin, 128
THORNTON, Benjamin, 99
THORNTON, Benjm., 22
THORNTON, Lemuel, 22
THORNTON, Lemuel, 99
THORNTON, Sterling, 128
THORNTON, Sterling, 99
THORP, Wm. A., 128
TIMMONS, Joseph B., 100
TODD, Willie, 128
TODD, Willie, 99
TODD, Wm., 128
TODD, Wm., 22
TODD, Wm., 46
TODD, Wm., 99
TOLBERT, James, 22
TOMLINSON, Henry, 100
TOMLINSON, Henry, 128
TOMPKINS, Isaac, 100
TOMPKINS, Isaac, 129
TOTTEN, Benjamin, 129
TOTTEN, Benjamin, 99
TOTTEN, _____, 89
TRACY, Joseph, 11
TRACY, Joseph, 87
TRANTHAM, Flowel, 22
TRANTHAM, Floyd, 129
TRANTHAM, Floyd, 46
TRANTHAM, Floyd, 72
TRAVIS, B., 101
TRAVIS, Fielding, 100
TRAVIS, Fielding, 128
TRAVIS, Fielding, 72
TRAVIS, M. B., 24
TRAVIS, M. B., 73
TRAVIS, Moses B., 128

TRAVIS, Moses B., 130
TRAVIS, Moses B., 48
TRAVIS, Moses B., 99
TRAVIS, Thomas, 48
TRAYWICK, Gibson, 128
TRENTHAM, Floyd, 100
TUCKER, Alexander, 128
TUCKER, Alexander, 163
TUCKER, Alexander, 22
TUCKER, Alexander, 99
TUCKER, Daniel, 100
TUCKER, Daniel, 128
TUCKER, Daniel, 22
TUCKER, Daniel, 47
TUCKER, Daniel, 72
TURNER, John, 129
TURNER, John, 72
TURNER, Phillip L., 51
TYLER, Wm., 22
UHLS, Frederick J., 100
UHLS, Frederick J., 129
UHLS, Frederick J., 73
UHLS?, Frederick J., 22
ULHS, Frederick J., 47
URY, Joseph, 129
URY, Joseph, 22
URY, Robert, 100
URY, Robert, 129
USEY, Edward, 57
VALENTINE, Thomas, 129
VAUGHN, John, 47
VAULX, James, 28
VINCENT, Abner, 100
VINCENT, Abner, 129
VINCENT, John M., 100
VINCENT, John M., 129
VINCENT, John M., 47
VINCENT, John M., 73
VINCENT, Joseph, 100
VINCENT, Joseph L., 129
VINCENT, Orien, 23
VINCENT, Orin, 129
VINCENT, Orren, 157
VINCENT, Orrin, 100
VINCENT, Orrin, 47
VINCENT, Orrin, 73
VINCENT, Perry, 100
VINCENT, Perry, 129
VINCENT, Perry, 139
VINCENT, Perry, 142
VINCENT, Perry, 23
VINCENT, Perry, 47
VINCENT, Perry, 73
VINCENT, negro, 145
VINVENT, Joseph, 73
VOUK, Jas., 40
WADE, Elijah, 100
WADE, Kenchen, 100
WADE, Kencher, 73
WADE, Kinchen, 129
WADE, Kinchen, 23
WAINSCOT, Andrew, 100
WAINSCOTT, Andrew, 24
WAINSCOTT, Andrew, 73
WALKER, Simeon, 24
WALL, Flemmin, 101
WALLACE, Andrew, 130
WALLS, Fleming, 130
WARD, Britton, 101
WARD, Britton, 130
WARD, Britton, 24

WARD, Britton, 51
WARD, Britton, 74
WARD, Elijah, 107
WARD, Elijah, 33
WARD, Elisha, 55
WARD, Elisha, 81
WARD, George, 101
WARD, George, 130
WARD, George, 74
WARD, Isaac, 130
WARD, J., 41
WARD, Jas., 16
WARD, Jas., 94
WARD, John, 131
WARD, John, 74
WARD, John B., 101
WARD, John B., 130
WARD, Messer, 101
WARD, Messer, 130
WARD, Messer, 23
WARD, Messer, 55
WARD, Messer, 81
WARD, Messrs., 47
WARD, Moses, 2
WARD, Mosser, 74
WARD, Roberson, 131
WARD, Robertson, 47
WARD, Robinson, 23
WARD, Robison, 73
WARD, Whitmore J., 100
WARD, Whitmore J., 129
WARD, Wm., 101
WARD, Wm., 101
WARD, Wm., 130
WARD, Wm., 24
WARD, Wm., 74
WARFORD, Samuel G., 24
WARNER, Mears, 100
WARNER, Mears, 129
WARNER, Mears, 148
WARNER, Mears, 23
WARNER, Mears, 47
WARNER, Mears, 73
WARNER, S. A., 133
WARNER, S. A., 134
WARNER, S. A., 139
WARNER, S. A., 165
WARNER, S. A., 166
WARNER, Samuel A., 131
WARNER, Samuel A., 138
WARNER, Samuel A., 23
WARNER, Samuel A., 47
WARNER, Samuel A., 73
WARREN, Benjamin, 102
WARREN, Benjamin, 74
WARREN, Edwin, 74
WARREN, John, 100
WARREN, John, 129
WARREN, Leroy, 74
WARREN, Samuel A., 102
WARREN, Wm., 74
WASHINGTON, negro, 168
WASHINGTON, negro, 168
WASHINGTON, negro, 170
WASHINGTON, slave, 164
WAT, negro, 168
WATERHOUSE, Richard, 100
WATERHOUSE, Richard, 129
WATSON, R., 63
WATSON, Robert, 110
WATSON, Robert, 28

WATSON, Robt. heirs, 47
WATTS, Marvel, 130
WATTS, Matvill, 74
WEBB, Amosa, 101
WEBB, Amosa, 130
WEBB, Amosa, 23
WEBB, Amosa, 48
WEBB, Amosa, 73
WEBB, Amosa, 80
WEBB, Bushrod, 80
WEBB, Elizabeth, 80
WEBB, George, 80
WEBB, Holland, 80
WEBB, Jesse, 80
WEBB, John, 23
WEBB, John, 48
WEBB, John, 73
WEBB, John, 76
WEBB, John, 80
WEBB, Mary, 80
WEBB, Nancy, 101
WEBB, Nancy, 130
WEBB, Nancy, 80
WEBB, Sarrah, 80
WEBSTER, Richard J., 73
WEIL, Wm., 74
WELCH, John, 24
WELCH, John, 74
WELCH, John, 87
WELLS, Andrew, 24
WELLS, Hayden E., 101
WELLS, Hayden E., 24
WELLS, Hayden E., 48
WELLS, Hayden E., 74
WELLS, Robert, 24
WELLS, Sarah, 101
WELLS, Sarah, 74
WELSH, John, 101
WELSH, John, 130
WELSH, John, 48
WENSCOT, Andrew, 47
WENSTON, George, 100
WERDON, Towner, 12
WESTER, Wm, 144
WESTER, Wm., 101
WESTER, Wm., 130
WESTER, Wm., 24
WESTER, Wm., 48
WESTER, Wm., 73
WHARTON, Jesse, 100
WHARTON, Jesse, 129
WHARTON, Jesse, 23
WHARTON, Jesse, 47
WHARTON, Jesse, 73
WHEELER, Mark, 48
WHELER, Mark, 73
WHELLY, Benjamin, 48
WHITE, Archibald, 24
WHITE, Henry, 23
WHITE, Henry, 30
WHITE, James H., 130
WHITE, John L., 24
WHITE, John L., 48
WHITE, John L., 74
WHITE, Kinchin, 167
WHITE, Lemuel, 131
WHITE, Tyrel C., 100
WHITE, Tyrel C., 47
WHITE, Tyrell C., 23
WHITE, Tyril C., 104
WHITE, Tysel C., 129

WHITE, Tysel C., 73
WHITE, Wm. W., 74
WHITLEY, Benjamin, 130
WHITLEY, John, 130
WHITLEY, John, 73
WHITLEY, Marcus, 24
WHITLEY, Marcus, 48
WHITLEY, alphens, 73
WHITSIL, Peter, 130
WHITUS, Mark, 101
WIGGINS, Benjamin, 129
WIGGINS, Benjm., 23
WILBANKS, Spencerd?, 163
WILKERSON, John, 100
WILKINS, Lewelen, 23
WILKINS, Lewelen, 47
WILKINS, Lewelin, 100
WILKINS, Lewelin, 73
WILL, negro, 145
WILLBANKS, Gardner, 130
WILLIAM, Sion, 40
WILLIAMS, Allen, 101
WILLIAMS, Allen, 129
WILLIAMS, Allen, 130
WILLIAMS, Allen S., 129
WILLIAMS, Allin, 23
WILLIAMS, Allin, 48
WILLIAMS, Allin, 73
WILLIAMS, Allin S., 101
WILLIAMS, Ann, 101
WILLIAMS, Ann, 130
WILLIAMS, Anne, 73
WILLIAMS, Arthur, 131
WILLIAMS, Bartlett, 101
WILLIAMS, Bartlett, 130
WILLIAMS, Bartlett, 24
WILLIAMS, Bartlett, 48
WILLIAMS, Bartlett, 73
WILLIAMS, Bennett B., 130
WILLIAMS, Bennit, 75
WILLIAMS, Briant, 101
WILLIAMS, Briant, 48
WILLIAMS, Charles, 48
WILLIAMS, Charles, 74
WILLIAMS, E.? P., 102
WILLIAMS, Elisha, 101
WILLIAMS, Elisha, 51
WILLIAMS, Elisha, 75
WILLIAMS, Gibson A., 23
WILLIAMS, Gibson A., 74
WILLIAMS, Jos. G., 23
WILLIAMS, Joseph G., 129
WILLIAMS, Joseph G., 157
WILLIAMS, Joseph G., 47
WILLIAMS, Joseph G., 73
WILLIAMS, K., 155
WILLIAMS, Kinchen, 100
WILLIAMS, Kinchen, 129
WILLIAMS, Kinchen, 152
WILLIAMS, Kinchen, 23
WILLIAMS, Kinchen, 47
WILLIAMS, Kinchen, 73
WILLIAMS, Kinchin, 152
WILLIAMS, Kinchin, 155
WILLIAMS, Kinchin, 156
WILLIAMS, Martin, 102
WILLIAMS, Martin, 48
WILLIAMS, Martin, 74
WILLIAMS, Martin H. S., 131
WILLIAMS, Martin H. S., 24
WILLIAMS, Mnna?, 48

WILLIAMS, Newborn, 101
WILLIAMS, Newborn, 130
WILLIAMS, Pet, 55
WILLIAMS, Peter, 101
WILLIAMS, Peter, 106
WILLIAMS, Peter, 130
WILLIAMS, Peter, 2
WILLIAMS, Peter, 2
WILLIAMS, Peter, 23
WILLIAMS, Peter, 28
WILLIAMS, Peter, 73
WILLIAMS, Peter, 81
WILLIAMS, R. C., 152
WILLIAMS, Rice, 137
WILLIAMS, Richard C., 148
WILLIAMS, Richard C., 149
WILLIAMS, Richard C., 150
WILLIAMS, Richard C., 151
WILLIAMS, Sarah, 156
WILLIAMS, Sarah, 73
WILLIAMS, Scion, 47
WILLIAMS, Sion, 106
WILLIAMS, Sion, 65
WILLIAMS, Sion, 82
WILLIAMS, Sion (heirs?), 119
WILLIAMS, Thomas, 101
WILLIAMS, Thomas, 130
WILLIAMS, Wm., 129
WILLIAMS, Wm., 30
WILLIAMS, Zachareal, 23
WILLIAMS, Zachariah, 101
WILLIAMS, Zachariah, 47
WILLIAMS, Zacheriah, 130
WILLIAMSON, Jno., 24
WILLIAMSON, Meredith, 130
WILLIAMSON, Meredith, 24
WILLIAMSON, Meredith, 47
WILLIAMSON, Merideth, 101
WILLIAMSON, Meridith, 74
WILLIAMSON, heirs, 28
WILLINGBLY, James, 47
WILLINGHAM, Isaac, 23
WILLINGHAM, Wm., 100
WILLINGHAM, Wm., 130
WILLINGHAM, Wm., 24
WILLINGHAM, Wm., 47
WILLINGHAM, Wm., 51
WILLINGHAM, Wm., 73
WILLIS, Andrew, 101
WILLIS, George W., 131
WILLIS, John, 119
WILLIS, John, 129
WILLIS, John, 28
WILLIS, John, 47
WILLIS, John, 73
WILLIS, Mark, 23
WILLIS, negro, 164
WILLIS, negro, 168
WILLOUGHBY, James, 101
WILLOUGHBY, James, 130
WILLOUGHBY, James, 74
WILLOUGHBY, Jas., 125
WILLOUGHBY, Jas., 97
WILLOUGHY, Jas., 20
WILLS, Hayden E., 129
WILSON, Alice S., 100
WILSON, Alice S., 73
WILSON, E. Robert, 118
WILSON, George W., 129
WILSON, J., 81

WILSON, Jason, 101
WILSON, Jason, 130
WILSON, Jason, 23
WILSON, Jason, 48
WILSON, Jason, 74
WILSON, John, 26
WILSON, Joseph, 100
WILSON, Joseph, 101
WILSON, Joseph, 130
WILSON, Joseph, 23
WILSON, Joseph, 48
WILSON, Joseph, 74
WILSON, Joseph, 81
WILSON, Lewis D., 100
WILSON, Lewis D., 129
WILSON, Lewis D., 28
WILSON, Lewis D., 47
WILSON, Lewis D., 73
WILSON, Sam'l D., 28
WILSON, Samuel, 47
WILSON, Samuel D., 48
WILSON, Samuel D., 73
WINCHESTER, Jas., 107
WINCHESTER, Jas., 23
WINCHESTER, Jas., 99
WINCHESTER, Jas. H. S., 47
WINNY, negro, 161
WINSTED, Johnson, 48
WINSTED, Johnson, 73
WINSTED, Johnston, 101
WINSTED, Johnston, 130
WINSTON, Candon, 163
WINSTON, Candon (f), 164
WINSTON, Condon (f), 163
WINSTON, David, 159
WINSTON, David, 163
WINSTON, David, 163
WINSTON, David, 164
WINSTON, David, 164
WINSTON, John, 101
WINSTON, Josiah, 100
WINSTON, Josiah, 129
WINTERS, Aaron, 74
WINTERS, Aron, 101
WINTERS, Aron, 131
WINTERS, Aron, 24
WINTERS, Aron, 48
WISDOM, Tavener, 71
WISDOM, Tavhere, 114
WOLF, Jonathan, 131
WONDER, negro boy, 1
WOOD, James O. K., 101
WOOD, Wilson, 130
WOODWARD, Geo., 23
WOODWARD, George, 47
WOOLBANKS, Hiram, 130
WOOTEN, Stephen, 101
WOOTEN, Stephen, 130
WOOTEN, Stephen, 23
WOOTEN, Wm., 101
WOOTEN, Wm., 130
WORKMAN, Pleasant, 23
WORKMAN, Pleasant, 48
WORKMAN, Pleasant G., 101
WORKMAN, Pleasant G., 130
WORKMAN, Pleasant G., 73
WRIGHT, Jesse, 101
YARBROUGH, David, 131
YARBROUGH, David, 24
YARBROUGH, David, 49
YARBROUGH, David, 75
YARBROUGH, Davis, 102
YARBROUGH, Seth, 74
YOUNG, A. B., 24
YOUNG, Abraham, 131
YOUNG, Abraham B., 48
YOUNG, Abraham B., 74
YOUNG, Harris, 131
YOUNG, Henry J., 102
YOUNG, Henry J., 131
YOUNG, Henry J., 48
YOUNG, Levi, 102
YOUNG, Levi, 131
YOUNG, Robt. C., 24
ZIMMERMAN, John, 102
ZIMMERMAN, John, 48
ZIMMERMAN, John, 74
_____, P. John, 13
_____, Wm. L., 13

www.ingramcontent.com/pod-product-compliance
Lightning Source LLC
Chambersburg PA
CBHW080432230426
43662CB00015B/2258